The Middlebrow Musical

The Middlebrow Musical

Between Broadway and Opera in 1940s America

JAMES O'LEARY

OXFORD
UNIVERSITY PRESS

Oxford University Press is a department of the University of Oxford.
It furthers the University's objective of excellence in research, scholarship,
and education by publishing worldwide. Oxford is a registered trade mark of
Oxford University Press in the UK and in certain other countries.

Published in the United States of America by Oxford University Press
198 Madison Avenue, New York, NY 10016, United States of America.

© Oxford University Press 2025

All rights reserved. No part of this publication may be reproduced, stored in a retrieval system, transmitted, used for text and data mining, or used for training artificial intelligence, in any form or by any means, without the prior permission in writing of Oxford University Press, or as expressly permitted by law, by license or under terms agreed with the appropriate reprographics rights organization. Inquiries concerning reproduction outside the scope of the above should be sent to the Rights Department, Oxford University Press, at the address above.

You must not circulate this work in any other form
and you must impose this same condition on any acquirer.

CIP data is on file at the Library of Congress

ISBN 9780190265212

DOI: 10.1093/9780190265243.001.0001

Printed by Marquis Book Printing, Canada

The manufacturer's authorized representative in the EU for product safety is
Oxford University Press España S.A., Parque Empresarial San Fernando de Henares,
Avenida de Castilla, 2 – 28830 Madrid (www.oup.es/en).

The publisher gratefully acknowledges support from the AMS 75 PAYS Fund of the
American Musicological Society, supported in part by the National Endowment for
the Humanities and the Andrew W. Mellon Foundation

For my parents

We were talking about *No, No, Nanette*. I said I thought there was such a thing as an Angry Bravo—that those audiences who stand, and cheer, and roar, and seem altogether beside themselves at what they would instantly agree is at best an unimportant thing, are not really cheering *No, No, Nanette*. They are booing *Hair*. Or whatever else it is on stage that they had and that seems to triumph. So they stand and roar. Every bravo is not so much a Yes to the frail occasion that they have come to make a stand at, as a No, goddam it to everything else, a bravo of rage. And with that, they become, for what it's worth, a constituency that is political. When they find each other, and stand and roar like that, they want, they want to be reckoned with.

Joe said, Isn't it possible they just want to say that they are having a good time? It's possible; one ought perhaps to take into account that it is fun to be part of an audience that wants to roar. Norma asked whether Joe had seen it. He said no. Norma said, "Well, then you don't know. It's not a musical audience roar. It's not an avant garde roar. It's a march roar. A rally roar. A parade roar."

—Renata Adler, *Speedboat*

Contents

Preface	ix
Acknowledgments	xv
1. "Damnably American": Defining the Middlebrow	1
2. Authentic, Autonomous, Popular: An Institutional Approach to Middlebrow Culture on Broadway	19
3. Heightened Realism: A Re-evaluation of the *Oklahoma!* Revolution	60
4. Jazz, Opera, and "In Between": Duke Ellington's *Beggar's Holiday* (1946) and the Black Middlebrow Tradition	100
5. "A More Human Development": Kurt Weill's *Street Scene* (1947) and the Integrated Musical	142
Conclusion: Further Steps Toward a Middlebrow Modernism	182
Notes	193
Bibliography	231
Index	247

Preface

Before the stacks of articles, essays, or monographs; before any archive expeditions; before sketches, outlines, drafts, or revisions, this book began at the piano. It began in rehearsals where I found myself harboring an inchoate feeling that, somehow, what I thought I knew about the mid-century Broadway musical did not fit with what I was hearing in it. The literature I had read about this subject typically located the mid-century musical's innovations in its "integrated" form: how closely songs and scenes fit together, how musical motives from one section would reappear somewhere else to create the effect of broad-scale unity, how a production's singing, dancing, and design advanced the plot or deepened the spectator's understanding of character, and so forth. A separate strain of writing pushed back, contending that these shows were not integrated but rather productively, excitingly disjointed. Both positions felt right to me, as far as they went: I could point to smooth, unified stretches in these productions, and also to moments when the stage erupted in a wild burst of song-and-dance energy, which is to say that most mid-century musicals, like earlier musicals, toggled back and forth strategically between the two modes. But the whole discussion seemed incomplete to me. The focus on large-scale construction effectively averted my eyes and ears away from what was occupying me day by day with directors and singers: individual songs, their unique flavors, the way they shaped my experience of time, the way they invited or foreclosed certain kinds of feeling or interpretation. These local, moment-by-moment qualities seemed as novel as any large-scale formal principle. Was there a historically sensitive way of describing these shows that could attend to both levels at once?

Answering this question took me far away from Broadway and back again. The outward-bound journey eventually brought me to literature, where contemporary critics were describing a style of writing that seemed analogous to what I was hearing in these musicals. In both domains, works were combining multiple stylistic registers that, to many people in the early years of the twentieth century, had seemed incompatible: the erudition of high art, the homespun sentiments of regionalism, and the commercial accessibility of popular culture. The most ardent defender of this literary style was Van Wyck Brooks, whose writing explored the relationship between present-day writers, their communities, and their customs, a topic that seemed especially urgent to him in a world that felt like it was charging forward at breakneck speed, where received mores became passé seemingly overnight. His subject was, in a word, modernism—but modernism flipped inside out: When Brooks was young, he had followed vanguard international literature with interest, yet he sharply rejected the experiments of James Joyce, T. S. Eliot, and others in the second decade of the twentieth century. High art, he argued, had once aimed to express society's loftiest, most idealist values (even if those values had always been in dispute), but in this new wave of literature, Brooks detected only obscurity, a blunt repudiation of tradition. Recoiling, he turned instead toward a sustained reflection upon the received literary tradition in the United States and he tried to figure out what it might still have to offer an era of self-proclaimed ultramodernism, when many of the most visible contemporary cultural figures considered nineteenth-century art to represent the rubble of the past. Brooks's writing instead encouraged mixing novelty and tradition, experiment and accessibility, highbrow and lowbrow. In doing so, he addressed both the received literary tradition and contemporary art at once, and the central subject of nearly everything he wrote was, at a fundamental level, the apparent conflict between the two.

The journey from the literary world back to Broadway began in the archives. Reading through Brooks's surviving letters—his jagged, diagonal, barely decipherable script—I found a trove of correspondence between him and Brooks Atkinson, the chief theater critic for the New York Times who presided over Broadway premieres for nearly four decades in the mid-twentieth century. In these letters, Brooks and Atkinson disclosed their critical ambitions to each other, poured out their career disappointments, and wondered whether the world would ever be open to middlebrow art, which in their eyes could be cutting-edge without alienating a broader public. One archive led to another, where I found correspondence between Atkinson and Oscar Hammerstein II, detailing a budding friendship based on their common middlebrow sensibilities. When I then reread Atkinson's published reviews, they seemed suddenly different to me: the public-facing branch of a much deeper, broader conversation rooted in debates about the relationship between art and society, in disagreements about our responsibility to the past, in urgent discourse about the weight of tradition on the present, all of which focused, not on literature, but on the Broadway musical. Atkinson, Hammerstein, Brooks, and their colleagues were searching for a style of writing that could speak to the present day's high-art trends while also remaining broadly accessible and popular, in dialogue with the rich traditions of the United States' heartland.

This book, then, examines the Broadway musical at a crucial period of its history, but it is equally the story of clashing modernisms: the modernism of experimental literature, theater, and music, and the middlebrow modernism of Van Wyck Brooks and his allies.[1] Debates about high modernism may seem far removed from the musical comedy, especially its composition and performance. And it is true that not every Broadway composer should be considered middlebrow in the sense it is being used here. Some, after all, still hewed to the cultural values of earlier musicals (a discussion of which lies beyond the scope of this book), and some had the goal of producing top-tier, musical-comedy entertainment *simpliciter*. This study is not about them. Many characters in this book, however, drew upon Brooks and his allies in their work on Broadway. Moreover, they insisted that they be included in this cultural debate by drawing explicit references to "classical" and "popular," and "folk" music in their shows, by claiming more (for lack of a better word) serious intentions for their work, and by inserting themselves into the discourse surrounding American opera during the 1930s and 1940s. Much of this comes to light through this book's archival investigation, which reveals often previously uncharted networks between major literary, theatrical, and musical critics of the early twentieth century on the one hand, and musical-comedy composers, writers, and producers of the same period on the other. The fundamental premise underlying the chapters that follow is that the profound changes in musical comedy of this time must be considered the result of a self-conscious and complex interaction between the popular-culture and high-art traditions. As Broadway composers and librettists began to interact more intentionally with the field of high art, critics increasingly began to view the musical as a repository for those very community virtues that recent experimental art had seemed to brush off. Thus the musical seemed newly serious, newly central to the tradition of art music, theater, and literature, which gave rise to discussions of a revolution in musical comedy (Chapters 4 and 5).

Buoyed by this new sense of seriousness, artists and producers began mounting edgier shows, even on the commercial Broadway stage. Draft

xii PREFACE

libretti show that the musicals featured in the final two chapters (Duke Ellington's *Beggar's Holiday* and Kurt Weill's *Street Scene*) began in an emphatically experimentalist vein. Both also began as provocatively political shows—radical, even. This should not be surprising; most of the musicians and writers involved in these shows, along with most of the producers, directors, choreographers, and designers who also worked on them, began their careers in the left-wing, Popular Front theater of the 1930s, the subject of Chapter 2. Moreover, many of them also had ties to the avant-garde scene in New York during the same decade. This book shows that these associations informed their musicals even after Broadway emerged from the war years. While histories of the Broadway musical generally view the mid-1940s and afterward as a return to entertainment that reaffirmed a stable social order, in this book I show otherwise: Broadway writers who began their careers as political firebrands emerged from the war still intent on expressing their political ideas, even though these ideas tended to change once the war ended.[2] These drafts reveal, however, that at this time, many of these writers and producers were also explicitly reconsidering how to convey their political thoughts, moving away from their avant-garde techniques toward something that struck them as affirmative toward cultural tradition, as middlebrow.

The middlebrow attitude toward culture may seem especially incongruous when considering traditionally underrepresented figures. Black artists such as Duke Ellington, Billy Strayhorn, Perry Watkins, and Langston Hughes all feature prominently in the pages that follow (especially Chapter 4). In the past, there has been a tendency to view their work as standing outside hegemonic culture, as resisting what has been categorized as a predominantly white strain of cultural production. In this book, however, I take a different approach, but the shift is subtle: While these artists protested contemporary oppression in the arts and society, the people featured in these pages also recognized and embraced the idea of an American tradition. Rather than stand apart from it, they insisted that their voices, their experiences, their struggles, and their opinions be included in it. Once again, their stance toward received culture was affirmative, even when they contested the prevailing culture's general outlines.

Although most of the artists in this book took a similarly affirmative approach to culture, they were hardly unified among themselves. Frequent disputes took place among the collaborators and critics about what exactly they were trying to express and about the most effective means for communicating their ideas. During the course of production, each creator was also forced to adjust the techniques he or she had used in the previous decade. The reasons behind these changes were not (or rather, not merely) to make their shows more popular, although that was often a consideration. Rather, each collaborator was trying to devise the most effective way to communicate during the age of postwar readjustment and the age of the so-called integrated musical on Broadway, the subject of Chapters 3–5.

Each chapter describes the dialogue between reviewers and composers, not because it somehow unlocks any "meaning" that the show may have held, but rather because it articulates a set of interpretive parameters that the composer, the writer, and the audience were negotiating at the time.[3] Analyzing the ways in which writers described shows, as "classical," or "popular," "commercial," or "opera," does not endorse or affix such labels (i.e., that a piece is highbrow, a composer is lowbrow). After all, whether a piece is "high" or "low" also depends on perspective; critics have always disagreed about such classifications, and the historian would be put in the impossible position of trying to settle these disputes retroactively. Rather, these words helped define a broad cultural field, they offer a glimpse of how art functioned in a wider marketplace of culture, they test the limits of art's communication, and they explain its political thrust or—crucially—its potential lack thereof.

Ultimately, the point here is not to "correct" the traditional historical view that the mid-century musical started a revolution, one which made musicals more coherent, more unified, more formally integrated, and thereby (if these qualities are seen as ideal) "better."[4] After all, even if evidence shows that musicals had already been formally integrated long before this point, the effect of the new musicals that emerged in the 1940s was to encourage composers and commentators to call attention to the integrated qualities of their shows, to "advertise" the formal properties of their productions—a formal revolution, but of a different sort. This book suggests instead that while there may not exactly have been a revolution in compositional form, there was indeed a change in how composers and critics read and interpreted musicals. These changes resulted from shifts in the way these groups understood which qualities were appropriate, at the most fundamental level, to the very notion of "Broadway musical." The new conceptual apparatus drew its terms from controversies taking place in other fields, which is to say that the musical was no bystander in the debates about modernism that roared through mid-century museums, concert halls, art galleries, and literary magazines. The musical was, in fact, a central player, and its intervention took place, not only on the level of large-scale form, but also at the level of sheer sound, in the remarkable tunes emanating from the pit orchestras of New York's theater district.

Acknowledgments

I am lucky to work in a field where so many colleagues have offered me their time, their ideas, their feedback, and their friendship. Sometimes even casual remarks—a quick email, a post-presentation chat, conversation over drinks—sent my work in vastly new directions. James Hepokoski oversaw the very first stages of this work, and although this manuscript has traveled a long way from those days, his mentorship and teaching have guided every sentence of this book. Thank you also to Tim Carter, Todd Decker, Naomi Graber, Brian Kane, Kim Kowalke, Jim Lovensheimer, Howard Pollack, Tom Riis, W. Anthony Sheppard, Larry Stempel, Michael Veal, and Trudi Wright.

I presented the earliest version of Chapter 1 at the Music and the Middlebrow conference in London in 2017, organized by Christopher Chowrimootoo and Kate Guthrie. Commentary from both Joan Shelley Rubin and Richard Taruskin helped me to shape this material into its current form. That same year, different portions of Chapter 1 were presented at the MC² conference organized by Marguerite Chabrol and Pierre Olivier-Toulza. The conversations I had there with Todd Decker, Adrienne McLean, and Steven Cohan helped me to reframe and revise this work. Chapter 2 began as a keynote address for the Transnational Opera Studies Conference in 2019. Isabelle Moindrot and Céline Firgau-Manning generously gave me ample space and resources to try out these new ideas, and Emmanuele Senici, Gundula Kreuzer, and Martha Feldman all provided enthusiastic and helpful feedback after that presentation. A very different version of Chapter 5 was given at the Transnational Opera Studies Conference in 2017, and Marco Beghelli's enthusiasm for the project, alongside Gundula Kreuzer's and W. Anthony Sheppard's insightful commentary, inspired the final version.

No academic book—and certainly not this one—comes into existence without librarians. I thank Kathy Abromeit, Susan Brady, Richard Boursy, Debbie Campana, Mark Horowitz, Bob Kosovsky, Suzanne Eggleston Lovejoy, Dave Stein, and the late Karl Schrom and Richard Warren, who were so generous with their time and resources. Along the way Stacey Hernandez,

Kathy Li, Shirley Tan, Andrew Wise, and Jessica Osborne all provided valuable research assistance.

Work on this book was supported by a Beinecke Library Summer Fellowship, an Oberlin College Grant-in-Aid, Oberlin College Research Status, and a Kluge Fellowship at the Library of Congress.

Thank you to Nick Betson, Bonnie Blackburn, Dan Blim, David Breitman, Bonnie Cheng, Chris Furman, Anna Gawboy, Sarah Gerk, Stephen Gosden, Jared Hartt, Megan Kaes-Long, Karen Leistra-Jones, Claudia Macdonald, Charles McGuire, Christopher Mirto, Bryan Parkhurst, Steve Plank, John Siciliano, and Sandy Zagarell, who all read portions of this book. My editor, Norm Hirschy, has run the entire race with me (both literally and figuratively), and I thank him for his patience with my pace.

So many friends have been willing to listen to me talk about the book over the years, and they picked me up even at the lowest points of the process: Debbie Doroshow, Tony Marchesi, Nicola Usula, Steve Cifranic, Chris Marx, Joseph Nunn, and David Kazimir. (And, of course, Porter.) Danielle Ward-Griffin has read almost every word of this book. Her eagle eye has made it better at every turn; her advice and friendship helped me to finish it. Vicki Shaghoian kept me close to the music all this time, and her conversation kept me energized about it. Julie Vatain-Corfdir's enthusiastic commentary, her kind invitations to speak at conferences, and her brilliance in so many fields continue to amaze and inspire me.

This book was completed amid hardship. I could never adequately thank Teresa Bejan for all she has done for me. I am grateful to Kieron Cindric's loving attention to detail and his brilliance. But even more than that: He made it all seem worthwhile.

And my dad—he truly knows.

1
"Damnably American"
Defining the Middlebrow

> Some people claim that [Broadway] is the forerunner of a new kind of opera; others insist it will never become opera, because it is not art, nor is it meant to be anything but light entertainment. Being a liberal, I can see both sides.
>
> —Leonard Bernstein, *The Joy of Music* (1956)

Written for a general mid-century audience, Bernstein's essay attempted to situate the Broadway musical between two expansive cultural categories: "art" and "light entertainment." Each term stood for distinct traditions of artistic practice, style, genre, and interpretation, all of which were so familiar, so fundamental that he could assume his readers would recognize them without further explanation. He had no problem placing Broadway, as it was understood at the time, firmly in the popular-culture class, yet he seemed unsure whether the musical would remain there in the future. To explain why, he outlined two opposing attitudes toward these types: The first attitude held high art to be incompatible with low culture; the second admitted that the two could profitably combine. Phrased in theatrical terms, the first maintained that opera and Broadway were two distinct genres; the second proposed that mixing them could produce "a new kind of opera." Yet as Bernstein's final quip suggests, choosing between the two was not merely a matter of taste. Beneath these categories lay conflicts among long-standing artistic value systems, which, in some way that he did not articulate, had become a flashpoint in broader contemporary cultural disputes.

In this book I investigate the multiple, overlapping conflicts that Bernstein described. My subjects are two related watersheds in the history of the

Broadway musical when the distinction (or lack thereof) between opera and Broadway became unusually charged. The first is so well known that nearly every history of American musical theater mentions it. On March 31, 1943, Richard Rodgers and Oscar Hammerstein II's *Oklahoma!* opened in New York, and in it critics immediately recognized a landmark shift in the way shows were composed, a change so drastic that, according to *The Oxford Companion to the American Musical*, "the history of the Broadway musical can accurately be divided into what came before *Oklahoma!* and what came after it."[1] For most historians the show has represented "the first fully integrated musical play," meaning that "the songs in *Oklahoma!* continued the plot and characterization, rather than interrupting them," or as Rodgers himself put it, "the orchestrations sound the way the costumes look."[2] With formal integration came claims of intricacy and sophistication, which marked the show, not as popular entertainment, but rather, according to the headline of *New York Times* critic Olin Downes's review, as "Broadway's Gift to Opera."[3] The show inspired a generation of imitators and an intensity of interpretation that, to many at the time, had seemed more appropriate for classical music.

The second revolution is so obscure that no other history of the Broadway musical describes it as such. It took place around the turn of 1947, when three musicals opened in quick succession: Duke Ellington and John Latouche's *Beggar's Holiday* (December 26, 1946, discussed in Chapter 4); Kurt Weill, Langston Hughes, and Elmer Rice's *Street Scene* (January 9, 1947, discussed in Chapter 5); and Burton Lane, E. Y. Harburg, and Fred Saidy's *Finian's Rainbow* (January 10, 1947). "In two swift weeks the musical theater has surged ahead of its high-toned contemporary, 'the legit,'" wrote *Sunday News* reviewer John Chapman. "The musical show, usually regarded as a happy refuge for the thoughtless and a trap for foolish angels, has been evidencing an artistic creativeness, a willingness to explore new paths, which make recent straight drama look pallid and uncertain in comparison."[4] These shows struck critics as unusually eager to deal frankly with social problems, and as trading in an experimental dramaturgy that had previously seemed out of place in the traditional musical comedy.

Most histories of Broadway subsume both moments under one umbrella concept of Broadway's "Golden Age," a period when Broadway was thought to have developed more sophisticated narrative forms that implied a tighter link between the script, score, and stage production. Around the edges of this story, however, has always lurked a faint shadow of skepticism. "You may

"DAMNABLY AMERICAN" 3

remember that the old musical comedy consisted of a story, songs, dances, scenery, girls and boys," quipped librettists Sam and Bella Spewack in the early 1950s. "On the other hand, the New Art Form consists of a story, songs, dances, scenery, girls and boys."[5] In this vein, many writers today continue to doubt whether a concept such as "integration" could ever adequately convey the innovations of *Oklahoma!* and other musicals of the 1940s. For example, Raymond Knapp, Scott McMillin, and many other scholars have asserted that, rather than the smoothness of unity, they "feel the crackle of difference" in listening to these shows.[6] Moreover, debate today tends to swirl around whether there were integrated musicals before *Oklahoma!*, and writers have cited *On Your Toes* (1936), *Chee-Chee* (1928), *Show Boat* (1927), the Princess Musicals (1915–1918), and George M. Cohan's musicals of the first decade of the twentieth century, to name a few.[7] As the proposed date creeps further back in time, formal integration begins to look less like a revolutionary achievement and more like a common, constant feature of the genre. Taken together, all of this suggests that, whatever revolution *Oklahoma!* may have inspired, integration as a formal concept cannot quite capture it.

In this book I adopt the general contours of Bernstein's discussion to make two broad, foundational shifts from previous Broadway histories. First, I argue that the primary concern facing a self-conscious group of experimental Broadway composers in the early 1940s was not form per se, but rather the wavering line between opera and musical comedy. Starting around this time, what had previously been a genre of enjoyment and extravagance became a forum for discussing rigorous construction and artistic bona fides, even in the mainstream press. Any change in the structure of the musical was a symptom of these shifting ambitions and priorities. Second, I describe the ways that, during the first half of the twentieth century, artistic categories such as "classical" and "popular" became increasingly tangled with political categories such as "the bourgeoisie" and "the people." By the late 1930s and early 1940s, as Broadway composers began to bump up against highbrow music, their previous strategies for interacting with audiences changed drastically, often eliciting blowback from critics. This permanently altered the very sense of what seemed appropriate subject matter for a typical Broadway musical, and it raised questions about the relationship between art and audience, between medium and message, between stage and society.

In other words, what happened when *Oklahoma!* opened was less a change in form and more a change in the very institution of the Broadway musical—a change in the way people talked about it, heard it, wrote it, produced it, and

4   THE MIDDLEBROW MUSICAL

understood it.[8] For example, although the Spewacks could detect no formal distinction between old and new musicals—both, after all, "consisted of a story, songs, dances, scenery, girls and boys"—they did note a difference of purpose: "The New Art Form require[s] a message."[9] By straddling classical seriousness and popular accessibility, and by mixing together concepts from high art, folk art, and popular art, musical-comedy composers asserted a new mission for Broadway, one that was both serious in intent and popular in appeal. The musical, at this moment, became middlebrow.

"Something New in History": Defining Middlebrow Culture

This book opens at a topsy-turvy moment in American cultural history. "The West has been won, the immigrants melted down, the factories and railroads built to such effect that since 1929 the problem has been consumption rather than production," claimed critic Dwight Macdonald in 1962. "The work week has shrunk, real wages have risen, and never in history have so many people attained such a high standard of living as in this country since 1945."[10] Along with prosperity came new access to education. Between 1900 and 1920, high school attendance jumped by 650%, and college attendance tripled.[11] The boom became an explosion; between 1940 and 1960, college enrollment tripled again. "Money, leisure and knowledge, the prerequisite for culture, are more plentiful and more evenly distributed than ever before," Macdonald wrote.[12] This meant that, by at least the 1930s, high, genteel culture—once consumed primarily by those who had sufficient means and time to spend on it—had become popular and salable.[13] New institutions rose to cater to the increased demand for literature, music, and art. The Book-of-the-Month Club combined slick advertising and university erudition to transform literature into mass culture.[14] Radio programs turned living rooms into lecture halls.[15] Subscription theaters and little theaters, offering the newest experimental American writers, replaced the vaudeville circuit.[16] Toynbee and Einstein became celebrities.[17] Sears sold Rembrandt prints.[18] Amid all this cultural activity, a British neologism from the mid-1920s came to spawn a veritable cottage industry of criticism in the United States: This was the era of "middlebrow" culture.[19] For Macdonald, "this [was] something new in history," and he marshaled a group of cultural critics to resist it.[20]

At the center of my analysis of the Broadway musical sits the concept of "middlebrow" culture. By way of introduction, a description follows of its

"DAMNABLY AMERICAN" 5

main features as they were articulated during an early 1940s dispute between the middlebrow's foremost detractor, Dwight Macdonald, and its foremost supporter, Van Wyck Brooks. Their debates began in the field of literature, but reverberated outward to art, music, and theater, including the Broadway musical. In the course of their arguments, they developed idiosyncratic ways of defining "middlebrow" that would prove influential among their contemporaries, and that differ in important ways from the way writers tend to use the word today.

For historians, one of the most difficult tasks has been ascertaining what *kind* of concept "middlebrow" was. Did it refer to a style of art? Did it refer to the taste of a certain economic or intellectual class of people? Or did it tend to be invective, a term that deflated the pretensions of art that purported to be serious? It was, at various times, each of these, and at times all of these. But throughout the term's history, the core, irreducible feature of the middlebrow was that it referred broadly to art that jumbled together popular appeal and highbrow erudition or technique. For example, studies of middlebrow culture and criticism often cite literary historian Lawrence Levine's famous study *Highbrow/Lowbrow*, which describes concert halls or minstrel shows that performed Shakespeare and Verdi.[21] Historian Ann Douglas and literary scholar Lauren Berlant describe the encroachment of sentimentality (typically gendered feminine) on the American novel in the works of Harriet Beecher Stowe, a kind of book that was sweeping in scope, sentimental in mood, literary in pretension, and popular in appeal.[22] Musicologist Christopher Chowrimootoo classifies Benjamin Britten as one among many mid-century composers who "[allowed] contemporary audiences to have their modernist cake and eat it: to revel in the pleasures of tonality, melody, sentimentality, melodrama, and spectacle, even while enjoying the prestige that comes from rejecting them."[23]

Another corollary feature of the mid-century middlebrow, which each of these studies has emphasized, is a pervasive sense of anxiety surrounding the word. It stems from its neither-here-nor-there logic, which bucks the familiar binaries between fine art and popular, serious and commercial, experimental and mainstream, highbrow and lowbrow.[24] Pioneering studies by cultural historians Janice Radway and Joan Shelley Rubin, for example, have described moments in United States history when critics worried that slipping too easily between classical and popular would make it difficult to distinguish so-called real culture from posturing.[25] They argued that classics had typically been prestigious not simply because of any inherent literary value or style, but also because certain institutions—the church, the university—had deemed them so.[26] However, in a country that has always lacked an official academy to designate some culture as prestigious, artistic pedigrees have been obscure and boundaries have been fuzzy; some worried that culture had lost the ability to anoint.[27] When markers of distinction became available for general consumption, supposedly stable hierarchies of class, gender, and race turned shaky, a condition that literary critic John Guillory once called the "ordeal of middlebrow culture."[28] Some segments of American society have long celebrated the dissolution of these boundaries, but those who had previously enjoyed privileged access to cultural prestige typically reacted against the climbing classes, seeking to reassert "real" culture (whatever that may have been) and rigid boundaries (however they may have been drawn).[29] This is to say that, whatever the aesthetic connotations of the "middlebrow" may have been, social and political controversy have always trailed closely behind.

Without abandoning those insights, in this study I focus more on the positive components of the middlebrow, portraying it as a set of active, affirmative, principled choices that linked art, economics, and politics into a coherent worldview.[30] According to Macdonald, these particular "middlebrow" theoretical elements coalesced around a group of critics in New York in the 1910s and 1920s, and Macdonald would eventually disparage their writing as representing the dominant, dangerous, and "damnably American" cultural development of the early twentieth century.[31]

From a broad perspective, when Macdonald used the words "highbrow," "middlebrow," or "lowbrow" to discuss these critics' writing, he rarely was referring to a style, genre, venue, or medium in any straightforward sense. Rather, these terms described two broad aspects of their work. First, they indicated a "critical mood," a manner of consuming art.[32] As such, the term consolidated far-flung works that were likely to be approached by audiences in the same way, even if they appeared otherwise unrelated—a cubist painting and a Beethoven symphony, for example, could each potentially strike somebody as having an "elevated" tone, an "abstract" style, or a "classical" sound, all of which could signal that a piece was highbrow. In labeling a piece highbrow, as opposed to middlebrow or lowbrow, the critic was essentially contending that it should be consumed according to a particular set of guidelines or attitudes: studied, not enjoyed; examined, not seen; listened to, not heard. "Middlebrow," in its most fundamental sense, connoted a critical mood that enthusiastically (or, for Macdonald, promiscuously) mixed

"DAMNABLY AMERICAN" 7

concepts, behaviors, expectations, vocabularies, and interpretive strategies that had traditionally seemed proper exclusively to either high art or low art. Second, Macdonald believed that middlebrow culture had a hidden social or political meaning that lay beyond a given piece's immediate subject matter. For him, refusing to discern between high- and low-art practices was alarming because it suggested that a particular artist or audience was unwilling to adopt a critical attitude, and thus was willing to assent to just about anything in art, good or bad, virtuous or harmful. "Masscult [a kind of middlebrow culture] is very, very democratic," Macdonald wrote; "it refuses to discriminate against or between anything or anybody. All is grist to its mill and all comes out finely ground indeed."[33] For Macdonald, resisting the "middlebrow" meant more than defending good taste. It was also a political act.

"They, the People": The Oppositional Approach to Culture

Categorizing culture by its broad "critical mood," and asserting the social and political implications of adopting that mood, had long been a feature of American criticism among then-famous writers such as Samuel Hopkins Adams, Jane Addams, Rollin Lynde Hartt, and Frederick Winsor, many of whom had also used terms such as "highbrow" and "lowbrow" to consolidate this art.[34] They had often argued, for example, that popular culture appealed to the baser, primal passions instead of the intellect, and in this context, terms derived from phrenology (such as "low-browed") linked race, ethnicity, or heritage with cultural grace (or lack thereof). Macdonald followed them in using these words to consolidate art based on its social function, but for him they did not carry biological connotations. Moreover, there was an additional important feature of Macdonald's criticism that his predecessors did not share: an emphatically oppositional stance that made him hostile to many established institutions and artistic traditions, a position that developed among critics in New York just as the word "middlebrow" entered the American lexicon. The gradual process of defining the middlebrow cannot be separated from the emergence of this new oppositional stance. Those who adopted the latter explicitly distinguished themselves against the former.

The first American to use the term "middlebrow" in print was probably the Pulitzer Prize–winning poet Margaret Widdemer, and she defined it from the point of view of somebody from the oppositional camp. She deployed it in 1933 to disparage art that tried to communicate any Message (capital M) whatsoever to its audience, and thereby she disavowed the clutched-pearl mores of Victorian art.[35] She claimed instead that true art should be "purposeless," that it should be written "*sub specie aeternitatis*." She considered any gestures toward usefulness, accessibility, or enjoyment to be a compromise with the masses—and thereby hopelessly middlebrow. Political justification for this hardline aesthetic stance followed: She argued that, in the "*bouleversée* world" after World War I when morals had gone askew, the only stable order to be found was in pure artistic technique. "Art or technique is in the saddle, dictator," she wrote (using language that would carry increasingly ominous overtones in the decade to follow). In a world gone mad, she suggested, art should divest itself of moral commitment altogether. "Art, as the Philistines, not to speak of Plato, always observed, is a dangerous guide for the mass. Art has always had to be without concern for any standards but its own."[36] The effect was to establish and occupy a critical vantage point that was set apart from both familiar literary trends and their attendant audiences, a move that she justified as a response to contemporary political hysteria.

Shortly thereafter, a more extreme version of this stance became the general position of the infamous New York intellectuals, a group of political thinkers who largely leaned toward the far left, and who counted Macdonald among their ranks. In part they picked up the general outlines of Widdemer's argument—her wariness of "usefulness" and popularity, her contempt of Philistine art for its presumed social effects, and her hope that a hypertrophic artistic technique could heal social wounds—but the New York Intellectuals would overlay her ideas with a critique of mass culture that had become increasingly common since the turn of the twentieth century. Their broad contention was that starting in the late nineteenth century, as Madison Avenue developed new techniques of advertising based on demographic research, art began to be sold as if it were a mass-produced good.[37] The effect was to turn, not just literature, but literacy itself into a salable commodity: Institutions began to market the idea of a classic as holding an attainable quality that could confer an air of sophistication on the consumer. In this atmosphere, they complained, classics became part of a transactional approach to culture, in which art paid a social subvention to its consumers in the form of prestige, sophistication, or expertise. The New York intellectuals feared that cultural institutions would turn away from preserving and promoting the excellence of this or that work of art per se and would turn instead thinking about how a particular customer might encounter that object, toward selling the experience of reading a kind of book, or toward the promise that some class of art or music could do something for a certain kind of reader.[38] In effect, art would no longer be an emblem of independent thinking; it would simply serve the marketplace, along with its established systems of power. They urged readers to resist these trends.

Unlike earlier critiques of mass culture, the New York Intellectuals, relying in part on Marxist ideology critique, argued that both popular culture and familiar classical culture were emblems of bourgeois authority, trading in familiar, predigested forms of art that required no thought from their audience, only passive acceptance and cash.[39] These critics believed that classical art and popular culture could be equally harmful depending on the attitude that producers and audiences adopted toward them. Somebody who "merely" accepted classical art as authoritative, great, or serious was as uncritical as somebody who was content "merely" to enjoy the latest release on the hit parade or bestseller list. For the New York Intellectuals, the middlebrow attitude was the epitome of being uncritical because it indiscriminately jumbled high and low without challenging the reigning practices of each. The middlebrow attitude may have seemed open-minded or even-handed, but these critics argued that it was actually authoritarian because it lulled the masses into acquiescing in a bourgeois social order that thrived on the inherent hierarchies of this literary marketplace.[40]

To combat the middlebrow, Macdonald and his fellow New York Intellectuals praised artists who flaunted flouting, who produced "genuine" culture—folk art, redolent of a time before the modern culture industry took shape, and thereby an emblem of resistance to it; and avant-garde art, which rejected traditional institutions, norms, and practices and thereby stood apart from salable, mass-produced art for general consumption and capitalist profit. For them, this art proudly occupied the uncorrupted, alienated margins against a vast mob at the center, and their goal was to cultivate a critical, discerning intellectual class that could create a bulwark against the culture industry. (Macdonald's pen name in Socialist Workers Party publications was James Joyce;[41] one of his earliest columns, written for New International from July to September 1938, was called "They, the People.") They encouraged artists to resist received culture and tradition, to create something autonomous, "valid solely in its own terms," "something given, increate, independent of meanings, similars, or originals," as Macdonald's

Partisan Review colleague Clement Greenberg put it in his famous 1939 article "Avant-Garde and Kitsch" (which, incidentally, began as a letter to Macdonald that Greenberg expanded for publication).[42] This negative stance toward received culture at large was the antidote to bourgeois art because, unfettered by shopworn institutions or ingrained habits of consumption, artists could "express [their] own peculiar personality" freely, without being stifled by modern, bourgeois society.[43]

Scholars have recently shown that, despite the oppositional modernists' apparent disdain for the mainstream organizations that distributed culture in the United States, they too used them.[44] By the late 1930s, the main figures of this movement were beginning to garner increasing attention in more mainstream outlets. This includes Macdonald, who stood at the nexus of "official" education, mainstream cultural journalism, middlebrow magazine publication, the Marxist backlash, the radical journals of the 1930s and 1940s, and the avant-garde. Starting in 1937, he rose to fame as one of the editors of *Partisan Review*, a left-wing magazine that tended to focus on the relationship between class struggle and broader American culture. Its circulation never topped 10,000, but nonetheless it has come to occupy a central position in the history of American letters.[45] Many of the writers who appeared in its pages in the late 1930s would become some of the most influential critics of the twentieth century. Clement Greenberg, Meyer Shapiro, Mary McCarthy, James Agee, and many others emerged from the *Partisan Review* to much larger audiences in later years, eventually holding prominent faculty positions around the country and writing for magazines such as *The New Yorker*, *Harper's*, *The New Republic*, *Time*, and *The Nation*. In addition, starting in the late 1930s and gaining speed with Macdonald's new magazine *politics* that he founded in 1944 (after he split from *Partisan Review*), these writers brought exiled, left-wing critics from the Frankfurt School to some of their earliest public attention in the United States.[46] They included Theodor Adorno, Max Horkheimer, and Leo Lowenthal, who had recently arrived in New York, and who had also begun to assume university positions in the United States, most famously at Columbia University. Although the New York intellectuals and the Frankfurt School differed in important details, at a broad level, both groups tended to seek out authoritarian tendencies in the aesthetic experience, and they largely believed that middlebrow culture was "compromised": it appeared to be entertainment, while it actually functioned as a tool of oppression used to control the masses.[47] The solution, they believed, was to promote art that stood altogether apart from these masses, from present-day politics and business—art that wore its autonomy as a bold badge of honor.

"A Usable Past": The Affirmative Approach to Culture

Starting in the late 1910s and early 1920s, writers in a set of popular magazines—*The New Yorker, Vanity Fair,* and others—began to develop what would become a rebuttal to the nascent mass-culture critique, and their arguments would eventually form the kernel of the middlebrow approach to art. They grouped the entire, disparate avant-garde movement under the umbrella term "modernism," based in part on the style or technique found in the art, and also on the artists' overarching disposition toward culture, society, and politics. In other words, the word "modernism" in their hands did the same kind of consolidating work that the term "middlebrow" would later do in the hands of the *Partisan Review* critics.[48] According to these authors, the central trait that bound each of these far-flung movements to "modernism" was their oppositional stance toward received culture, tradition, and familiar artistic institutions.

Middlebrow writers, however, did not merely consolidate "modernist" art under one umbrella concept of "opposition." They rebuked it. This group rejected rejection, negated negation, and took an explicit, principled, and public stand against certain strains of experimental art.[49] If the oppositional approach was anathema to sentiment, subversive of authority, and suspicious of beauty, middlebrow culture accepted past canons of beauty and quality, explicitly situated themselves within tradition, recognized and respected cultural authority, and approached culture open to learning, feeling, and experiencing. If highbrow texts demanded that the reader take part in the production of meaning, middlebrow texts encouraged readers to identify with the text, to learn from it, to understand it, or even to enjoy it.[50] And if the oppositional avant-garde marshaled these cultural arguments into a critique of bourgeois society, the middlebrow tended to marshal their aesthetic opinions into a different political approach, one that sought to unify a society that had splintered along cultural lines.

By the late 1930s, according to Macdonald, the middlebrow was legion, but he singled out Van Wyck Brooks as its leader. Brooks belonged to an earlier generation of literary radicals than Macdonald, one that formed prior to the Great Depression and before the influx of European émigrés

12   THE MIDDLEBROW MUSICAL

rocked the intellectual scene in New York City. Brooks was born in 1886 in Plainfield, New Jersey ("a suburb of Wall Street," as he would call it[51]) and attended Harvard University, which at the time was a hotbed of philosophical Pragmatism. The general mood of this intellectual movement—which made abstract rigor responsible to personal experience; which insisted upon academic inquiry that was socially conscious and avowedly democratic—left its mark on Brooks's later middlebrow criticism about American literature.[52] (Many of the critics in the chapters that follow who were sympathetic to Brooks's ideas also studied at Harvard around this time, including Gilbert Seldes, Brooks Atkinson, and Alain Locke.) In 1908, just after he graduated from college, Brooks renounced his capitalist past, moved briefly to England, and published his first book of criticism, *The Wine of the Puritans*. In this book Brooks identified the central problem that would occupy him for the next five decades: Could the United States claim an artistic tradition that was specifically American? The answer, he argued, was no. "For the Americans alone among all the races of the world, cannot seek for any interpretation of life in their own remote antiquity, simply because the childhood of America is the childhood of another country," he wrote. "We seek in [our ancestors] virtues to be copied, and we find their virtues negative, necessarily negative; noble for them because adapted to their situation, but obsolete and ill-adapted for ours."[53]

Many writers had previously addressed the question of American tradition, but Brooks approached the problem differently. He focused (much like Macdonald would do thirty years later) on the ways that artists situated their work in broader political, social, and economic contexts. He turned his attention toward established artistic institutions, which, in his 1915 book *America's Coming of Age*, he divided into two groups: the highbrow and the lowbrow. He argued that, on the one hand, the highbrow "vaporous idealism" of university education pursued cold, lofty, theoretical rigor, while on the other hand, the lowbrow "self-interested practicality" of the business world chased immediate gratification and personal gain. Each considered the other useless.[54] However, while previous critics had tended to endorse either the highbrow's genteel theory or the lowbrow's Pioneer practicality, Brooks dismissed both as "equally unsocial."[55] His goal was to find a "middle path" between the two, to bring to a practical, mundane world "those personal instincts that have been the essence of art, religion, literature—the essence of personality itself—since the beginning of things," and to do so in a way that would "directly concern the mass of men as a whole."[56] This, in fact, is the crucial, defining feature of the middlebrow: Not merely a style, class, or set of practices, "middlebrow" signified a critical mood that believed highbrow and lowbrow art could combine without obliterating the special qualities of each.

Equally important for Brooks was the reason to combine these separate categories of art. He believed that American society had fractured into incompatible sects, differentiated not only by ethnicity or class, but also by learning, taste, and culture. An art that could bridge these divides could potentially rejoin the American public. In his hands, terms such as "organic," "wholeness," and "unity" signified, not a tightly constructed artwork or internal referential structure, but rather sympathy between art, creator, and audience, and in the 1910s he began to offer suggestions for how literature could help foster what his colleague Randolph Bourne called a "beloved community."[57] Joining together various strands of his previous arguments, Brooks began to argue that the impediment to any collective American tradition was rampant highbrow experimentation—literary "anarchy," he called it—which had become an end in itself, autonomous, and thereby cut off from a sense of any broader "cultural economy," from any "body of critical understanding," or from "any sense of inherited resources."[58] "We want bold ideas, and we have nuances," he wrote. "We want vitality, and we have intellectualism. We want emblems of desire, and we have Niagaras of emotionality. We want expansion of the soul, and we have an elephantiasis of the vocal organs."[59] The solution, he argued, was to fuse highbrow theory and lowbrow practicality. Early in his career, he described this process in oracular, mystical, reverential terms. "Art as an institution," he wrote, referring to "classical" or "highbrow" culture, "dissolves toward pure soul."[60] However, as he started writing for radical magazines in New York City (including *Seven Arts*, *The Freeman*, and *The Dial*), he developed a more concrete historical method, which he outlined in his 1918 article "On Creating a Usable Past." First, while he had claimed previously that the United States had no literary past, he changed his position subtly: At this point, he started to claim the United States has no *suitable* literary past. The cause for this, he said, lay not in any actual lack, but rather in what he called the "almost pathological vindictiveness" of contemporary critics.[61] According to him, they promoted an idea of tradition that, rather than describing a common heritage, served merely as a cudgel to abuse young writers by "[comparing] the 'poetasters of today' with certain august figures of the age of pioneering who have long since fallen into oblivion in the minds of men and women in the world."[62]

14   THE MIDDLEBROW MUSICAL

Second, he reframed the entire discussion in psychoanalytic terms. He argued that present-day literary pathology could be treated by analyzing the past. Thereby tradition would be *useful* to the present in a therapeutic sense: The historian could heal today's literary maladies by rooting out their latent causes. "Why not trace these elements back," he asked, referring to underdeveloped or inchoate artistic ideas in the present day, "analyzing them on the way, and showing how they first manifested themselves, and why, and what repelled them?"[63] For Brooks, even as the psychological component fell away in subsequent years, it remained central to his middlebrow approach that present-day art and criticism should be responsible to a broader community, sensitive to its past and its traditions, part of the community's collective culture, even when it attempted novelty or experiment.

"The Middlebrow Counterrevolution": A Clash of Modernisms

Both the affirmative middlebrow and oppositional modernist camps articulated their core beliefs during the 1920s and 1930s. Soon after, the two groups came into direct conflict. In 1935 Brooks joined the League of American Writers, and as a member he banded together with authors Lewis Mumford and Malcolm Cowley to steer the league away from hardline Communism and toward a more middlebrow discussion of America's literary (and liberal) heritage.[64] Also starting in the mid-1930s, Brooks turned his critical attention on the avant-garde literary scene (especially William Faulkner, T. S. Eliot, Gertrude Stein, and Ezra Pound). In two speeches, "On Literature Today" (first delivered at Hunter College in June 1940) and "Primary and Coterie Literature" (delivered in September 1941),[65] Brooks denounced these writers: They were "maladjusted," "dilletanti," "*des enfants qui se sucent le pouce*" supported by "camp-followers"; their abstruse work was "baby-language," "gibberish," "crossword puzzles"; their oppositional stance was a "death-drive," a "dead hand," "the ash of a burned out cigar." They were narcissistic: "They implied a general denial of progress . . . [because] if there was no progress, there was nothing to prevent them from taking their personal bent for the primary thing."[66] They were amoral: Because their writing "evaded the whole world of values, which is justly the concern of criticism, it lay outside the field of literature. It was properly a discipline in the field of science."[67] His contemporaries found these words shocking, and they ignited a literary battle that divided the critical world.[68]

Macdonald organized a coordinated response against Brooks. In public, he called Brooks the leader of a regressive, "circular pattern of the entire modern movement in American letters," a "Middlebrow Counter-Revolution," or "counterattack" against oppositional, avant-garde art. Between 1939 and 1941 alone, *Partisan Review* published no fewer than four essays attacking Brooks specifically, and eventually the magazine would produce dozens of articles aimed at attacking middlebrow culture in general.[69] A middlebrow victory, Macdonald argued in one essay, would portend an era of oppression in which critics would "impose on the writer *from outside* certain socio-political values, and ... provide a rationalization for damning his work *esthetically* if it [failed] to conform to these *social values*."[70] Show trials would surely follow, he believed, which would purge dissenting, critical intellectuals in favor of bourgeois, totalitarian rule. Behind the scenes, too, Macdonald fumed, and he marshaled comrades-in-arms.[71] For example, in a letter to critic Edmund Wilson dated November 1941, Macdonald wrote:

I take it you agree it's a serious matter, going far beyond Brooks's own personal failings and asininity—a symptom of growing cultural repression and regimentation. And in that case, it would seem the responsibility of writers on *our* side of the fence to stick their necks out now, to speak out publicly against this sort of thing. Personal letters don't do the job at all.[72]

At the most basic level, Macdonald objected to the very idea that "modernists" or the "avant-garde" could be consolidated under a single label. After all, avant-garde art was supposed to be irreducible, independent of familiar classification based on familiar ideas, responsible only to itself for logic. However, despite his dudgeon, Macdonald did acknowledge the classification. "It is true that the approach of the coterie writers to the specific historical values of modern society is negativistic, cynical, sceptical [sic], destructive, etc.," he wrote.[73] No matter that Macdonald adopted this pose as a point of pride; middlebrow writers such as Brooks exposed his attitude as a pose, a stance toward culture with familiar, reproducible contours, regardless of how individual it claimed to be. Worse, according to middlebrow writers, both the critical mood and social agenda of the oppositional camp threatened to deepen American's rifts along cultural lines.

Thus were the battle lines drawn by the early 1940s, and they divide nearly all the critics in the pages that follow. Ultimately the point here is not to endorse one theory or the other. Rather, it is simply to observe that the divide between the oppositional modernist attitude and the affirmative middlebrow attitude toward culture is not a *post hoc*, retrospective historiographical heuristic. It was well recognized at the time, both in public and in private correspondence, and by the early 1940s this dispute divided the critical world. Like Macdonald, Brooks counted powerful critics among his supporters in many fields of criticism, including Brooks Atkinson, Waldo Frank, Alfred Kazin, Alain Locke, Archibald MacLeish, Paul Rosenfeld, Gilbert Seldes, and René Wellek. During the heat of battle, Brooks won a Pulitzer, a National Book Award, and appeared on the cover of *Time* magazine (the caption: "He is rediscovering the American Past").[74] Lionel Trilling, who wrote for *Partisan Review* and often disagreed with Brooks, nonetheless allowed in 1954 that Brooks was "of significance that, for our time, is perhaps unique."[75] In 1958 even Macdonald had conceded defeat at Brooks's hands: "by 1940 the avantgarde had run out of gas."[76]

He need not have worried. The avant-garde side of the feud tends to remain well known to scholarship today, and many of its defenders entered academia during the second half of the twentieth century. Brooks's reputation, however, generally has not fared well among recent critics and academics.[77] Brooks died in 1963, and already by 1968 his own biographer would claim that Brooks had moved "from the center to the farthest margins of literary influence."[78] Only three years later, this same biographer would call Brooks's influence "pernicious" because it led "to the celebration of a style of literary culture, middlebrow, in which contrarieties are denied. It is a view, too, which bolsters an ideal of social order, in the style of Lyndon B. Johnson or Richard Nixon in which in the name of consensus radical conflict is ignored or suppressed."[79] Since then, many critics have claimed that after 1930, when Brooks emerged from a fallow period to criticize the avant-garde, he slid into a bland jingoism or cultural shamanism in which critic-prophets murmured visions of a mystical better world where all mankind enjoyed a specifically American spiritual unity.[80] Today Brooks's works remain peripheral to American criticism.[81] For all intents and purposes, Macdonald won his war.

In part, the goal of this book is to revive and reconsider the other side of the debate, Brooks's side, and to describe how he and other middlebrow critics, musicians, and artists fought back. Well-known oppositional writers like Macdonald were quick to dismiss the middlebrow affirmative attitude as vapid or "uncritical," but when the debate about middlebrow culture erupted in public in the early 1940s, Brooks's influence spread much more widely than Macdonald's, albeit among different groups: newspaper and magazine

"DAMNABLY AMERICAN" 17

critics, critics of modernism who had fallen out with the avant-garde crowd, and composers of popular culture in the United States, including Broadway. In 1941, for example, critic Alfred Kazin joined the fray against the oppositional (or, his word: "isolated") stance of the New York Intellectuals. He lamented that critics like Macdonald believed that alienation was itself a virtue. "There is no criticism in America today," he wrote, "there are only critics; and though the best of them have invested criticism with an expertness, a grace, an austerity, never known before in America, their work has a kind of high, solemn futility."[82] He would continue to see the oppositional attitude as the central problem of literary criticism for the next twenty years, arguing that these critics "would never feel that they had compromised, for they believed in alienation, and would forever try to outdo conventional opinion even when they agreed with it."[83]

Journalist and editor Russell Lynes also joined in the debate on Brooks's side, most notably with his famous essay "Highbrow, Lowbrow, Middlebrow" in *Harper's Magazine*, which would become so popular that it would eventually inspire a Broadway revue (*Touch and Go* by Walter and Jean Kerr from 1949).[84] Lynes turned on its head Macdonald's assertion that popular culture was any more authoritarian than highbrow culture or folk culture. "If we ever have intellectual totalitarianism, it may well be the lowbrows [roughly, folk artists] and the highbrows who will run things, and the middlebrows who will be exiled in boxcars to a collecting point probably in the vicinity of Independence, Missouri," words which, on the heels of World War II, must have been especially striking.[85] Lynes instead wrote in praise of the dilettante, "the kind who brings to art intelligent critical interest, an excitement for what is both serious and new, and respect for historical development without a frenzied belief in the sanctity of the past—or of the present, for that matter."[86] He, in other words, praised Brooks's middle path; he praised those who situated their own personal tastes within a larger tradition and community, who were both individual and social at the same time.[87] "And when there is a sufficient group of people more interested in art than in looking as though they were interested, then perhaps there will be a climate in which art will find itself the legitimate concern of a great mass of people who will accept it as a necessary part of the pleasure of living."[88]

Brooks's influence, however, was not limited to debate in public fora. Behind the scenes, he kept up a lively correspondence with most of the famous literary figures of his day, including many of the writers who will appear in the chapters that follow. What emerges is a network of critics and artists who took an active part in debates about high art and its relationship to popular art. Like intellectual Marxism, which encompassed a wide range of supporters, from pink enthusiasts to fellow travelers to apparatchiks, middlebrows also ran the gamut from the generalist to the theorist, bound together by certain core beliefs about tradition and the ideal relationship between popular culture and high art, between art and audience. They also tended to reject the kind of avant-garde that would dominate critical discourse in the second half of the twentieth century.

For scholars today, the middlebrow offers a cogent rebuttal to some of the early theories of the avant-garde. It is only by understanding what Brooks and his colleagues hoped to achieve in popular culture that we can understand why 1947 might have appeared to be a middlebrow theatrical revolution, and it is only in understanding why a different kind of critique supplanted middlebrow thought in historical writing that we can understand why 1947 no longer seems a watershed in Broadway history.

2

Authentic, Autonomous, Popular

An Institutional Approach to Middlebrow Culture on Broadway

During the 1920s and 1930s, the middlebrow cultural values introduced in Chapter 1 spread outward from literature to music, art, poetry, and theater, including the Broadway musical. Even in these other media, the central disputes persisted, transposed into the discourses of other artistic fields: Critics continued to debate the ideal relationship between artist and community, the proper attitude toward tradition, the ways in which art could address modern social problems, and so on. Moreover, the two archetypal positions that Dwight Macdonald and Van Wyck Brooks had sketched in their writings remained intact: first, Macdonald's oppositional point of view that rejected what he perceived to be hoary techniques from the past in favor of something startlingly, bracingly new; and second, Brooks's middlebrow point of view that sought to incorporate artistic experiment into a broader, shared cultural tradition.

Understanding this process of generalization requires looking beyond the well-documented disagreements between Brooks and Macdonald, and focusing instead on their often overlooked points of agreement, a set of mutual understandings that was just as remarkable and consequential as their surface rancor. Both Brooks and Macdonald, for instance, rarely aimed to assess the aesthetic merits of this or that work for its own sake. Instead, they considered individual pieces to be instantiations of an artistic macrocosm, which they divided into "highbrow" and "lowbrow." Although they used each term differently, at a broader level these words functioned in the same way for both writers: They adumbrated general artistic "institutions" that encapsulated an entire cluster of linked ideas: the attitudes, habits, behaviors, vocabularies, expectations, and generic or stylistic categorizations that supported interpretive norms across a wide range of media.[1] To borrow a phrase from cultural theorists Peter and Crista Bürger, Brooks and Macdonald both described how "the institution functions within the work, just as the work functions within the institution."[2] With this in mind, Brooks's and Macdonald's shared vocabulary of "highbrow" and "lowbrow" amounted to shorthand for describing familiar, otherwise tacit institutional patterns of thinking about, producing, describing, and consuming art.

For both writers, each institution represented a set of conceptual boundaries that separated art (in the strong sense) from mere culture, and both critics drew those boundaries in strikingly similar ways.[3] At the heart of these distinctions lay two broad questions. First: Was art to be aloof from workaday life, consigned to private contemplation, or was it to be an active part of daily activity and political thought? This was the question of art's "autonomy," which, over the course of the nineteenth century, had often come to mean that the value of art lay in its abstract, formal ingenuity. Autonomous works gave the impression of being sui generis, self-sufficient, organic, and independent of shopworn convention;[4] the meaning of these works often lay in their purported distance from prosaic activity, giving rise to familiar claims of transcendence or spiritual insight, in which art became an antidote for the fallen, modern, mundane world.[5]

Second, and overlapping: Was art to be a part of the modern cultural marketplace (both the literal and figurative), or was it to resist that market? This was the question of art's "authenticity," which rejected the merely popular, the merely commercial, the merely modern, in favor of something that was supposedly folkish, communal, essential, and "original." As ethnomusicologist Philip Bohlman has noted, these supposed "origins" always remained intentionally—and productively—vague. Rather than pinpoint these origins to any particular moment, critics tended to defer them constantly to some prelapsarian time: before modernity, before industrialization, before mass culture. Therein lay its validity: Authentic art supposedly remained untainted by the cynicism, individualism, chaos, and commercialism of the urban, modern world.[6]

Across the board, both Brooks and Macdonald (and, as will become clear, many of their contemporaries) answered such questions more or less the same way, and therefore recognized the same three prevailing institutions: first, autonomous or highbrow art; second, authentic or folk art; and third, popular culture or mass culture, which fit into neither category and which may not have been art at all (see Figure 2.1).[7] The institutions of autonomy and authenticity struck these critics as two sides of the same untendered coin. Both were idealist in conception. If autonomy located true art "beyond" the here and now, authenticity located true art "before" the here

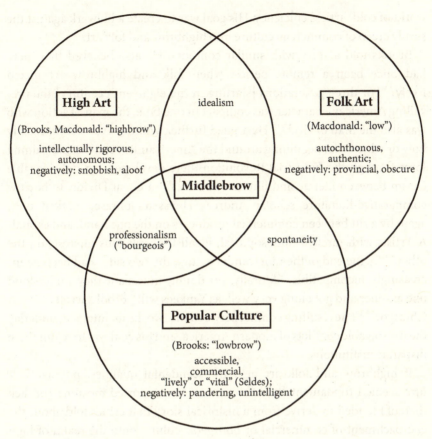

Figure 2.1 Overview of institutions of art and culture.

and now.[8] Macdonald, for example, claimed that both categories represented an antediluvian artistic culture, which, prior to the industrial age, was enmeshed in small communities and imbued with an aura of personal association and immediate emotional significance: court, church, folk. "There could obviously be no mass culture until there were masses, in our modern sense," Macdonald wrote. "The industrial revolution produced the masses. It uprooted people from their agrarian communities and packed them into factory cities.... Up to then, there was only High Culture and Folk Art."[9] As industry encroached upon these local communities during the nineteenth century, and as people moved from small communities into large cities, their handiwork transferred from workshops to factories. In Macdonald's telling, instrumental reason turned a world aflame with personal associations into a world of cold, artless efficiency. His goal was to create a bulwark against the steady creep of commercial culture into highbrow and folk art.

Brooks told a story with similar contours. He also believed that there had once been a remote period when folk and highbrow art mixed freely: "For three generations [starting in the eighteenth century] the prevailing American character was compact in one type, the man of action who was also the man of God."[10] He argued further, without ever stating exactly how or why,[11] that beginning around the American Revolution and gaining force through the Industrial Revolution there developed "an unbridgeable chasm between literate and illiterate America"—a Great Divide, to borrow comparative-literature scholar Andreas Huyssen's phrase, marked once again by a rift between commercial producers on the one hand, and capital-A Artists with rarefied philosophical, idealist, or religious interests on the other.[12] By the end of the nineteenth century, the two sides had become increasingly incompatible. "Morally, no doubt, in Jaalam they understood one another and got along very well, as Yankees will," Brooks wrote. "But in Chicago?"[13] The resulting conflict between the two, he maintained, underlay the irresolvable conflicts of modern America, and his goal was to rejoin these disparate institutions.

If highbrow and folk art held transcendental qualities, popular culture seemed fundamentally different, and its purported meaning (or lack thereof) tended to derive from a historical story that critics told about the encroachment of commercial or bourgeois culture onto the realm of high art.[14] At the end of the eighteenth century, the story goes, composers, artists, and writers forsook their courtly patronage and began to compete in the wider marketplace of culture. To differentiate their own work from mere low culture, bourgeois artists began to create works that advertised (so to speak) their distance from commercial amusement, insisting on principles of self-sufficiency, complexity, and organic unity in their art.[15] They sought to mark out a kind of distinction—"true gentility" or "self-culture," as historian Joan Shelley Rubin has called it—that could not be purchased on the wider marketplace.[16] Concepts of beauty, which in the eighteenth century had typically referred to art that gave pleasure to sensitive palates, became increasingly abstract, otherworldly, sublime, idiosyncratic, personal, inward, and formal. Conservatories and special venues arose to inculcate people with the practices of high art and to shield initiates from the pressures of the marketplace, while the experience of this art became increasingly imbued with a transcendental fervor that, had it not been secular, could have been mistaken for religious.[17] Therefore, if autonomous and authentic art represented a safe haven outside the marketplace where spiritual, social, and moral values reigned supreme, modern popular culture supposedly wallowed in commerce, and therefore tended to represent a dearth of such transcendent values—an anything-for-a-buck vulgarity. "It is non-art," Macdonald fumed. "It is even anti-art."[18]

During the first few decades of the twentieth century, however, popular culture—and especially Broadway—began to represent something entirely different. A number of critics and composers in and around New York (introduced in the pages that follow) began to locate a special quality within the institution of popular music. Some called this quality "vitality," some called it "intensity," some called it "liveliness," and each word described a feeling akin to immediate, uncoerced enjoyment, or even frenzy.[19] It required no interposition of the intellect, it required no formal training, and therefore this quality began to be imbued with a political and social charge: It represented the music of today's "people," the music of a newly world-ascendant, American democracy. According to this group of critics, art within the institutions of autonomy and authenticity was aloof or obscure, and as such tended to blunt or overlook this vital quality. Some of these writers went so far as to fault autonomous and authentic art as being too stolid, too distant from audiences in the present day. Even more controversially, a few of them muddled institutional values by evaluating high art and folk art, not only by their supposed transcendental values, but also by whether they elicited a here-and-now popular-culture spark. These onlookers viewed the encroachment of popular-culture standards upon the art world as a liberation of feeling, or as a liberation of the popular consumer within the world of classical art; for others, however, it was invasion.

This divide also marks the fundamental difference between Brooks and Macdonald. Although they referred to the same cultural institutions in very similar terms, they disagreed about the proper attitude toward them: Should high art, folk art, and popular culture remain separate institutions, or could they be joined without destroying their special, individual qualities? Macdonald sought to keep these categories separate for fear of damaging the unique attributes of each, ultimately with the purpose of saving high art from the encroachment of popular culture, and the purpose of preventing art's "total subjection to the spectator."[20] For him, if high art and folk art resisted popular culture, they could proffer a glimpse of some alternative to the status quo and avoid getting bogged down in the muck of the present day. Therefore, he represented an "oppositional" point of view, and he tilted at any art or critic that sought to combine the values of these institutions, lambasting them as "middlebrow." Brooks, however, represented an "affirmative" point of view. He was trying to forge a "beloved community" along a "middle path" of culture, wherein the most sophisticated of arts would nonetheless boast some popular appeal, situated within a living tradition even while retaining some genuine sophistication (however he might have defined that). He believed that from institutional divisions flowed social divisions, "a mutual contempt between theory and practice" which "[confirms] us all either in the one extreme or in the other": "Between university ethics and business ethics, between American culture and American humor, between Good Government and Tammany, between academic pedantry and pavement slang, there is no community, no genial middle ground."[21] His goal as a critic was to pioneer that middlebrow ground by mixing different artistic institutions, providing a common cultural tradition that could heal modern, divided America.

The following pages describe how the terms of their debate spread outward beyond literature to other fields, including to Broadway, a site where popular culture, autonomous art, and authentic art mixed in especially stark terms, and where the boundaries between these institutions seemed especially fluid. Although many composers and writers witnessed these battles, the story in this chapter will focus primarily on four critics. The first two, Gilbert Seldes and Mike Gold, tried to define institutional boundaries for a modern, American world. The former (a colleague of Van Wyck Brooks) did this by claiming that Tin Pan Alley and jazz represented, not just commercial music, but a modern-day popular–folk hybrid culture; the latter (a Communist) did this by excoriating classical musicians and encouraging them instead to devise music that would be imbued with "purer" folk-like qualities, thereby accessible to the masses, specifically to the proletariat, but still resistant to commercial culture.

The second two critics each took different attitudes toward these cultural institutions, the first a middlebrow, affirmative attitude, the second a modernist, oppositional attitude. *New York Times* theater critic Brooks Atkinson (a confidant of Van Wyck Brooks) took the middlebrow approach, cheering the dissolution of institutional boundaries because doing so would take what was otherwise aloof (autonomous or authentic culture), situate it within a living tradition, and thereby make it accessible to present-day audiences, which he conceived of as a community of Americans. Theater critic Eric Bentley, however, took the oppositional approach, praising classical, folk, or popular culture only insofar as they were purely classical, purely folk, or purely popular. Mixing the values of these institutions, he argued, would only dilute the benefits of each separate category, ultimately leading to social and political degradation: He and his colleagues issued ominous threats that a popular culture without any stable non-commercial aesthetic counterpoise would hitch hearts and minds to mass media and corporate capitalism.

From a broad perspective, in this chapter I describe how a handful of musical-comedy writers, composers, and critics in New York began to make incursions from the realm of popular musical comedy into the realm of folk and high art. While I will focus on contemporary debates about Broadway, the critics who appear here drew the terms of their arguments from many different genres and different institutions: symphonic music, opera, folk music, regionalist literature, popular dance, ballet, agitprop theater, expressionism, and so forth. Importing institutional values from these fields ultimately tested received notions of what seemed appropriate content for the Broadway musical.

Sociologist Paul DiMaggio once issued a warning about such institutional stories: The "explanations of social phenomena that posit the existence of unseen structures are by themselves merely models of reality and little more than attractive metaphors, unless one can explain how purposeful, reasoning, self-interested actors contribute, in pursuing their own subjective ends, to the maintenance of these structures."[22] Therefore, instead of portraying folk, fine, and popular culture as regulatory categories that functioned abstractly in the background, so to speak, I follow flesh-and-blood composers and writers, showing that the institutional categories they debated were historically contingent, fragile, and mutable, rather than transcendental, durable, or fixed.[23] What follows intervenes in actual contemporary debate about the Broadway musical to show how each writer forged allies and enemies in early twentieth-century New York.

"An Eternal Impulse of Humankind": Authenticity and the Musical Comedy

"As late as 1910," reported musicologist Benjamin Filene, "most Americans would have been surprised to hear that America *had* any folk music."[24] His point was not that folk music was simply unfamiliar. Rather, for many at the time, the very idea of an "American folk" was a contradiction of terms: Folk, they believed, belonged to the "old world." Yet between the turn of the century and 1925, an increasing number of contemporary writers would claim to uncover an American folk tradition, and they would also gradually extend the boundaries of that tradition to include modern and commercial music: blues, jazz, ragtime, and the songs of Broadway.[25]

At the end of the nineteenth century, Harvard professor Francis James Child dominated the academic field of folk studies and assembled a mammoth collection of ballad poetry that still remains a cornerstone of British and American scholarship today. Yet he was also important as a theoretician who established a set of parameters that distinguished "folk" from "nonfolk," charging these categories with moral imperatives that would remain influential for generations. First, Child believed that folk culture was fundamentally remote from the present day, from modern society, and from any modern nation—and by implication, remote from the relatively young United States.[26] Echoing Enlightenment-era philosophers such as Johann Gottfried Herder, Child argued that folk art belonged to an idealized past and an idealized community in which "the people [were] not divided by political organization and book-culture into markedly distinct classes, in which consequently there [was] such community of ideas and feeling that the whole people [formed] an individual."[27] In light of this, to describe a work as authentically folk was not merely to make a historical claim about its age or provenance. It was to argue that, properly read, folk culture could impart a specific kind of knowledge about the essences of a people, about a society, even about humanity writ large, often with an eye toward how conditions in the present day have been corrupted by comparison (and, among successive generations of scholars, with all the ominous political connotations that a word like "corrupted" could suggest).[28]

Second, Child believed that folk culture's spontaneity distinguished it from art. He argued that spontaneity was the primary vehicle behind the evolution of individual folk songs. He did not object to this change per se; all folk scholars have recognized that ballads undergo variation from generation to generation and from place to place. But he believed that only certain kinds of changes were proper to folk music. For example, he argued that folk ballads had once been naturally "highly polished and constructed," but in modern times had degraded into something "thoroughly despicable and worthless," a "low kind of *art*."[29] The epithet "art" suggested adaptations according to the whims of the aristocracy or the pressures of a marketplace, deference to convention or decorum, with the goal of personal glorification or academic cultivation.[30] For Child, the only acceptable kinds of changes (the only kinds proper to folk music) were those that were made according to a community's immediate needs or desires, uncoerced by market pressures; or in the words of folklorist Cecil Sharp, made by the "*spontaneous* and intuitive use of untrained faculties."[31]

Finally, Child believed there existed a strong barrier between folk and "popular," a word which, since the eighteenth century, had signified culture that was commercial, professionalized, and fashionable—the culture, not of the authentic folk, but of the "rabble" and the rising middle class.[32] According to Child, "professional singers," "modern editors," and modern technology (including even the printing press, which appeared in England in 1475) had destroyed pre-commercial culture by making "willful change" "without scruple," thereby obscuring the ways in which these ballads had once expressed "what is permanent and universal in the heart of man."[33] Academic work in this field, he argued, could restore this work to its premodern form, helping folk culture to "survive the fluctuations of taste," which in turn would serve today's world by "[recalling] a literature from false and artificial courses to nature and truth."[34]

In the years following his death in 1896, Child's students (and his students' students) spread his ideas beyond the confines of academia by publishing collections of folk songs in editions intended for a wide, popular market. This younger generation also studied music that lay beyond the core repertoire of "Child ballads," claiming that this other music, too, was folk music, even though Child would most likely have rejected this material as too modern, too popular. Historians today cite figures such as William Wells Newell, Cecil Sharp, George Lyman Kittredge, Robert Winslow Gordon, Ralph Peer, and John Lomax for expanding the genre of folk: Each argued that the United States harbored a living, present-day folk culture; each turned away from British ballads toward the study of Black American, Indigenous American, and cowboy songs, as well as the music of various immigrant groups; and many of them used modern technology to create recordings of this music for urban, commercial audiences.[35] Despite these changes, however, this younger generation never rejected Child's theories outright. Instead, they often took pains to assure fellow folklorists that these new repertoires were fundamentally in keeping with Child's theories of authenticity. Debates raged about how far these theories could bend without breaking.

Historians have also described the ways in which folk music gradually began to lose its idealized quality by becoming increasingly concerned with worldly matters of the present day, especially politics. During the first two decades of the twentieth century, for example, writers in rural colleges (the Commonwealth Labor College, Brookwood Labor College, the Highlander Folk School, and so on) and in various organized labor organizations (the Industrial Workers of the World, National Textile Workers, and so on) began to rewrite the words of familiar church songs, ballads, and local community songs for use by a burgeoning left-wing labor movement, creating a large repertoire of anti-capitalist contrafacta.[36] Meanwhile, during the early decades of the twentieth century, folk music made inroads into urban centers through an explosion of recordings, concerts, and sheet-music publications, culminating in the national renown of Woody Guthrie, Pete Seeger, the Almanac Singers, and others, starting in the 1930s and 1940s.[37] By the midcentury folk-music revival, these earlier singer-songwriters would become nearly mythic: John Handcox, Lee Hayes, Joe Hill, Aunt Molly Jackson, Margaret Larkin, Ella May Wiggins, Tom Tippett, Claude Williams, and so on.[38]

Along these lines, but less familiar to scholarship, are the ways in which a generation of critics in the 1920s began to import the language of authenticity from folk studies into their treatment of the modern, popular, urban, commercial Broadway musical comedy. One of the earliest was journalist Gilbert Seldes, whose influential 1924 book *Seven Lively Arts* argued that America's popular arts—vaudeville, revues, movies, comic-strip cartoons, jazz, ragtime, popular satire, newspaper humor, music-hall dance, musical comedy (he listed far more than seven)—should be considered modern, urban forms of folk art.[39] "The folk song hardly exists in America to-day. The songs of the Kentucky mountains (English in provenance) and the old cowboy songs are both the object of antiquarian interest," he argued, referring obliquely to the work of both Child and Lomax; "they aren't as alive as the universal *Hail, Hail, the Gang's All Here* or *We Won't Go Home 'til Morning*. If we refuse to call our ragtime folk music, then we must face the fact that we are at a moment in history when folk songs simply do not occur."[40]

For some, the idea that modern America had no folk music would have been self-evident: Ragtime and Tin Pan Alley struck them as modern and commercial, not universal and timeless. Yet Seldes argued that ragtime and other popular music actually did conform to many of the parameters that Child had laid out. First, even though it was emphatically contemporary, this music did contain an idealized element: It represented, Seldes claimed, the essence of the American people. Jazz, for example, he called "the symbol, or the byword, for a great many elements in the spirit of our time—as far as America is concerned it is actually our characteristic expression," capturing, as he put it, "our independence, our carelessness, our frankness, and gaiety."[41] From there he extrapolated outward, arguing that what was essentially American also revealed something universally human: In slapstick comedy, for example, the "gross caricatures are perhaps truer than the realism of the theatre. I see a Rabelaisian madness in the millions of broken plates. In a thousand flying custard pies I recognize an eternal impulse of humankind."[42]

Like Child and other folklorists, Seldes shared a special disgust for the merely commercial, despite his appreciation for popular (commercial) culture. On almost every page, he used the language of money and economics to lambast art he disliked. Dull art, for example, offered not "ecstasy," but rather "social *subventions*," cachet "which *repays* the deadly hours of boredom we spend in the pursuit of art."[43] For Seldes, the element that transformed a merely popular work into authentic lively art was excitement, "intensity": direct, honest expression, which he likened to being "possessed," a frenzy he felt "in religious mania, in good jazz bands, in a rare outbreak of mob violence," "at a prize fight," "on the Stock Exchange," and "in our skyscraper architecture."[44] This was his version of uncoerced spontaneity, the very quality that Child and other folklorists had long used to separate folk art from studied art. The implication was that certain (although not all) popular culture was only incidentally tied to the marketplace, containing a spirit that also transcended it, making it a modern folk art.

The opposite of "intensity" was "intellect," a category about which Seldes was ambivalent. On the one hand, overemphasizing intellect could stultify art, and Seldes warned about the "poison of culture," the "lorgnettes of prejudice provided by fashion and gentility," the "touch of 'art' which makes all things false and vulgar," an attitude toward art reminiscent of Child's.[45] On the other hand, the intellect could create a "definitely perceptible structure" that would result in a "greater intensity of effect."[46] It could also act as a civilizing force to temper or harness wild intensity: "There will always exist the wayward, instinctive, and primitive geniuses who will affect us directly, without the interposition of the intellect; but if the process of civilization continues (will it? I am not so sure, nor entirely convinced that it should) the greatest art is likely to be that which an uncorrupted sensibility is *worked* by creative intelligence."[47] Seldes called culture which successfully mixed professional production with folk spontaneity the "lively arts." "The good revue pleases the eye, the ear, and the pulse," he wrote; "the very good revue does this *so well that it pleases the mind*."[48]

In many ways, Seldes's category of "lively art" may appear to adopt the same affirmative attitude toward culture as Brooks, advocating the mixture of different institutions of art. After graduating from Harvard College in 1914 (six years after Brooks), Seldes joined a generation of writers, including Walter Lippmann, Randolph Borune, H. L. Mencken, and others, who extolled the virtues of popular arts while turning an iconoclastic eye toward what was traditionally called the high arts.[49] Like many in that generation, including Brooks, Seldes seemed to be searching for a middlebrow institutional path that lay between highbrow gentility and lowbrow authenticity, a place where they would converge. He believed he had found it in his category of the "lively arts": "The popular song takes its place between the folk song and the art song," he declared, echoing the "middle path" that Van Wyck Brooks had outlined in 1915 when he wrote *America's Coming of Age*.[50] (Seldes had served as an editor at the literary magazine *The Dial* from 1920 to 1923, where he had been Brooks's colleague.) If there was a difference at this time between Brooks and Seldes, it was a matter of degree, not kind. Seldes focused more on popular writing, while Brooks focused on literature: Seldes wrote that Brooks was "an invaluable critic for America; yet one wishes that he, too, could see Mr. Dooley's place in our literature; one still hopes that he will begin to enjoy Ring Lardner," referring to then-famous figures in popular doggerel and sports commentary.[51] In the years that followed, Seldes would continue to combine high art with popular entertainment, writing pieces for Broadway, including an African American jazz adaptation of Shakespeare called *Swingin' the Dream* (1939); publishing regular columns for middlebrow magazines such as the *Saturday Evening Post* and *TV Guide*; and serving as the first director of television for CBS.

Yet Seldes is difficult to pin down. There were aspects of his writing that stood at odds with Brooks's middle path, especially later in his career. While "lively art" was successful at melding intensity and intellect, Seldes also recognized a different kind of art that failed: "bogus art," which mixed highbrow sophistication with folk sentimentality, becoming a form of pretentiousness and snobbery. He turned all his critical fire upon this category. Continuing with the analogies to commerce, he described the bogus as "counterfeit currency," and he cited Gresham's Law—a principle of economics that explains how counterfeit currency drives out legitimate money—to describe why this was harmful to society. "It is the lively arts which are continually jeopardized by the bogus, and it is for their sake that I should like to see the bogus go sullenly down into oblivion."[52] What the bogus lacked, which the lively had, was the "vital" spark from popular music: The "sullen" bogus played on the clout of both autonomous and authentic art, thereby appealing to social climbers who posed as sophisticates, but offering none of the enjoyment of popular culture. More broadly speaking, even though Seldes cheered the increasingly blurred distinctions between the various cultural institutions, and even though he never went so far as to maintain that different artistic institutions should be held strictly separate, he, too, increasingly sensed that blending them could be radical or even dangerous. In 1941 Seldes read the work of Theodor Adorno for the first time, which, he reported, decried almost all popular music as "standardized." Seldes admitted to being "startled" and "intimidated" by this claim, but nevertheless insisted, "I *do* feel originality within the standard patterns; melodies run in one way for Porter, in another for Kern. And in Rodgers and Hart—assuming that the writer of words helps to mold the line of music, I almost never feel the stale pattern—maybe it isn't there."[53] By this point, the attack on mass culture as mind-numbing and crypto-authoritarian had become a recurring refrain in the writing of the New York Intellectuals, and in 1961 Seldes would echo them outright, claiming that modern media had the potential to harm "autonomous thought and individualism," even though he was, and had long been, one of the country's most prominent figures in television, radio, and popular theater.[54]

His ambivalence stands as a reminder that no matter how much the definition of "authentic" expanded during the first three decades of the twentieth century, no matter how many popular genres it came to include, there nevertheless remained a strong, often academic (and often self-consciously embattled) "purist" position, as early twentieth-century folklorist Maude Karpeles called it. As late as 1951, she gave a speech to an enthusiastic audience in which she cited "industrialism," "general education," and the radio as threatening "the continuity of the musical life of the peasants and country people." Because the Western world now lacked traditional folk societies, she argued, it fell to scholars to reclaim "the purest folk music [...] which has been submitted to the crucible of tradition, and which emerges as a complete artistic unity." Again, this all had moral implications. She believed that "by selecting the best and most authentic folk music, we may in some measure counteract the damaging effects produced by modern conditions."[55] Folk music, for her, was the music of an uncoerced, free, unspoiled people, while commercial wares were foisted onto the modern public by slick advertising. Throughout this period, everything that "authenticity" had implied in the nineteenth century—the remoteness, the allegiance with autonomy, the political and moral justifications—remained intact, and some even redoubled their allegiance to "pure" folk with renewed intensity against those who would imbue it with popular culture and lively art.

Seldes's ambivalence also points to a paradox that lay just beneath the surface of his writing. At one point in *Seven Lively Arts*, he promised to describe "general principles" that would allow the critic to examine a work and pronounce it either "lively" or "bogus" with some degree of certainty—in other words, to establish "lively art" as a stable artistic category.[56] He never actually offered any. How could he? "Liveliness," "vitality," and "frenzy" spoke to immediate individual experiences and tastes, and to claim some kind of universality for them would be to collapse popular culture back into the institutions of authenticity and autonomy. In practice, however, he did argue that "liveliness" or "vitality" was a feature proper to all *art*, including autonomous art: "The existence of the bogus is not a serious threat against the great arts, for they have an obstinate *vitality* and in the end—but only in the end—they prevail."[57] In doing so he scrambled critical values, suggesting that a valid way of critiquing capital-A autonomous art was to test its appeal to audiences of the present day, thereby placing joy, popularity, and relevance on truly equal footing with other supposedly pure, aesthetic, transcendental qualities. Whether this was supportable became a central point of artistic debates over the next two decades.

"Falling Between Two Stools": Autonomy and the Musical Comedy

Scholars, critics, and artists have long recognized that, by the early twentieth century, high art and popular culture had never seemed so far apart.[58] "[By] the early decades of [the twentieth century]," wrote historian Lawrence Levine in his now classic study of American culture, *Highbrow/Lowbrow*, "the masterworks of the classic composers were to be performed in their entirety by highly trained musicians on programs free from contamination of lesser works or lesser genres."[59] However, at this time, artists and critics also began clamoring to collapse this distance. In 1938, for example, composer and activist Elie Siegmeister tasked his contemporaries with "breaking down the age-old division between learned or art music on the one hand, and folk or popular music on the other," thereby joining an ongoing movement in other media that sought to "reintegrate" high art into everyday life; to pull highbrow art beyond the studio, beyond the stage, beyond the concert hall and into modern society; to tackle new subjects and new styles; and to mount it in new venues—including upon the Broadway stage.[60]

"Reintegration" took many forms in the United States during the early decades of the twentieth century. First, for some at the time, reintegration meant situating high art explicitly within modern society instead of construing it as a timeless, universal, or abstract genre. As such, high art would become a genre that could provide uplift by giving conservatory training a present-day social purpose. Starting in the late nineteenth century, settlement houses across the country brought humanistic education, including the study of classical music and theater, into the hands of poor immigrants.[61] Closely connected to these venues was the Little Theater movement, which blended aesthetic experimentation with community improvement around the country, and in New York included the Neighborhood Playhouse (which grew out of work being done at the Henry Street Settlement), the Washington Square Players (out of which came the Provincetown Players and the Theatre Guild), and so on.[62] For those accustomed to the typical aloof nature of high art, these projects seemed incongruous. In 1927, for example, after a performance of Jacques Copeau's adaptation of *The Brothers Karamazov* at the Theatre Guild, one critic complained: "I thought I was coming to hear a talk on the theatre: instead I find myself at the Salvation Army."[63]

Second, for others, "reintegration" meant rejecting past canons of "pure" beauty or "timelessness" by composing in a style, language, or technique redolent of the here and now. In 1916 the first issue of the journal *Seven Arts* featured an encomium to America by French writer Romain Rolland, who believed that the United States was unusually poised to produce a truly modern art: "You are free of traditions. You are free of that vast load of thought, of sentiment, of secular obsession under which the Old World groans.... There is in you no weariness of the Yesterdays; no clutterings of the Pasts."[64] (His editor was Van Wyck Brooks.) *Seven Arts* was part of a network of so-called "little magazines" established during the first two decades of the twentieth century to promote literary experimentation. Musicians followed suit and formed groups outside the established orchestral societies. Their goal in doing so was to reject the techniques and habits of the major European conservatories. This "maverick tradition," as music historian

Michael Broyles has called it, drew inspiration from the burgeoning field of psychology (Leo Ornstein); new mathematic theories of resonance (Henry Cowell and Charles Seeger); modern technology, industry, and engineering (George Antheil, Edgard Varèse); contemporary popular music (Louis Gruenberg, Aaron Copland); and so on.[65] Claire Reis helped found one such group (the League of Composers, 1923), and in an article for *Eolian Review* she advocated turning away from audiences who held "aesthetic standards which belong to the past," and instead appealed to the uninitiated "man on the street," the kind of audience that "can sense an art belonging to his age because it is part of his life, because he has not been educated to accept *definite laws based on tradition*."[66]

But these debates about "reintegration" extended beyond conservatory-style art; they were also visible on the Broadway stage. During the first four decades of the twentieth century, the conceptual gulf that separated the Metropolitan Opera House from the rest of the theater district became a common theme and a common source of satire in musicals and revues. In this music and in these shows, if opera evoked memories of the old country, popular music represented the ultramodern American city. If opera seemed sophisticated and intellectual (or snobbish), popular music seemed entertaining and energetic (or salacious—and proudly so). If opera was beautiful, popular music was, to use the common phrase of the day, "vital." Victor Herbert's *The Debutante* (1913), for example, features a "Cubist Opera," which begins with a parody of dissonant modernist music sung in solfège, before gradually morphing into an equally modern rag ("not a melody found in a single line / of this futurist opera of mine").[67] The second-act finale of Irving Berlin's *Watch Your Step* (1914) features five characters, each singing ragtime arrangements of well-known operatic pieces. Suddenly the ghost of Verdi appears on the balcony, singing "Please don't rag my melody," to which the chorus responds "We hate to tantalize you / But we mean to modernize you."[68] George and Ira Gershwin's "When Do We Dance?" from *Tip-Toes* (1925) declares: "I'm fed up with discussions / About the music of the Russians / And I'm most unhappy when you talk about art," and that "Just can't help swaying—I must begin / When they are playing Kern or Berlin."[69] Examples are legion. Such spoofs did not really collapse the distance between artistic institutions. None, for example, made any claims of transcendence or authenticity for popular music, which would have mixed the familiar institutional values of each field. Instead, they delighted in the foibles of each institution as they stood.

However, some Broadway composers did go further by seeking to narrow the divides between institutions. As musicologist Jeffrey Magee has shown, in 1913, 1924, and 1925 Irving Berlin announced plans to write a tragic opera entirely in ragtime, a project that never materialized. (Scott Joplin's *Treemonisha* was probably unknown to him.[70]) According to Berlin, "beautiful thoughts can best be expressed by syncopation. It alone can catch the sorrow—the pathos—of humanity."[71] "Beauty," "pathos," "sorrow," "humanity": Few, if any, at the time would have associated these words with Tin Pan Alley ragtime.

Even more disruptive to the institutional divide, however, was George Gershwin, whose famous jazz-inflected concert music—*Rhapsody in Blue* (1924), the Concerto in F (1925), the three piano preludes (1926), *An American in Paris* (1928), the Second Rhapsody (1931), the *Cuban Overture* (1932), and *Variations on "I Got Rhythm"* for piano and orchestra (1934)—famously mixed institutional values, leading theater historian David Savran to call him "the first (and perhaps definitive) crossover artist."[72] As Gershwin wrote in 1930:

> The only kinds of music which endure are those which possess form in the universal sense [i.e., formally composed art music] and folk music. All else dies. But unquestionably folk songs are being written and have been written which contain enduring elements of jazz. To be sure, this is only an element; it is not the whole. An entire composition written in jazz [i.e., popular music] could not live.[73]

Here Gershwin picked up on many of the debates about authenticity and autonomy—including the supposed "eternal" aspects of highbrow and folk music, and the ephemeral nature of popular music (the broad, hard-to-define term "jazz")—and combined them. Moreover, he often did this using language very similar to Seldes's. For example, writing in response to critics who eyed jazz as a dangerous dance craze that had taken over American culture, Gershwin declared that after bringing it to symphonic writing, "[t]he employment of jazz will no longer dominate but only vitalize. It is for the trained musician who is also the creative artist to bring out this vitality and to heighten it with the eternal flame of beauty," thereby combining popular-culture liveliness with the logic of Walter Pater's *l'art pour l'art* aestheticism.[74] The resulting critical mood was quintessentially middlebrow.

Gershwin brought this same crossover mentality to his writing for the Broadway stage.[75] When composing his first full-length Broadway score, Gershwin claimed that he wanted to "write an absolutely new type of musical show, with modernistic words as well as modernistic tunes," and the resulting string of productions—including *Lady, Be Good!* (1924), *Tip-Toes* (1925), *Of Thee I Sing* (1931), and its sequel *Let 'Em Eat Cake* (1933)—mixed operetta, foxtrot, ragtime, jazz, and blues.[76] Critics were flummoxed. In 1924 critic Linton Martin argued that Gershwin "practices a sort of tonal jiu-jitsu," producing sounds which "elude" labels, a fact that placed Gershwin's music in an entirely different category than the typical Broadway musicals of the early 1920s: "Right in the middle of a bit of bouncing jazz he will insert an echo of the whole tone scale, hitherto heard only in the ultra-modern music of symphony concerts."[77] For Gershwin and his supporters, this "kaleidoscope" of sounds comprised an affirmative (middlebrow, although they did not use that word) modernism, mixing highbrow technique with popular forms to portray something authentically American.[78] Gershwin himself believed that this middlebrow approach carried social implications, representing "our vast melting pot, of our incomparable national pep, our blues, our metropolitan madness." For his detractors, it was, according to Savran, "cultural miscegenation," which threatened to jumble traditional artistic boundaries that had been fortified by long-standing social distinctions between the elite and the masses, between the wealthy and the poor, between white and minority, between Gentile and Jew.[79]

Especially controversial was Gershwin's "folk opera" for Broadway, *Porgy and Bess* (1935), which purported to mix the authenticity of Black folk music, the autonomy of opera, and the popular culture of jazz.[80] Despite Gershwin's efforts, however, many in the press still found these institutions incompatible.[81] For some, *Porgy and Bess* was not highbrow enough, and they took issue with Gershwin's compositional technique: his development of leitmotifs (or lack thereof), his large-scale formal designs (or lack thereof), and so on. In a 1935 review of the show, composer and critic Virgil Thomson recapitulated the long-standing critique of Gershwin's music from the concert hall that "he hadn't learned the business of being a serious composer."[82] For Thomson and others, autonomous art could not rest on popularity or tunefulness, and they believed that the purely formal component of Gershwin's music was appallingly thin.

For other commentators, however, *Porgy and Bess* was not authentic enough. Thomson, once again, dubbed it "fake folklore" with "gefiltefish orchestrations," a whiff of anti-Semitism reminding readers that Gershwin was Jewish, not Black.[83] According to these critics, what made *Porgy and Bess* inauthentic was exactly the quality that previous writers had long argued separated folk from highbrow music: sophistication. (Ironically, in retrospect, this was also the very quality that highbrow critics had found lacking in Gershwin's score.) Duke Ellington, for example, described the inauthenticity of *Porgy and Bess* by analogy, disparaging Gershwin's opera as a musical version of "fifteen-dollar words" that did not capture the spirit of its subject: "how could you possibly express in decent English the same thing I express when I tell my band, 'Now you cats swing the verse, then go to town on the gutbucket chorus'!"[84] Black composer and arranger Hall Johnson claimed that the "sophisticated intricacies of attitude," associated with the largely white institution of classical music, "could not possibly be native to the minds of the people who make up his story," and that it lacked "authentic Negro musical language."[85]

Yet for others still, *Porgy and Bess* was not popular enough. In the *New York Times*, Brooks Atkinson argued, first, that it was indeed authentic, calling it "a fairly objective narrative of a neighborhood of Negroes" (a position that separated him from most of his Black contemporaries), and second, that it was indeed highbrow opera (a position that separated him from many of his classical-music contemporaries). But he found opera itself to be "cumbersome," and he wanted Gershwin to stick to unadulterated musical comedy. "Turning 'Porgy' [i.e., the play on which *Porgy and Bess* is based] into opera has resulted in a deluge of casual remarks that have to be thoughtfully intoned and that amazingly impede the action," he wrote. "Why do composers vex it so?" The parts of the score that most resembled Broadway music, he argued, served best because they were "personal" (a word he emphasized three times in his review): "In sheer quality of character they are worth an hour of formal music transitions."[86] Opera and folk music were, to him, abstract and aloof, but popular music spoke directly to modern-day audiences. For him, the classical-music components threatened to snuff out the show's popular-culture spark.

Taken as a whole, most of the critics who wrote about *Porgy and Bess* tended to recognize that different institutions produced different kinds of meanings—be they the abstractions of autonomous or authentic art, or the intensity of popular art—all of which, they believed, were incompatible. Thomson, again: "I don't mind his being a light composer, and I don't mind his trying to be a serious one. But I do mind his falling between two stools."[87] This, as the following pages attest, generally started to shift later in the decade.

"Glass Splinters of Pure Technic": Labor and the Oppositional Approach to Broadway

During the second decade of the twentieth century, the argot of the newly ascendant Communist Party burst onto the arts scene in New York. Although the familiar distinctions between high art, folk art, and popular culture remained broadly recognizable, and although the debate between the affirmative and oppositional attitudes continued apace, a new wave of communist artists and critics would inflect these concepts in explicitly political and economic terms. At the most fundamental level, what non-communist composers had been characterizing as "old-world" or "elite" in highbrow culture, the far left started to label as "bourgeois." In the Depression, as more artists turned toward communism, the Party's politicized aesthetics became increasingly visible to mainstream audiences. Part and parcel with increasing visibility was an increasing awareness of the Party's shifting approach to the Broadway musical, which had been the commercial genre par excellence.

The story of how the ongoing debates surrounding middlebrow culture adapted to the rise of communism is anything but straightforward. The official cultural stance of the Party lurched back and forth between oppositional and middlebrow points of view, first advocating that high art, folk art, and popular culture be kept apart as strictly separate institutions, and then eventually, during the period known as the Popular Front, suggesting that artists and composers combine these previously distinct kinds of art. Moreover, in the United States, even artists who did consider themselves to be communist did not always fall in lockstep with the Party's official cultural pronouncements, meaning that year by year within communist circles there was considerable disagreement about the relative merits of the oppositional and middlebrow positions. Despite this, the overall trend was that during the 1920s, the official Party stance was more or less oppositional, either construing experimental high art to be a rejection of the previous century's bourgeois art, or construing folk art to be an authentic expression of the proletariat. At that time, popular music and familiar classical music, according to official Party doctrine, represented the music of the old, crumbling, capitalist order. During the 1930s, however, communists increasingly adopted a middlebrow attitude, which finally became official party policy starting around 1935. At this point, the Party sanctioned both familiar classical music and popular music as legitimate tools for advancing the movement.

To parse this story in greater detail: Starting around 1920, a crush of "front organizations" raced to envision what a truly committed communist performing arts scene would look like. At first, like their non-communist counterparts, many of them embraced the modernist moment, endorsing a welter of styles with little in common except that they stood apart from the bourgeois institution of "classical" music. At this point, both aggressive experimentation and collectivist, folk-like spectacle could serve to reject received canons of bourgeois beauty. In theater, this ranged from the stylized agitprop productions of the Prolet Bühne and the Workers' Laboratory Theater (later called the Theater of Action) to the professional left-wing productions of the Theatre Union; in dance, this ranged from the ballet of the New Dance Group to the mass amateur dance spectacles and competitions ("spartakiades") of the Workers' Dance League; in music, this ranged from the avant-garde Composers' Collective to the bands and choruses that made up the Workers' Music League and the Pierre Degeyter Club.[88]

Amid this veritable beehive of committed artists, Mike Gold emerged early on as the most forceful Communist cultural critic, and he presided over the wide New York arts scene at the time when the Communist Party reached its apex of influence and was searching for an artistic practice to serve its social mission. Born Itzok Isaac Granich in a Lower East Side tenement in 1893, Gold began his career taking part in the pre-communist experimental arts scene in New York, writing emphatically modernistic poetry and commentary for the radical magazine *The Masses* in 1914, as well as short plays for the experimental Provincetown Players starting in 1916.[89] In this early stage of his career, he believed that this radical, experimental art could scrub away the residue of the decrepit, capitalist world. By 1921, however, he changed paths and condensed his developing aesthetic theories into a landmark article called "Towards Proletarian Revolution." In it he announced his mission to produce a specifically communist kind of art, and he outlined the foundation of what would become his cultural and critical project over the next two decades.[90] He laid out two basic criteria, both of which were radical at the time, even among the far left. First, Gold took aim at "bourgeois individualism," which he characterized negatively as highbrow and autonomous. "The old moods, the old poetry, fiction, painting, philosophies, were the creations of proud and baffled solitaries," he wrote. "The tradition has arisen in a capitalist world that even its priests of art must be lonely beasts of prey—competitive and unsocial," a word that echoes Van Wyck Brooks's 1915 description of "highbrow" and "lowbrow" art (cited in Chapter 1).[91] Second, he overlaid his theories of collectivism with a disdain for art that he considered too slick, too professional, too academic. Here Gold parted ways with Brooks, denouncing the latter's journal *Seven Arts* as a "hot-house" that "based its hope on the studios" rather than "in the fields, factories and workshops of America."[92]

Instead, he advocated a communist-inflected folk style that he called, in a now-famous article, "Proletarian Realism" (1921), which he described in terms that would have been broadly familiar to many folklorists at the time. He said the style would be defined by "honesty alone, frank as an unspoiled child's"; that it would be distinct from high art (he called Proust "master-masturbator of bourgeois life"); that the material would be drawn from "life," and that the writer should "feel this intensely"—all phrases that suggest the spontaneity of folk art.[93] Yet there were two important differences that distinguished Gold's writing from others at the time. First, unlike previous folklorists, Gold believed that "the nationalist idea [was] dying," to be replaced by "class ideologies," meaning that an international working class (the "world proletariat") would eventually replace ethnic or racial communities as the source of validity in authentic art.[94] Put differently, he believed that ethnically derived folk music spoke to the old, debased world, not to the proletarian future of an international federation of united workers.[95] Second, he believed that the ideal artistic style of the Party "[would] never [be] pointless," never purely aesthetic, never purely entertaining; it "[would have] a social purpose" that should be expressed directly "as a social theme."[96]

He brought this sensibility to his writing about musical comedy. In general, he believed that most Broadway music was irredeemably popular, capitalist, and bourgeois. (In a typical rhetorical flourish, he deemed Tin Pan Alley "an overlay of filth" applied to folk materials.[97] He once published a poem called "The Shame of Jazz" which stated "Wah, wah! in shrieking dance halls / I hear that sad mean capitalist wah."[98]) Yet he was not always consistent. In a move resembling (but distinct from) Seldes's, he did argue that some popular music, under very specific conditions, could essentially stand as a proletarian folk music, even if it was in written a popular, commercial idiom. He wrote, for example, that he was "knocked off [his] pins" by the 1937 revue *Pins and Needles*, with music by Harold Rome and mounted by laborers in the International Ladies Garment Workers' Union. Even though the show was politically moderate, Gold found it to be "a bright, charming, thoroughly proletarian musical review." "I would say half the appeal of the show comes from the fact that you know the actors aren't professionals," he wrote, distancing the show from other commercial theater. He even praised the playbill for "proudly listing [the performers' union] affiliations," which further made this production feel far from high art or popular culture. "This is something that makes every worker proud of his class and causes every bourgeois to take a fresh view of the people who work in factories."[99] Gold admitted this was an unusual production, which managed to be a spontaneous eruption of proletarian sentiment within the otherwise capitalist context of musical theater—an exception that essentially proved the rule.

Gold had consolidated his position as one of New York's most powerful Communist critics during so-called Third Period Communism (1928–1935) when the Party was asserting that capitalism was near collapse. At this time, official policy toward high art grew increasingly hostile: Proletarian artists were to mount a united front against bourgeois culture, or, in the frequently uttered phrase, art was to be a class weapon. At a meeting of the International Union of Revolutionary Music, Lev Lebedinsky equated "bourgeois individualism" with "modern experimentation" and denounced both.[100] Official Communist publications began to disavow both modernist (autonomous) technique and professional (popular) polish, even when they purported to serve sympathetic ideological ends. This meant that the experimental theater, art, literature, and music that had been produced in the Party's name for the previous decade suddenly fell afoul of Party policy. Gold, however, was overjoyed. This new policy was suddenly in line with his folk-like "Proletarian Realism" from earlier in the decade, and he drummed this new official decree from his perch at the *New Masses* starting in 1926, and then from the *Daily Worker* starting in 1933. On painting: "I just don't like cerebral art, and don't believe I ever will."[101] On dance, in 1934: "Do you think you can keep this up forever, this labelling a grey standardized sterile dance by Martha Graham by a hundred different titles—Scottsboro, Anti-fascism, etc., and make us accept the product as revolutionary?"[102] On music, two days later: "When one sings, 'We must unite! We must fight!' is there any excuse for employing a melody full of geometric bitterness and the angles and glass splinters of pure technic?"[103]

By the middle of the 1930s, the Party stood divided between those who followed Gold toward Proletarian Realism, and those who tried to rescue conservatory technique and turn it toward popular, Communist ends. This latter position would open the possibility for a committed middlebrow attitude that would seek to combine the anti-bourgeois experimentation of classical art with the popular culture of rank-and-file workers—in other words, and to rephrase it, in Brooks's parlance, to forge a communist middle path.[104]

"The Idealistic Point of View": Broadway and the Middlebrow Aesthetic

During the Third Period, many party-member and fellow-traveler composers in New York bristled against the Party's official stance toward high art, even though they did not abandon the communist cause. They often tried to salvage classical art from its bourgeois background for left-wing purposes. The most concerted effort along these lines came from the Composers' Collective, a subdivision of the Communists' Workers Music League, which met between 1932 and 1935, and which sought to combine classical technique with popular culture—including the Broadway musical— to produce sophisticated, committed art for the amateur worker to consume and perform.

One of the Collective's members, composer, ethnomusicologist, and critic Charles Seeger, agreed with the Party that "professionalized art" had tended to be "used to perpetuate the peculiar relationships upon which the dominance of the class depends, [even though] its actual producers are drawn from the ruled classes." Yet given that so many workers took part in producing professional music, he had his doubts about the Party's official proscription: "How true a reflection and how efficient an instrument is this art for the purposes of the ruling class? May not elements hostile to it creep into the little understood fabrics especially of the non-linguistic arts?"[105] "Creeping in" was essentially a synonym for "reintegration," and the Composers' Collective believed that professional artists qua professional artists could do their part by blending the institutions of autonomous art, authentic art, and popular culture. To jog these professional techniques out of their familiar capitalist contexts, the Composers' Collective struck a delicate balance: Songwriters had to avoid merely duplicating the capitalist commercialism of musical comedy on the one hand and the bourgeois individualism of modernist music on the other.[106] As musicologist Carol Oja has shown, particularly important to this group was the example of composer Hanns Eisler, who arrived in the United States in 1935. (In 1947, the House Committee on Un-American Activities dubbed him "the Karl Marx of Music" and the government asked him to leave the country the following year.) Eisler developed a style of composition in his mass songs that was tuneful enough to attract workers, but unconventional enough to feel experimental, and thereby critical of received "bourgeois" practice.[107]

Some in the Composers' Collective tried to apply the mass-song model to musical comedy. Seeger again:

> That was one of the things we tried to do in the Collective: to use ordinary fragments of technique in an unusual way, because we thought *that* was revolutionary and therefore suitable for the workers to use. We didn't give them those same patterns in the usual way, which was what Broadway did. Broadway just handed out a certain number of formulas in the usual way; but we took those same formulas, simply used them differently, and hoped that we were doing something revolutionary. Lots of compositions were in that type. They had unusual harmonic progressions in them, but usual chords. Or if there were some unusual chords, they put them in conventional patterns.[108]

By 1935 one member of the collective, Marc Blitzstein, brought this style to Broadway. He contributed the song "Send for the Militia" to a revue called *Parade* (dubbed the "Red Revue" in the wings), produced by the Theatre Guild.[109] In the words of musicologist Howard Pollack, Blitzstein's piece "[employed] dissonant harmonies, changing meters, and disjointed phrases (including a quote of 'Columbia, the Gem of the Ocean' nestled in the chorus), all framed by jazzy gestures and scoring."[110] The satirical song portrayed a ladies' club doyenne who is liberal enough to discuss socialism, birth control, and poverty in the abstract, but who flamboyantly gasped and denounced any actual concrete action on each of those issues, calling such moves scandalous, immoral, and (in some imprecise, catch-all way) communist. Such mixtures of comedy and politics, along with mixtures of popular and avant-garde music, were still foreign to Broadway at the time. Brooks Atkinson, about five months before he reviewed *Porgy and Bess* for the *New York Times*, complained that *Parade* lacked "homogeneity," saying "it was neither, fish, flesh, foul [sic?], red herring[,] nor Jimmy Savo," who was the show's comic star. "In Fourteenth Street it might have a revolutionary timbre that would leave a single impression," he wrote. "But in Fifty-second

Street it is a strange brew of dance abstractions, strident music and political mummery."[111] Bourgeois Broadway and agitprop modernism were still, according to Atkinson, incompatible institutions.

However, in August 1935, at the Seventh World Congress of the Comintern, the Party once again issued an abrupt about-face, turning away from its previous antipathy to popular, commercial culture. Instead, it now officially advocated a more middlebrow attitude. Georgi Dimitrov maintained that "the masses cannot assimilate our decisions unless we learn to speak a language which they understand," and urged Communists "to speak simply, concretely, in images which are familiar and intelligible to the masses," to "refrain from abstract formulas."[112] This began the period called the Popular Front, during which, according to literary historian Morris Dickstein, "the divisive language of class-consciousness gave way to the more fuzzy vocabulary of populism, and even Communists began referring to themselves as 'liberals' and 'progressives' (as some of the survivors of that period would continue to do for the rest of their lives)."[113] In the United States, Earl Browder, leader of the Communist Party USA, made his famous pronouncement that "Communism is 20th-Century Americanism," meaning that the Party was no longer staking its cultural claim outside America's popular culture.

For artists, writers, and musicians in the Party, this meant a turn away from Mike Gold's Proletarian Realism, and a turn instead toward a style that was closer to that of the Composers' Collective, which embraced a combination of professionalized music, conservatory-style music, and high-gloss popular music—including Broadway—all without being branded bourgeois. It opened the door for an affirmative, middlebrow approach to cultural institutions, which would blend classical technique, folk art, and popular appeal. All of this was to be in the service of present-day liberal and far-left politics, which during the Popular Front became increasingly difficult to disentangle. The most visible example of this progressive style at the time was the massive Federal Theatre Project, which was coordinated at the national level but directed at the local level, and which between 1935 and 1939 employed more than 13,000 theater workers, dispensed some $46 million dollars as relief ($42 million of which directly furnished workers' salaries), produced more than 1,200 productions, and played to more than 30 million people around the entire country in a "federation of theaters" that would have otherwise remained dark during hard times.[114] For example, their production of *Power*, a Living Newspaper (discussed below), reached far-flung cities such as New York, Chicago, and San Francisco; in Seattle it was so popular that the mayor declared a special *Power* week.[115]

Scholarship surrounding the Federal Theatre Project has tended to consider its productions outside the Broadway orbit.[116] This is partially true. For instance, the Federal Theatre Project was largely unable to hire professional, working Broadway artists because the government required just about all of the collaborators to come from relief rolls, which meant that the Federal Theatre Project was largely unable to hire professional, working Broadway artists.[117] Other regulations (later relaxed) also forbade the Project from charging admission in order to prevent competition with professional Broadway theaters.[118] However, according to Willson Whitman's contemporary account of the Project, *Bread and Circuses*, many at the time did not consider the Project wholly distinct from Broadway. He argued that the professional theater had become decrepit before the Project opened and cited the alarming statistic that in the 1932–1933 season alone, 82 percent of productions folded.[119] In light of these dire circumstances, he and others at the time believed that the Project could represent either a rejuvenation of Broadway or a welcome substitute for Broadway, and as such could point to where New York theater might turn in the future. Along these lines, in 1937 the critic for *Fortune* magazine also dismissed old, familiar production methods in favor of the Project's model. "From any point of view save that of the old-line box-office critics to whom nothing is theatre unless it has Broadway stars and Broadway varnish, the Federal Theatre is a roaring success."[120] Moreover, many of the people who began their careers working for the Project would emerge as composers, producers, designers, and writers for commercial productions on Broadway after the war, and to some degree they would import the Project's sensibilities into the commercial theater (the subject of Chapters 4 and 5). Generally speaking, then, even though the Federal Theatre Project's production methods and style were different from the typical Broadway modus operandi, many critics, writers, and musicians saw the Project as either a critique of or an extension of the commercial musical theater.

At the Project's helm sat national director Hallie Flanagan, who not only organized the national theater's logistics around the country, but who also provided some general artistic guidelines for its productions, imbuing the Broadway stage with a decidedly middlebrow, affirmative attitude. First, Flanagan attempted to reintegrate theater into the economic, political, and social context of the Depression years. "The theatre must become conscious of the implications of the changing social order," she wrote, "or the changing social order will ignore, and rightly, the implications of the theatre."[121] This was not merely an economic initiative as part of the New Deal; she believed that this had aesthetic implications. "It would be supreme sentimentality to become so involved in the human values of our project that we failed to see that these human values can be continued only if we achieve theatre results," she wrote in one of her monthly bulletins to the local branches of the Federal Theatre Project.[122]

Second, Flanagan recommended that a substantial proportion of the Project's shows should avoid "realism." She maintained: "The panorama of life today cannot be imitated, nor has our theatre committed itself to imitating reality. We have tried to set up a new reality on stage, in accord with, but not descriptive of, the life of our days and our years."[123] For her, this meant producing shows that were avowedly experimental, that mixed components of many kinds of theater at once. Toward these ends, the central federal office released monthly bulletins to local branches of the Project, consisting of play catalogs grouped by theme (anti-war plays and Jewish plays, to name only two), theatrical resources (costume technique, Southern folk song, and so on), or historical and national styles (Greek or Japanese, among others) to aid local projects in exploring new ways of approaching the theater.[124] *Variety* even began to allude to a recognizable Project style, and it described certain commercial, non-sponsored plays as being "down the Federal Theatre's alley."[125] (It was not a compliment.)

Following these guidelines, the Project produced a number of musicals, including Blitzstein's infamous, much-studied "play in music" *The Cradle Will Rock* (1937) about a labor strike led by Larry Foreman against the industrialist Mr. Mister; the "topical revue" *Sing for Your Supper* (1939), featuring the wildly popular "Ballad for Americans" by John Latouche and another member of the Composers' Collective, Earl Robinson; and Oscar Saul, Lou Lantz, and Oscar Walzer's children's musical play *Revolt of the Beavers* (1937), which the *New York Times* called "Mother Goose Marx," and which later featured prominently in Flanagan's testimony before Congress about communist infiltration in the arts.[126] All of these productions conspicuously blended different genres of theater, from high to low, and music, from classical to popular.

Perhaps the Project's most identifiable productions were its Living Newspapers, each of which combined music and experimental stagecraft to scrutinize a pressing topic of the times. Although the exact origins of these shows remain obscure, most historians agree that they emerged from some combination of discussions between Flanagan, playwright Elmer Rice (who would later lead the Project's regional office in New York, and who appears in Chapter 5), and Morris Watson, head of the Newspaper Guild.[127] The surviving archives give a clue to the unit's working methods. In steel cabinets there still exist more than 3,000 envelopes, assembled by the project's professional newspaper staff, each containing clippings on a wide variety of subjects, including "Girl Scouts," "accidents," and "nudism."[128] Writers combined these clippings with academic research and quotations from congressional records to produce scripts that would identify a major social problem, lay out its historical background, and often suggest a course of action to address it. At least thirty-two scripts survive in various stages of completion, touching on topics that include the Fascist campaign into Africa (*Ethiopia*, which closed after its dress rehearsal, 1936), agrarian reform (*Triple-A Plowed Under*, 1936), union policy (*Injunction Granted*, 1936), electricity (*Power*, 1937), the Black experience in the United States ("Liberty Deferred," written, planned, but unproduced, 1938), housing (*One Third of a Nation*, 1938), and syphilis testing (*Spirochete*, 1938).[129]

In drawing from actual news articles, the goal, according to the Project's literature, was to lend these productions a core of authenticity. "Few bravura scenes have the convincing impact of an adroitly presented fact. *Authenticity should be the guiding principle on Living Newspaper production*. Let it be kept in mind that some of the most fascinating and also dramatic statements are to be found in the daily columns of newspapers."[130] Once again, the claim of authenticity here retains certain familiar features from the eighteenth- and nineteenth-century definitions of the term from literature on folk art: first, that these shows avoid the "artiness" of highbrow theater; second, that they be relevant to a specific community; and third, that they represent the community in a spontaneous way. The model for this was the 1920s "dramatized newspaper" tradition from Vienna, which arrived in New York in 1931, and which developed out of Jacob Moreno's theories of a "Theater of Spontaneity" (*das Stegreiftheater*). In this tradition, performances that summarized and responded quickly to a given day's events were proof to audiences that the improvisatory productions were immediate, spontaneous, and unfiltered by scripts, rehearsal, or any other sort of artifice.[131] While the Living Newspapers would not be so improvisatory, their productions were designed to be as current as possible, and their scripts could be updated with new developments as necessary.

In addition to its modern folk elements, the Living Newspapers also famously drew upon experimental, avant-garde techniques of the left-wing theater. Scholars frequently cite the influence of the Soviet Blue Blouse troupes, named for the worker's uniforms they wore, which emerged in 1923 at the Moscow Institute of Journalism. These productions provided rousing performances of the day's news for illiterate workers in a collective, montage style, with symbolic masks representing general archetypes, and rousing songs that were anti-bourgeois in sentiment. The goal was that "little by little, the tunes boring everybody [would] be squeezed out." "Down with naturalistic costumes," ran the group's manifesto. "We are against bright beauty and realistic sets and decoration (no little birch trees and rivers), no clumsy props and set."[132] Scholars also cite influences from the German-language Prolet Bühne in New York, which, with the crash of the stock market, became politically activist and imported the staging techniques of Germany's agitprop theater, especially those developed by Erwin Piscator. "We, as revolutionary Marxists, cannot consider our task complete if we produce an uncritical copy of reality, conceiving of theater as a mirror of the times," he wrote in language reminiscent of Flanagan's.[133] For each of these groups, social critique and aesthetic critique were inseparable, and the experimental methods of highbrow, avant-garde art served to challenge the past and distance their productions from bourgeois commercial theater.

Drawing upon each of these influences, the Living Newspapers mixed experimental art (often based on European models) with folk and popular art. These shows tended to be episodic, like a theatrical montage, with abstract settings that changed quickly. They largely featured "everyman" characters, loudspeaker narrators (usually called "the Voice of the Living Newspaper"), and projected stills, cartoons, and films. Most productions left the audience with a pointed question. In *Power*, for instance, a recurring character known only as Consumer tries to figure out what exactly determines his electricity rate, and the show follows him as he navigates complex distribution networks. In the final moments of the play, the assembled cast takes a step forward toward the audience as a huge question mark is projected onto them, and they demand (originally printed in all capital letters): "What will the Supreme Court do?"[134]

The bulk of the music in the Living Newspapers was incidental or melodramatic, supplied by a live orchestra. However, some featured actual songs interspersed in the scenes. For example, at the end of the first act of *Power*, behind a scrim showing projected photographs and film clips of the

Tennessee Valley Authority, a character steps out and sings what Atkinson described in the *Times* as a "mountain ballad" replete with "band music and flag waving." Immediately following this singing, the orchestra brings the first act to a close in completely different musical terms. Departing from the I–IV–V harmonies of the song, the orchestra veers quickly to sonorities that lie far away from the prevailing F-major of the ballad, turning instead toward a concluding tag that breaks the eight-bar regularity of the song with a nine-measure phrase, and that disrupts any sense of a steady beat with over-the-bar ties (see Example 2.1). This style—mixing folk with highbrow dissonance—was essentially in line with the Composers' Collective and their middlebrow approach to committed theater.

In his *New York Times* review of the production, Brooks Atkinson described the show in terms that mixed institutional values. First, he praised its conspicuously high-art components, acknowledging its experimental form, its "mastery of narrative style," its mastery "of photographic backgrounds to set the fleeting scenes, of expository symbols on the stage, of the truculent loudspeaker, of exciting and commenting musical scores, of street parades and

Example 2.1 "T.V.A. Song," *Power*, Federal Theatre Project Collection, Music Division, Library of Congress, Washington, DC, Container 1308.

50 THE MIDDLEBROW MUSICAL

Example 2.1 Continued

campaign songs—even the uses of sardonic humor, have been learned from a year of active experience and they have been perfected." Second, he noted its folkish aspects, claiming that the end of the first act drew inspiration from the "joyous folklore of the South" with the "sound of cracking whips and a dramatic rattle of hoof-beats." Finally, what truly set *Power* apart for him was that, despite its claims to authenticity and autonomy, it was nonetheless popular. What Seldes would have called the show's "intensity," Atkinson called "exuberance"; "Minsky has nothing quite so hot to offer in this jejune vicinity."[135] Put differently, Atkinson essentially believed that this show succeeded where Gershwin had failed, that it managed to combine rigorous form and authentic subject matter in a popular, rather than operatic, idiom. For him, it represented Brooks's middle path.

Atkinson remains a ubiquitous figure in most Broadway studies as one of the most influential theater critics of the twentieth century, but few have recognized that his ideas were part of a systematic, theoretical program derived in large part from the middlebrow writings of Van Wyck Brooks. Born in 1894, Atkinson graduated from Harvard in 1917 (nine years after Brooks, three years after Seldes) and began his career in 1920 working for the magazine *The Freeman*, where he wrote his first essays about naturalism and Henry David Thoreau. Even in these earliest essays, a recurring theme in his work was a rapprochement between the transcendent values of high literature and the immediate vitality of casual or popular writing. In 1920, for example, he wrote: "One day we extol idealism to the skies; the next it is less idealism we want and more of the practical," and two years later, he praised Thoreau for being "rude and classical, provincial and universal, ingenuous and sophisticated."[136]

It was at the *Freeman* where he first encountered Brooks, who was an associate editor of the journal ("chief of the literary desk," as one of the journal's founders called him).[137] The *New York Times* hired Atkinson in 1922 and he served as their chief theater critic from 1925 until 1960 (with only two brief breaks as a foreign correspondent). Throughout this entire period, he and Brooks maintained a glowing correspondence, in which the two of them confided in one another about their career disappointments and their general impressions of literary criticism. According to Brooks, Atkinson's writing resonated with him because it belonged to a tradition of "the best old American writings," and not to the annals of "sophisticated," abstruse, autonomous art.[138] Atkinson confirmed this general characterization in his reply, and he denounced "radical" and "reactionary" literature, using two words that implied an oppositional (as opposed to an affirmative) stance toward culture, and added, in terms that would have resonated with Brooks, that the "idealistic sort of essay" could provide "spiritual sustenance" for their readers.[139] A decade later, Brooks would probably have characterized Atkinson's writing as "primary," grounded in tradition and appreciable by a wider public (affirmative, middlebrow), as opposed to "coterie," experimental, obscure literature written for high-art initiates (oppositional, modernist) instead of a broad theatrical audience.[140] This basic affirmative stance informed Atkinson's criticism for the next decade, and predisposed him toward theater that, no matter how modern or experimental, was also both popular and situated within a community and its traditions.

Along these lines, Atkinson maintained that theatrical experiment was not an end in itself. Instead, it was to be a tool for expressing ideas "vigorously," taking into account a longer tradition and established practice: "a sense of time, a sense of dramatic architecture, a sense of motion and emphasis, a knowledge of what actors can say or do, a feeling for the response of audiences. Some of these things can be learned by a study of craftsmanship or technique. A great deal more can be learned by acting or working backstage in the company of theatre people."[141] Also along the lines of Brooks's middlebrow theories, Atkinson believed that the purpose of theater was civic, drawing people toward a common humanity. During the war, for example, Atkinson wrote a column defending comedy in dark times. "But a sense of humor understands that human nature is not only wonderfully varied but wonderfully imperfect, and that it falls absurdly short of the nobility to which we aspire. The sense of humor forgives, tolerates, makes mutual adjustments in a spirit of good-will and sweetens community living."[142] Like Brooks, he believed art could serve a civic function and draw together an otherwise split society.

Each of these ideas informed Atkinson's complicated, guarded enthusiasm about the Federal Theatre Project. On the one hand, he praised the Project for being civic: "The Federal Theatre is broadminded enough to be interested in people and alert enough to throw open its doors where large numbers of people congregate. It is interested in public good-will. The commercial theatre has not yet become that farseeing."[143] On the other hand, he lamented that many people involved in the Project seemed "more interested in politics" than in art. He did not necessarily object to the political positions themselves; Atkinson was avowedly liberal. But while his ideal theater may have been civic, it was not partisan. Politics, he believed, was divisive and dangerous to community cohesion. "If the theatre were limited to plays of social significance," he wrote, using a common term at the time for politically controversial theater, "it could not fulfill its traditional function of drawing people out of themselves and into an imagined world in which wit, humor, romance, excitement and audacity are as valid as reality."[144] When he felt a play had pushed too far toward politics, he became reactionary, usually recommending that writers retreat, to whatever degree, back into the "unsocial" realm of pure art or pure entertainment as a corrective. In this vein, he changed his mind about the Project once he began to feel it was overly political: "It is urgent that some standards of competence be specifically incorporated into the bill [that would perpetuate the Federal Theatre]. A Federal Bureau of Fine Arts can never be anything but a headache unless the people it employs are genuine artists."[145] "Genuine art" represented a kind of antiseptic theater, pure entertainment that would stand apart from committed, divisive theater.

Atkinson would remain the most vocal proponent of Brooks's "middle path" for the next three decades, continuing even after he retired as the paper's drama critic in 1960. In 1961, he wrote an article about Brooks's aversion to formal, autonomous, modernist writing (here represented by T. S. Eliot and Ezra Pound), a class of art that Brooks considered to be a "betrayal of the American spirit." "In the last half century [Brooks] has never wavered in his conviction that humanism and liberalism are the essence of the American spirit," Atkinson wrote. "He would rather believe too much than too little."[146] When Brooks died in 1963, Atkinson wrote the obituary for the New York Times, in which he claimed that the elder writer's main contribution to scholarship was that he "defined an American literary tradition, which he felt was lacking although he believed that it was essential to a healthy body of literature."[147] As the following chapters will attest, this "middle-path" mentality, which sought to situate artistic experiment within a civic-minded cultural tradition, would guide the rest of Atkinson's career, and would thereby dominate the opening-night reviews of almost every play and musical on Broadway for decades.

Ferocious Formalism: The Oppositional Backlash

The close collaboration on Broadway between the far left and the liberals during the Popular Front sparked both political and aesthetic objections. Many suspected that the New Deal cultural programs harbored communists, and they began to worry that the overt civic liberalism touted by the arts projects was, in fact, covert Marxism. For example, writer Irving Howe, a Trotskyist who opposed both mainstream communism and Rooseveltian liberalism, decried the "Trojan-horse" attack from the entertainment sector; others feared "mass hypnotism"; some called artists "dupes," plying their trade unwittingly for the purpose of subconscious propaganda, and they generally feared "subtle efforts . . . to inject subversive propaganda" into art, music, dance, and theater.[148] In 1938, the House of Representatives established the Dies Committee to root out communist influence in the arts and in government. "They even sing Communism," claimed one witness before the House Committee on Un-American Activities on August 16, 1938, the fourth day of hearings. "Here is [a phonograph record called] the Soup Song, and this is entitled 'We Shall Not Be Moved.'" The chairman blurted, "That is an old-fashioned religious song," to which the witness replied, "It used to be."[149]

For some, the solution to this creep of subversive politics was to halt reintegration and to return to the purest forms of authenticity, autonomy, and non-political entertainment. According to their logic, neither high art of the past, nor pre-modern folk art, nor unalloyed entertainment, held any truck with modern politics. These kinds of art were, therefore, safe. As historian Victoria Grieve has shown, this issue came to national attention with the debate over two proposed bills in Congress: the Coffee-Pepper Bill in August 1937 and the Sirovich Bill in June 1938.[150] At this point, Republicans had regained control of Congress and threatened to roll back many of Roosevelt's Works Progress Administration programs, including the Federal Theatre Project. Both bills sought to retaliate against the Republicans' plans by establishing a permanent Federal Bureau of Arts, which would perpetuate the Works Progress Administration's Federal One arts projects in their then-current form. Both bills failed. Composer Walter Damrosch cheered their defeat in the name of aesthetic autonomy, defying the kind of public-oriented arts organizations that had been in existence since the Settlement House movement of the late nineteenth century: "Relief of the indigent must go on, but there should be no compromise between art and relief. Any bureau that is established should minister to the finest and holiest there is."[151] Such objections were not unique to conservatives. Many on the far left, including Dwight Macdonald and his colleagues at the *Partisan Review*, also advocated for the purity of institutions. "So let the masses have their Masscult [popular middlebrow culture], let the few who care about good writing, painting, music, architecture, philosophy, etc., have their High Culture, and don't fuzz up the distinction with Midcult [middlebrow art that more convincingly imitates highbrow culture]," Macdonald wrote—an approach, he said explicitly, that was completely at odds with Brooks's middle path, which sought to blur those boundaries.[152]

Yet the New York Intellectuals went one step further. In the nineteenth century, the fundamental separation between art and everyday life had usually led to analogies about transcendence, idealism, or spiritual uplift. The New York Intellectuals, however, dismissed these analogies as insufficiently autonomous. Poet Margaret Widdemer, for example, wrote in the *Saturday Review of Literature*, "You cannot discuss art in terms of morality or immorality"; to do so was to speak "like a common garden-club reader."[153] Poet Louise Bogan wrote that true artists should not try to popularize their works, but should instead hunker down in an aggressive crouch within the ivory tower, "the workshop, stronghold, and place of meditation" for the "brave fighter, sensitive thinker, and good workman known to all ages as the artist."[154] Art critic Clement Greenberg, Macdonald's colleague at *Partisan Review*, was even more emphatic: "Content is to be dissolved so completely into form that the work of art of literature cannot be reduced in whole or in part to anything not itself."[155] This was drastic: To purge art of its popular tendencies, it purported to purge art of meaning altogether, a kind of ferocious formalism that would guard against any potential propaganda. (Greenberg famously extolled the work of abstract formalists.)

Despite the purported purity, however, their emphasis on autonomy had social, political, and economic (read: aesthetically impure) motives. For some, drawing a "magic circle" around art would shield it from the blandishments of politics and money, which would represent an act of opposition or rebellion against the modern entertainment industry, an approach that musicologist Richard Middleton once called "an outraged and deliberately esoteric response to the new drive toward commodification."[156] By standing apart from mainstream audiences, by rejecting sentiment or direct communication or entertainment, high art would adopt a radically critical pose, not necessarily opposed to any specific idea, but instead opposed to the entire business-oriented, stratified "status quo" tout court.

Macdonald and the New York Intellectuals were similarly strict about the institution of authenticity. "Folk Art was the people's own institution, their private little kitchen-garden walled off from the great formal park of their masters," Macdonald wrote. "But Masscult [middlebrow culture] breaks down the wall, integrating the masses into a debased form of High Culture and thus becoming an instrument of domination."[157] Two of Macdonald's colleagues at *Partisan Review*, Bogan along with novelist and journalist James Agee, would make more or less the same argument about mixing folk art and popular culture. In Bogan's words, "the folk tradition has become thoroughly bourgeoizified," thereby producing, in Agee's words, the "pseudo-folk." Both argued that commercial folk art was not just an artistic problem; it was also a political problem: It "dangerously corrupted" the "peasants themselves," Agee argued, and he feared that commercial folk could become a manipulative tool for demagogues who wanted to burnish their political messages with the patina of folk authenticity and the glint of popular appeal: "We may have a jew's-harp President yet," he warned.[158] Once again, the solution was to advocate for a kind of folk purity that stood outside the modern marketplace of culture. As Agee wrote, "The folk artist and the non-folk artist have this in common: that their living—if they try to get it from their work—all but entirely depends upon an audience which, if the artist succeeds with them, virtually assures the destruction of his art."[159]

Although it may seem unexpected, critics in these circles brought these same standards of "purity" to popular culture, including Broadway. One such writer was Eric Bentley. In a career that spanned some seven decades, he garnered a reputation as an avant-garde snob, partially for his association with Theodor Adorno in California, partially for translating and promoting Bertolt Brecht's experimental and political plays, and partially for his infamous contrarian tone.[160] (As critic Walter Kerr wrote in the *New York Herald Tribune* in 1953, "Brecht speaks only to Bentley, and Bentley speaks only to God."[161]) But in fact, his tastes were more complex, and he expounded on them in the popular press as a staff writer for *Harper's* (1945–1948), for *Theatre Arts* and *The Kenyon Review* (1948–1951), and for *The New Republic* (1952–1956). Like both Brooks and Macdonald, Bentley argued that there was once a time when drama was unified. "Until the modern period great drama has possessed not only those deeper and subtler qualities which reveal themselves to the careful analyst and which constitute its greatness, it has also possessed more generally available qualities," he wrote. "It has appealed to the connoisseur *and* the amateur, the critic *and* the public."[162] Also like them, he believed that economic changes over the past two centuries had caused a rift between "theater" (which is a visual, musical, or scenic art) and "drama" (which is a literary or poetic art): "As the public was stratified into what we now call high- and lowbrows, the theater was similarly split."[163] Following Macdonald's logic, he wrote that the rise of middle-class society pushed drama more toward spectacle and entertainment, arguing that "the extension of literacy to the previously illiterate majority created, not a nation of philosophers, but a nation of newspaper readers."[164] To avoid being completely swallowed by the entertainment industry, Bentley offered a bunker mentality: "We may have to stay outside the theater as it is now financed and organized, and accept a special, limited audience."[165] Like the writers at *Partisan Review*, he believed that mixing different institutions—the middlebrow approach—was a problem. "Disorder reigns, and impurity," he complained. "In our theatre, you seldom see *anything* in its purity. Nearly always there is an effort, instead, to combine the best of both, and indeed all, worlds. Our lighter comedies are ruined by a moralism which has no proper place there. Musical comedies begin to put on the airs of operas, if not of oratorios."[166]

Yet Bentley did not entirely reject musical comedy in favor of something more highbrow. Quite the opposite, in fact: "*Guys and Dolls* is so glorious a piece of entertainment that it almost makes me fall down . . . and worship solid, fleshy, lowbrow America," he wrote. "One has to admit that as a piece of art it far surpasses all Broadway's deliberate attempts at the artistic."[167] He was enthusiastic about "pure" entertainment, which eschewed anything except unalloyed enjoyment as its goal. "I refuse to be lectured by a musical comedy scriptwriter on the education of children, the nature of the good life, and the contribution of the American small town to the salvation of souls," he railed. "I regard such a gaffe simply as an opportunity to get out of the theatre before the crowd. I deplore the death of the king in the *King and I*; it was definitely his duty to stay alive and amuse us."[168] Yet Bentley also believed that such "purely" entertaining musicals could indeed hold a civic function, albeit one that was entirely abstract. Consider, for example, his assessment of Bert Lahr's performance in a 1946 revue called *Burlesque*:

> Mr. Bert Lahr need only show us a tithe of his extraordinary talent and we are transported to a realm that no entertainment-monger could possibly be interested in. Mr. Lahr's performance has about it a very embarrassing quality—beauty. His mere presence on the stage is something more meaningful than anything in the play he has to pretend to be a part of. Worst of

all, his personality—like that of all first-rate comedians—expresses a criticism of life and thus calls into play a faculty even more formidable than the aesthetic sense: the intellect. While such things go on, the show business cannot be as watertight and foolproof as it wants to be.[169]

Whatever social use this kind of musical comedy could have, whatever "criticism of life" it could offer, it was necessarily indirect: By remaining above the fray, so to speak, pure entertainment could silently critique the fray itself. Even though Bentley described this kind of entertainment as "pure," there was something "impure" about his conception of it. Although he was describing entertainment, he drew his terms from high art, describing the "beauty" of Lahr's performance, which suggests a quasi-Kantian form of pleasure that stood apart from worldly matters, in this case, from the modern capitalistic work of "entertainment-mongers" in "show business." Yet whereas Kant associated "beauty" with the disinterested pleasure one typically experiences in observing the formal properties of an artwork, here Bentley's concept of beauty lay closer to Kant's "agreeableness," a quality of an object that satisfied one's desire to be pleased. Whether Bentley actually meant "beautiful" or "agreeable" is beside the point. Rather, he probably used the term to emphasize that whatever joy one derived from popular musical theater should be immune to the ideological intrusion of modern politics or contemporary social issues (or, to adapt Kant's language once again, that it should be "purposeless" in a political or social sense), which for Bentley meant privileging an almost precognitive, radically sensual, nearly instinctual response to the show at hand.

From a historian's perspective, Bentley's tone was as notable as the content of his critiques. He and his comrades (including Agee, Bogan, Macdonald, and others) suffused their writing with a reactionary feeling, which pitted them against a massive middlebrow movement that sought to mix high art, folk art, and popular culture. For them, such mixtures would distort the special qualities of each individual category. Today, apart from the merits of their arguments, the intensity of their writing stands as a testament to how pervasive, recognizable, and controversial their middlebrow enemies had become. Equally telling was that their response was to impose strict conceptual boundaries between each artistic institution—stricter, perhaps, than anything that had existed in the previous century.

At a broad level, this chapter has shown that the consequence of this debate over the proper attitude toward the distinctions between high art, folk art, and popular culture was that seemingly familiar genres suddenly seemed open to new compositional techniques and new modes of interpretation, drawn from other genres that had previously seemed incompatible. On Broadway, for example, the trend toward middlebrow mixing meant that, by the end of the 1930s and the beginning of the 1940s, the seemingly fundamental principles governing the composition and interpretation of the musical had emerged into open debate in the mainstream press. In the most general sense, this was nothing new; critics had long argued about the Broadway musical's style and content. Yet the terms of those arguments changed at this historical moment: Was the Broadway musical, properly speaking, a form of entertainment, or could it aspire to be high art or folk art? Could it aspire to participate actively in the most pressing social and political issues of the day? Could it claim the level of sophistication or seriousness of intent that had seemed proper to classical music? Could it resonate deeply within the soul or tap the very roots of American identity, as folk music had done? Previously these questions had had mostly stable answers, even as Broadway's dominant styles had changed: Broadway was entertainment. But at the start of the 1940s they reared up as stubbornly open questions.

This instability provides the backdrop for the dawning of what would come to be known as Broadway's Golden Age. At this point in history, a show premiered that thoroughly muddled artistic institutions: a popular musical comedy, which was set in the dusty plains of the West with folksy dialect and music, and which critics at the time also hailed as the first true American opera. That musical was *Oklahoma!*.

3

Heightened Realism

A Re-evaluation of the *Oklahoma!* Revolution

Since its premiere in 1943, *Oklahoma!* has carved out territory somewhere along the heavily patrolled border between high art and popular culture. On the one hand, at a stylistic level, the show bears almost no resemblance to "classical" music: Its songs (with the possible exception of "Lonely Room") sound emphatically American, emphatically popular. On the other hand, at a conceptual level, critics have long claimed that the show boasts a formal sophistication that elevates it to the status of opera. With unmistakable Wagnerian overtones, commentators have argued that all components of this show—the script, the costumes, the sets, the dance, the lyrics, the score, the arrangements—are "integrated," that is, conceived as a single entity that serves the story and its characters.[1] In practice, "integration" has signified a few things: a production in which song and dance advance the story instead of providing respite from it; a show with songs that cannot easily be separated off from their surrounding context in the play (sold as individual hits or plugged individually on the radio); a musical in which song and scene flow seamlessly into one another.[2] All of these, various scholars have argued, can apply to *Oklahoma!*. For most, the show's formal integration set it apart from previous musicals, the majority of which had comprised a looser collection of individuated songs, acts, and cameos. Therefore, while *Oklahoma!* may have sounded and looked like a popular musical, albeit a highly original one, beneath the surface lay unusually complex craft. As Oscar Hammerstein II famously put it, "The art of this thing is to get in and out of the numbers so that the audience isn't aware that you are jumping from dialogue to singing. The art, you understand, is not to jump but to ooze."[3] The operative word, repeated for emphasis, was "art."

Around this aesthetic principle has hovered an entire constellation of corollaries which, taken together, have lent *Oklahoma!* some of the prestige of high culture. The most prominent claim has been that attaining the integrated form amounted to an artistic revolution. For musicologist Joseph

Swain, *Oklahoma!* heralded Broadway's "maturity," standing as "the first work of an important series, like the First Symphony of Beethoven."[4] For director and theater historian Sheldon Patinkin, *Oklahoma!* "almost single-handedly changed everyone's understanding of what a musical should be."[5] For musicologist Ann Sears, the show possessed "a dramatic unity and momentum that had hardly been present in American musical theater before 1943, and thus [announced] the arrival of the 'musical play.'"[6] Alongside a new seriousness of technique came a new seriousness of purpose. In musicologist Larry Stempel's estimation, the show "both created and fed on the very possibility that a Broadway musical could come to matter in the cultural life of the nation."[7] For Stephen Sondheim, Hammerstein was a "morality playwright" who aimed for something beyond entertainment: "He taught everybody: he sang for us all."[8]

Nearly as often as historians have articulated these formal principles, however, they have also acknowledged that some of the details do not entirely withstand scrutiny. From an aesthetic point of view, theater historian Scott McMillin has doubted just how integrated Rodgers and Hammerstein musicals could have been given that they still marked a break between speech and song, between action and reflection, between naturalistic movement and dance, between linear plot and repetitive song, and between "progressive time" and "lyric time."[9] From a historical point of view, scholars have attributed the integrated form to shows before *Oklahoma!*, including works written by George Gershwin, Jerome Kern, and George M. Cohan, among others, and they have also found evidence for the integrated form in the earlier works of both Rodgers and Hammerstein.[10] Instead of a linear evolution from episodic musical comedy to integrated musical play, this research depicts a theatrical field in the early decades of the twentieth century in which multiple genres existed on a continuum, ranging from vaudeville sketch to topical revue, to musical comedy, to plotted operetta: distinct in concept but slippery in application, available to composers and librettists to be mixed as an expressive choice.[11] This is to say that there may never have actually been an integration revolution at all, at least not in the familiar formal sense of the term. (Summing up, and borrowing the words of musicologist Kim Kowalke, "Not even the exclamation point in the title was a first."[12])

From all of this research and commentary emerges another paradox, a historiographical one: In 1943, without the distance of time, it should have been especially clear that formal integration did not burst onto the

Broadway scene with *Oklahoma!*. Nonetheless, contemporary critics touted *Oklahoma!* as a revolution, which many at the time attributed to some kind of integration. Historians have suggested a couple of ways to square this circle. First, some have written that even if the individual components of the musical—including not only its overall formal integration, but also certain features of its choreography, dialogue, and so on—turned out not to be completely novel on their own, the composite effect of them all gathered into a single evening's performance pushed Broadway in new directions, amplified by the show's unprecedented box-office and critical success.[13] For others, the claims made at the time about the formal ingenuity and operatic ambitions of *Oklahoma!* were part of a mystique created by the production team as part the show's advertising. Not all may survive historical investigation, but even so, the *Oklahoma!* story nonetheless remains influential in the way that legends are. In musicologist Tim Carter's apt words, "even the untrue contains its truths."[14]

In this chapter I propose another solution. Re-examining contemporary sources reveals that when *Oklahoma!* opened, Hammerstein and his contemporaries never actually claimed that formal integration was itself innovative, at least not in the way most understand the term today. When Hammerstein did write about formal integration, it served as a means to an end, one cog in a larger theatrical theory that he called "heightened realism," and *this* was what he and others claimed in 1943 was revolutionary. Heightened realism was not primarily a formal theory, although it did imply a certain (now familiar) formal cohesion. Instead, it referred to integration of a different kind, a style of theater that brought together qualities that would have seemed otherwise incompatible: the dazzling ("heightened") production values of popular musical comedy and the idealist authenticity of folk art ("realism"), a combination of institutions that, according to Hammerstein, had not existed on Broadway before (except, perhaps, in certain of his earlier works such as *Show Boat*, *Rainbow*, and *Music in the Air*). He believed that the theory of heightened realism opened new potential for expression and meaning in the musical, and these expanded interpretive possibilities, this new air of importance, encouraged some reviewers to call *Oklahoma!* operatic, even though the production did not sound or look like opera. Fundamentally, then, this theory of heightened realism meant that *Oklahoma!* was, in the sense introduced in the previous two chapters, a middlebrow musical that blended the institutions of high art, folk art, and popular culture—and self-consciously so.

The task here is not merely to refine the familiar definition of integration and distinguish between "formal" and "institutional" kinds. Rather, recognizing heightened realism as the primary innovation of *Oklahoma!* requires a shift in analytical lenses. Returning to the opening argument, if the distinction between highbrow art and popular culture has long been at the center of the show's legacy, the distinction between folk art and popular culture has been less prevalent. Insofar as it has appeared in the commentary surrounding the show, it has tended to reside at the level of style, as an acknowledgment that the script and score have an air of Americana about them. As will become clear, however, theories of folk authenticity also operated at a deeper, conceptual level, contributing to the way the creative team conceived the production and to the way that the earliest reviewers received it. Conceived as folk music, *Oklahoma!* seemed capable of articulating homespun American values, deep spiritual truths about the American people, which had seemed all but foreclosed to urbane musical comedies of earlier decades.

Hammerstein developed his theory of heightened realism gradually over more than a decade, during the period outlined in the previous two chapters when seemingly stable institutions of high art, folk art, and popular culture were shifting, blending. In fact, both Rodgers and Hammerstein acknowledged a debt to many of the critics who appeared in those pages, especially Gilbert Seldes and Brooks Atkinson. When Rogers and Hammerstein began collaborating in the early 1940s, they drew upon these critics' ideas and influences, aiming to blaze what Van Wyck Brooks (introduced in Chapter 1) would have termed a "middle path" between modern, urban, and commercial popular culture on the one hand, and the idealist values of folk and classical art on the other. Middlebrow critics who cheered *Oklahoma!* believed that no matter the degree to which these categories blended, folk art could still retain some of its fundamental idealist properties and stand as an authentic emblem of homier times: an antidote for or reprieve from the fallen, modern, commercial, war-ridden world, a recovery of stable values amid chaos—even in the context of a Broadway comedy. Grasping onto these traditional values, many of them also believed that the combination of folk and popular music helped *Oklahoma!* pioneer a form of American opera that would be of the people, by the people, and for the people. This claim carried international implications. For them, *Oklahoma!* modeled a way to reclaim opera, a genre that in European hands had become increasingly obscure or obscene in the early decades of the twentieth century, and to return it to its purported folk roots, albeit roots transplanted from Italian, German, or French soil to the vast expanses of the American West.[15] For others, however, classical, folk, and popular culture remained blatantly contradictory. Melding them threatened to destroy the special properties of each and would effectively collapse high art and folk art into mere commodity, rendering opera incapable of providing a true glimpse of a life that was not beholden to rampant commerce, politics, or war. According to these critics, *Oklahoma!* and its success were ominous.

"Youth, ambition—and, well, just plain voltage": Richard Rodgers before *Oklahoma!*

A few months after *Oklahoma!* opened, Rodgers recalled that the show's producers had been "scolding" him for over fifteen years. "The work you're concerned with is too trivial," he remembered them saying. "You must find a subject-matter of more importance. Get something truly American, something that will have a lasting quality."[16] He claimed that they had "conditioned" him since at least the mid-1920s to seek out serious projects, and *Oklahoma!* represented only his latest attempt to do so. Statements like these may seem dubious in retrospect, typical of the hype surrounding a show's premiere. Surviving historical sources, however, suggest that Rodgers was not exaggerating. They confirm that earlier in his career, he had frequently discussed how to develop a more "serious" kind of musical theater with his writing partner, lyricist Lorenz Hart. Broadly speaking, two general strategies emerged from their collaboration. First, they sought to reimagine (or, in their minds, improve) the typical features of popular music in their day, conducting what amounted to "experiments in the vernacular, snickering with irony," as Atkinson described them.[17] Second, they occasionally made forays into "classical" music (ballet, opera, symphonic music, and so on), using these genres to tackle forms and subjects that would have seemed unusual for popular musical comedy of the time. In both cases, no matter how important a given project may have seemed to them, their primary goal remained to preserve the "liveliness" that critics associated with contemporary musical comedy. Although the way Rodgers thought about "seriousness" would change when he met Hammerstein, some of his basic strategies in that later context would derive from his previous work with Hart.

According to Hart, most popular-music lyrics in the 1910s and early 1920s were "fairly stupid and had no point," were awash with Victorian sentiment and tired clichés, and were out of touch with American audiences—or, as Rodgers later recalled from their first meeting in 1919, these songs were often "cowardly, responded only to formula, and said nothing."[18] For Hart the fundamental quality of good theater was "Spontaneity" ("spell it with a capital 'S,'" he told a reporter in 1926[19]), and he praised popular theater that had "vibrating energy," that "[rushed] madly" and that traded in the "places, names, colloquialisms, and the popular news topics of the day," which could "touch American soil."[20] To this end, he crafted lyrics with current, everyday words, topical references, and slang. "Find something *living*, a word everyone uses," he said. "People don't go around talking about 'love' and 'dove.' ... I try to make [song lyrics] as fresh and as natural as ever, as close to earth as may be."[21] He also saturated his lyrics with rhyme, even going so far as to claim that the actual meaning of what he wrote was less important than the effect of its sound on the listener. "In a song of this sort the melody and the euphonics of the words themselves are really more important than the sense," he said.[22] The goal was a veritable frenzy of words, one that focused less on abstract significance than on sonic effect—a radically lively approach to writing.

Rodgers emphasized these qualities by incorporating syncopated rhythms imported from dance music, rhythms which drew attention to the internal rhymes within each line. The phrases in his songs often comprised a single, repeated, transposed, or transformed motivic cell, often lasting less than one measure.[23] Hart tended to set each of these individual short gestures with interlocking rhyming words.[24] In other words, rather than rhyme every four or eight measures, as was the norm at the time, each small gesture (one measure or less) could be linked by assonance and emphasized by rhythm. In his autobiography Rodgers cited "Blue Room" from *The Girl Friend* (1926) as an example of all of this (reproduced and annotated in Example 3.1a). "I begin the second, third, and fourth bars on a C natural [. . .] and followed it with a note rising a half tone [sic] in each successive bar," he wrote. "This gave Larry the idea of using a triple rhyme on the repeated C note, and then, for emphasis, repeating the word 'room' on the rising half tones."[25] Rodgers touted the economy of means—the individual cells lasting a single measure, the rapidly recurring multi-syllabic rhymes—as the formal innovation that made their approach to standard chorus forms seem new and exciting.[26] In his autobiography, he also cited "Thou Swell" as a piece that featured a fresh

Example 3.1a–b. Richard Rodgers, Lorenz Hart, "Blue Room" and "Thou Swell," adapted from *Rodgers and Hart: A Musical Anthology* (Milwaukee: Hal Leonard, 1995), 84, 127–28. See also Rodgers, *Musical Stages*, 80.

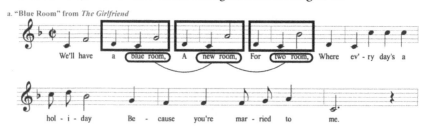

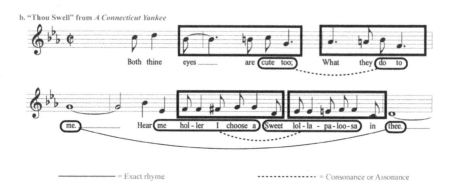

approach to otherwise standard thirty-two-bar forms. Although he did not elaborate, the strategy appears similar. As shown in Example 3.1b, the recurring melodic cell comprises three chromatically rising notes followed by a descending fourth. Each group receives an internal, multi-syllabic slant rhyme, punctuated by an exact rhyme at the end of the line. The result was a speedy, rat-a-tat effect produced by a constant spray of internal rhymes and recurring small, rhythmic motives, the kind of song that sparked constant attention because nearly every syllable and nearly every small cell of notes resembled something that came before or something that would come after.

All of these values—the spontaneity, the frenzied excitement, the relevance, the intensity, the American quality—were in line with the "lively" values of popular culture that Seldes spelled out in his book *Seven Lively Arts* (1924). As discussed in Chapter 2, Seldes believed that popular music was tantamount to urban folk culture: It was modern and commercial music, but also capable of expressing something essential about people living in America's steel-and-glass-skyscraper cities. In fact, Rodgers and Hart acknowledged Seldes's influence explicitly by dedicating the second-act opener of *The Garrick Gaieties* (1925) to him. Titled "The Joy Spreader," its plot pitted two kinds of joy against one another, the abstract joy of classical beauty and puritanical virtue against the carnal joy of modern, popular culture. The aptly named Mr. Price extols the first kind of joy, championing hard work, thrift, self-denial, and Christian morals. "Although the modern rage is / A cry for higher wages, / I pay you less to keep you from temptation!" he sings as he awards a Bible to his most industrious worker. The second kind of joy comes from his employee Mary, who, after reading a love story, tells a co-worker that she has come to understand something about her workaday life: "We aren't really—really *alive*, dear." That night Mary finds herself inadvertently locked inside the store with a colleague. The two of them sway to strains of jazz, and when Price discovers them the next morning *in delicto*, he fires them. The young couple is overjoyed ("We fire ourselves!"), and, accompanied again by jazz, lead their co-workers in a rebellion against Mr. Price, overthrowing him with a sarcastic "Amen!"[27] The imagery was hardly subtle. The sketch's title alone ("The Joy Spreader") suggests that their goal was to supplant abstract puritanism with dance-music liveliness.

Liveliness became a recurring refrain in the commentary surrounding *The Garrick Gaieties*. Actress and writer Edith Meier, who helped direct and assemble some of the sketches, attributed the revue's success to these lively qualities, or in her words, to "youth and ambition—and, well, just plain voltage."[28] As historian Ann Douglas has described, Hart found himself in good company in a "culture of momentum" alongside writers including H. L. Mencken, Ring Lardner, Dorothy Parker, and F. Scott Fitzgerald, all of whom were exploring new possibilities for the American vernacular, raising doggerel to a level of sophistication and intensity rarely seen before in American letters.[29] Dorothy Hart, Lorenz Hart's sister-in-law, attested to this when she wrote, "I fell in love with Scott Fitzgerald and Lorenz Hart in my very early teens," and added, crucially, "They made language *alive*."[30] What emerged from all of this was a mode of expression that could claim both formal intricacy and pop-culture currency, a combination of values that Rodgers would also attempt (in a different way) with *Oklahoma!*.

Rodgers and Hart also tried to write more "serious" pieces during the 1920s and 1930s by engaging in formal experimentation, which at times made their work appear partially in line with highbrow genres such as ballet and sung-through opera. One such piece, in fact, was "The Joy Spreader" from *The Garrick Gaieties*, which alternated between short songs and recitative, and which they billed as an "American Jazz Opera." Other examples included their "symphonic narrative" *All Points West*, first performed at the Philadelphia Academy of Music and then at the Hippodrome in 1936, and the *Nursery Ballet*, which premiered at Carnegie Hall in 1938, and which largely reused instrumental music from their musical *Jumbo*.[31] Rodgers explained at the time that he took on these projects because he and Hart "wanted to do something with more freedom. We wanted to escape the conventions that hedge in the musical-comedy song."[32] In part, Rodgers was referring to experimenting with the standard thirty-two-bar form, and in a high-art venue, audiences could expect formal experimentation to be an end unto itself. For example, after the premiere of *All Points West* in Carnegie Hall, critics focused on the piece's formal novelty, and they reached deep into their musical dictionaries for the occasion: One unsigned review claimed that *All Points West* was "not recitative, nor does it bear much resemblance to 'recitative stroment,' less to the 'aria parlante,'" and then proclaimed it to be "a new form"; critic and composer Deems Taylor called the piece a "combination of orchestral tone poem, dramatic aria, and recitation."[33]

Yet, broadly speaking, no matter how inhospitable Rodgers and Hart found musical comedy in the early part of the twentieth century, and no matter what form their experiments took, they had no intention of leaving the field. Throughout this period, even as they were producing more "serious" work, they also mounted a half dozen shows and revues that spoofed high art, suggesting that they found high art as uncongenial as current popular music.[34] At most, they sought to situate themselves somewhere between high art and popular culture. Both *All Points West* and *Nursery Ballet*, for example, were collaborations with the famous bandleader Paul Whiteman, whose goal was avowedly middlebrow, not highbrow: He sought to carve out a "third stream" of concert music that lay somewhere between classical music and jazz.[35] Moreover, as musicologist Dominic Symonds has amply demonstrated, Rodgers and Hart had already incorporated formal experimentation ("dialogue lyrics," continuous underscoring, and other strategies of blending story and song) into their musical comedies since their earliest collaborations, including *Poor Little Ritz Girl* (1920) and *Chee-Chee* (1928), the latter of which included the often-cited program note: "The musical numbers, some of them very short, are so interwoven with the story that it would be confusing for the audience to peruse a complete list."[36] Taken together, it appears that even though Rodgers and Hart criticized accustomed *practices* of the institution of popular culture, they rarely questioned its *values*—its immediacy, its currency, its allegiance with feeling, its opposition to abstraction and aloofness, its liveliness.

Nevertheless, in 1940, despite all of his previous work to stand apart from run-of-the-mill musical comedy, the Theatre Guild was still pressuring Rodgers to set more "serious," "lasting," and "American" works. In 1941 novelist Edna Ferber approached Rodgers, Hart, and Hammerstein about adapting her novel *Saratoga Trunk*, a sweeping story about nineteenth-century New Orleans and New York with a similar scope and Americana atmosphere as *Show Boat*, another novel by Ferber that Hammerstein had previously adapted for the musical stage with Jerome Kern. *Saratoga Trunk* ultimately fell through, and Hart became increasingly incapacitated from alcoholism. However, something Hammerstein mentioned to Rodgers continued to resonate. "Specifically," Rodgers wrote to him, "you feel that I should have a book with 'substance' to write to. Will you think seriously about doing such a book?"[37]

"A Rich Vein for Musical Play Metal": Oscar Hammerstein II, *Couleur Locale*, and Integration

In fact, by 1941 Hammerstein had long been thinking about doing such books. Like Rodgers and Hart, Hammerstein began his career squarely in the field of popular musicals, working on shows that one reviewer at the time described as "full of melody, jazz, girls, and comedy."[38] Like Rodgers and Hart, Hammerstein was frustrated with the genre. He complained that "musical comedy standards were [not] as high," that the genre "followed a rigid construction formula," that "the field of libretto writing [. . .] was filled with hacks and gag men who extended the tradition of ignominy attached to musical comedy books."[39] Despite these similarities, however, he ultimately conceived of "substance" differently than Rodgers and Hart. Unlike Hart, who believed that musical comedy had fallen fundamentally out of touch with its American audiences, Hammerstein's central complaint was that "the general attitude [. . .] toward musical comedy was cynical." He continued, "Neither the public nor the critics expected more than a display of girls, jokes, and tunes," and he believed that most songwriters of this generation pandered to their audiences, "[indicating] a lack of integrity in the musical comedy of those days."[40] If Hart's overall goal had been to reignite a lively spark in contemporary musical comedy, then Hammerstein sought to restore the genre's respectability.[41]

Equally important to Hammerstein at this point in his career, however, was to attain respectability while also distancing himself from high art, which he generally considered to be aloof or stuffy.[42] He argued this explicitly in a 1925 *Theater Magazine* article, written shortly after his operetta *Rose-Marie* opened:

> Is there a form of musical play tucked away somewhere in the realm of possibilities which could attain the heights of grand opera and still keep sufficiently human to be entertaining? I have an extravagant theory that little light opera, a healthy youth all alive and ambitious, can be so developed that he can come in at the back door and give his big brother, grand opera, a stiff battle for artistic honors—certainly the younger one has a great advantage. He is continually moving and progressing.[43]

In part, Hammerstein was joining a long list of people who complained about opera's stodginess at the time and who sought to make it more accessible, a list that included his infamous grandfather (and namesake), whose Manhattan Opera House nearly brought the Metropolitan Opera to ruin in the first decade of the twentieth century.[44] Among this crowd, as musicologist Annegret Fauser has shown, common strategies for reforming opera at the time included lower ticket prices, English translations, and other tactics designed to make European opera seem more accessible to the broader public. Others attempted to be relevant to local audiences by writing serious-minded operas on specifically American themes.[45] Others struck an irreverent pose, writing "hot jazz" versions of classic operas (including both *Swing Mikado* in 1938 and *Hot Mikado* in 1939) that often featured Black singers, dancers, and musicians.

Hammerstein's approach, however, was fundamentally different. He sought to forge a new kind of hybrid theater out of two seemingly incompatible components. First, he sought to retain popular entertainment's "sufficiently human" qualities, a phrase that recalls Van Wyck Brooks's arguments that high art had become "unsocial" and aloof from its audiences (see Chapter 1). Second, he sought to imbue this popular form with some kind of "artistic honors." Instead of turning to highbrow opera to supply these qualities, however, Hammerstein turned increasingly toward folk music. It was in this context that critics began to use the term "integration" to describe his work, not strictly as a formal term, but rather as a word that signified a combination of musical-comedy entertainment with wholesome folk art—genres that, for many of Hammerstein's early reviewers, seemed incommensurable.

Hammerstein's journey to folk art began in operetta. Somebody once asked him why he did not write comedies like Rodgers and Hart. "You mean one that takes place in a New York penthouse?" he asked. "Mostly because it doesn't interest me."[46] Starting in the early 1920s, Hammerstein distanced himself from popular musical comedy by writing operettas set outside the modern, urban, commercial world of New York City, and he collaborated with composers who distanced their scores from modern-day Broadway by outfitting them with sonic emblems of "local color."[47] None of this was strictly accurate in the ethnographic sense. (An example of particularly eye-popping orientalism comes from *The Desert Song*, in which the Vietnamese femme fatale dances a hula.) Rather, these were essentially special effects, just convincing enough to give a sense that these shows represented a world far outside of quotidian city life. Indeed, by 1928, when his Gold Rush musical *Rainbow* opened, one critic wrote, "Atmosphere appears to have been definitely added to the list of ingredients a successful musical should have."[48]

In his work as librettist, Hammerstein found two additional ways to distance his writing from "penthouse" musical comedy. First, he adopted a style of language that stood far afield from Broadway argot, and early on, critics complained that he often toppled into grandiloquence. Alexander Woollcott, for example, wrote that in Hammerstein's play *Gypsy Jim* (1924) "lyric speech became so contagious that the authors were in grave danger of seeing the newspapers break out this morning in a rash of notices such as this: 'Oscar Hammerstein 2d and [co-author] Milton Gropper / Wrote a comedy that came an awful cropper.' "[49] Second, Hammerstein's shows typically delivered some homey life lesson, often in the form of what musicologist Stephen Banfield has called an "act-two sermon."[50] The danger in all of this was that the elevated tone would seem out of keeping with the genre of musical comedy to critics. The *New York Times* reviewer, for example, described the script to *Wildflower* (1923) as "practically never funny, and now and then even a little dull"; he complained that the script to *Golden Dawn* (1927) was "ponderous and mannered" (another critic, Walter Winchell, dubbed it "The Golden Yawn"); and he found the script for *The New Moon* (1928) "[weighed] a little on the entertainment after the first act."[51] The challenge of finding a balance between "seriousness" and "liveliness" would continue to dog Hammerstein throughout the 1920s and 1930s.

In all of this, Hammerstein was on the leading edge of a wave of musical productions, identified by composer and historian Mark Grant, that washed over Broadway during the mid-1920s.[52] They mixed the folkish atmosphere of the South or frontier West with serious-minded plots and music. One of the first of these was W. Franke Harling's "native opera" *Deep River*, which opened on Broadway in October 1926, starring Jules Bledsoe (who would later star as Joe in Hammerstein's *Show Boat*), and which featured a libretto by Laurence Stallings (who would later write *Rainbow* with Hammerstein). Atkinson's review in the *New York Times* encapsulates the general attitude critics took toward the production, calling it a "rather too pretentious native opera," reiterating his general displeasure with opera's supposed stuffiness, and previewing his later complaints about *Porgy and Bess* (discussed in Chapter 2). Crucially, however, Atkinson did praise the score for "occasionally [accenting] the prancing rhythms of jazz," and he also wrote that its "score seems most native when it develops folk-themes, sometimes with the flavor of the negro minstrels, and when it invokes the superstitious spells of the voodoo queen with cabalistic chants and prayers to the evil gods." At these moments, according to Atkinson, the show "[pointed] the way to a rich mine of American material."[53]

Between 1927 and 1928, Hammerstein opened two shows that worked this rich mine: *Show Boat* and *Rainbow*. Both stressed the "local color" of frontier, Western, or Southern life. However, they both also incorporated musical-comedy entertainment. Atkinson raved that in *Show Boat*, Hammerstein achieved an ideal balance between popular culture and folk art. In his 1927 review, Atkinson stated as a general principle that "whatever its theme, a musical play must include all the variety of that *lively* form of entertainment," and praised the show on these grounds. Yet, according to Atkinson, hand in glove with modern entertainment came backwater wisdom. He called it a musical show that "developed logically out of a fragment of folklore."[54] When it came to mixing the popular culture and folk music in *Show Boat*, Atkinson believed that despite "eccentric dancing," "slapstick," and "sundry cajoleries," "the producers have kept everything in tune, subordinating wit to humor and cleverness to entertainment."

For Atkinson, tempering both the showbiz and folklore elements (keeping both "in tune") amounted to Hammerstein's primary achievement in *Show Boat*, and he called this "integration": "For such musical drama no tin-pan clatter of eclectic melodies suffices. In providing 'Show Boat' with a full complement of 'song hits' Mr. Kern has not violated his sense of the fitness of things," and added, "Even the jazz tunes become *integral* parts of the score."[55] In using this word, Atkinson's main point was neither that each song helped advance the story, nor that the dialogue and music fitted together smoothly, although he did believe that the show was well constructed. Rather, this word suggested that the show was, in his phrase, "perfectly blended" between popular culture and folk culture, and that this feature opened up new potential for meaning. "'Show Boat' is not sophisticated," he wrote, using a word that tended to carry negative connotations of cynical urbanity in his correspondence with Van Wyck Brooks (as described in Chapter 2). Instead, he argued, "the romance is full and uncritical; the humor is hardly more than a relish of fun."[56] Backing away from the (sometimes salacious) musical-comedy "sophistication" of Rodgers, Hart, and others of that generation, Hammerstein's show struck Atkinson as sincere and "exuberantly good natured."[57]

This line of commentary continued in his review for Hammerstein's next show, *Rainbow*, which premiered in 1928. During out-of-town tryouts the show had earned a reputation as the next *Show Boat* because it mixed musical comedy, a folk atmosphere, and a serious plot.[58] According to critic Burns Mantle:

> Laurence Stallings is credited with the yarn, and there are traces of the sort of thing you would expect the author of "What Price Glory?" to write. But not all of it is his. Some of it belongs, by program, to Oscar Hammerstein 2d. And Oscar's part, it is easy to assume, includes a kiss-'em-'till-they-faint scene for a mule-skinner comedian, a Times Square hymn and other occasional lapses into the lower Broadway school of musical comedy.[59]

Although Mantle still associated Hammerstein with the "melody, jazz, girls and comedy" of his earliest Broadway ventures, he nonetheless emphasized that that the show alternated the Broadway comedy segments with the serious dialogue along the lines of Stallings's war play *What Price Glory?* (cowritten with Maxwell Anderson). The result was a show with a new mood that sat somewhere between broad comedy and high drama. Others found this equally remarkable. Critic and playwright St. John Ervine, for example, believed that *Rainbow* was billed as a musical play because of the "ambition of its authors to rescue musical plays from the pool of twaddle in which the plots of most of them are thoroughly soused."[60] Dance critic Herbert Miller described it as "American, but not flag-waving, expensive but not too gaudy, and huge because it presents a spectacle of one of the most romantic periods in this country's history," and argued that it was superior to unalloyed entertainment "because *Rainbow* has a book, something that musical comedies rarely possess."[61] Howard Barnes likewise declared, "Laurence Stallings and Oscar Hammerstein 2d fashioned the book of this new musical play and with such gusto that the conventional musical comedy pattern was ever in imminent peril of being rudely shattered."[62]

Atkinson followed suit. He acknowledged the show's lowbrow musical comedy. "You may scantly wish that it were less obsessed with the masculinity of our pioneer civilization and less prone to ribaldry. In between the musical serenades 'Rainbow' abandons itself to shootin' and cussin' and drinkin' and wenchin'—rough-hewn and coarse with all the swagger of border life."[63] Still, he considered this show a landmark. "Although [*Rainbow*] is long, to the point of tedium, it yields robust entertainment that never succumbs to the general musical comedy fol-de-rol," he wrote, and continued: "Not to be unduly secretive, it is a *lively* fun," boasting a "roistering book." Crucially, according to Atkinson, the "integrity" of *Rainbow*—the element that tempered the broad musical comedy—derived from its pervasive folk atmosphere (its Gold Rush "pioneer" setting, its downhome dialect, its "swagger of border life"), and this quality "opened a rich vein for musical play metal," echoing almost verbatim the sentence that he had used to describe *Deep River*.[64] If Hammerstein was incorporating these folk elements to make the show seem more serious, it worked: About two weeks later, Atkinson declared in print, "Oscar Hammerstein 2d never writes for the musical stage without distinction"—a far cry from "melody, jazz, girls and comedy."[65]

In 1930 Hammerstein and Atkinson began corresponding directly (and potentially even meeting in person) to discuss theater. Only a few letters between them survive, but in one of them Hammerstein wrote, "I have a vaguely pleasant feeling of coming closer to a critical mind—a type of mind, which God knows, seems pathetically far away on mornings after my opening nights," and added, "I should like to have lunch with you some day and figure out what you like in the musical play. Please forgive me for being so in earnest about such a trivial subject but somebody ought to be."[66] What exactly they discussed is impossible to know, but from this point on, Atkinson began increasingly to describe Hammerstein's shows as both integrated and artistic. When Atkinson enumerated Hammerstein's "artistic honors," he mustered the most august terms he could. "At last the musical drama has been emancipated," he wrote in his 1932 review of Hammerstein and Kern's *Music in the Air*, calling the show "an organic work of art," and praising its "beauty" and "craftsmanship." He never explained this jargon; he never described what made *Music in the Air* so well crafted, never discussed formal integration, and never elaborated on what exactly the music theater had been emancipated from. One suspects, however, that these terms were not exactly literal, but instead were emblems of highbrow sophistication. Yet what Atkinson did explain clearly was how *Music in the Air* blended seemingly incompatible kinds of theater: popular theater and opera. "By the beauty of the music, the artlessness of the story and the simplicity of the acting it goes directly to the playgoing heart," he wrote.[67] The revolutionary aspect, in other words, was that the purportedly artful mixed so well with the purportedly artless. According to Atkinson, at a basic level, the resulting production felt different from other musicals: It boasted "effortless craftsmanship" that was also "remarkably spontaneous" with "sentiment and comedy" that did not "fall back into the cliché's [sic] of the trade."[68]

Shortly thereafter, Hammerstein and Rodgers began corresponding about plays of "substance," and when they did, there were already a few basic ideas hovering in the background. First, Hammerstein was trying to find ways to improve the quality of Broadway shows without tipping over into aloofness or undue seriousness. At the same time, he was also searching for the abstract "artistic honors" that would lend his plays distinction, and he had begun to find them, not in grand opera, but in folk music replete with "local color." Second, Rodgers had occasionally indicated that he was interested in incorporating some formal experimentation into his work, and like Hammerstein he was trying to strike a balance between sophistication and lively popularity. Third, from the critical point of view, Atkinson had been following Hammerstein's work and for more than a decade had praised it as "integrated" in the sense that it traveled a middle path between folk, opera, and musical comedy, even when these values seemed otherwise incommensurable. It was this project, integration as a middle path, that Rodgers and Hammerstein took up together when writing *Oklahoma!*.

"A Tightrope Between Life and Fantasy": The Theory of Heightened Realism

Rodgers and Hammerstein spent the initial weeks of their collaboration devising an approach for their new work.[69] They carried out most of this work in person, and many of the exact details have been lost to time. However, on February 4, 1943, just as *Oklahoma!* was entering rehearsals, the newspaper *PM* published a short article providing a glimpse into some of the ongoing behind-the-scenes discussions:

> Unlike the regulation musical comedy, the show (which, by the way, hasn't been named) won't be broken into tap numbers, ballet numbers, comedy spots, etc. [Agnes] de Mille is trying to work the dancing right into the story, so that folk dances and pageantry will be in keeping with the book. Mr. Rodgers, too, is scrupulously avoiding "set" musical numbers.[70]

At first it may appear that the primary issue facing the creative team was formal integration, referring to the process of fitting the show's various elements (here, dance) "right into the story." Context, however, suggests that this was only one small part of a much broader discussion. By the early 1940s such announcements about "avoiding 'set' musical numbers" had become almost routine. In some form, they had already appeared in the programs for Rodgers's *Chee-Chee* and Hammerstein's *Rose-Marie*, *Desert Song*, and *Golden Dawn*.[71] Moreover, in another article written a couple of months later, Hammerstein maintained that formal integration was only remarkable in comparison with Lynn Riggs's *Green Grow the Lilacs* (1931), the play on which *Oklahoma!* was based, but not in comparison with other musicals:

> [The eleven songs in *Green Grow the Lilacs*] were delivered incidentally, sung by the characters at a party and by a cowboy chorus to cover scenic changes. The songs we were to write [in *Oklahoma!*] had a different function. They must help tell our story and delineate characters, supplementing the dialogue and seeming to be, as much as possible, a continuation of the dialogue. This is, of course, true of the songs by any well-made musical play.[72]

This final sentence is crucial. It suggests that formal integration had been de rigueur for any composer or librettist working in plotted musical theater, and while Hammerstein would surely devise new ways of moving between scene and song in *Oklahoma!*, the concept itself was not innovative.[73]

Returning to the *PM* article from February 1943, other seemingly less remarkable details point to more pressing issues beyond formal integration. For instance, the sheer number of different genres that appear in this short paragraph—"regulation musical comedy," "tap numbers," "comedy spots"; "folk dances," "pageantry"; "ballet"—bespeaks a fundamental conceptual disagreement about the production: Should it be considered popular culture, folk art, or high art? Glimpses of this same backstage debate also emerge in other contemporaneous sources. A few weeks earlier, for example, the *Daily News* had reported that "the immediate problem is how to tag the show. It falls into the category of 'American folk opera,'" the label George Gershwin had used with *Porgy and Bess*, which the Theatre Guild had also produced.[74] Yet the same article had also noted that "the Guild [did not] want to call [*Oklahoma!*] an opera," a sentiment echoed in director Rouben Mamoulian's production notes, probably written around this time: "Guild afraid to be highbrow."[75]

Why all this anxiety? Two months after the *PM* article appeared, Jo Heidt, the Theatre Guild's press representative, would explain in an interview:

> First thing not to do [when advertising *Oklahoma!*] was to scare customers away by advertising a musical as an opera.... In original release, "Porgy and Bess" was stressed as a George Gershwin opera of American life.... And it was priced at a $4 top.... There was only a small audience available for such an offering, and George denied himself the greater audience that was available by refusing to let radio broadcast the wonderful tunes in the show.... Miss Helburn and Mr. Langner [the producers of *Oklahoma!*] decided that these mistakes should not be made again.[76]

Heidt associated "opera" with "small audiences," and he associated "tunes" on "radio broadcasts" with "greater audiences," thereby calling to mind the familiar institutional characterizations of highbrow art as esoteric and elite, and popular art as entertainment suitable for the masses. When the Theatre Guild's production of *Porgy and Bess* tried to escape these categorizations eight years earlier, the company failed at the box office. So, learning from experience, they advertised *Oklahoma!* in popular terms as "a lusty, swashbuckling" "morale booster," as "an antidote for war jitters," as "bright and breezy" entertainment.[77]

At the same time, however, some members of the production team expressed misgivings about billing the show as straightforward entertainment. This was especially clear in the discussions surrounding the show's title, also alluded to in the February 1943 *PM* article, which stated that the show "[hadn't] been named." In fact, around the time when that feature was written, the show did acquire a name, "Away We Go!," but producer Theresa Helburn felt that it did not fit. She wrote to Riggs on March 2, 1943, requesting "ideas for titles that would have more quality than *Away We Go!* and yet a gaiety and a lightness that would suit a musical version."[78] Four years later, she would provide even more detail about why the original title seemed inadequate, and what "quality" she was trying to capture. On the one hand, she deemed the original working title, "Oklahoma," "heavy and geographic," reminiscent of "dust bowls, oil wells and Grapes of Wrath." On the other hand, the other titles people in the production office suggested ("Cherokee Strip," for example) were too "jaunty," in danger of leading audiences to believe that they "were doing an old time 'Hurrah Girls' revue" (or worse, according to Helburn, that they were doing a "strip tease").[79] If the title was supposed to signal to the audience what to expect once the curtain rose, both the "heavy" and "light" titles would have been misleading because, in its conception, the show was neither highbrow *nor* popular, but rather both highbrow *and* popular. The Guild's ultimate solution was to split the difference, to use the "heavy" title "Oklahoma" but to insist upon a leavening exclamation point, punctuation long familiar to musical-comedy marquees. So careful was the team about striking the exact right tone with their title that, in the days before the premiere, Heidt sent letters to the major regional newspapers reminding them to include the punctuation in their articles. The strategy worked. The *Brooklyn Eagle* published an opening-night review of the show titled, "'Oklahoma!' Opening at the Saint James [Theater] Lives Up to its Exclamation Point," and another reviewer in New Jersey exclaimed, "When time and space permit this department will go further and make it 'Oklahoma!!—Whee!'"[80]

Amid all the juggling between musical comedy and opera, Hammerstein himself began communicating to the press, but his approach differed from his colleagues' in the production office. He framed the discussion, not as a distinction between musical comedy and opera, but rather as a distinction between musical comedy and folk music. He did this in two extended articles, one for the *Boston Post* on March 14, 1943 (just after the show finished tryouts in New Haven), the other for the *New York Times* on May 23,

1943 (about seven weeks after the show had already opened to rave reviews). Both essays drew upon dramaturgical ideas that he had been developing during the previous two decades, and they offer a clear snapshot of what Hammerstein viewed to be the major artistic problems he was facing with *Oklahoma!*.

Hammerstein stressed that he was drawn to the folk elements of Riggs's original play, the "well-defined American characters whose talk was at once earthy and lyrical." The conflict, he said, lay between the broadly theatrical qualities of popular musicals on the one hand, and the "lyric beauty" and the "honest-to-goodness American feeling" of his source material on the other. "A musical play has in addition to its story, music, lyrics, a cast of actors, more glitter in its production and a great brilliance in costumes and scenery, to keep pace with the higher key into which music pitches a play," he wrote, and added that the modern, popular elements could potentially obliterate the fragile, idealistic elements of the production: "To thus heighten reality is almost an obligation for a musical production. To accomplish it without becoming completely false is difficult."[81] His job, he maintained, was to avoid falsity by mediating between these two styles, a process he called "integration." "The labor was to preserve these qualities and add to them the heightened values of music; to create songs that were, in themselves, amusing and tender as songs should be, and at the same time *integrate* them into the story so that they would seem as natural and indigenous to the play as the dialogue itself."[82] Important here is the subtle distinction between this kind of "integration" and the formal integration typically cited as the primary innovation of *Oklahoma!*. Hammerstein's concern was not strictly to blend song, script, and scene (even though he did discuss this as a regular part of crafting any musical). Rather, his concern was to blend the seemingly incompatible institutions of folk art and popular culture, to blend the "indigenous" with the "amusing."

To do this, he devised a dramaturgy that hinged on a subtle distinction between three closely related terms: "realistic," "literal," and "believable." He wrote on March 14, "The most fundamental decision we made [...] was our determination to be realistic without being literal. By that too concise statement, I mean that we wanted the story and the characters to be presented in a believable manner." The general concept involved a resemblance between the onstage world of *Oklahoma!* and the offstage world of Oklahoma, a kind of similarity that would persist even when the former did not exactly reproduce the latter. In these terms, Hammerstein's "realistic" is vague, general, or unwieldy (and could be applied to just about any production). However, he clarified his ideas on May 23. "Deriving from a source that is real," he wrote, "the whole production is lifted a plane above literal reality." The "source" was *Green Grow the Lilacs*, and in this play the term "reality" carried two special meanings. First, Riggs's opening stage direction described the play's mood as "partly true and partly a trick of the imagination focussing [sic] to keep alive a loveliness that might pass away," suggesting that whatever "true" qualities he was accessing in his script, he conceived them as remote, in danger of slipping beyond memory into oblivion. Second, these "real" qualities were also abstract and idealist (in Riggs's words, they constituted "a flow of spirit"; in Hammerstein's words, they lay in "a plane above literal reality"), suggesting a kind of essential truth about humanity that lay somehow "beyond" appearance, "beyond" the quotidian. By referencing Riggs's "realistic" source material, Hammerstein was making a bold claim: The musical comedy could legitimately access those other kinds or modes of idealist "reality," which had previously seemed proper to folk art and high art, but not to popular culture.

Put differently, Hammerstein's overall goal was to write a show with a different "mood" than previous musical comedy. He said that he wanted to write a piece that was "essentially good-natured" despite being, to whatever degree, a musical comedy. The wording is important. "Good-natured" echoed the phrase that Atkinson had previously used in his reviews to describe *Show Boat* and *Sweet Adeline*, in both cases as an antonym to "sophisticated." Moreover (as described in Chapter 2), in Atkinson's correspondence with Van Wyck Brooks, "sophisticated" had been a pejorative term for literary works that they deemed too clever, which thereby had lost touch with the homey "idealism" of the American people. Even if the similar language was inadvertent, there exists other evidence to suggest that Hammerstein was trying to create a new mood for musical comedy by blending the institutional expectations of folk art, high art, and popular culture. For example, Hammerstein wrote on May 12, "Much of the flatness commonly found is due to the erroneous ideas of what you can't do in a musical play. It has been proved again and again that if the story is bright, and gayety [sic] surrounds the story, the events of the story can be as dramatic or tragic as anything found in a play without music."[83] Hammerstein believed that a homey or comic tone could temper subject matter that typically lay out of bounds for musical comedy. This blend between musical comedy and folk, between popularity and idealism, marked the unusual style of *Oklahoma!*. (For that matter, it would remain the hallmark style of his two subsequent

Broadway productions with Rodgers, *Carousel* and *Allegro*, discussed briefly in Chapter 4.)

Beyond the libretto, Hammerstein's theory of heightened realism informed all aspects of the production. This is to say that formal integration, in the familiar sense of blending all the elements of the show, served this broader aim of a kind of institutional integration. "Otherwise you would think you were seeing two different shows," Hammerstein explained.[84] All collaborators on the show sought to create an atmosphere of "heightened reality" and blend folk art with musical comedy. Director Rouben Mamoulian, for example, jotted the phrases "theory of unreality" and "uplifted realism" in his notebook just as *Oklahoma!* was entering rehearsals, and he wrote a list of examples from his earlier productions that he believed had achieved a similar balance.[85] For example, two items on this list, "Symphony of noises" and "shadows," both referred to his Broadway production of *Porgy and Bess* from 1935.[86] The "symphony of noises" (called the "Occupational Humoresque" in the original production) began with everyday street sounds (cleaning, sweeping) but gradually transformed into unaccompanied, percussive, coordinated, full-cast choreography; the "shadows" referred to the exaggerated lighting and rhythmic swaying that lent an almost expressionistic quality to the cowering crowds in the hurricane scene.[87]

In this same set of notes, it was clear that Mamoulian was already thinking of ways to create the effect of "heightened realism" in *Oklahoma!*.[88] Along these lines he scribbled the phrase "recitative in Kansas City" and the word "technicolor."[89] It is unclear which portions of "Kansas City" would have become recitative, but the general line of thinking was clear: Recitative heightens realism by sitting between naturalistic speech and out-and-out song.[90] "Technicolor" strikes a similar balance, exaggerating naturalistic hues into more vibrant ones. This term could easily have described the costumes of *Oklahoma!*, which in black-and-white photographs appear to be run-of-the-mill cowboy hats and chaps, but in color reveal unusually vivid paints and dyes (so bright, in fact, that the set designer asked the costumer to tone down the "bitch pink" shirts).[91] The sets also straddled the line between photographic and "heightened" realism, with vivid backdrops reminiscent of the Regionalist landscapes of Thomas Hart Benton and Grant Wood.[92] As Hammerstein wrote, "This is a Western landscape, and no question about it. Yet the style of these designs and the manner of painting are essentially modern. It is Indian Territory at the turn of the century expressed in the stage-design idiom of 1943."[93]

According to Hammerstein, Agnes de Mille also applied this theory to the choreography. He wrote, "The 'photographic' approach would have limited [de Mille] to reels, jigs, and hoe-downs as they were danced in Oklahoma at the turn of the century. Well, dear public, however much you might think you would like an evening of these authentic gyrations, take our word for it, you wouldn't!" He described the professional dancers in the show, and continued, "Shall we waste them on a series of square dances that you or I could do? Would that satisfy you as a full, rich evening of dance?"[94] Their purpose here was to mix the professionalism of Broadway choreography with rough, spontaneous, traditional folk dance—again, two institutions that may have seemed fundamentally incompatible.

Beyond giving folk dances a professional luster, this kind of choreography offered audiences new potential for interpretation. Hammerstein wrote that de Mille "infused into her dances an unmistakable feeling of the Southwest. There are undertones of earthiness, roots of reality, beneath her subtle, rhythmic impressions." Again, "roots of reality" here signifies something beyond photographic reproduction, an ineffable quality of American authenticity. Likewise, in a 1979 interview, de Mille described her work in similar terms, focusing on one of the gestures from the dream ballet at the end of Act I, the moment when Laurie's friends rush out to celebrate her wedding announcement: "And you'll see the little fluttering, the quivering, pulsating movements that became quite famous. They're not just flat hands patting the ground, patting the Earth. They're hearts beating. They're Laurie's heart. They're bird wings. They're Laurie's throat."[95] Under de Mille's direction, these gestures assumed multivalent meanings, both literal (as an excited, waved-hand greeting) and more cryptic (as a gesture toward the soil and as a gesture toward Laurie's inner emotions, both of which symbolized "essential," "natural," or even complex psychological meaning) that could not be represented by imitative movement—and which would have been unusual in musical comedy of the previous two decades.

Hammerstein also applied the theory of heightened realism to his work with Rodgers on the score. On May 23 he wrote, "Our problem in this case was to write words and music that would convey the flavor of the West and the feeling of the period, and yet not be slavish imitations of the Western songs that had been interpolated in the original. We didn't want to write second-hand hillbilly ballads. They wouldn't be as good as the real ones."[96] Years later, in his autobiography, Rodgers would make nearly the same point about his music, using the language of authenticity explicitly. "I remember that shortly before beginning the score Oscar sent me an impressively thick book of songs of the American Southwest which he thought might be of help. I opened the book, played the music of one song, closed the book and never looked at it again. If my melodies were going to be authentic, they'd have to be authentic in my own terms."[97] His own terms had until that point been the sophisticated, lively comedy of Hart, which suggested that his score to *Oklahoma!* would to some degree incorporate the techniques he developed for Broadway 1920s and 1930s, but would also deploy them toward folkish ends.

The clearest example of how he achieved this balance appears in the opening number, "Oh, What a Beautiful Morning," which Rodgers and Hammerstein tackled first in their collaboration, and which, according to both, provided a blueprint for the work that followed.[98] The broad contours of this song differ from Rodgers's previous Broadway songs, which tended to feature short, relatively free introductory verses, followed by longer choruses in some standard thirty-two-bar format. Yet, as musicologist Graham Wood has noted, the verse and the chorus of "Oh, What a Beautiful Morning" are the same length, a mere sixteen triple-time bars, an unusually short chorus with only one precedent in Rodgers's oeuvre before 1943.[99] Moreover, unlike any of Rodgers's songs with Hart, the words of the chorus are invariable. The overall effect was old-fashioned, more in keeping with songs from the turn of the century than with the contemporary pop charts.[100]

In fact, "Oh, What a Beautiful Morning" follows the same general format as "Whoopee Ti-Yi-Yo, Git Along Little Dogies," the same folk song that opens Riggs's *Green Grow the Lilacs*. In John Lomax's transcription, this piece contains a verse and a chorus of equal length, eight measures in compound time. Moreover, the most salient melodic feature of "Git Along Little Dogies" is its single chromatic note, the pungent flat-seventh scale degree to open the chorus. The result is an unusual harmonic effect: It injects into an otherwise tonic–subdominant–dominant harmonic field an applied dominant, which briefly draws the song toward IV. In "Oh, What a Beautiful Morning" there is likewise only one chromatic note in the melody, again the flat-seventh scale degree, projected over the subdominant chord in the chorus (see Example 3.2).[101] Could "Git Along Little Dogies" have been the song Rodgers turned to in his "impressively thick book"? Could this book have been Lomax's famous compilation Western of folk songs?

Even though the general features of "Oh, What a Beautiful Morning" resemble the folk tune "Git Along Little Dogies," smaller details lend the former

84 THE MIDDLEBROW MUSICAL

Example 3.2a–b. John Lomax, *Cowboy Songs and Other Frontier Ballads* (New York: Sturgis and Walton Company, 1911), 90; Richard Rodgers and Oscar Hammerstein, *Oklahoma!* Vocal Score, ed. Albert Sirmay (New York: Williamson Music, 1943), 17.

the professional polish of a Broadway song. Consider, first, the voice leading. Every chord in Lomax's "Git Along Little Dogies" appears in root position, and its verse toggles between I–IV–V–I, one chord per large beat in regular four-bar blocks. Likewise, as seen in Example 3.3, the verse of "Oh, What a Beautiful Morning" follows the one-chord-per-large-beat pattern and each motive also lasts four bars. The harmony at the outset is similarly straightforward, swaying back and forth between I and V. However, instead of mimicking the blunter root motion of the folk song, the opening bass line of "Oh, What a Beautiful Morning" rocks gently back and forth stepwise between scale degrees 1 and 7 (between I and V^6). In measure 6, halfway through a four-measure motive, the bass line begins a stepwise descent that lasts six bars. The effect is to break the four-bar block pattern of the song, and to elide the presentation portion with the continuation portion of the phrase.[102]

Example 3.3. The harmony sketched here comes from the second verse of the song (in the vocal score, the first verse is unaccompanied until the word "eye"). Rodgers and Hammerstein, *Oklahoma!* Vocal Score, 16–19.

Rodgers's professional polish also appears in the internally referential design of the verse and chorus, a technique reminiscent of his previous work with Hart. At first, the tone of Hammerstein's lyric might appear a world apart from Hart's dazzling chains of urbane rhymes. Rodgers, however, picked up on the fleeting Hart-esque details in Hammerstein's lyric: the chains of true rhymes ("high," "eye," "sky"; "day," "way"), the repeated lines ("There's a bright golden haze on the meadow," "Oh what a beautiful..."), the slant rhymes ("morning"/"feeling"). In response, he produces a taut, economical melody that connects these details through similar or recurring

Example 3.4a–b. "Oh, What a Beautiful Morning": a comparison of the verse's and chorus's contours.

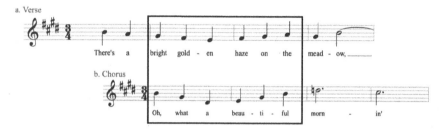

melodic gestures. However, unlike the small, syncopated cells of less than a single measure that Rodgers had written with Hart earlier in his career, the recurring pattern in "Oh, What a Beautiful Morning" lasts two complete measures. As seen in Example 3.3, this pattern consists of three descending quarter notes, followed by three ascending quarter notes. Moreover, this same contour appears in both the verse and the chorus, the difference being that the chorus inflates the verse's stepwise motion into swooping motion by thirds (see Example 3.4).

This intricacy, this economy of means, this self-referential structure grants "Oh, What a Beautiful Morning" some of the "liveliness" of a Rodgers-and-Hart song, but does so without the motivic virtuosity of Rodgers's earlier music. Subtly, however, it also provides a point of convergence with "Git Along Little Dogies," which likewise has a self-referential structure that links the verse to the chorus, albeit in a less intricate way. In the folk song, the striking minor third that launches the chorus also appears as the opening two notes of the verse, the difference being the range (the chorus increases the intensity of the gesture by transposing it up a fourth) and the fact that the verse's minor third is diatonic (the fourth scale degree) while the chorus's minor third is chromatic (the flat-seven scale degree). Moreover, the first two measures of both the verse and chorus in "Git Along Little Dogies," shown in Example 3.5a–b, also follow the same general intervallic pattern. This means that Rodgers's setting of Hammerstein's lyric does not lie completely outside the realm of authentic folk material, even as his song adds some gleam of professional craft.[103]

Zooming out from each individual component in the production, the theory of "heightened realism" marked a significant departure from Hammerstein's previous attempts to blend folk culture and musical comedy.

Example 3.5a–b. "Whoopee Ti Yi Yo, Git Along Little Dogies": a comparison of the opening intervals in the verse and the chorus.

In his earlier shows from the 1920s and 1930s, Hammerstein had used folkish special effects in both the music (*couleur locale*) and dialogue (act-two sermons, lyric speech) to distance his shows from Broadway. The effect, as contemporary reviewers attested, had been to toggle back and forth between Broadway "melody, girls, jazz, and comedy" on the one hand, and the kind of folk attitude that squinted far into the distance beyond New York. *Oklahoma!*, however, *blended* the two: Its main characters, Curly and Laurie, trade witty banter without losing their drawl ("People Will Say We're in Love"); the supporting roles, Will Parker, Ado Annie, and Ali Hakim, engage in musical-comedy double entendre using vernacular language ("I Cain't Say No"). They all sing folk songs with a New York orchestra; they all square-dance in chaps, spurs, and character shoes. Folk art in *Oklahoma!* no longer distanced the show from Broadway musical comedy; it incorporated musical comedy.

At this fundamental level of dramaturgy, however, *Oklahoma!* was different from Riggs's *Green Grow the Lilacs*. Riggs believed that an author should tap into idealist content about the essence of the American people, but he argued that the playwright should avoid interfering with the "flow of spirits." Instead, the goal was to marvel at it, to present it to an audience unadulterated. Riggs portrayed himself as a passive playwright, one who merely recorded what his idealized characters were doing on some transcendental plane, separately from him. "I let them go ahead acting out their simple tale, which might have been the substance of an ancient song," he wrote; "And sometime, [the playwright's] characters may do stirring things he could never have calculated. And sometime, if he is fortunate, he may hear from the people he has set in motion (as Shakespeare and Chekov often heard) things to astonish him."[104] He believed that such theater had moral implications: To bear witness to elemental forces without imposing the values of modern society upon them was to aim for "humility and abnegation," and thereby to become "wise."[105]

While Riggs stressed that the playwright's job was to work "in a limbo beyond the knowledge of applause," Hammerstein explicitly considered how spectators were likely to respond his musical. He did so on principle. He was writing a Broadway musical, after all, and he sought to prevent the show from becoming aloof or, in the most literal sense of the word, unpopular. He therefore made changes to Riggs's script with the potential audience in mind. For example, Hammerstein worried that Riggs's famous "shivoree" scene, in which rowdy cowhands and farmers haze the newlywed couple, contained a "vaguely Freudian flavor" that might repulse musical-comedy audiences. His solution was to retain it in "compromised form": "The laughter is lusty and boyish rather than smirky," he wrote, implying that the tone of his adaptation was ingenuous, free of the smart double-entendres of Broadway musical comedy or the edgy sexual overtones of Riggs's play.[106] At times, though, he was willing to push harder against the musical-comedy tradition. For example, describing the scene where Curly kills Jud, he wrote, "We realized that an actual killing is something the average musical playgoer doesn't bargain for when he buys his ticket." In this case he kept the murder, but adapted the trial scene that followed, making it "funny, reasonably just and fair and common-sensible," and thereby entertaining, accessible, and popular enough to appeal to Broadway audiences.

Ultimately Hammerstein's theories of a new kind of popular-folk hybrid were not as aloof from the quotidian world as Riggs's, but they were equally high-minded. He believed that the purpose of "heightened realism" was never purely dramaturgical. It was also moral. Hammerstein sought to create a kind of dramaturgy that would touch both everyday life and idealist essences, thereby imbuing popular musical comedy with a new seriousness, but without tripping into remoteness. In charged language, he differentiated the commercial elements of a show ("encores," "numbers," "specialties") from the "integrated" components:

> Otherwise, what will happen when a number takes five or six encores and "stops" the show? If it is not an integral part of the story it may literally stop the show, and the show may never start again. An unrelated musical number or specialty can do untold damage to a play. The more the audience

likes it the less they will welcome the return to the story after the number is over. They have been led into another medium, vaudeville.[107]

His ominous language ("untold damage," the image of "being led") suggests that just beneath the surface of *Oklahoma!* lay ethical implications. Imbuing all aspects of the show with folk sensibilities would counteract what he had described as the "cynical" tendencies of slick, modern, popular Broadway theater ("vaudeville"), a testament to the new kinds of meaning he believed musical theater could reasonably attain.

In the years that followed, both Rodgers and Hammerstein would continue to tap into idealist language to portray themselves as near "mystics," to use Hammerstein's term; as untainted by commercial theater; as visionaries recalling a better, healthier past.[108] Rodgers (who once praised his own business acumen by saying, "I roll success around in my mouth like a piece of candy") proclaimed that his music expressed fundamental, earthy truths about the world: "I think that the sunset, the mountain, the experience, all go inside and may not come out for fifty years. But they become *part* of your knowledge, *part* of your personality, *part* of your education, *part* of your technique. And eventually you express yourself."[109] For his part, Hammerstein described to an interviewer what he had been trying to express in his shows: "Our interest, our belonging to one another, the oneness on earth is the same thing as our oneness with God. God is that oneness, in my conception. He is all of us, and we are all of [H]im."[110] These claims testify to how far they had moved away from the shows they had written earlier in their careers. Whether anybody else was willing to follow, whether anybody else was willing to recognize musical comedy as capable of expressing such ideals, would only become clear after *Oklahoma!* opened.

"A Living Opera, Expressive of People": *Oklahoma!* and American Opera

Hammerstein wrote his two articles to train spectators to interpret this new kind of production properly. He admitted as much during the show's Boston tryouts in a letter he penned to his son. "All this is said in the hope that a handful of beer-stupefied critics may not decide that we have tried to write a musical comedy and failed," he wrote. "If they see that this is different and higher in its intent, they should rave. I *know* this is a good show. I cannot believe it will not find a substantial public. There! My neck is out."[111] His risks paid off to a degree he could never have imagined. In the months following the premiere, critics acknowledged that the show's primary innovation was blending musical comedy and folk art. On March 12, for example, even before the New York premiere and before Hammerstein published his first article in the *Boston Globe*, one critic had already recognized this quality and used the term "integration" to describe it:

> Here is no synthetic stuff created on Broadway in what someone weakly imagines is the West for the purpose of selling it to urban yokels nurtured on Western movies. It is the West of father's day moved into Broadway, not Broadway reaching for the west. The same thorough artistic *integration* evident in all other parts of this musical entertainment is to be found in the dances for the creation of which Agnes deMille is responsible. Ballet effects are a natural part of this musical comedy with which they are dealing here, not something good for almost anywhere brought in to help decorate. Every dance movement is carefully and consistently made a part of the whole effect.[112]

Once again, formal integration was secondary. It served the broader goal of sustaining a folk atmosphere in a popular tone without resorting to any modern-day musical-comedy sophistication, which would have broken the illusion of authenticity. Other critics made similar observations. Henry Simon at *PM*, for example, made a similar claim on April 19: "It's the best Rodgers score I've heard, chiefly, I think, because it is the simplest and least Broadwayish. [...] They're fine, folk-like tunes Rodgers has composed."[113]

Gradually, however, another kind of argument began to emerge in the press: that *Oklahoma!* was opera. By and large, however, contemporary critics did not justify the show's operatic bona fides with evidence of its formal sophistication or its similarities to European classical music. Instead, they tended to argue that *Oklahoma!* was operatic by dint of its allegiance to folk music—an argument that may seem paradoxical today. For critics at the time, however, it made sense. Many of them were embroiled in an ongoing, wider critical debate about opera in America. The main issue was whether there could be a genre that was both recognizably operatic in the grand style and recognizably American at the same time, or whether pieces that sounded like "grand opera" could only amount to mere imitations of European music that were irrelevant to American life.[114] For many, *Oklahoma!*, with its down-home sentiment and folk-like tunes, confirmed the latter position.

Lewis Nichols, who briefly served as theater critic for the *New York Times* (while Atkinson was abroad as a war correspondent), kicked all of this off in his opening night review. "Possibly in addition to being a musical play, 'Oklahoma!' could be called a folk operetta," he wrote; "whatever it is, it is very good."[115] The designation "folk operetta" acknowledged the show's folk tone and popular-culture appeal, but it also linked *Oklahoma!* to the genre that audiences would have associated, at least in part, with European composers such as Jacques Offenbach, Johann Strauss II, and Arthur Sullivan. In the weeks that followed, critics forged more explicit connections between popular culture, folk culture, and European music theater—and increasingly, the specific type of European music theater they referenced was opera, not operetta. One critic, for example, asserted that musical comedies "spring naturally out of American life, they speak our idiom dramatically and musically, they come in answer to a spontaneous popular demand, not a forced one. They suggest that, if we are to have a native 'grand' opera in America, it will grow out of our genius for musical comedy, not out of our lack of genius in the idioms of Verdi and Wagner. It will be found in the Ozarks, not the Apennines."[116]

A more radical version of the argument stated that on both sides of the Atlantic, "real" opera had always sat closer to the campfire than to the concert hall, and that the now-familiar grand style of European opera was merely a distortion of "true" opera. For critics who followed this line of thinking, *Oklahoma!* seemed closer to such "real" opera than, say, the repertoire of the Metropolitan. Nobody made this claim more forcefully than Olin Downes, the widely read, widely disseminated classical-music critic for the *New York Times* from 1924 until the end of his life in 1955. Underlying his review was an aesthetic theory that overlapped considerably with the middlebrow, affirmative modernism of Van Wyck Brooks (introduced in Chapter 1). No correspondence between the two critics survives, but they did turn to many of the same authors for inspiration, which may account for their similarity. Like Brooks, Downes believed that there had once been a time when there existed no real separation between folk, classical, and popular culture, a time when "a babel of tongues and races, and every rank and type of citizen, were thrown together in the welding of the nation." Under these circumstances, music "became the language alike of the educated and the illiterate, the aristocrat and the commoner."[117] Downes foresaw a time in the future when the arts would rejoin to help reclaim that unified social condition, at which point, he argued, "melodic insignia of race and nation disappear, to be transformed and sublimated in a way which is a distillation of the popular expressions, in forms of highly developed art."[118]

Addressing the United States specifically, Downes tended to ask a more pointed question, analogous to the one Brooks had asked of literature: Could the United States harbor its own, unique, musical tradition? Downes agreed with Brooks that contemporary academic writing, which by and large had projected only disdain for American culture, impeded any development of a homegrown musical lineage, and thereby impeded any hope of unifying a fractured society: "The notion, advanced by a majority of foreign-born artists and teachers, that there is no such thing as American music has been parroted through the length and breadth of the land," he fumed, "especially by individuals hardly capable of recognizing such a racy and original folk-tune as 'Dixie' if they met it walking down the street, and who, even then, would not acknowledge its acquaintance unless the introduction were sponsored by an unquestioned musical authority, preferably a European."[119] His goal: to unearth an American tradition and to advocate for its down-home excellence, which in turn could provide some abstract, spiritual insight into the manner by which people from widely different backgrounds could come together under the banner of American music and form a unified cultural democracy. He wrote, "It was not until the founding of the American nation, wherein classes, types, and races mingled in a great polyglot, that we perceive the genuine diffusion of democratic essence, not only in our society, but in the body of our national music."[120]

Downes (again, like Brooks) took inspiration from French writer, critic, artist, and philosopher Romain Rolland and argued that, to achieve this broadly human music, highbrow music should aspire to the community spirit of folk music.[121] In an article he wrote in 1945, Downes cited Rolland's theory that true opera (whatever that may have been) had originated in two genres, which long ago had been unified but over time had gradually drifted apart: "sacre rappresentazioni" and "maggi," "the former to be seen in Florence and other cities, the latter on the plains of Tuscany, where the life was rural." For Downes, rejoining these two genres—one urban, one rural; one sacred, one secular—was not just an aesthetic or historical project, but rather a "moral vision." "It is a plea for brotherhood that failed," he wrote.[122] In his estimation, this rift between "sacre rappresentazioni" and "maggi" had continued to the present day, to the point where modern opera had become so experimental, so elite, so highbrow that it now lay utterly outside the experience and understanding of its audiences. Any advancement in the genre, Downes argued, should mark a return to their combined state, which in modern terms would suggest that the most sophisticated means of expression would nonetheless remain popular, accessible, and recognizable by the broader public.

For Downes, this meant combining art music with folk music, the latter of which he described as "the song that a people cherishes and sings."[123] This definition was broad, but he narrowed it with two additional stipulations. First, according to Downes, folk songs in their purest forms were distinct from present-day art music. "[Folk songs] are not belles-lettres, and they do not represent the classical education. They were not written by people trying to be artists," he wrote. "The song served the turn of the moment, or the crisis of the heart."[124] Second, Downes did not believe that folk songs were entirely distinct from popular culture. He argued instead that Broadway songs could potentially act like genuine folk music, and he cited Kern and Hammerstein's "Ol' Man River" as an example.[125] The result (which, again, may seem paradoxical) was that folk songs and popular songs could both provide a conceptual foundation for specifically modern, American, democratic opera.

This theory about the relationship of folk music, popular music, and opera provided the intellectual backdrop for his review of *Oklahoma!*, entitled "Broadway's Gift to Opera." There were two main components. First, regarding form, Downes praised *Oklahoma!* for pulling together disparate media into a single piece, which is to say that he praised what critics have come to call the show's formal integration (although for him, the word "integration" signified something else, described below). He also inherited this idea from Rolland, who had argued that "sacre rappresentazioni" and "maggi" had both combined music and dance. Rejoining these two components, according to Rolland, might create a new kind of musical theater, which would be as capable as the earlier genres of expressing meaningful ideas to broad swaths of society. In a similar vein, Downes waxed enthusiastic about the dance in *Oklahoma!*, arguing that the way it combined with music might also create a new kind of musical theater. "The songs [. . .] serve as a springboard for the dance numbers and the singing that usually goes with them. It is all of a piece [. . .] it is the sum of the piece, and not the component details, that counts, and indicates a direction that American opera of native cast might take in the period before us."[126] Yet his purpose was not only to admire the suave combination of dance, score, story, and design; rather, it was also to say that *Oklahoma!* produced an entirely new kind of dance, distinct from ballet. "The [classic] ballet is in itself a completely conventionalized design," he argued, "whereas these dances [in *Oklahoma!*] emanate from the music and the situations and do not merely stylize them but interpret them." This new kind of dancing was also distinct from typical Broadway choreography, which, he claimed, had tended to be as decorative as ballet. (He may have had the precision chorus lines of Busby Berkeley in mind.) He wrote, "And the inclusion of the dance, escaped here from the insipidities of the pretty musical show, as also from the confines of the purely decorative aspect being integrated with the story and the score, is most important."[127] In formal terms, then, *Oklahoma!* was reaching back toward the "sacre rappresentazioni" and "maggi" by combining dance, folk music, and drama, and the resulting form of dance struck him as capable of new kinds of expression that were inaccessible to either ballet or traditional Broadway choreography alone.

All of this comprised only half of Downes's theory, and to this point it is largely indistinguishable from any other theories of integration or *Gesamtkunstwerk* that existed at the time. The second component, however, was different. Downes believed that a truly American opera should combine folk music, highbrow music, *and* popular music. *Oklahoma!* did just this, he raved. "The music is not folk-music, but that of a Broadway composer writing in a popular vein, free, skillfully, and with taste, and a fortunate relinquishment of the jazzeries of previous fashion," he wrote. "It is to an older, homelier, more truly ancestral source that Mr. Rodgers has gone for the melodic elements of his score." He likewise praised the dances' "folk substructure," which he called "new burgeoning from an old root, and never merely realistic or photographic." In doing so, *Oklahoma!* also recaptured the preindustrial, prelapsarian spirit of Rolland's "sacre rappresentazioni" and "maggi," thereby providing a glimpse of the unified society that had been lost to modern America.

For Downes, combining both the high-art and the folk components offered a new direction for opera on both sides of the Atlantic, which, if emulated, could allow opera to become a tool for unifying the splintered modern public. He wrote:

> [R]eal national opera has always begun somewhere in the vicinity of the position now occupied by "Oklahoma." The Grand opera was the classical thing, ceremonious, weighty, more or less international in idiom. But when "Serva Padrona" of Pergolesi, and a thousand other little pieces of its kind, were produced in Italy—little comedies, patter pieces, diversions of a patois

sort with conversation as well as singing in the eighteenth century—then a living opera, expressive of people and not courts or churches or social ceremony, came into being. This kind of opera has knocked the stiltedness of grand opera silly, time and again.[128]

Conceptually, he argued that the folk quality of *Oklahoma!* set it apart from previous attempts at American opera, which had tended toward orotund self-importance. Downes singled out Gershwin's *Porgy and Bess* as one example of a piece that had failed to achieve the goals of an American opera. Although Gershwin's piece had been billed as a "folk opera," Downes felt that there had been nothing folkish about it, and declared that it "survives by its melodies and not by the dramatic appositeness of the score." He continued: "[Gershwin's] comedy 'Of Thee I Sing' is much finer and better *integrated* and more reflective of period and environment."[129] Again, integration here does not necessarily mean that the script and score were wed seamlessly together. It more likely meant what Atkinson had also taken it to mean, that the highbrow aspects, the folk aspects, and the popular aspects blended more smoothly in *Of Thee I Sing* and *Oklahoma!* than they did in *Porgy and Bess*, which Downes found stilted, overblown. All told, Downes believed that *Oklahoma!*, not *Porgy and Bess* or any other piece in the grand-opera vein, was capable of uniting modern America's fractured society because it combined high-art idealism, popular-culture accessibility, and folk authenticity into a single work, thereby communicating across a wide swath of the American public.

Downes was only one of many critics to argue that the combination of folk music and popular music in *Oklahoma!* suggested new directions for American opera. Dance critic, philosophy professor, and editor of *Theater Arts* magazine George Beiswanger, for example, argued in 1944 that *Oklahoma!* was "leading us eventually toward our own opera" by drawing from sources beyond the "legitimate" theater:

> In the immediate background [of *Oklahoma!*] are two decades of the Broadway musical show, whose development from pieces hardly worthy of serious attention to the best light musical theater I have from time to time recorded in [the journal] *Theatre Arts*. But the roots run deeper than that, to vaudeville, song that has assimilated a surprising amount of all the music traditions, dance of every kind, and much that comes straight from the folk.[130]

Music historian Cecil Smith followed suit in 1950, noting the "sunny homeliness of Hammerstein's book and lyrics," along with Rodgers's "friendly melodies" and "folk feeling, even though [the songs] were not literally based upon folk idioms." He also maintained that this opened new forms of potential meaning for the genre. "Rodgers took a long step away from Broadway toward a more universal and less insular type of light music," he wrote. "Without losing touch with his audience and their predilections, he made of *Oklahoma!* more of an operetta and less of an out-and-out musical comedy than any of his earlier works."[131]

Four years after *Oklahoma!* opened on Broadway, Atkinson, having returned from war, made a similar argument, substituting ballet for opera. He began by asserting that formal integration "was really an old idea—as old as Wagner at least." He continued:

> But [formal integration] could never be fulfilled on the popular musical stage until the American ballet had developed into the expressive instrument it has become today. Once an esoteric art for coterie enjoyment the ballet has become a form of popular expression with a wide range of ideas. Beginning most conspicuously with "Oklahoma!" it has revolutionized the musical stage.[132]

The key word is "popular," which he uses twice. The broad contours of his argument are similar to Downes's and Rolland's: Ballet (like opera) had become so "esoteric" that it was incapable of maintaining any real contact with its audiences. Atkinson's word "coterie," in fact, was probably borrowed from Van Wyck Brooks, to whom it signified a formal, esoteric art understandable only to initiates.[133] For Atkinson, any revolution in ballet would arrive, not in the form of more sophisticated techniques, but instead by situating itself in popular culture, and in this revolution, *Oklahoma!* was the shot heard round the world.

Even the rare critic who disliked *Oklahoma!* recognized that joining popular culture and folk art was its main innovation. One such writer was Eric Bentley (introduced in Chapter 2), who wrote an article for *Partisan Review* on this subject shortly after *Oklahoma!* opened. "Here is a revived and jazzified Wagnerism which does not omit Wagner's nationalism and praise of the soil," he declared in words that would have been especially intense during and after World War II.[134] He continued to argue the same point throughout the following decade. "The term Grass Roots was always used [to describe *Oklahoma!*]—as if Messrs. Rodgers and Hammerstein were cowboys. Invited to accept *Oklahoma!* as an American, or rather Amurrican, *Magic Flute*, some of us could not resist the temptation to reject it as that and as anything else it might pretend to be."[135] Also in *Partisan Review*, novelist and film critic James Agee (introduced in Chapter 2) warned that *Oklahoma!* portended an ominous development in American arts. (He actually reviewed the show without seeing it "because [he] felt sure [it] would be bad."[136]) Whatever its supposed merits, he rejected the show on principle as mere "pseudo-folksy charm," which he believed to be "hopelessly detached from, and benevolently interested in, and unconsciously patronizing toward 'the folk,' like Roosevelt."[137]

Beneath both writers' invective lay a shared anxiety. They worried that the emotional appeal to American roots through popular culture could become a tool for manipulation, and that a broader public might be willing to accept just about any message as long as it felt homey. The guise of authenticity, they warned, could become a dangerous weapon. Bentley placed Rodgers and Hammerstein alongside a roster of demagogues that included Aimee Semple McPherson, William Randolph Hearst, and Josef Goebbels.[138] Agee was equally intense, fuming that the type of consumer who enjoyed *Oklahoma!* was likely a "'democrat' who, if he happens to read these notes, will wish to call me an anti-Negro, an anti-Semite, a Nazi, and whatever other overdigested derogatives remain in his vocabulary."[139]

Bentley, however, believed that *Oklahoma!* was only one symptom of broader theatrical problems that beleaguered modern American theater. Like Downes, Brooks, and Macdonald, Bentley believed that centuries ago there had been a "unified theater" that was both highbrow and lowbrow at the same time:

> Until the modern period great drama has possessed not only those deeper and subtler qualities which reveal themselves to the careful analyst and which constitute its greatness, it has also possessed more generally available qualities. It has appealed on different levels. It has appealed to the connoisseur *and* the amateur, the critic *and* the public. It has functioned as mere entertainment for some and as the highest art for others.[140]

Since then, however, the theater had divided to the point where "art and commodity have become direct antagonists."[141] Like the other authors, Bentley sought to reunite these split institutions, and like these other authors, his solution was inspired by Romain Rolland. But he understood Rolland differently than Downes or Brooks had. Borrowing terminology from Rolland, Bentley proposed to create a "People's Theater," which would be both entertaining and energizing, and which would inspire audiences to critical thought and action instead of allowing them to remain passive. Yet he introduced a crucial distinction. Rolland had advocated that all ranks of society collaborate on this new kind of theater equally. "By the people! Yes, because there can be no great popular work except where the poet's soul collaborates with that of the nation, and receives nourishment from the passions common to all," Rolland wrote. In mystical language reminiscent of Brooks, Rolland continued, "Let everything be presented to the people, but only on the condition that they see themselves somewhere in it, and through the present and the past become part of the universe, and that all forms of human energy may flow through them toward the common weal."[142] Bentley, however, instead applied Macdonald's "they-the-people," oppositional logic. He argued that a People's Theater should be led by a cadre of intellectuals, stationed outside (or above) hoi polloi, and that this upper intellectual class should direct the new theater in order to raise the audience's intelligence. "Talk of raising the masses is mere demagogy in the mouth of a man who does not claim—in stated respects at least—to be superior," he wrote. "Without the prior existence of standards of excellence, without the prior existence of minority culture, no general development is possible. Without aristocracy, no democracy."[143] The first step toward making this happen, he argued, would be to return to a literary theater, a "drama of substance" that engages the critical intellect, and to turn away from a visual or musical theater, a "drama of artifice" that merely titillates.[144]

With this as his stated goal, *Oklahoma!* and its integration of high art sophistication and lowbrow entertainment struck him as retrogressive. He considered it the latest and most potent example of "theatricalism," a kind of theater that primarily aimed to overwhelm spectators with theatrical effect. The potency of "theatricalism" derived from intensifying the events of the text with musical effects, with scenic brilliance, and so on. The result was not a drama of ideas, but rather a drama of the senses, a drama of experience, a drama of emotions.[145] Bentley worried that if an audience could attend the theater without engaging their critical faculties, and if they could be easily manipulated by song and scenery, then they could be encouraged to applaud just about anything. Following this logic, the folksiness of *Oklahoma!* was merely a special effect that dazzled the heart and quieted the brain. Given recent events in Europe, which he believed had been underscored with constant Wagnerism, a theatricalist approach to "Amurrican" nationalism struck him as especially dangerous.

Was Bentley's panic overwrought? It may seem so today. After all, whatever *Oklahoma!* was, its generally sunny tone and boy-meets-girl plot were hardly subversive politics. Later in the decade, however, Bentley's saw his fears confirmed. After *Oklahoma!* premiered, more shows opened that explicitly sought to combine folk music, opera, and popular culture. Worse, a subset of these shows was unmistakably political. Faced with these new productions, even critics who did not share Bentley's panic—even critics who applauded *Oklahoma!* for introducing new expressive modes and potential interpretive possibilities into the Broadway musical—would all be forced to confront which topics would be appropriate for the post-*Oklahoma!* musical, and which best lay beyond the pale.

4

Jazz, Opera, and "In Between"

Duke Ellington's *Beggar's Holiday* (1946) and the Black Middlebrow Tradition

> The fabulous success of "Oklahoma!" was bound to have its effect on the Broadway musical market. Let's face it. We are in for several seasons of intensely old-fashioned quaintness, most of it with choreography by Agnes deMille.
>
> —Wilella Waldorf

Almost immediately after *Oklahoma!* opened, composers and writers rushed to reproduce its middlebrow combination of folkish wisdom, highbrow ballet, and popular appeal.[1] In the months and years that followed, journalists repeatedly heralded the arrival of "another *Oklahoma!*" in their pre-premiere articles, and their post-premiere reviews repeatedly debated whether the show in question had measured up to the hype. Four such musicals opened in quick succession, each of which reunited members of the original cast and creative team of *Oklahoma!*: the Civil War–era musical *Bloomer Girl* (1944),[2] the folk-song comedy *Sing Out, Sweet Land* (1944),[3] Rodgers and Hammerstein's regional romance *Carousel* (1945), and their small-town musical *Allegro* (1947).[4] This wave of folkish musicals swelled to the point where, by 1963, librettist Alan Jay Lerner could complain, "Because *Oklahoma!* had mined its gold in American soil, and early American soil at that, from *Bloomer Girl* down to *The Music Man* [1957] and *The Unsinkable Molly Brown* [1960] hardly a season passed on Broadway without girls having fellers and everyday singin' and dancin.'"[5] (His own gold-mining musical, *Paint Your Wagon*, had premiered in 1951.)

At issue for critics was more than these productions' "intensely old-fashioned quaintness." For those who were not exhausted by the post-*Oklahoma!* craze, the show's hallmark mixture of folk content and popular comedy had sparked a wide reconsideration of what musicals could (or, for some critics, should) sound and look like, and therefore what musicals could (or, for some critics, should) potentially mean. If the Broadway musical had previously tended to feature "melody, jazz, girls, and comedy" (to repeat a phrase from Chapter 3), *Oklahoma!* convinced them that the genre could now articulate homey American values sincerely, at a human scale, without entirely abandoning comedy. To encourage this trend, critics' reviews patrolled these new institutional borders, guarding against too much urban, urbane Broadway shtick, which would upset the folksy, ingenuous, innocently comic mood and scuttle any potential for broaching more "serious" content. Louis Kronenberger, for example, wrote in *PM* that *Bloomer Girl* struck the right balance because it "prefer[red] the bygone to the brash, and [was] willing to blend high spirits with picturesqueness."[6] Critics Olin Downes and Lewis Nichols of the *New York Times*, however, argued that *Sing Out, Sweet Land* failed to live up to the *Oklahoma!* exemplar because the script's stream of one-liners was "studiously coy for the material they discuss," deploying a kind of showbiz sensibility that was out of keeping with the folk-music score that "came up from the people."[7] The same standards also applied to Rodgers and Hammerstein's newest productions.[8] Brooks Atkinson at the *New York Times*, for example, described the first act of *Allegro* as "lovingly presented like an American legend" or "like a religious rite," but faulted components of the production's second act that "vulgarized" it.[9] The result: "'Allegro' is no longer a religious rite, but a smart Broadway musical show."[10]

In just a few weeks at the end December 1946 and the beginning of January 1947, however, three productions opened in quick succession that challenged these prevailing standards: *Beggar's Holiday* by John Latouche and Duke Ellington (December 26, 1946, the focus of the present chapter); *Street Scene* by Langston Hughes, Elmer Rice, and Kurt Weill (January 9, 1947, covered in Chapter 5); and *Finian's Rainbow* by E. Y. Harburg, Fred Saidy, and Burton Lane (January 10, 1947). Some critics believed they were witnessing a revolution. Atkinson proclaimed a "remarkably fruitful, perhaps even an epochal, season on the musical stage" that "broke the Broadway formula."[11] *Life* magazine described these shows as a "gust of excitement"; "all three [productions] are far off Broadway's beaten paths, proving that a good deal of the freshness and originality in the U.S. theater today is contributed by musical shows."[12] In the *Journal American*, Robert Garland attested to feeling newly inspired by these productions: "a theatre able to display a 'Street Scene' and a 'Finian's

Rainbow' on successive evenings is a theatre to admire. Ungrudgingly!"[13] Likewise John Chapman in the *Sunday News*: "I do not recall any other period in which three such stunning offerings as *Beggar's Holiday*, *Street Scene*, and *Finian's Rainbow* appeared in such quick succession. Every one of them is an artistic as well as a financial gamble."[14] For Rosamond Gilder in *Theater Arts*, these three weeks surrounding the new year were no less than "a minor miracle."[15]

Why such excitement? First, although these musicals incorporated (often explicitly) key facets of the *Oklahoma!* model, they used its methods toward new ends. Like *Oklahoma!*, these shows tended to mix high art, folk art, and popular culture, deploying the inherited connotations of each institution strategically. In general terms, emblems of a classical style could imply sophistication and sincerity (or snobbishness); folk music could imply down-home wisdom and a sense of community (or crude simplicity); popular culture could imply relevance and excited liveliness (or brash commercialism), all depending on how the composer and librettist situated them in the production. Unlike the Rodgers and Hammerstein exemplar, however, these shows usually did not aim to maintain a smooth stylistic unity throughout. In doing so, these postwar composers and writers encouraged audiences to toggle between different modes of reception, between different strategies of meaning-making. This meant that the burden of signification often shifted to the style of music, dance, or language, which inflected the manner by which audiences were to interpret the musicals' semantic content. For some critics, like Atkinson, this was noteworthy. "If the musical stage continues to improve, it will no longer be necessary to speak dialogue," he wrote. "Everything essential can be said in song and dancing."[16]

Second, these shows represented a shift in the general approach to political material on Broadway. Many of the producers, writers, composers, designers, and performers involved in these three productions had begun their careers in and around the Federal Theatre Project, and they emerged from the war years eager to pick up where they had left off. That proved impossible; Broadway was not the same place in 1945 as it had been in 1939. Behind the scenes, each creative team worked to negotiate between, on the one side, the demands of postwar, commercial Broadway, which tended to eschew partisan politics; and on the other, their enthusiasm for the socially conscious prewar left-wing theater. The result was a musical with a new mood: civic, if not overtly political; a mixture of ideal content and present-day social consciousness. Some critics, however, took a dim view of these developments. To them, these productions were proof that the post-*Oklahoma!* show was wielding its folksy charm and comedy toward political manipulation. "Nowadays you get social significance mixed with your musicals whether you want it or not," carped George Freedly in *The Morning Telegraph*.[17] Taken together, both the breathless praise and intense invective offer historical insight into a more fundamental issue: contemporary negotiations over the range of acceptable topics and the bounds of appropriate interpretation for the postwar, post-*Oklahoma!* musical, which amounted to sweeping discussions about genre that emerged into open discussion in the press at this time.

Few musicals tested the limits of Broadway convention to the same degree as Ellington's and Latouche's *Beggar's Holiday*. Because this production was an updated, Americanized version of John Gay's satirical *Beggar's Opera* (1728), it was not surprising that, at its core, *Beggar's Holiday* took aim at modern American values. But instead of satirizing polite society and high culture as Gay had done, *Beggar's Holiday* broached issues of postwar racism, violence, and poverty. In doing so, the show pulled Broadway into what recent scholarship has called the "long" civil rights movement, a term that refers to the struggle to end segregation that stretched back decades before the movement's more familiar, "classic phase" in the 1950s and 1960s.[18] In this earlier period, even among those who agreed on the same general social and political objectives of racial equality, fiercely competing claims arose about how best to realize those goals, including how best the arts could contribute to the cause. What follows will situate *Beggar's Holiday* as an emphatically middlebrow response to those debates. On the one hand, Ellington and Latouche deployed recognizably popular swing and Broadway idioms to speak to a broad-based, multiracial, multiethnic American audience. On the other hand, they encouraged those audiences to reflect deeply on what they considered to be a postwar American social psychosis that lay at the root of racism, a critique they delivered through avant-garde stagecraft and operatic music. Ultimately, whether reviewers would accept the social commentary of *Beggar's Holiday*, and whether they would agree more broadly that such topics could be fair game for post-*Oklahoma!* Broadway entertainment, remained an open question as they generally puzzled over how to understand or interpret such an audacious, unusual production.

The "Tone Parallel": Duke Ellington and the Black Middlebrow

Six years before beginning work on *Beggar's Holiday*, Duke Ellington, leader of one of the nation's most prominent jazz orchestras, published a series of three articles in *Down Beat* magazine. His opening salvo was explosive: "The most significant thing that can be said about swing music today is that it has become stagnant." He called for "musical progress," he encouraged "constant experimentation and innovation," but he also argued that an intractable obstacle stood in the way: "causified critics" who held "certain preconceived conceptions" or "prejudices" about what jazz should be.[19] Ellington singled out one writer for particular opprobrium: John Hammond, Jr.—and Ellington was uncharacteristically fierce. He had reason. Four years earlier, in the same magazine, Hammond had blasted Ellington's large-scale work *Reminiscing in Tempo* as "vapid and without the slightest semblance of guts" because Ellington had "purposely kept himself from any contact with the troubles of his people or mankind in general."[20] In response, Ellington alleged that Hammond's judgment was warped by his strong political sympathies because he "[had] consistently identified himself with the ... underdog in the form of the Communist party."[21] (This proved one step too far. Hammond may have affiliated with the far left, but he was not a Communist. Ellington wrote a retraction.[22])

This was merely one tense episode in a long-standing musical and political debate on jazz in the 1930s and 1940s in which Ellington and Hammond had become the most recognizable figures, and in which *Beggar's Holiday* would become yet another point of contention. At issue: Was jazz folk music or popular music? Could jazz merge with classical music without abandoning its core identity? Neither of these questions was purely musical. In Hammond's hands, Ellington's music became a stand-in for commercialism, for exploitation by the popular-music industry, for internalized racism. For others, especially for philosopher and critic Alain Locke, Ellington came to symbolize something else, a new generation of Black musicians who were expressing themselves with sophistication and pride after centuries of oppression. For both sides, the most notable (or notorious) feature of Ellington's career was that he roamed freely through the sounds and discourses of popular culture, folk music, and classical music, and this controversy would follow him from the world of jazz clubs to the world of the post-*Oklahoma!* Broadway musical. In both places, negatively or positively, critics considered him middlebrow.

Is it appropriate to apply the term "middlebrow" to Ellington? Or is any similarity merely superficial? Are the debates between Dwight Macdonald and Van Wyck Brooks, and the controversies surrounding the early 1940s Broadway musical, too far removed from the swing-music scene to have any real bearing? Previous scholarship has stressed caution, arguing that Harlem Renaissance critics in the 1920s and 1930s had long appreciated jazz's cultural currency, but had generally considered it to be unalloyed popular music. For them, their goals of cultural uplift had been better served by combinations of classical music, spirituals, and folk music—genres they had not associated with Ellington.[23] (An important exception to this has always been Langston Hughes, discussed in Chapter 5.) Without abandoning these insights, in this chapter I join a group of scholars who focus instead on points of contact, and in doing so will demonstrate that Ellington's music helped draw swing directly into contemporary debates on middlebrow culture.[24] Ellington and many of his supporters, introduced below, believed that combining the popularity of jazz with the highbrow sophistication of classical music could unite each genre's distinct audiences into a thoughtful, multiethnic cultural community built upon mutual understanding (if not agreement). They ardently rejected any music or criticism that would split society into separate audiences whose core interests and tastes were characterized as fundamentally incompatible or incommensurable.

In the 1930s, as Ellington and his orchestra were emerging into the national spotlight, Hammond was also establishing his reputation as jazz's most forceful critic. For jazz historians, Hammond stands as the leading figure in a generation of writers who helped pull swing, boogie-woogie, and "hot jazz" out of niche markets (race records, Harlem nightclubs) and into the (white) mainstream.[25] Hammond did this partly by advocating for Black musicians in his writing, partly by encouraging white musicians to emulate their style, partly by funding and producing music featuring Black musicians, and partly by encouraging swing bands to integrate racially. All of this activity was grounded in a complex set of principles that linked aesthetics, politics, and history—an effort, on Hammond's part, to correct social and cultural problems that dated back to the earliest years of the United States. For many decades after the country's founding, he argued, there had existed no infrastructure to support non-commercial art, meaning that folk musicians had been forced to compete in a broad marketplace. They often had done this by mixing folk art with commercial appeal. The consequence, however, was that Black folk music had often been altered to accommodate a largely white marketplace. "During the nineteenth century [Black music] reached the white public in the thoroughly distorted form of the cakewalk, the 'coon' song, and its most ludicrous caricature, by white men with their faces painted, in minstrel shows," Hammond wrote, and he argued that such distortion continued into the present: "In this twentieth century [Black music] has its most stirring forms—blues, boogie woogie piano, and swing—and the misconceptions promptly took new shapes to accommodate the change."

He called the commercial form of Black music "sweet jazz" ("a commodity rather than an art"[26]), and distinguished it from folk, or "hot," jazz ("un-buttoned" and "never-too-disciplined"[27]). Hammond, to stem further cultural corruption, sought to promote hot jazz and protect it from popular music. He turned all his fury against "the jitterbug millions, lurching along on their new Children's Crusade, [who] have scared a lot of people away from hot jazz."[28] He heaped equal disdain on symphonic jazz, especially upon George Gershwin and Paul Whiteman.[29] "While the intelligentsia has been busy trying to water our scrawny cultural tree with European art and literary movements, [hot jazz] has come to maturity unnoticed," he argued.[30] According to Hammond, mixing symphonic music with jazz only served "to suppress the genuine thing."[31] Hammond believed it artistically and politically important to keep broad cultural institutions separate from one another: hot jazz (folk music) from sweet jazz (popular culture) from symphonic jazz (highbrow music), a defiantly oppositional attitude toward prevailing cultural institutions.

This oppositional attitude, tinged with politics, underlay Hammond's critique of Ellington. He argued that Ellington had become too commercial, that his "music [was] losing the distinctive flavor it once had, both because of the fact that he ha[d] added slick, un-negroid musicians to his band and because he himself [had been] aping Tin Pan Alley composers for commercial reasons."[32] Hammond also alleged that Ellington was chasing the prestige of art music. He wrote, Ellington "has introduced complex harmonies solely for effect and has experimented with material farther and farther away from dance music, and although he has earned the fervent praise of trade paper critics he has alienated a good part of his dancing public."[33] According to Hammond, the demands of popular culture and classical music corrupted the special folk qualities of Ellington's jazz, proof that folk music was essentially incompatible with other cultural institutions. More than that, he claimed that Ellington himself had essentially become inauthentic by chasing success among large commercial (often white) audiences via popular music, and by chasing prestige among (often white) specialists via highbrow sophistication.

At the same time, however, another writer was offering a competing assessment of Ellington's music: Alain Locke, remembered today as a pragmatist philosopher who made lasting contributions to theories of value, and as the "father of the Harlem Renaissance" for his writing about the arts.[34] In private correspondence, he invited Ellington to perform in a concert he was organizing, which, he said, would provide "a chance at last to give a real Negro version [of their music] without having to have any white producer intruding his ideas or particular whimsies," probably a reference to Hammond.[35] Although the concert never came to fruition, the invitation stands as a testament to Locke's enthusiasm for Ellington. More than that, it demonstrates racial politics playing out in aesthetic terms: Hammond may not have intended it, but his oppositional stance ran the danger of confining Black performers to a narrow range of cultural production in the name of musical authenticity. When Locke lionized Ellington, however, he praised exactly what Hammond condemned: He considered Ellington "the pioneer of super-jazz and the person most likely to create the classical jazz to which so many are striving."[36] At its most basic level, "super-jazz" and "classical jazz" implied a music (and, concomitantly, a composer) that could roam freely through genre and style, from popular to classical, thereby opening avenues of expression for Black musicians than had traditionally been almost entirely closed.

Beneath Locke's praise of Ellington lay complex cultural theories, which mixed art and social consciousness, and which had their roots in the middle-brow writings of Van Wyck Brooks. Locke hailed from an earlier generation of critics than Hammond. He graduated from Harvard in 1907 and later that year enrolled at Oxford as the first Black Rhodes Scholar. At both universities he was Brooks's classmate, and according to historian Nathan Huggins, evidence suggests that they began their careers with similar literary goals.[37] For example, what Brooks had identified as *America's Coming of Age*, Locke called a "Spiritual Coming of Age" for Black America.[38] Locke described this in his seminal collection of essays, *The New Negro* (1925), which forged a civic-minded cultural criticism that, like Brooks's, rested upon fine distinctions between high art, folk art, and popular culture. He later defined these terms explicitly in his book *The Negro and His Music* (1936): classical music, "music in the universal mode without trace of folk idiom and influence"; folk music, "produced without formal musical training or intention by the greatest and most fundamental of all musical forces, – emotional creation"; and popular music, which he characterized as "broad but shallower" than the other two categories.[39] Also like Brooks, Locke's attitude toward these institutions was fundamentally middlebrow: Instead of cordoning off hot jazz from classical music, he recommended merging them. "Eventually the art-music and the folk-music must be fused in a vital but superior product," he wrote.[40] The resulting music would mix these institutions, meaning that musical abstraction and experimentation would arise directly from the popular traditions and desires of the broader community.

But Locke's argument also contained a feature that Brooks's did not. Brooks believed that the end result of combining high art, folk art, and popular culture would be a more "universal" form of art. Locke, however, advocated that prior to striving for any universality, Black musicians should produce their own kind of high art, with their own standards of excellence, independently of white culture.[41] Since his earliest writings, he called this "parallel evolution," which he explained by analogy: "Each tradition if it is organic must be exclusive—to illustrate, Japanese art and western art must be the consistent development of two different art principles," he wrote, "and the true cultured attitude toward them is not the eclectic blending of the one with the other, but a distinct sense of the parallel evolution of the two."[42] What was true for visual art was also true for music. Locke believed "classical" music was best understood, not as a particular style, but rather as a way of thinking about music, one that submitted the raw materials of folk or popular music to a process of abstraction, similar to the way that Bach created intricate, contrapuntally dense suites out of existing folk dance forms. Inputting either European or Black folk music into such a procedure would ultimately produce different sounds, even though the "classicizing" processes of abstraction would be qualitatively the same (or "universal") for both kinds of music—or, using Locke's words, the processes would be "parallel." On a concrete level, Locke believed that a Black classical music would abstract its raw materials from dance or folk music into complex forms, cutting-edge rhythms, and novel approaches to harmony and melody. He wrote: "Certainly for the last fifty years, the Negro has been the main source of America's popular music, and promises, as we shall see, to become one of the main sources of America's serious or classical music, at least that part which strives to be natively American and not derivative of European types of music."[43]

For Locke, the most important musical and social progress toward a "serious" Black art music came from Ellington. Locke joined a group of critics who believed that Ellington was using the raw materials of jazz to produce new musical forms. Locke cited Constant Lambert, who wrote that Ellington's music constitutes "not just decorations of a familiar shape but a new arrangement of shapes"; he cited Robert Goffin: "the technique of jazz has been rationalized by Ellington," "he has gradually placed intuitive music under control"; and he cited R. D. Darrell: "Delightful and tricky rhythmic effects are never introduced for sheer sensational purposes, rather they are developed and combined with others as logical part and parcel of the whole work."[44] Each believed that Ellington transformed the sensual, physical, dance characteristics of jazz into something intellectually rigorous. Such developments were only possible, according to Locke, if musicians like Ellington could access classical-music resources (such as ensembles, venues, and so on) and enjoy the encouragement to experiment. "Cultural opportunity and appreciation are just what for the moment the Negro musician critically needs," he wrote.[45] In other words, blending popular music, folk music, and classical music was tantamount to social or political advocacy for Black Americans.

By 1940, at the hands of Locke, Hammond, and their colleagues, Ellington had become more than a famous bandleader. He had become a symbolic figure in a broad debate about the future of American music: about the proper relationship between popular music and classical music, about the proper understanding of Black culture within the broader American artistic landscape, about the proper role that politics should play in art, and so on. Yet the precise degree to which Ellington himself actively intervened in these debates is difficult to discern. Ellington was famously elusive in interviews, an effect that musicologist Mark Tucker once described as an "effusive verbal smoke screen."[46] Nevertheless, around the edges of Ellington's commentary exists evidence of his more specific cultural priorities, and the composite picture they paint is, first, of somebody who was sympathetic to middlebrow culture, even if he was not one of its main theorists, and second, of somebody who rejected the oppositional approach. These core middlebrow beliefs, and the increasingly acrimonious debates surrounding them, constituted the background for his involvement in *Beggar's Holiday*.

First, we know that Ellington was at least aware of—and enthusiastic about—the major literary figures in the Harlem Renaissance, many of whom featured prominently in Locke's *New Negro*. In his first published article from 1931, for example, Ellington cited "Countee Cullen and others in literature" for "great achievements over fearful odds," work that he considered "long overdue."[47] In 1941, Ellington also spoke publicly about another Harlem Renaissance figure who had featured prominently in *The New Negro*, Langston Hughes. Hughes's celebration of Black vernacular was radically different from Cullen's self-consciously classical verse. But Ellington detected a broad connection: Hughes's poetry, like Cullen's, was a civic-minded celebration of Black culture. Ellington, in fact, envied how direct these poets could be in their medium about social issues: "[M]usic is my business, my profession, my life ... but even though it means so much to me, I often feel that I'd like to say something, have my say, on some of the burning issues confronting us, in another language ... in words of mouth."[48] In this spirit, Ellington frequently composed pieces that had political undertones, including his musical revue *Jump for Joy* (1941), which sought to undercut Black stereotypes that were familiar to musical theater at the time; *Black, Brown, and Beige* (1943), which Ellington described as a musical depiction of Black American history; *Blutopia* (1944), which he described as representing the "yearning of the people of the world for the Utopia of the brotherhood of man"; and the *Deep South Suite* (1946).[49]

Second, like these writers, Ellington wrote music that would speak to the Black American experience—partly by choice, because he considered himself a proud representative of his race; and partly by circumstance, because others scrutinized his music in racial terms. "When we [Black people of his generation] went out into the world, we would have the grave responsibility of being practically always on stage, for every time people saw a Negro they would go into a reappraisal of the race," he wrote in his autobiography.[50] In this spirit, Ellington occasionally described his compositions as folk music. To be clear, the *sounds* of his music, as well as the modes of dissemination he deployed, tended to sit within the sphere of popular culture, but at a conceptual level he believed it *functioned* like folk music, as a music that expressed the essence of his "people" and their traditions. As he said in an interview with a Scottish newspaper reporter in 1933: "My contention about the music we play is that it also is folk music, the result of our transplantation to American soil, and the expression of a people's soul just as much as the wild skirling of bagpipes denotes a heroic race that has never known the yoke of foreign dictatorship."[51]

Third, like Locke and other middlebrow theorists, Ellington resisted fixed institutional boundaries. "As you may know, I have always been against any attempt to categorize or pigeonhole music, so I won't attempt to say whether the music of the future will be jazz or not jazz, whether it will merge or not merge with classical music," he said. "There are simply two kinds of music, good music and the other kind."[52] Over time, the idea that his music was "beyond category" became a cornerstone of Ellingtonia, and it remains one of Ellington's most frequently cited bon mots today.[53] Less frequently mentioned is how similar he was in this respect to Locke, who once argued, in language very similar to Ellington's, "that the important distinction is not between jazz and classical music but between the good, mediocre, and bad of both varieties."[54]

This is to say that Ellington had no interest in maintaining Hammond's style of folk purity. He had long been interested in placing his compositions in dialogue with symphonic music. In the 1920s and 1930s, some of the pieces Ellington wrote bore the words "symphony" or "rhapsody" in their titles: Ellington's *Rhapsody Jr.* (1926), *Creole Rhapsody* (1931), *Symphony in Black: A Rhapsody of Negro Life* (1935); others were extended-form or multi-section works: *Reminiscing in Tempo* (1935), *Bird of Paradise* (1935), *Diminuendo and Crescendo in Blue* (1937), and *American Lullaby* (1942); one was partially commissioned by Paul Whiteman: *Blue Bells of Harlem* (1943); another by the august conductor Arturo Toscanini: *Harlem* (1950). Musicologist John Howland's study of these works has described how Ellington's manager and publicist encouraged him to write extended-form symphonic-jazz pieces to compete with Paul Whiteman, George Gershwin, and other white jazz composers of the 1920s.[55] Ellington's goal, however, was not merely to write in that style, but rather to inflect the prevailing symphonic-jazz style with some of the "hot-jazz" or jam-session sensibility from his experience in Harlem nightclubs: "Our band came along ... just when Paul Whiteman and his orchestra had popularized the symphonic style.... But ... we came in with a new style. Our playing was stark and wild and intense."[56] Ellington's enthusiasm about mixing symphonic jazz with "hot" jazz was a key element that distanced him from Hammond and drew him toward the middlebrow.

Finally, Ellington stated that he never sought to imitate European highbrow composition in symphonic jazz. Instead, he wanted to derive a new kind of classical music from specifically Black traditions. Probably referring to concert spirituals, he once said, "arrangements of historic American Negro music have been made by conservatory-trained musicians who inevitably handle it with a European technique. It's time a big piece of Negro music was written from the inside by a Negro."[57] For him, this meant submitting Black folk music, not necessarily to the compositional procedures of European classical music, but rather to a self-consciously Black form of composition. In other words, it suggested Locke's "parallel development." In fact, Ellington often appended the phrase "tone parallel" to his extended, classically minded compositions: *Black, Brown, and Beige: A Tone Parallel to the History of the*

American Negro (1943), *New World A-Comin'* (1943, a parallel to a book by Roi Ottley with the same title),[58] *A Tone Parallel to Harlem* (1950), and *Such Sweet Thunder* (a parallel to Shakespeare, 1957).[59] At the most basic level, Ellington used the term "parallel" both formally and conceptually. Formally, it referred to a work comprising multiple sections or movements that referenced a historical or literary subject. Conceptually, according to musicologist Graham Lock, parallels made possible an alternative interpretation of a familiar subject "in which accepted notions of language, history, the real, and the possible are thrown open to question and found wanting."[60] In *Such Sweet Thunder*, for example, Ellington and his collaborator Billy Strayhorn provided a distinctly Black perspective on Elizabethan poetry, pointing out similarities between Shakespearian poetics and modern jazz. "Somehow, I suspect that if Shakespeare were alive today, he might be a jazz fan himself—he'd appreciate the combination of team spirit and informality, of academic knowledge and humor, of all the elements that go into a great jazz performance."[61]

All of this—Ellington's political advocacy, his genre-bending middlebrow sympathies, his desire to create high-art music with specifically Black musical materials, his idea of a "musical parallel," and his disagreements with Hammond—culminated in the 1943 Carnegie Hall premiere of *Black, Brown, and Beige: A Tone Parallel to the History of the American Negro*. The piece traced the history of the United States—the arrival of enslaved people, plowing the frontier, the Revolutionary War, the Civil War, and so forth—from a distinctly Black perspective. In an early article about the piece, the reviewer described the Civil War section: "The predominant musical note struck here is that of humor, light laughter-ringing pathos sounded only in the strain of bewilderment and fear involved by the frightened old folk, told to go free and uncomprehending where or how to proceed."[62] The combination of "humor" and Civil War might have struck some readers as odd, but this piece represented the perspective of an enslaved person recently freed by the Emancipation Proclamation. It amounted, in other words, to an alternative ("parallel") way to feel about the Civil War from a distinctly Black perspective.

Musically, too, it represented a proudly Black interpretation of classical music. "The things we use . . . are purely Negroid—we want to stay in character. . . . We are not attempting . . . to produce a magnificent affair. We desire to remain true to self. The music was inspired by the character of the playing of the men in the band and is characteristic of ourselves, and, we hope, the saga which motivates our effort," Ellington said.[63] It was not merely that the sounds of *Black, Brown, and Beige* derived from the harmonic, melodic, and rhythmic palette of jazz. Rather, the phrase "inspired by the character of the playing men in the band" suggests that Ellington was also providing an alternative way of understanding how such works could be composed, a riff upon (or parallel to) the process of classical-music composition. Ellington elaborated in a now famous description from 1944:

> When I get an idea, I write the melody and often work out the arrangement, too. But sometimes the band and I collaborate on the arrangement. I write the melody down and play it at rehearsal. Then the boys will start making suggestions in a "free-for-all." One of them might get up and demonstrate his idea of what a measure should be like. Then another one of the boys will pick it up and maybe fix it a little. Sometimes we'll all argue back and forth with our instruments, each one playing a couple of bars in his own way.[64]

This approach blends the score-based, composer-centered method familiar to European conservatory training (he invented the initial melody, he ultimately oversaw the score's compilation and put his name on it) with the improvisation of a jazz club (the band rearranged the melody, tried out different instrumentation, varied it, and made other suggestions). Ellington's sounds fell between popular and classical music, but also his entire approach to creating and performing music fell between the two institutions.

By the time Ellington began writing *Beggar's Holiday* in late 1945, the politicized cultural disputes surrounding his work had become even more intense. In 1943, when *Black, Brown, and Beige* premiered, Hammond wrote a review called "Is the Duke Deserting Jazz?" He recycled some of his earlier complaints: "My feeling is that by becoming more complex he has robbed jazz of most of its basic virtue and lost contact with his audience."[65] Alongside Hammond sprang a generation of critics even more extreme than he was.[66] Nicknamed the "moldy figs" by critics and jazz historians, these writers considered anything except New Orleans or Dixieland Jazz to be counterfeit culture.[67] In 1947 critic Ernest Borneman described this group as "fundamentalists" who held that jazz "began to decline when the musicians learned to read and gave up collective improvisation on blues and ragtime themes for written arrangements of Tin Pan Alley tunes."[68] In their early days, the moldy figs critiqued swing, especially Ellington, and later would claim that bebop was as decadent, as inauthentic, as swing had been.

Scholars have typically held that after *Black, Brown, and Beige* received largely negative reviews in 1943, Ellington became cautious and backed away from large-scale symphonic pieces, at least for a while; that he felt bruised both by those who claimed his work was insufficiently related to jazz and by those who claimed his work insufficiently rigorous enough to be symphonic.[69] Yet at the time, Ellington insisted in the press that critics misunderstood him. He claimed that he was never really trying to write European symphonic music, but rather trying to write *in parallel* to the symphonic tradition. In 1944 he wrote, for example, "If I seem a little shy about being displayed on a critical platform with the classical big shots, let me also dispel the notion that I hesitate to place the jazz medium in a top musical category.... To attempt to elevate the status of the jazz musician by forcing the level of his best work into comparisons with classical music is to deny him rightful share of originality."[70] It was at this point, in September 1945, that Ellington signed a contract to write an unusual, experimental Broadway production that combined the titles of two of his earlier extended pieces—*Reminiscing in Tempo* and *Black, Brown, and Beige: A Parallel to the History of the American Negro*—both of which had elicited Hammond's most severe critiques. The show would be called *Beggar's Holiday: A Parallel in Tempo to John Gay's Beggar's Opera*. Hardly a retreat, collaborating on a midtown musical was a further betrayal to the moldy figs' folk ideals. It would be the embodiment of Ellington's middlebrow ideals, a civic-minded Black musical conceived of as both classical and popular. The title alone would have been a red flag to Hammond's bull.[71]

"The Idiom and Tempo of Today's America": Early Drafts of *Beggar's Holiday*

"Confirmed Ellingtons [sic] commitment to do music for an opera prepared to sign contract," ran an undated telegram from producer Perry Watkins to his co-producer Dale Wasserman.[72] Official paperwork followed on September 28, 1945, and the next morning an article appeared announcing Ellington's involvement in an "ambitious ... modern version" of John Gay's *Beggar's Opera* (1728).[73] At this point, aside from a broad concept, very little else of the show existed. The production team was small, comprising

Watkins, Wasserman, a press agent, and, probably starting in the summer of 1945, librettist John Latouche. Details were hazy; from the surviving desultory notes scattered among the archives, it seems that the creative team was even unclear as to whether they were adapting *The Beggar's Opera* or some combination of that play and its sequel, *Polly* (1729).[74] This is to say that before any dialogue, before a plot, before any music, before even a title, there existed a fundamental set of seemingly incommensurable ideas: a high-art, high-minded, "ambitious" script in dialogue with classic literature, but set against the generic backdrop of modern Broadway and swing. Sketchy though they were, however, these early materials already brimmed with heady enthusiasm. They promised "a revolution in the production styles for musicals"[75] and "a rebuke to the existing musical comedy."[76] According to one early typed summary, "Properly done, 'The Beggar's Opera' can do for that sterile, sad, retrogressive form of theatre known as the musical comedy what it did for the grand opera of 1720. It can, by demonstration of the virtue of proper marriage (of libretto and music) make an honest woman of the whore."[77]

When Ellington first agreed to work on *Beggar's Holiday* in late summer or autumn 1945, he probably knew only the most general details about the developing production. Watkins later recalled approaching Ellington spontaneously to compose the score, at a restaurant where he had spotted the composer and his entourage. He laid out his idea for a show based on *The Beggar's Opera*, dropped Latouche's name, and mentioned a commission. Ellington, he said, accepted on the spot.[78] Any follow-up discussions have been lost to history. Scattered early sketches, notes, synopses, and press releases give a sense of what the creative team may have told Ellington when he signed on. Taken together, these documents reveal a show that would speak to Ellington's preexisting middlebrow cultural priorities. By signing his contract, Ellington became an active participant in the postwar, post-*Oklahoma!* interpretation of the middlebrow musical, which would blend the institutions of high art, folk music, and popular culture to offer a new, specifically American perspective on the long tradition of political satire in the theater.

First, Ellington knew that *Beggar's Holiday* was conceived of as a "parallel" (a word, however, that the producers would actually adopt only a year later), an alternative way of viewing a literary classic from the point of view of modern-day America, or as the earliest advertisements put it, "a biting satire adapted to the American scene."[79] According to Latouche, he calibrated his script so that it would remain true to the eighteenth-century source material and also to the contemporary mood, and this latter feature was to distinguish his version from previous modernizations, including Bertolt Brecht's and Kurt Weill's *Der Dreigroschenoper* (1928), which had been written for their own contexts. He wrote in one synopsis:

> Bitterness can be overdone. The version [of *The Beggar's Opera*] by Brecht and Weill, which captured so admirably the desperate cynicism of German audiences after the last World War, reflects how far this interpretation can be carried—but the present American mood demands a different interpretation. It should partake rather of that anxiety, that mixture of dread and hope, which is the keynote of this [i.e., post–World War II] transitional period.[80]

It was not merely that Latouche was working behind the scenes to capture the right mood. In fact, the show's mood itself was to be a central theme of the production. In the very earliest surviving sketches, John Gay himself served as a narrator, and the opening scene was to feature him arguing with one of his central characters, the magistrate Peachum, about the proper tone for the story.[81]

> Gay protests vigorously, albeit as a mincing gentleman of the period, that this is neither his opera, nor can he countenance its use as such a bitter, blasphemous vehicle. He argues that the opera was conceived in literary charm, not in macabre humor. Peachum listens patiently, points out that times have changed, that the immediacy of Armageddon or catastrophe prevents being merely charming; that modern tempo precludes superficiality.[82]

Although Gay and this dialogue would disappear in later versions of the script, certain elements of this scene remained. In the final version of the script, for example, the narrator opened the show by singing a song ("Inbetween") and delivering a monologue, both of which served a similar function, to describe the central mood: a hard-boiled, gangster noir set in that uncertain moment between twilight and nightfall, a time of day that also represented the uneasy state of the modern soul.

Second, Ellington knew that this production was to be a satire. In part, he would have understood this from the people he was signing on to work with.

Watkins, Wasserman, and Latouche had all begun their careers working in the popular, populist, experimental labor musical theater of the 1930s and the Popular Front. Watkins had worked in the Negro Theater of the Works Progress Administration; Wasserman had worked closely with Katherine Dunham, a Black dancer who choreographed left-wing political musicals such as the 1939 labor revue *Pins and Needles*; and Latouche had taken some of his earliest writing jobs in the Federal Theatre Project, the left-wing Theatre Arts Committee, and, alongside Wasserman, the long-running revue *Pins and Needles*.[83] The creative team they eventually assembled after Ellington signed his contract also largely hailed from the 1930s political theater. Director John Houseman had worked in the Negro Theatre Unit of the Federal Theatre Project (before breaking off to found the Mercury Theater company in 1937), and his assistant Nicholas Ray had been a member of the Theater of Action and then part of the Federal Theatre Project. That they all hailed from the same general background was not an accident, according to an actor from *Beggar's Holiday* named Perry Bruskin (who also had begun his career in the left-wing Worker's Laboratory Theater and the Federal Theatre Project). He said, "I think it reflected Houseman's attitude towards the theatre of the 1930s, because those were his most exciting days, and Nick [Ray] and I came from that same background. He and Latouche represented that same period. There was a dynamic reason for the grouping of those people."[84]

Yet *Beggar's Holiday* did not merely continue prewar practices. The production team tried to update the dramaturgy of the prewar political theater for a postwar world. In terms of style, Latouche wanted *Beggar's Holiday* to put a new spin on some of the recognizable stylistic features of 1930s political theater. To give just one example, in 1942 Latouche told *Mademoiselle* magazine that he had grown frustrated with the stock device of the narrator in political theater, both on stage and on the radio:

> It is time that a jaundiced eye was cast at one cliché that has evolved out of radio's invisible domain: the cliché of the Little Man. The Little Man is always footballed around by the radio Homers the minute democracy comes into the picture. Whenever any governmental or political problem is explained, the Little Men rush in with merry whoop and lazy drawl to have it explained to them. The ordinary citizen must rather resent this coy title since most of those I've met considered themselves fairly important in the jobs they were doing.[85]

His goal was to create a different kind of narrator, one that would still situate the show's themes in present-day context, but not passively or naively. To this end, the narrator in *Beggar's Holiday* does not educate the audience, but rather poses questions directly to them, implicating them in the proceedings.

Third, and closely related, Latouche also wanted to experiment with a new kind of political engagement, and Ellington probably knew this when he signed on. Whereas the Federal Theatre shows had tended to take aim at specific political figures or policies, *Beggar's Holiday* remained purposefully inchoate. "There will be no direct preaching," according to an early synopsis, written before Ellington signed on; "any moral conclusions will occur, as they always must anyway, in the minds of the onlookers."[86] According to a later synopsis, written after Ellington joined the team, "no specific character will be satirized, as, let us say, John Gay satirized Walpole"; "for each Walpole, we can find a dozen prototypes in the contemporary scene."[87] Latouche maintained this stance even after the show opened. In his "Letter to John Gay" in the *New York Times*, he described a broad swipe at a new "jittery" postwar world: "We can no longer point to a Walpole as the author of our unrest. In this jittery era, one can present no single man as a Peachum.... Accordingly, I aimed my sights at a contemporary type, the huckster of power. His antics and contradictions cannot disguise his emotional deep-freeze, his moral bankruptcy."[88] The end result was not a political satire that advocated any particular idea, but rather a show that took a broad swipe at contemporary life—civic but not explicitly partisan; socially minded but not explicitly activist. As such, it aimed to be critical but not divisive, a kind of civic critique that was in line with middlebrow writers such as Brooks and Atkinson (discussed in Chapter 1 and Chapter 2, respectively).

Ellington was no stranger to this kind of political expression that avoided "direct preaching." In 1941 he had joined forces with what he described as "a team of scholarly Hollywood writers [who had] decided to attempt to correct the race situation in the U.S.A. through a form of theatrical propaganda," a revue called *Jump for Joy*.[89] He later recalled that when he had worked on *Jump for Joy*, he had already insisted that whatever commentary the play might make, that it be delivered in oblique terms. "I think a statement of social protest in the theater should be made without saying it, and this calls for the real craftsman," he wrote.[90] He wrote in his memoirs that casting the major roles in *Beggar's Holiday* without regard to their race was tantamount to a political statement, leveled obliquely:

Again it was a matter of saying things without saying them. If you had white and black people on the stage together at that time, one of them was supposed to call the other a bastard, or something. There was none of that in this show. People were cast according to their ability. Alfred Drake played the part of Macheath the mobster, and the chief of police and his daughter were both black. Mack and the colored girl fell in love. Now that's a silly show in 1947! There were no such things then.[91]

According to musicologist Graham Lock, this oblique "saying without saying" became one of Ellington's "guiding aesthetic principles," which he continued to deploy for decades.[92]

Fourth, Ellington probably knew that this show's stagecraft was going to be experimental, edgy. For Latouche, a new kind of broadminded satire called for a new dramaturgy, and in his original conception, all components of the show were to give the impression of what he called the "universal." As an early synopsis stated, "The elements that comprise the piece are in themselves universal, geographically, and timeless," and continued: "Emphasis on timelessness. This means consequent de-emphasis upon period. Exactitude as to period is extremely unimportant, nor is consistency of chronology a virtue. The time doesn't matter. Mix them if it adds anything."[93] Therefore, regarding settings, Latouche wrote: "The place, like the time, is not definite"; regarding costumes, he wrote: "It is anyplace in the United States where the political corruption is taken for granted by the honest citizens."[94] These would gradually disappear in later versions of the script (which eventually skewed toward a gangster noir), but one universalizing component remained: the casting, and it became one of the most noted aspects of the show, both at the time and in later scholarly studies. The earliest press releases and synopses, dating from September 1945, announced that production would have a "mixed-race cast," and by January 1946 a story ran that described one of the show's "novel" features as its "interracial cast including Negroes, Malaysians, Chinese and Japanese, as well as the white members, all in speaking and singing roles."[95] The reason, according to one early synopsis (written before Ellington signed on), was that *Beggar's Opera* "is characteristic of no race more than any other. It's [sic] vices are man's. But an all Negro production, for instance, might invite an undesirable association in the minds of the already prejudiced. The solution is this; the cast shall be mixed."[96] As Watkins said it, to capture "the idiom and tempo of today's America," he believed that a "bi-racial" cast "expressed the integrated cross-sectional spirit of the true

American scene," and in the press described it as "proof of the universal character of the arts and artists of the theater."[97]

Fifth, and inseparable from the political components of *Beggar's Holiday*, were Latouche's gestures toward group psychology in *Beggar's Holiday*. "We live in a civilization that is very aware of itself, demanding to know more and more about itself," Latouche wrote. Self-understanding, projected onto a social level, had long been a goal of the middlebrow critical movement that centered around Van Wyck Brooks and Alain Locke, among others (introduced in Chapter 1). Latouche was continuing in this vein. In a 1945 article, for example, Latouche argued that the reason he mixed folk and experimental writing was to speak to modern audiences at a psychological level. On the one hand, he argued, folk music and folk ballads would speak to spectators' primordial, deeply ingrained, shared cultural identity. "Traditionally, the ballad has been the method of unlettered people for transmitting information—you can follow the whole history of America in the ballads of the Southern and Western mountain regions," he wrote. "To stir people's deepest understandings the poetic medium must be invoked." On the other hand, he believed that combining it with avant-garde techniques would make it speak to specifically modern audiences in modern terms. As he put it, "Utilizing the enormous verbal and psychological range opened by the experimentalists, [younger writers] are revitalizing the hackneyed forms of our national expression."[98]

From his early conversations with Latouche, Ellington would have known that the production was conceived in terms of modern psychology. In his pioneering biography of Latouche, musicologist Howard Pollack described Latouche's analysis of the modern temperament as residing at the level of the spiritual and the psychological, and he believed that an effective way to access it was through yoga, hypnotism, and dream analysis.[99] On the surface, this called for an expressionistic style that would enable the American subconscious to emerge. The producers described the general style as "fantastic and wonderful," a "visualization" "consistent with the vivid imagination of the beggar-minstrel" who was to narrate the show.[100] Moreover, throughout the production, the narrator was said to be "commenting with wisdom and tolerance on the hectic saga which is actually being *dreamed* up in his mind."[101] In one early synopsis, Latouche described the ending of the production:

> In dialogue with Peachum he [i.e., the Beggar] demands to know whether it isn't he, himself, who is dreaming this opera. The answer is yes, of course, The [Beggar] is positive in that case he can *dream* any kind of an ending

he wishes—so MacHeath is to be set free, since in morality there is little to choose from.[102]

There is a political point here, but at this stage it was difficult to discern—something about comparing the arbitrariness of modern morality to the arbitrariness of dreams. Latouche would continue to hone it as he wrote later drafts. Yet whatever the script's ultimate moral or political stance would eventually become, dreams and dream analysis remained an important feature of the production.

Fifth, even before Ellington signed on, the score was projected to be middlebrow. Early sketches, written before Ellington signed his contract, feature a guitar-playing ballad-singer narrator: "He looks, acts and sings like Leadbelly. In fact, he should be Leadbelly," the blues guitarist and singer, suggesting that the show was originally conceived broadly in terms of Black folk music alongside opera.[103] This may explain why Watkins and Wasserman had approached Latouche to write the book. His successful Broadway musical *Cabin in the Sky* (1940) had woven spirituals into a good-versus-evil battle over the soul of its drinking and womanizing main character. As *Beggar's Holiday* took shape over the next year, Latouche never entirely lost sight of this original idea, and he wrote a "Letter to John Gay" in the *New York Times* after the premiere that reiterated these folk elements: "You based your melodies on street-cries and traditional tunes. I wove in and out of my lyrics moods and phrases from folk rhymes, hobo ballads like 'Big Rock Candy Mountain,' and blues improvisations I remember having heard along Southern streets during my childhood."[104]

But once Ellington signed his contract, the central musical conceit of the show changed. "Musically, it will be a 'jazz' opera, rather than a folk work," a new synopsis stated, "although certain folk elements will be retained, depending on the needs of the character."[105] Writing a show that blended jazz with opera probably appealed to Ellington, who had wanted to write an opera since at least the early 1930s.[106] This fact became part of the show's advertising materials once Ellington signed his contract. One synopsis announced, for example, that Ellington saw in *Beggar's Holiday* "the opportunity for a great American jazz opera" which would "[consolidate] his influence on modern music."[107] A press release distributed eleven months before the premiere spun this provocatively: "It was Ellington who stated in print that *Porgy and Bess* was neither Negro nor jazz, and that some day he would himself write a jazz opera."[108] It is difficult to parse precisely what "opera" meant to the production team in these early days, whether it referred to European-style grand opera, British ballad opera, or something else. At the very least, however, this term signaled to readers and potential backers that the show would—in some yet unclear way—walk a fine line between high art and popular culture.

All of this—the civic sensibility, the goal of self-understanding, the mixture of high art and popular culture—situated this production squarely within the middlebrow tradition, and self-consciously so. Yet in addition, the show also responded to changes in middlebrow writing that had taken place during the war. In 1940 the Pulitzer Prize–winning poet and the Librarian of Congress Archibald MacLeish had given a speech that became instantly famous—and infamous. In broad outline, it assumed many of the themes that Brooks had been advocating for decades, discussed in Chapter 1. But while Brooks had framed his arguments in spiritual or psychological terms, MacLeish framed his arguments in terms of the present-day political situation. World War II, he argued, was not primarily a political battle; it was a cultural one. To him, fascism represented "a revolt against the common culture of the West," and he insisted that artists defend it.[109] Yet modernist, obscure, abstruse, opaque, avant-garde writing did no such thing—in fact, he argued, modernist art was also in revolt against received traditions, and as such only abetted the enemy. In his formulation, it represented "the pure, the perfect type of irresponsibility," and he advocated instead for an artist "admittedly responsible for the defense of the inherited tradition, avowedly partisan of its practice."[110] (Brooks approved wholeheartedly with these developments, distributed copies of the speech to major intellectuals of the day, and maintained a close professional relationship and a warm correspondence with MacLeish for years.[111])

During the war, Latouche wrote an article in which he praised MacLeish's radio scripts, which, he believed, captured the sensibilities of the mid-1940s.[112] Like MacLeish, he took issue with modernist writing. He admitted to admiring James Joyce's, Gertrude Stein's, Ezra Pound's, and T. S. Eliot's "Revolution of the Word," but he considered their style out of touch and out of date. "Through repeating, with increasing obscurity, the revolt of yesterday, they [i.e., avant-garde writers] have become the academic moderns of today," he wrote, accusing modernist poets of "writing waspish verses for a circle of fellow-poets to dislike."[113] His goal was to situate genuinely experimental writing within the broader American community, especially through radio and musical comedy, and thereby to gain broader civic significance.

This is to say that, with both Ellington and Latouche at the helm, *Beggar's Holiday* was not to be the story of a charming criminal who marries a prostitute and a magistrate's daughter, aimed at lampooning the mores of the higher classes. It was instead to be a middlebrow commentary on American postwar society via a socially minded critique of high art and popular culture, designed to expose America's modern, psychological maladies.

"That's the Symbolism, That's the Highbrow Stuff": Late Stages of *Beggar's Holiday*

Latouche began working on the first draft of the libretto starting in late October or early November 1945, and by January 1946 the show's press agent described the show as "in its final writing stages."[114] This was untrue; no script appeared for months. To speed the writing process along, starting on or around February 1, 1946, the producers sent Latouche to join the Ellington orchestra so that the two could work together while the composer was on tour.[115] By March, the production team once again projected an opening night in the press, this time in June.[116] That date, however, came and went and still the producers had no script or score, at which point the historical record goes dim for nearly three months. What little information survives from this period suggests that the spring and summer of 1946 were difficult for the creative team. According to later recollections by his collaborators, Latouche started drinking, was juggling multiple projects, became increasingly erratic, and even disappeared briefly.[117]

Finally, in late summer 1946, Latouche submitted a complete first-draft script, accompanied by many (the exact number is unclear) musical numbers by Ellington, labeled according to their corresponding pages in the libretto.[118] A few key moments still needed to be written (including MacHeath's climactic speech at the end of the second act), and many of the songs contained only melody and sketched chords. However, these materials faithfully translated the ambitious middlebrow ideas that had been set out in the synopses and press releases from the previous autumn, and they retained the central goal of describing and analyzing America's anxious postwar mood. In this draft, the narrator (called the Beggar) serves as a psychoanalyst errant, prodding the characters and audience with cryptic or pointed questions, alerting them to their own neuroses. In the opening moments of the production, for example, before the curtain rises, he walks to the edge of the stage and begins to sing:

> Inbetween
> Neither happy nor tearful
> You're inbetween
> Neither confident nor fearful
> Half in a mist and half wide-awake,
> You wait for the moment when something will break [...]
> You're a feather in the air, waiting for a breeze
> To blow
> To show
> You which way you're gonna go—
> But you aint sweet or mean
> You're jes inbetween
> And you don't know...[119]

The "you" in question was the audience. In this version of the script, the somnambulant quality of the production becomes a state of the modern soul—the anxious, directionless, "jittery" mood that Latouche had described as the hallmark of the postwar era, underscoring the production's social critique, which he states here clearer than he had in any of the previous notes, sketches, or synopses. During the scene that follows, the Beggar and the main character converse:

> BEGGAR
> Times like these, dream things and written things and real things all git mixed up in my head till I can hardly tell who from which. Why try?
> MACHEATH
> Real things—they're pretty ugly. Most people won[']t look at 'em straight; they want life covered over with dream-icing, before they can work up an appetite for it. That's where guys like me step in, and get the goodies—cause we don't need the trimmin's.[120]

In this production, MacHeath's main virtue (aside from charm) is practicality, a willingness to act—either for good or bad—while others merely slumber or hide from the real world. The full critical import of existing in this state appears only in the final execution scene, in an elaborate final speech, given by the Beggar, in which they look out from the stage over the audience.

> [BEGGAR]
> You see how it is, Mac. Look at the lathered pack of mankind, hysterical, jittery, anxious—jumping this way and that, snapping and biting at whatever passes before their furious jaws ... looking for a blame in this man's color, a scapegoat in that man's race, running frantically before the shadow of their illogical fear—trapped in the arid gulleys [sic] of their hatred.... The deed has been done by all of us—the hates hated by all of us—the bombs released, the triggers pulled, the mines laid, the victims destroyed—by all of us. The one thing we equally share in this inequal world is guilt.
> MACHEATH
> But you are the guiltiest of all. [...]
> [BEGGAR]
> What have I done? [...] I just sat back and let things happen.
> MACHEATH
> And that is the greatest crime of all.
> [BEGGAR]
> If that is true then we are all criminals.[121]

Once again, "we" implicates the audience and describes them as complicit in present-day atrocity simply by doing nothing. Yet, as promised in the early material, the production never encourages the audience to act according to some partisan notion of good. Instead, the script's goal seems simply to be civic self-awareness, a diagnostic of the modern condition that traced postwar racism to deep-seated mania.

To create this dreamlike atmosphere, Latouche and Ellington kept their promise to establish a novel relationship between song and score, with continuous underscoring that frequently bubbled up into musical numbers, some of which lasted only a few bars before receding back into underscoring once again. (Later, Ellington would claim that they had written fifty songs for the show—perhaps true, if "songs" refers to "cues."[122]) Speech flows freely between prose, verse, recitative, and song.[123] In one scene, for example, the crooked magistrate and the chief of police have an argument. "The music takes up their denunciations. A double-bass and a Bflat [sic] clarinet develop the fury of the duo to a vibrating climax of anger, while PEACHUM [the magistrate] and LOCKIT [the chief of police] pantomime a rage they cannot even voice."[124] In other scenes, characters accompany themselves on instruments, and at one point a "one-man band . . . wanders on" from the wings to announce the entrance of the magistrate and, simultaneously, to underscore a duet for MacHeath's scorned lovers.[125] Speaking broadly, the script and score toy with diegesis throughout. On the one hand, as is customary in musicals, when music appears, it often marks a switch into reflection mode, a kind of musical time when action largely gives way to expression, when the characters express but do not consciously recognize that they are, in fact, singing.[126] On the other hand, there are also times in the show when characters do hear music as such, a "sung song." In the first draft of *Beggar's Holiday*, however, the distinction is often productively unclear, residing on the border between action and reflection—"in between" different modes of reality.

To blur these two kinds of time in the musical, Ellington's songwriting often avoids a firm sense of cadence, and thereby the sense of a closed song form that typically separates action from reflection. For example, the music of "Inbetween" creates a sense of suspended animation, in which large sections of the song seem poised to cadence but never do, even in the final bar. Like most Broadway songs, the piece divides into a verse and refrain. The latter, however, does not fall into the normative ABAC or AABA pattern, but instead into an atypical AAB format: the A section (mm. 13–20), a repeat of that A section (mm. 21–30) with a small extension (mm. 25–27, leading to a "crux" moment at m. 28 where the phrase once again corresponds to the first A phrase), followed by a closing B section (mm. 31–37). Ellington treats every formal joint in the refrain (m. 20, m. 30, m. 37) conspicuously, leaving it open and unresolved. Each phrase of the refrain ends with repeated accents and triplet rhythms that stand out against an otherwise duple context, emphasizing the same recurring harmony, pictured in the left side of Example 4.1.[127] This chord eludes easy labeling. While it could potentially be given many names, affixing a functional label to this chord would obscure its most salient quality: the ambiguity that stems from the fact that its root lies, literally, "in between" the subdominant and dominant. Because Ellington deploys it as the final harmony for both the A and B sections (including the final measure of the song), the overall effect is that this song seems not quite finished—as if it were actually an AABA song, but the final A remains unspoken, unsung. So conspicuous was the feeling that this song was left floating in air that in one of the two surviving demo recordings of the piece, the pianist adds a tonic E-flat to provide the sense of an ending that the original manuscript lacks.[128]

What Latouche and Ellington considered a novel relationship between script and score, director Houseman considered unfinished. "Latouche... had written a number of lyrics but only the roughest draft of our first act and almost nothing of the second," he recalled. "Ellington, teeming with tunes and mood pieces, still had not faced the necessity of composing a complete musical score."[129] The operative word is "complete." For Ellington's part, he had provided dozens of musical cues and probably expected to work them into a score during rehearsals, the standard working method he deployed with his orchestra (described above). To this end, he dispatched Billy Strayhorn, his long-time writing partner, who arrived in New York City on September 10 to oversee this work while Ellington himself continued on tour.[130] Meanwhile, on September 4, 1946, the press department announced that John Houseman had been hired to direct *Beggar's Holiday*, and according to his memoirs he arrived around this time in New York to begin working with Latouche to revise the script. On September 17, 1946, Latouche wrote to friends that he was "slaving away at the script of *The Beggar's Opera*," a statement the surviving sources corroborate.[131] In a stack of script fragments there remains new typewritten material dated between September 14 and September 26.[132] This process of revision was difficult. "Latouche was of little help to us," Houseman wrote in his autobiography. "He argued and whined in defense of his non-existent script. Then he vanished for ten days. When he reappeared he quibbled with us over what we'd done in his absence."[133]

This second version of the script reined in some of the more avant-garde aspects of the first draft. The orchestra became confined to the pit, and instead of weaving short snippets of song in and out of the dialogue, the songs tended to fall into more familiar closed forms, with clear beginnings, middles, and endings.[134] Instead of expressionistic props, sets, and costumes, the show became a parody of gangster films. The narrator's new first speech, for example, evoked the genre's hardboiled dialogue and street-lamp-lit slums:

> Slummin', eh? Got your eyes peeled? What ya lookin' at? Who you 'spect to see comin' around that corner? Jack the Ripper? Gargles? You like Alan Ladd? Bogie? I do! You like best sellers? Psychological thrillers? I do! This is the place that kind of stuff's supposed to happen, ain't it?[135]

In the previous version of the script the narrator interrogated the characters and audience about their dreams, but in this version of the script the narrator tended to discuss the expectations of genre, lending

128 THE MIDDLEBROW MUSICAL

Example 4.1 Comparison of "Inbetween" and "Tomorrow Mountain" from *Beggar's Holiday*.

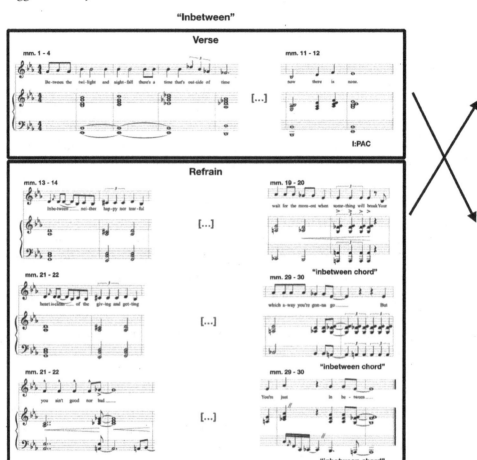

Example 4.1 Continued

the show a self-referential quality. For example, in the beginning of Act I, after MacHeath's elaborate back-alley wedding ballet, the narrator ambles onstage. "Hey, that's a hulluva situation! We're just about gettin' started—and we run into a climax! [MacHeath] slipped that one over on me. Didn't know he was that practical," he says to the audience. "That's why I like to dream up these things.... You can push your hero around and you know everything's gonna be all right." He then tells the audience that any good story needs a "heavy":

You just pick out a face.

(He looks out over the audience.)

Maybe it's some guy who's shoved you around—wouldn't give you a buck for a cup of coffee—maybe it's some joe you never saw before—some joe with the sweetest, nicest look in his eyes—(Savagely—with grim relish)—and you make him the meanest, dirtiest, lousiest, crookedest son-of-a-bitch....[136]

This cues the entrance of comedian Zero Mostel in the role of Peachum (an entrance accompanied by a fugue). In each of these moments, the tension lies between what should happen according to generic expectations (weddings tend to conclude musicals, the heavy is a "son-of-a-bitch") and what actually happens in the show (the wedding occurs in the beginning, the heavy is a charming magistrate). The narrator tries to impose regularity but the characters refuse, meaning that the play explicitly thematizes genre, thematizes what supposedly should happen in comedies, dramas, classics, musicals, and so on. The characters, however, refuse to conform—and, as will be seen, they occasionally argue with the narrator about it. It was from this kind of dialogue about generic expectations that the specifically middlebrow point of view emerged: Because genres not only implied expected forms and styles, because they also tended to be associated with highbrow or lowbrow culture, debating genre implied debating the accustomed practices—and the merits—of high art and low culture.

Moreover, the script was clear that such moments of tension about genre were supposed to have social implications. In the final (unwritten) scene of the show, for example, when MacHeath goes to the electric chair, the diversion from what is expected in a musical comedy and what has happened onstage becomes especially stark.

The Beggar harangues the audiences. He relates his day-dream to present-day American life; explains his phantasy in terms of the fashions and foibles of our times. It shouldn't take long—not more than a minute of time—but it will point and clarify the meaning of *The Beggar's Opera* today.

(This speech is still being polished and worked on until the very last minute. It will depend to a great extent on the impact and reaction-quality of our play.)

At the conclusion of this little speech, the Beggar, knowing that the audience obviously and rightly expects a happy ending, agrees to give them one. They shall have the most goddam happy ending they've ever seen.[137]

Upon which the dead characters rise, the crooked are thrown in jail, unhappy marriages are annulled, the Beggar reveals himself to be MacHeath (escaped from the chair), and the whole cast faces front to sing "Utopiaville," which describes a "mighty big nation" where "the whiskey fountains play / and there ain't no bills to pay / and it's Christmas every day."[138] This scene is very similar to the ending of Gay's original *Beggar's Opera*. Both have happy endings that are forced onto the plot by a *deus ex machina* (in Latouche's case, the Beggar) and justified by arbitrary rules of genre (in Latouche's case, that musical comedies need happy endings). Yet while Gay's work had implicated a corrupt social order throughout ("it is difficult to determine whether ... the fine Gentlemen imitate the Gentlemen of the Road, or the Gentlemen of the Road the fine Gentlemen," according to the final scene[139]), Latouche's musical carries psychological implications: Whatever order rules over the production at the end of the evening is as arbitrary as a dream. Once again, Latouche's (and Houseman's) main point appears to be that social order is an illusion that barely covers an underlying unpleasant reality.

It is likely that this script was used in the early rehearsals of *Beggar's Holiday*, which started on October 14, 1946.[140] Glimpses of the process, gleaned through scattered announcements in the press, suggest that behind the scenes the situation was tumultuous. In late October 1946, the *Tribune* announced that the show would open for its out-of-town preview in late November, first in Buffalo, then in Cleveland. By early November, however, the itinerary changed to New Haven on November 21 and Newark on November 26.[141] As the date approached, the later engagement was canceled and replaced with tryouts in Hartford and Boston.[142] Logistics aside, the show's finances were out of control. One year earlier, in September 1945, producers had budgeted the show at $150,000. Four months later, the price tag rose to $200,000.[143] By the time the show entered previews, it rose even higher; as one reporter wrote, "$250,000 [was] trembling on the drama critics' verdict."[144] Just days before the show opened on Broadway, the number climbed to $300,000.[145] Especially embarrassing was news that the show might have to suspend work because producers could not cover the required Equity bond of $40,000 (which would pay two weeks' salary to the performers in case of a default).[146] In the middle of this financial crisis, as they were scrambling to find a theater, producer Dale Wasserman left the show and sold his share to John R. Sheppard.[147] This was November 4, 1946, during the third week of rehearsals, about two and a half weeks before the show was slated to open for its New Haven tryout.

Facing negative out-of-town reviews and in arrears at least $40,000, the producers decided to nudge the show in the direction of clear-cut musical comedy.[148] First, they changed the show's title. During the early rehearsals they called it *Beggar's Opera*, which may have been a placeholder title. By the spring of 1945 they had changed it to *Street Music*, but changed it again to *Twilight Alley* by the time the production opened in Boston, perhaps playing upon the noir atmosphere of the show.[149] In New York, however, they ultimately called it *Beggar's Holiday* (a title that had been used for months behind the scenes), with the word "holiday" emphasizing entertainment.

Second, they fired Houseman, the original director, and hired George Abbott to revise and restage the show before its New York opening. Abbott's nickname was "Mr. Broadway," and he was known for fast-paced, lavish, and commercially successful productions. Abbott famously had no truck with the avant-garde theater of the 1930s. (Once, when a dutiful actor asked what his motivation was in a particular scene, Abbott replied, "Your job."[150]) His changes were drastic. As the *New York Tribune* reported, "Lines and whole scenes have been cut, new lyrics have been added and the material has been worked over to such an extent that even the members of the cast don't recognize it as the same show."[151] First, he replaced the lead actress, chanteuse Libby Holman, two days before the premiere.[152] Second, to make *Beggar's Holiday* more straightforwardly entertaining, he excised almost all of the narrator's social commentary about the anxiety of the present age. Third, he eliminated all the formalist aspects of the show that were redolent of the Federal Theatre Project style. Most conspicuously, he pared down almost all the narrator's monologues (eliminating the final speech entirely) and cut almost all the narrator's dialogue with MacHeath.

Emblematic of Abbott's changes was the end of the first act. Before Abbott became involved, it had ended with a solo reprise of the song "Take Love Easy," in which MacHeath brushed off one mistress's concern that he was married to another woman. By the time the show reached Broadway, however, the solo number had been replaced with two spectacular dances. First was "On the Wrong Side of the Railroad Tracks," an interpolated number for the secondary comic leads (played by Marie Bryant and Avon Long). Second was the full-cast "Tomorrow Mountain," with words reworked from the previous draft's "Utopiaville," in which the gangsters sing about a paradise "Where suckers are glad / When they are had / And it's Christmas every day."[153] This spirited number ratcheted up the energy, building to a brisk finish that brought down the curtain.

This change may appear only to alter the tone of the show, emphasizing fast-paced song over avant-garde stagecraft by placing two up-tempo pieces just before the curtain. But in fact, it points to even deeper revisions. "Tomorrow Mountain" was actually a re-composed version of "Inbetween." Strayhorn, as arranger, took the open-ended refrain of "Inbetween" and transferred it to the later song's verse, and took the earlier song's harmonically stable verse and used it as the refrain for "Tomorrow Mountain." Instead of the irregular AAB form of "Inbetween," the new song's chorus now fell into a familiar AABA format, and instead of ending each phrase with the harmonically ambiguous "Inbetween chord," each phrase of "Tomorrow Mountain" ended with a relatively standard half cadences or perfect authentic cadences (see Example 4.1 above). The effect was to stitch together the seams that had been open in the first draft, when the score moved freely between speech and song, between action and reflection. In Abbott's version, the floating, dreamlike musical atmosphere all but disappeared.

Abbott, however, felt that he had not been able to carry out all the revisions he wanted (and he requested that his name be removed from the program).[154] Even as the show edged closer to typical musical comedy, certain experimental elements remained. First, the show retained its broad critique of American life. For example, MacHeath was given a song called "The Hunted":

> No matter where I hid[e]
> I see on every side
> Kids chasing big dogs
> Big dogs chasing little dogs
> Little dogs chasing cats
> A game of cops and robbers
> Is the universal plan
> And top dog in the scramble
> Man chases man.[155]

Second, the reflexive references to genre remained in the script. In the final moments of the production, the hooded and shackled character of MacHeath took his place center stage in an electric chair. He gave no speech, and when the executioner threw the switch, the jail plunged into darkness. Suddenly a carnivalesque flash burst forth from the chair, and the stage lights returned to reveal the once-somber cell festooned in colorful bunting. In the chair sat, not MacHeath's corpse, but the show's narrator. "I can't go bumping off the hero," he told the audience, "not in a musical comedy." "Who is he, Daddy?" asked one of the witnesses. "That's the symbolism. That's the highbrow stuff. . . it gives meaning, or something," replied the magistrate, who then turned to the audience and said, "Get this—this is the novel twist!" The narrator suddenly ripped off a mask to reveal that he was, in fact, MacHeath all along. "It's ridiculous!" objected the magistrate. "But it's a happy ending," MacHeath retorted, and closed the evening by leading the cast in the high-spirited finale.[156]

Finally, although the production team added "Tomorrow Mountain" to the show, they never removed the song it had been based upon, "Inbetween." According to a running order that was typed up on January 5, 1947 (almost two weeks after the show's opening), the song was still performed before the curtain rose, leading Atkinson to grumble in the *New York Times* that the show "was cursed with a prologue."[157] This suggests two things: first, that vestiges of the original, unusual harmonic approach that Ellington seems to have planned for the production remained in its premiere; second, that both a popular-song version and a more experimental version of the same background material appeared in the score. Blending the experimental with the popular in this way suggested that the show remained middlebrow, perhaps even despite itself.

Satire and Burlesque: The Reception of *Beggar's Holiday*

Mixed reviews are hardly rare in the annals of Broadway, but *Beggar's Holiday* elicited an unusually divided response. For every critic who complained that the writing "stumbles when it begins to take itself seriously,"[158] another argued that the writers "seemed afraid to take themselves seriously";[159] for every critic who complained, "it does not add up to a successfully integrated musical comedy, operetta or music-drama,"[160] another argued that the "work [was] an integrated affair, rather than a series of musical numbers hopefully offered for the juke box trade";[161] for every critic who complained about "the generally low level of the musical,"[162] another argued that "occasionally the lyrics try too hard and become too clever";[163] for every critic who complained that *Beggar's Holiday* and Gay's original "have no more than a nose-thumbing acquaintance,"[164] another argued that the musical "is at its best when farthest from its source, when it is a matter of pure 20th-century jazz and jive."[165]

Beneath this surface disagreement lay a recurring concern about genre, specifically about whether this show was best categorized as satire (a serious-minded show that skewered society's vices, usually with humor) or burlesque (entertainment which lampooned other shows, in this case Gay's *Beggar's Opera*).[166] Critic Elliott Norton laid out the terms of the discussion in his review of *Beggar's Holiday*, which he wrote after seeing its out-of-town tryout:

> Where John Gay found fun by deriding the corruption of the courts and rulers of his time, the present librettist, John Latouche, seems to be jeering only at his own story. Let him do so, if he likes, providing it is funny. But what reason is there for using the ancient work as the basis unless he finds some parallel to shoot at? Or is this burlesque instead of mere satire?[167]

Norton's question of genre (burlesque or satire) breaks down into two separate points of confusion. First, was this show meant to be interpreted politically? The sheer fact that *Beggar's Holiday* was based on a satire suggested the answer should have been yes, but because the creative team had intentionally dodged any direct references to specific politicians, and because they had opted instead for a broad swipe at American society, typical modes of reading satire seemed unavailable to Norton. Second, was this show intended to be a serious-minded work of art, or was it mere popular musical comedy? The phrase "jeering only at his own story" suggests that he may have found the self-referential dialogue about the show's genre ("I can't go bumping off the hero, not in a musical comedy," and other such lines) to have scrambled categories enough to make it unclear whether this show was a highbrow satire or a pop culture gangster potboiler. Such confusion followed the show as it finished its out-of-town tryouts and opened on Broadway. After the New York premiere, for example, Richard Watts wrote in the *Post*, it "never quite makes up its mind whether to be social satire, melodramatic burlesque or just plain musical extravaganza, and while such an objection may seem academic it is justified by the confusion of treatment displayed in the show."[168]

Distinguishing between these categories was not merely a fusty terminological issue. For these critics, genres suggested more than a set of normative stylistic traits for a group of similarly classified works. More fundamentally, these labels also carried with them a repertoire of interpretive strategies, which delimited the kinds of readings or questions that would be appropriate from the kinds that would seem out of bounds. Because *Beggar's Holiday* was so unconventional, these critical concepts—which in the normal course of a review were typically automatic, bedrock—seemed suddenly up in the air.

Some critics cleaved to their interpretive norms in the breach. While they acknowledged that *Beggar's Holiday* broached serious social commentary, they also refused to engage with it on principle because, they argued, popular culture precluded such interpretation a priori. "Maybe there are morals or messages," wrote one critic, "but if there are they're kept hidden under a great deal of music with the unmistakable stamp of the one and only Duke Ellington."[169] An even stronger stance came from Robert Garland in the *New York Journal American*. He correctly surmised (probably from pre-premiere theater gossip columns) that the show had changed drastically between its more avant-garde early drafts and its final version, and he assumed that in this process, Broadway song-and-dance had essentially replaced the high-minded commentary:

> If, at the Broadway Theatre, *Beggar's Holiday* had the courage of its unorthodox convictions, today's would be a different story. Let no one tell you that the John Latouche-Duke Ellington revamping of the John Gay ballad opera didn't start out to be one thing and end up by being another. Somewhere along the way, the song-and-dance play had its fearlessness removed . . . between the first act and the second, the conscience which makes cowards of most of us sets in. Satire turns to slapstick.[170]

Critic Eric Bentley (introduced in Chapter 2 and Chapter 3) also ascertained that the show had changed between the first draft and the final version, and like Garland he assumed that as the show was being revised, entertainment had shouldered out highbrow art:

> I gather that Mr. Latouche began with an intelligent musical satire based on John Gay's 'Beggar's Opera,' that his overlords thought the job too 'highbrow,' and called in George Abbot to transform 'art' into 'amusement. The result is incoherence. The play is neither one thing nor another.[171]

No matter how astute Garland and Bentley were in sensing the changes in the show's style, they were fundamentally incorrect about two things. First, Latouche's mix of satire and burlesque was not a blunder that he backed into because his producers forced his hand. In fact, his own copy of *Beggar's Opera* contained an introductory essay written by English literature scholar William Eben Shultz in 1923, and in it he underlined the following passage:

> If satire and burlesque were absent, the play, with its disreputable characters, might indeed be revolting. With both of these agencies present, it becomes picturesque and even attractive. The burlesque is not broadly comic; it is intellectual, and elusive without proper understanding.[172]

Second, popular culture had never been a *substitute* for high-minded political work; it had always been intended as *part* of its broadside against American values, a mechanism for capturing the modern mood and communicating directly to a modern Broadway audience. Yet these critics were unable or unwilling (or both) to read *Beggar's Holiday* in the way the authors intended because, for them, serious art and popular culture were incompatible institutions, and their combination could only lead to (Bentley's word) "incoherence."

Yet there also existed an equally strong middlebrow response to *Beggar's Holiday*, which, at a basic level, did not hold satire and burlesque to be as incompatible as Bentley, Garland, Norton, and others were suggesting. Atkinson, for example, began his review in the *New York Times* by doing what others had done in the wave of post-*Oklahoma!* shows: patrolling the production to test whether serious theater and popular musical comedy were balanced enough to allow both to shine. His language was slightly different from others'. Roughly, what others had described as a mix of "satire" and "burlesque," Atkinson described as a mix of "prestige" and "entertainment." Atkinson's verdict was mixed. On the one hand, he held no affection for Gay's *Beggar's Opera*, which, he claimed, "has always had more prestige than entertainment," and he complained that certain components of *Beggar's Holiday* were likewise overly concerned with prestige. The script, for example, "never quite breaks through the restraints of a sophisticated attitude toward music and showmanship."[173] Yet he also argued that other parts of the show wallowed in puerile "entertainment," especially comedian "Zero Mostel's grotesque and sweaty posturing."[174]

Nevertheless, he believed that, on the other hand, the show did strike a successful balance, largely because of Ellington's score. On the "prestige" side, Atkinson remarked how well "composed" the piece was. ("The word 'composed' is used here advisedly," he emphasized.) As a sign of careful planning, he noted that, despite the score's variety of material ("wry romances, a sardonic lullaby, a good hurdy-gurdy number, a rollicking melody that lets go expansively"), it nevertheless sustained a consistent modern, jazzy, urban mood "without altering the basic style." "No conventional composer," Atkinson wrote, "he has not written a pattern of song hits to be lifted out of their context, but rather an integral musical composition that carries the old Gay picaresque yarn through its dark modern setting."[175] Hand in hand with careful composition came what he called "exuberance": "Given a literary theme steeped in evil, Mr. Ellington has expressed it in febrile music that is more dramatic than anything John Gay wrote and that gives 'Beggar's Holiday' the rhythm of a wild and sinister carnival for a thieves' market."[176] As Atkinson did with so many other middlebrow musicals featured earlier in this book, he praised the show both in terms of its careful compositional planning (emblematic of its highbrow rigor) and in terms of its entertainment value (emblematic of its popular appeal).

Others agreed with Atkinson that *Beggar's Holiday* was middlebrow. This kind of critique appeared especially clearly in the Black press, where reviewers saw the show as both an artistic success and civic triumph. Broadway historian Allen Woll described two general trends that underlay these reviews: First, by the late 1940s, racially integrated shows on Broadway had become increasingly normal, and Black actors became employed in major Broadway shows to a degree unknown in recent years.[177] (This trend would reverse starting in the early 1950s, but this later phase lies beyond the scope of this book.) Second, these musicals (unlike Black musicals from earlier in the century) were almost always written and produced by white people, who used them to explore their conceptions of Black life.[178] Therefore, among the various journalists, watchdog agencies, and appointed commissions who investigated such matters at the time, the main civil-rights issues facing the New York stage tended to be, first, ensuring that Black artists be employed in jobs of high quality (especially when compared to their white colleagues), and second, exorcising belittling, *Amos 'n' Andy*-style stereotypes from the airwaves and the stage.[179] For many reviewers, the fact that *Beggar's Holiday* was mounted by an interracial team, that it offered both leading and supporting parts to Black actors, that it traded in both literary classics and popular music, and that it cast Black performers in both serious and comic roles, made it a landmark.[180] The *New York Amsterdam News*, for example, noted that the show "presents Negro and white performers in a stage relationship quite different from anything usually seen here and abouts, and does this so well that no raised eyebrows were permitted to remain so too long."[181] And according to Richard Dier in the Baltimore *Afro-American*, "You need go no further for proof that colored actors and actresses, if given roles on par with whites without racial identification, can handle them just as capably and effectively than in the gay and tuneful modern version of *Beggar's Holiday*."[182]

Atkinson agreed, but he pursued this point to different ends. For him, this show served an important civil-rights function, which became clearest three months later in his review of a different production. The play was *Tin Top Valley* by Walter Carrol and it was produced by the American Negro Theater. It told the story of a fraught (and ultimately deadly) friendship between a poor white boy and poor Black boy. Atkinson found the production dull, simplistic, and difficult to hear. This was doubly disappointing to him in the contemporary theatrical climate. "Broadway and Hollywood are constantly criticized for typing Negro actors as entertainers," he wrote, frustrated that this play did not offer Black actors a better opportunity to display their talents in serious drama. He continued:

> But this is a production of the American Negro Theatre, which is regarded as one of the most progressive in Harlem. If it cannot infuse vitality into an ordinary drama about common people, there is not much point in looking down on such exuberant, racy entertainment as the Negro parts of "Beggar's Holiday." The "Beggar's" culture may be low, but at least it moves and it makes sounds that can be heard in a public theatre.[183]

Behind this statement lay Atkinson's conviction, described in Chapter 2, that the purpose of theater was to draw the audience out of their individuated lives into shared, mutually respectful society. Anything that alienated spectators—from divisive politics to poor craftsmanship—made this impossible.[184] In his view, the sheer entertainment value of *Beggar's Holiday* made it more useful to the cause of Black performers than *Tin Top Valley*, no matter how serious, up-to-date, or politically righteous the latter may have been. *Beggar's Holiday*, he argued, encouraged multiracial audiences and creators to enter into the same community based on mutual enthusiasm for the talents of its performers and creators. This is to say that, according to Atkinson, not only its style but also its cultural effects were middlebrow.

Plucking out individual voices from the vast chorus of critics who responded to *Beggar's Holiday* is not exactly the point here. Critical opinion ran the gamut from praise to pan, and no single voice can be said to represent some consensus about the show that never actually existed. Neither is the point, even after having lavished so much attention on *Beggar's Holiday* in this chapter, to claim a broader influence for this musical in the history of American culture that the evidence cannot bear, no matter how intrinsically interesting the show may have been. After all, *Beggar's Holiday* ultimately faded into relative obscurity shortly after its brief post-Broadway engagement at Chicago's Shubert Theater in mid-April 1947, and it inspired no compositional imitators in the way, say, *Oklahoma!* had done. Instead, its historiographical interest lies elsewhere. Despite the critical confusion surrounding it, despite its oddball status, it struck many at the time as a watershed, an early example of a broader revolution taking place on the New York stage. It stood alongside a clutch of shows that represented an alternative mood toward political theater, one that embraced high art, folk art, and popular culture to draw together audiences into a mutually respectful conversation about the controversial problems facing modern American society. In the decades that followed, as the avant-garde was repudiating mainstream theatrical traditions in the name of political progress, Ellington and Latouche never quite disavowed mainstream Broadway norms in their later works. Likewise, in the 1950s and 1960s, as political music increasingly turned away from pop culture toward folk music, gospel music, and bebop (all music advocated by Hammond), Ellington remained firmly committed to the political possibilities of the American hit parade, convinced that the middlebrow language of communal spirit, group psychology, community tradition, high ideals, and civic enthusiasm could be a valuable tool in the struggle for civil rights.[185]

Equally important to the show's legacy is the critical disagreement that surrounded its premiere. Such confusion, similar to the kind that greeted *Beggar's Holiday*, also continued to follow Ellington. His middlebrow approach struck many in the civil rights movement as overly conciliatory, and it would remain controversial long after *Beggar's Holiday* closed. English scholar Julius Fleming has noted that Ellington would continue to disavow divisive "politics" in favor of "social significance" decades later, at the tensest moments of the civil rights movement, much to the consternation of his colleagues.[186] Later still, Ellington's own son would look back and note this as a general trend in his father's later works—one that he regretted: "To my mind, if Pop was ever wrong it was on occasions when he let the artistic character of his works obscure the statement being made, blunting its effect on the audience. *Beggar's Holiday* was a case in point."[187] Regardless of whether one agrees with Ellington *fils*, the legacy of *Beggar's Holiday* lies partially in that note of regret: After the show faded into obscurity, the middlebrow terms that informed the show's writing, composition, and criticism remained central to cultural and social debate. *Beggar's Holiday* is merely one example of art that attempted to level social critique in middlebrow terms, that is, in a manner that would encourage group reflection while still drawing audiences together into a unified society, even at moments in American history when such gestures struck many as naive or counterproductive—moments such as the hottest points of the civil rights era. Although the show was undeniably unusual, it was hardly alone.

5

"A More Human Development"

Kurt Weill's *Street Scene* (1947) and the Integrated Musical

Kurt Weill emigrated to the United States in 1935 and immediately embarked upon a project of self-fashioning, which involved both adapting his previous practices to the New York theater and convincing its major producers that his experience in Germany would be valuable to them. In Berlin he had established himself, on the one hand, as an inheritor of the German high-art tradition in opera, and throughout his life he would insist that he was working within this lineage, exploring its inherited "form problems" as a source of musical and dramatic insight.[1] On the other hand, he had also established himself as one of that tradition's foremost skeptics. From his early encounter with the writings of French philosopher and novelist Romain Rolland, Weill had railed against what he had called the "lies, against the hyperemotionality of German music, even in Bach, Wagner, and the rest,"[2] preferring instead music that spoke more directly to contemporary audiences in a style that drew from the trends of the present day. Reconciling these seemingly incompatible positions between high art and popular culture had given Weill's work its striking cast, at least in part: At the height of his renown in Germany, philosopher Theodor Adorno had described his music as "revealing cracks in the social totality . . . without giving them the benefit [of the illusion] of aesthetic totality" by "avail[ing] itself partly of the style of expression of nineteenth-century bourgeois music and partly of present-day consumer music."[3]

Nazism disrupted all of this. Uprooted to New York, Weill began the delicate cultural negotiations necessary to forge a career in his new home. At the most fundamental level, he never abandoned the project he had begun in Berlin: In interviews and published essays, he continued to embrace the idealist tradition, burnishing his high-art bona fides as an opera composer, while at the same time casting himself as a maverick who embraced the accessibility of popular music. In 1936, for example, shortly after he arrived in the United States, he gave a lecture to the Group Theater:

> I feel that I can here at last continue what I have built up in Europe, that I can bring to you my experiences and be certain that you will use them in the right way, and that your experiences will be helpful to me in my efforts towards the goal which I have set for me since the beginning of my career: the creation of a musical theatre for our time.[4]

Or, as he described it in an article he published less than a year later, "the building of a new (or the rebuilding of a classical) form."[5] Yet if Weill were to continue this work in the United States, he would have to convince potential collaborators that he was no mere parvenu in the New York theater, but rather that he was an insider, capable of writing American-style popular music that would appeal to a broad, but local, public. Behind the scenes, his position within the cutthroat, high-stakes, hit-tune marketplace required constant supervision and maintenance, and his correspondence attests to how assiduously he nurtured connections, royalties, collaborations, funding, contracts, and critics, as well as his emphatically American persona.[6] His ultimate success in this is a matter of record; judging by how frequently his music graced the charts, he became one of the most popular Broadway composers of the late 1930s and 1940s.

Equally important to Weill, however, was to convince his new colleagues that the operatic component of his project would seem relevant to New York audiences, where so-called classical music had a more limited appeal and was still dominated by European imports. Toward this end, he repeatedly made the argument that musical theater and opera were two sides of the same dramaturgical coin. "If we substitute the term 'music theatre' [for opera], the possibilities for development here, in a country not burdened with an opera tradition, become much clearer," he wrote in one of his earliest American articles, insinuating that the Broadway musical could be as artistically significant as old-world opera without giving up its identity as popular entertainment.[7]

This ongoing project put him in direct competition with Richard Rodgers.[8] In the heady years following the premiere of *Oklahoma!*, reviewers increasingly claimed that Rodgers's music was in dialogue with an international operatic tradition, even if that dialogue was carried out in a distinctly American dialect (described in Chapter 3). Such claims reached a new level of intensity after Rodgers and Hammerstein's *Carousel* premiered to rave reviews in 1945. Obviously rankled that the press was treating Rodgers as a pioneer (and still stinging from the negative reviews of his most recent show, *Firebrand of Florence*), Weill wrote a now famous letter to his wife, actress Lotte Lenya, in May 1945:

> So Rodgers "is defining a new directive for musical comedy." I had always thought I've been doing that—but I must have been mistaken. Rodgers certainly has won the first round in that race between him and me. But I suppose there will be a second and a third round.[9]

The competition's next round would begin in earnest later that summer when Weill started work on *Street Scene*. As Weill himself would later attest, and as this chapter will demonstrate, this show would mark an important watershed in his career: In this context, partially in response to Rodgers, Weill would reconceive the compositional methods he had originally developed among the Berlin avant-garde for the postwar, post-*Oklahoma!*, middlebrow musical.

By this point, "integration" had become the conceptual foundation for Rodgers's reputation as an innovator, and once *Carousel* opened, Weill fixated on the term in public and private, a signal that he was confronting Rodgers on his own turf. Weill used the word in two closely related ways, both of which implicated Rodgers's work (as described in Chapter 3).[10] First, "integration" held formal implications for him: About a year before *Street Scene* premiered, Weill wrote to the original director of *Oklahoma!* asking him to take part in the developing show. "I know you have always been interested in this form of musical theatre, where music and drama are completely *integrated*," by which he meant a show where "the dialogue will be spoken, but underscored, so that the audience should never know where the dialogue ends and the song starts."[11] Second, Weill almost always coupled his discussion of form with references to different genres, different styles, different venues, all of which would situate his music conceptually between opera and Broadway. In an article for the *New York Times*, for example, he wrote that the integrated form "allows [the composer] to use a great variety of musical idioms, to write music that is both serious and light, operatic and popular, emotional and sophisticated, orchestral and vocal."[12]

Even though the immediate topic of each of these passages was ostensibly the Broadway musical, Weill still framed the broad project as one with European roots. Just before *Street Scene* opened, for example, he wrote in the *New York Times* that the music of George Gershwin (and tellingly, not Rodgers) had convinced him that "the American theatre was already on the way to the more integrated form of musical that we had begun to attempt in Europe," and that *Street Scene* was the culmination of this work.[13] It was here where Weill could outdo Rodgers: Whereas Rodgers's musicals had been only indirectly "operatic," Weill could actually claim direct experience in the European "grand opera" tradition.[14] Thus in the days before *Street Scene* premiered, Weill once again touted his European operatic pedigree in public, writing in the *New York Times* that he "start[ed] out as a composer of grand opera" but also that he "soon discovered the limitations" of that genre and instead devoted his energies to "other fields of musical theater," namely the American musical.[15] He emphasized that the show was not a "dramatic musical" (despite its billing); it was, in fact, a "Broadway opera." Weill seemed poised to attempt what *Oklahoma!* had not: If *Oklahoma!* had mixed folk art and popular culture toward new expressive ends, *Street Scene* would blend sounds and styles that were drawn from the European grand opera tradition with American popular music. If, as described in Chapter 3, *Oklahoma!* was operatic only in an abstract way, *Street Scene* would actually sound operatic. Such claims essentially flipped the script: It was Rodgers, not Weill, who was the outsider in this arena.

More was at stake here than a private competition about who could rightly lay claim to the "integrated" form. (In fact, Rodgers probably knew nothing about this rivalry.) As with *Oklahoma!*, assertions of a more "serious" form came hand in hand with assertions of a more "serious" purpose. In the surviving correspondence and notes for *Street Scene*, this serious purpose was the expression of what Weill and his collaborators called the show's "philosophy," which they hoped would make this show relevant to postwar American society. The show's philosophy amounted to a broadly optimistic feeling about the power of American democracy to foster a more peaceful, more prosperous, more loving world, or, as the group of collaborators described it, optimism for the American "melting pot." As a self-standing group of concepts, this philosophy was as sincere as it was blunt. But subtlety (or lack thereof) was beside the point—in fact, its forceful simplicity was one of its virtues. More important was its powerful effect on audiences. As this chapter will demonstrate, Weill and his team had been developing strategies for using musical theater to draw together what they perceived to be a factionalized society into a common community, linked by common values and common feeling.

Such a goal bears witness to Weill's attempts to adapt to the post-*Oklahoma!* middlebrow musical. In part, it was a natural fit. What had gradually emerged as the central values of these musicals during the 1940s aligned with many cultural commitments Weill had already made while working in Germany. First, his early, enduring fondness for Romain Rolland, for example, echoed similar enthusiasms from critics cited in earlier chapters, especially *New York Times* critics Olin Downes and Brooks Atkinson (both of whom, in fact, would become friends with Weill; Downes would also collaborate with Weill on the folk opera *Down in the Valley*). Inspired by Rolland, Weill had construed nineteenth-century German classical music to be a "coterie [*gesellschaftlichen*] art," invested more in obscure experimentation and overheated emotionalism than in communicating with its audiences. He had argued instead that opera should "turn toward the interests of the broader public,"[16] that it should become a *gemeinschaftsbildenden* ("socially formative") art.[17] Second, scholars have long noted the nuanced, provocative ways that Weill had created what he had called in 1926 a "Zwischengattung," a "mixed genre" that incorporated both art music and popular music to make opera seem relevant to a broader European public.[18] Similar experiments (albeit with different individualized solutions in each production) would find an enthusiastic reception in New York after the premiere of *Street Scene* among people who had already generally embraced the high-low mixtures of the middlebrow musical. All of this—the goals of producing civic-minded, community-building art that was situated between high and low culture—resonated with his middlebrow contemporaries.

Yet where Weill differed from his middlebrow counterparts was just as important as where he aligned with them. As this chapter will demonstrate, Weill envisioned *Street Scene* not just as a blend between grand-opera style and the popular Broadway musical, not just as a way to explore ever more innovative ways to blend scene and score, not just as a way to express political beliefs about postwar American society (all of which have been discussed at length in earlier scholarship), but also as an experiment in the *function* of a musical: a new way of thinking about how a show could interact with its audiences, about what kind of effect it could have on society—all in ways that diverged from the *Oklahoma!* exemplar. Surviving correspondence and notes from the production detail the degree to which Weill attempted to calibrate this show to postwar New York. Weill and his collaborators situated this production on the wavering line between civics and politics, between the kinds of statements that could engender broad community spirit among the show's spectators, and the kinds of statements that could encourage audiences to take concrete action on behalf of some segment of broader society.[19] As described in Chapter 2 and Chapter 4, critics such as Brooks Atkinson had regarded overtly political statements as dangerous because they risked alienating members of the audience who either disagreed or simply would not countenance any preaching from the musical-comedy stage. Yet Weill and his creative team approached such topics differently, seeking to inspire civic feeling so overwhelming that in turn it could have an indirect political outcome: that it would make audiences more attuned to poverty, more sympathetic to those who were suffering—a kind of engagement with contemporary life that *Oklahoma!* had not attempted. Perhaps counterintuitively, the grand opera tradition proved to be an important tool for Weill in realizing these goals. As described below, in the years leading up to *Street Scene*, Weill had experimented with alluding to different kinds of European operatic idioms in his works for Broadway. By the time he wrote this show, European-style opera had become a key tool for Weill: an emotional intensifier, an idiom that ennobled the characters onstage, that universalized them. Weill and his collaborators' work consisted of calibrating the smallest details of their show—the forms of songs, the placement of lines, the orchestration, the design, and the staging—to achieve this intense emotional effect, all in hopes of bridging the gap between the Broadway stage and the realities of postwar American life, thereby endowing Broadway with new relevance in shaping postwar New York.

From Operetta to Broadway Opera: Weill and the Light Opera Boom

"It's my opinion that we can and will develop a musical-dramatic form in this country, but I don't think it will be called 'opera,' or that it will grow out of the opera which has become a thing separate from the commercial theater, dependent upon other means than box-office appeal for its continuance," Weill said in early 1940.[20] Less than four years later, however, his opinion had changed. He wrote to his wife in July 1944: "It looks more and more as if [*The Firebrand of Florence*] might become what you and I have been waiting for: my first Broadway Opera."[21] Ultimately the production (billed as "a musical in two acts") was almost universally recognized by critics as an operetta, not as an opera. But even if *The Firebrand of Florence* did not realize Weill's ambitions to write Broadway opera, it fostered an important shift in his thinking: the idea that Broadway had become hospitable to European-style opera.[22] For Weill, the conceptual road to Broadway opera and *Street Scene* traveled, at least in part, through operetta.

Early in his career, Weill, like many others of his generation, had considered "opera" and "operetta" to be distinct genres. The former belonged to high art: resistant to the marketplace, grand (or grandiose) in scope, often serious in pretention, self-consciously artistic, taking part in a long line of serious-minded forebears. The latter belonged to popular culture: commercially viable, often satirical, self-consciously accessible, and entertaining. Thus, in his early articles Weill had described operetta as a genre of "apparent secondary importance" ("äußerer Zweitrangigkeit"), as "dusty" ("verstaubt"), as music of a bygone era ("der gestrigen oder vorgestrigen Generation").[23] Yet as Weill began to solidify his iconoclastic stance against the German high-art tradition, his attitude toward operetta changed. In part, his newfound affection for operettas by the French Jacques Offenbach and the Austrian Johann Strauss II may have been part of a rebellious cosmopolitanism, especially during an era marked by intense German cultural nationalism.[24] But in addition, Weill also began to imbue operetta with some of the conceptual heft typically reserved for high-art music. In 1925, for example, he wrote an article arguing that operetta would be perfectly at home on radio programs that were otherwise devoted to classical music (as much a sign of his respect for operetta as it was a sign of his frustration with wide swaths of the German classical-music tradition).[25] In 1926 he maintained that the zany parody of Offenbach's operettas masked "serious, philosophically-based content" ("ernste, philosophisch begründete Inhalte"), amounting to "serious parody" that placed Offenbach among the ranks of other revered satirists such as Miguel de Cervantes and Charlie Chaplin.[26]

During the mid-1920s, Weill also came to find operetta increasingly relevant to present-day society, despite its age. "Offenbach's witty banter can be interpreted in many ways," he wrote in 1925. "It need not be limited to his time; it can apply to certain ridiculous things in our day."[27] But there also emerged in his writing a sense that operetta's relevance could be more abstract, more idealist. "In terms of content, [Strauss's operetta] scarcely says anything to us anymore, contentwise; it is based on moral concepts of the 80s and therefore strikes us as naïve and childish," Weill wrote in 1925. "And yet, no sooner have the first tones of the overture sounded than we are put under a spell. Something reverberates in this music that springs from the realm of the highest art, something human, the vibration of a wide, world-encompassing soul."[28] By collapsing the distance between opera and operetta, Weill was already assuming the maverick pose that would make him famous in his collaboration with Brecht a few years later. Yet there was an important distinction: Broadly speaking, with Brecht, Weill would effectively evacuate the genre of opera of its metaphysical pretensions by undercutting it with a quirky, jazz-inspired popular idiom; here, however, Weill imbued popular operetta with idealist qualities that had typically been reserved for classical music. He would eventually return to this second strategy, and it would become especially important to him in the mid-1940s after he had moved to the United States.

Finally, on a practical level, operetta had helped Weill to develop the concrete, compositional terms of his rebellion against the German highbrow tradition, which he first explored in Ferruccio Busoni's masterclasses between 1921 to 1924. For Busoni, rejecting the "profundity," the "personal feeling and metaphysics"[29] of late nineteenth-century German art music had implied "the definitive farewell to thematicism and the reclamation of melody,"[30] an attitude he often described as "italianità" or "New Classicality."[31] More specifically, Busoni believed that returning to clearly projected melodies could scrub the classical tradition of its obscure, experimental excrescences, revealing more primordial forms of "Urmusik" underneath. Such terminology would appear in Weill's writings for decades ("Urform," "Urtyp," or, after he moved to the United States, fundamental "form-problems").[32] According to musicologist Tamara Levitz, Busoni also believed that "[t]he melodic germ expressed an eternal and spiritual truth, in the way Luther's word expressed God's will in Protestant Church music."[33] Such lofty language also crept into Weill's writing about Johann Strauss. He marveled at Strauss's "melodies of . . . intensity" and "voice leading that we only find in the most brilliant inspirations of the greatest musicians," which elevated "his will to dance" to "a creative force (Schöpferkraft)."[34] So strong was Weill's appreciation for operetta that in 1928, when a German newspaper offered to write a feature about him with the title "Weill als Humperdinck" (his former teacher, a famous Wagnerian), Weill rejected it and suggested an alternative: "Von Offenbach zu Weill."[35]

Weill finally embarked on his own operetta, *Der Kuhhandel* (usually translated as *Kingdom for a Cow*), in February 1934.[36] In April of that year, he described this project as "far away from that Viennese operetta trash," but also, in a different letter a few days later, wrote that this piece "finally picks up again on the best tradition of operetta, which had been buried for decades."[37]

Importantly, Weill was distinguishing between two kinds of operetta, aligning himself with what he called "klassicher Operettenmeister" (Johann Strauss, Franz von Suppé, Jacques Offenbach, Arthur Sullivan, and others who rose to prominence in the 1870s and 1880s) and distancing himself from "Viennese Operette" (Leo Fall, Franz Lehár, Oscar Straus, and others who dominated musical theater around the turn of the twentieth century).[38] The two traditions differed in attitude. "Classic operetta" (which later scholars have often referred to as "Golden Age" operetta) tended to be satirical, zany; "Viennese operetta" (which later scholars have tended to call "Silver Age" operetta) tended to be sentimental, nostalgic.[39] *Der Kuhhandel* falls squarely into the first type. Its score is a collection of popular tunes: lullabies, anthems, marches, and, in place of Offenbach's cancans or Strauss's waltzes, calypso. It tells the story of a humble Caribbean couple, Juan and Juanita, whose cow is confiscated by their authoritarian government to pay a war tax. When Juan sets off to retrieve his cow, he inadvertently becomes embroiled in a coup, and, after crossing a populist dictator, winds up before a firing squad. Juan ultimately prevails when all of the guns malfunction at once; a wedding quickly ensues, and the curtain falls on a frenzied rejoicing worthy of Offenbach's zaniest ensemble finales.

The circumstances surrounding the production of *Der Kuhhandel* were chaotic, and despite high hopes, the production was largely a critical and financial failure. It remained a source of personal disappointment for Weill.[40] Yet he did not abandon operetta. On the contrary, operetta remained a strong conceptual grounding point for his work. Just over three months after the premiere of *Der Kuhhandel*, Weill moved to New York, where he embarked on his career in the American musical theater. As he jockeyed for contracts in the New York theater scene, he argued to his potential collaborators that the experiments he began in Germany to build a serious, relevant, and yet popular musical theater could continue in the United States, and that operetta could provide the ideal model. "Gilbert and Sullivan in England, Offenbach in Paris, and Johann Strauss in Vienna have proved that a musical theatre culture of high merit can arise from the field of light music," he wrote in an article from 1937.[41]

If Weill's earlier efforts in operetta had tended toward Offenbachian satire, during the early 1940s he would turn toward sumptuousness, old-world nostalgia, and emotional intensity. Roughly put, Weill's journey from his first operetta, *Kingdom for a Cow* (1935), to his second operetta, *Firebrand of Florence* (1945), also brought him from Offenbach to Lehár, from satire to sentiment, from "Classic operetta" to "Viennese operetta." This was part of a broader trend in Weill's work. With Bertolt Brecht, Weill had famously eyed emotional manipulation suspiciously. He maintained, for example, that his ideal audience had comprised thinkers, not feelers, the type of person "who, since he really wants to think, perceives any demand on his pleasure centers [*Genussnerven*] as an annoyance."[42] Satirical operetta had aligned well with these goals, encouraging audiences to view the status quo with skepticism. By the time he arrived in the United States, however, Weill had begun to emphasize what he called a "human" element: "Music can only express human sentiments," he wrote; "I write to express human emotions, solely."[43] In a letter that Weill would write to friends and former collaborators about six months before *Street Scene* premiered on Broadway, he would say, "I almost never see Brecht. He is still the old egomaniac and obsessed with his idiotic old theories, without any sign of a more human development," confirming that he had traveled a long conceptual distance from his earlier work.[44] In 1941, summing up his ideas, he told an interviewer that "music has a more binding, uniting power than the spoken or written word because it appeals to the common emotions of the people—and that's what this country needs at this moment."[45]

For these newer goals, the sentimentality and high-flown emotions of Viennese operetta would come to seem more appropriate. In part, this was also because Broadway became newly hospitable to such works in the early 1940s. Decades earlier, operetta had represented a popular rebellion against what Americans had loosely called "grand opera" (not to be mistaken for the French genre of the same name), which generally referred to large, imposing works in the art-music tradition. But by the mid-1930s the two genres were merging once again: Romantic operetta increasingly struck critics as just as old-fashioned, old-world, and old-hat as the stuffiest of operas.[46] For its dwindling adherents, this, in fact, was one of the genre's primary virtues. According to operetta composer Rudolph Friml, "When I write music for the theatre ... I like books with charm to them, and charm suggests the old things—the finest things that were done long ago. I like a full-bodied libretto with luscious melody, rousing choruses, and romantic passions."[47] Yet, as Broadway historian Gerald Bordman has shown, once jazz musicals increased in popularity, most critics came to dismiss operetta, to the point that in September 1943, *New York Times* critic Lewis Nichols could proclaim that "operetta and Broadway no longer are marching side by side," and one day later, *PM* critic Louis Kronenberger could quip (with a dig at Friml's

1934 operetta *Music Hath Charms*), "Music Hath Charms, But Its Charms Have Limits."[48]

Two major events upended operetta's otherwise steady decline into irrelevance. First, fueled by a wave of European émigrés, Broadway quite suddenly witnessed what *Time* magazine called in 1942 a "light-opera boom."[49] In part, this was because the Federal Theatre Project and Federal Music Project had taken on the mission of democratizing European musical theater, a mission that included operetta. The goal of bringing operetta to a broader public transferred to the private sector in the early 1940s after Congress shuttered the Federal Projects.[50] After that, there arose a group of producers in the early 1940s who began to mount lavish productions of operettas on Broadway. The most prominent was the New Opera Company. Befitting an organization that arose from the spirit of the Works Progress Administration, it began as an avowedly civic endeavor: first, as an attempt to put unemployed musicians (especially singers) to work and to cultivate their skills so they could compete in a competitive professional marketplace; second, to become an incubator for American composers and singers to develop a specifically American form of opera.[51] In fact, their original goal was to produce European-style grand opera, and they included an updated version of Offenbach's *La vie parisienne* only as a light-hearted closer for their season in the spirit of an encore.[52] Antal Doráti, who conducted the performance in New York, would later write, "so delightedly did the public take to it that we received an offer from a commercial theatre company to buy the production for a Broadway run," which, ultimately, "was ignored by the snobbish Board."[53] Their next season followed a similar pattern. None of the operatic works drew much attention, but their closer, a "lighter work" (which remained unnamed in their initial publicity) once again became so unexpectedly popular that the company extended its run and continued to move it from Broadway theater to Broadway theater for more than a year.[54] The piece was *Die Fledermaus*, renamed *Rosalinda*, and recognizing its success, the New Opera Company quickly followed it with an enthusiastically received revival of Franz Lehár's operetta *The Merry Widow* in 1943. Together, *Rosalinda* and *The Merry Widow* completely recouped the loss of over $260,000 they had incurred with their grand opera productions.[55] They never produced another grand opera again.

"What has been accomplished with a piece which first opened here some thirty-five years ago [i.e., *Die Fledermaus*] is a freshening of pace," wrote critic Howard Barnes.[56] (As *Time* reported, the piece "set its opening-night audience to swaying in their seats, [and] caused at least one white-haired fan, Walter Damrosch, to go shagging down the aisle like a Habsburg jitterbug."[57]) Most reviewers agreed, and they attributed this to the New Opera Company's showmanship: to the choreography (by George Balanchine), the wild costumes (by Walter Florrell), the sets (by Howard Bay), and the conducting (by Erich Korngold). Moreover, in the throes of World War II, old-world nostalgia struck some critics as fashionable, necessary, current.[58] As Robert Bagar put it, "If the present times warrant escapism in the theater, one can think of no lovelier or fuller measure of it than to spend an evening with *Rosalinda* and Johann Strauss."[59] In the wake of these shows appeared a wave of operetta revivals and new works in the operetta style, including *The Student Prince* (1943), *Blossom Time* (1943), *Song of Norway* (1944), *Helen Goes to Troy* (1944), *Polonaise* (1945), and *The Vagabond King* (1945). The overall effect was that operetta, long considered old-fashioned, began to seem like it had a new life, even a new civic purpose.

Weill monitored these developments closely. He found himself involved in no fewer than four potential operetta projects during the spring of 1942, including a sendup of petit bourgeois mores "on the Offenbach line" called *The Tinted Venus* (later to become the musical-comedy spoof of American prudery, *One Touch of Venus*, in 1943), and an adaptation of Ludwig Fulda's 1912 German comedy *Der Seeräuber* for Alfred Lunt and Lynne Fontanne called *The Pirate* (the musical version of which foundered amid contractual and personal disagreements).[60] At the same time, producer Russell Lewis and Oscar-winning actress and singer Grace Moore approached Weill to establish a repertoire theater that would produce opera and operetta for broad, popular audiences. They placed themselves in direct competition with the New Opera Company by planning to revive another Offenbach work, *La belle Hélène*, and they asked Weill to arrange it.[61] Weill turned it down, writing that he had seen the New Opera Company's *La vie parisienne* and was "shocked how stale and how dated the Offenbach music sounded."[62] Undeterred, Lewis tried to interest him in a parallel venture. In August 1942 he and Moore announced in the press that they had approached Kurt Weill to compose a new operetta for them.[63] No contract existed until October 1942, at which point Weill signed on, alongside lyricist Ira Gershwin and librettist Edwin Justus Meyer, to produce an operetta about the seventeenth-century English courtesan Nell Gwynn.[64] According to a page of notes Weill made about the project, they conceived of the project as an Offenbachian commentary on twentieth-century geopolitics: "The theme should be somewhat around: How empires are being made—namely in the bedrooms of the kings. This would have great significance in a time where the whole idea of empires—and the empires themselves are breaking down."[65] The writers tabled the project for most of 1943, each working on separate projects with more pressing deadlines, and when they took it up again in April 1944, Weill described it as "an intimate romantic-satirical operetta for the international market" about the bedroom exploits of Italian painter and sculptor Benvenuto Cellini, an adaptation of Meyer's play *The Firebrand* (1929). The word "romantic" suggested that it may have started conceptually to tilt in the direction of Viennese sentimental operetta, even though it nonetheless remained "satirical."[66]

Yet this started to change in early July 1944. At this point, the *Billboard* Donaldson Awards honored Hammerstein's *Carmen Jones* (1944) with the award for best score, snubbing Weill's *One Touch of Venus* (1943). Adding insult to injury, *Carmen Jones*, a modern adaptation of Georges Bizet's *Carmen* with an all-Black cast, did not even have a newly written score (and indeed, the original production team insisted in the press that any slight changes to the score would "hardly be noticeable," and critics largely described the music as "pure and undefiled").[67] Even more frustrating, the press raved that with this production Hammerstein achieved many of the goals that Weill had long been pursuing. First, they described *Carmen Jones* as a successful blend of opera and Broadway, of high art and popular culture (see Figure 5.1).[68] Second, the press largely agreed that *Carmen Jones* made European opera seem suddenly relevant again. "For years I have thought of that ancient structure on Broadway at 39th St. [the Metropolitan Opera] as a kind of ancestral tomb," wrote socialite and critic Elsa Maxwell. "But now I realize that it is as alive, by comparison, as the Grand Central Station the day before Christmas."[69]

On July 7, days after the award ceremony, Lenya wrote to Weill (in her idiosyncratic English):

> I was so mad, when they gave Carmen Jones the Bilboard award for the best score. Those snobs. Especially what the[y] did with that score. It makes me furious to think, how little they know about you. But maybe after the war you will have a chance to write operas again and then see what will be left of that Hillbilly show 'Oklahoma.' The music sounds dummer and dummer every time I hear it. There is something about tradition and it can't be pound into people. It has to grow t[h]rough centuries.[70]

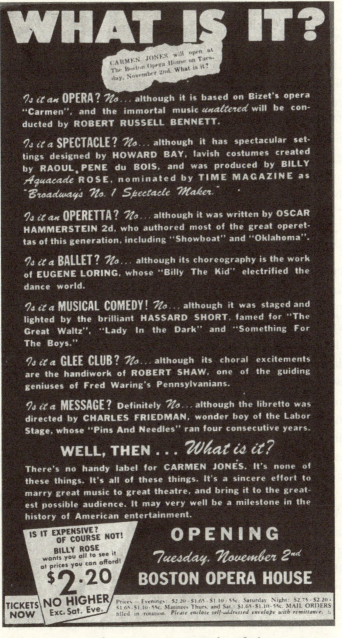

Figure 5.1 Advertisement for *Carmen Jones*, unidentified newspaper. Contained in the show's clippings file at the Billy Rose Theater Collection, New York Public Library, New York, NY.

Mentioning *Oklahoma!* fanned the sense of competition between Weill and Rodgers, and Lenya suggested different strategies Weill might follow to best his rival. She discouraged faux folk in the style of *Oklahoma!* because such tunes were neither authentic nor autochthonous. (Weill apparently disagreed; he had frequently used folk and folk-like tunes in his earlier works, and in 1945 he would compose the first version of his folk opera *Down in the Valley*.[71]) Yet the suggestion about opera did appeal, and in a letter he wrote five days later, he referred to his current project, *Firebrand of Florence*, as "a real Broadway opera." What exactly he meant by opera becomes clear in subsequent letters he wrote to Lenya while he was working on the piece. First, "opera" signified an expanded scope: "The score will have the size of an opera," as he put it.[72] In part, this simply meant that there would be a great deal of music. "It will probably become almost an opera because I hear music almost all the way through, except for the comedy scenes."[73] Second, the term "opera" also linked this score to a tradition of European classical music. Weill told Lenya that his score would have the same "flavor" as *Les Contes d'Hoffmann*[74] and the lush, erotic score of Strauss's *Der Rosenkavalier*;[75] he told her that different scenes drew from sixteenth-century madrigals and Italian folk dances,[76] from tarantellas ("Italian and Spanish at the same time," as Weill described them[77]), from Palestrina.[78] At one point, Lenya compared Gershwin's in-progress lyrics to François Villon and *Don Giovanni*.[79] These far-flung references speak less to any coherent musical idiom than to a general sense that this music would seem broadly European, and not American.

Finally, and closely related, the word "opera" also implied that Weill was composing "without any attempt to write American popular songs," as he explained to his wife in a letter shortly after the Donaldson Awards.[80] This is not to say, however, that he envisioned this show to be anything but lively. After all, he praised his collaborator Gershwin as a good "showman," and he saw this production as "an entirely new combination of first-class writing, music, singing and acting," production values that critics were then associating with the New Opera Company's revivals.[81] But it does represent two bold shifts in Weill's thinking. First, narrowly, if most of the operetta adaptations of the previous seasons had, to some (usually gentle) degree, updated the material for a modern New York audience, the team decided to go in a different direction: "[Ira] says: lets [sic] make this a 'classic,' not a one season show for Broadway but something lasting—and you know that goes down like honey with me," Weill wrote to Lenya.[82] This would suggest that any topical references, any winking toward present-day audiences, any slang (all Gershwin specialties) would be out of keeping with the overall mood. In other words, the team had moved decidedly away from the satirical, Offenbachian style of operetta they had originally envisioned when they started work on this project. Second, more broadly, although Weill had once viewed operetta as a counterpoise to the European high art tradition, he now saw the two as potentially aligned. Put differently, he now sought to smuggle the values and sounds of European-style opera into the Broadway theater via operetta, creating a piece that was lively enough for modern audiences who had been reared in the values of American entertainment, but nonetheless including music that looked back to a long tradition of European classical music. The resulting production had all the outward features of Viennese operetta—the old-world setting, the lush orchestration, the ensemble finales, the large choral scenes, the romantic and comic couples, a score that did not call for belting or crooning, the lavish sets and costumes—but it also had the risqué wit of a Gershwin comedy.

Weill and his collaborators, however, miscalculated. In the end, almost all reviewers praised the show on technical merits but nevertheless found that it "lack[ed] sparkle, drive, or just plain nervous energy," as the *New York Times* review described it; "it is a little like an old-fashioned operetta, slowly paced and ambling."[83] Nevertheless, in the course of working on *Firebrand of Florence*, Weill came to believe that grand, old-world style, emotionally intense European opera could indeed appear on Broadway, even if *Firebrand of Florence* was ultimately unsuccessful. In January 1947, just days before *Street Scene* opened, Weill looked back on the year that *Firebrand of Florence* had premiered and described it as turning point: "Opera was now a popular entertainment, [and] the public had become more interested in singing."[84]

On July 12, 1945, after *Firebrand of Florence* premiered, Weill jotted down prospects for his next work on a piece of scrap paper.[85] Three items—*Don Juan* (which he crossed out), *School for Wives*, and *Blue Danube*—suggest that he may have been interested in writing another European-style comedy or operetta along the lines of *Firebrand of Florence*. Two other items suggest that he was still thinking in civic or outright political terms: "Robeson show," probably referring to *Ulysses Africanus*, a script he had been working on with his former (and future) collaborator, Maxwell Anderson; and "Sezhuan," perhaps referring to Brecht's *Der gute Mensch von Sezuan*, which he had, off and on, considered working on since 1942.[86] Next to this entry, Weill wrote the name "Hughes," implying that the poet may have been on his mind as a possible collaborator. Finally, *Gone with the Wind* and *Farmer Takes a Wife* were also scribbled on the page, and years later, Weill's wife Lotte Lenya would incorrectly recall that *Huckleberry Finn* and *Moby Dick* appeared there as well.[87] They did not, but her recollection may suggest that, in private conversation, Weill was especially keen on Americana. Regardless, all of this would converge in his next project: Americana flavor, politics, Hughes, and—after years of resisting it—grand opera.

"That Means: Not Abstract!!!": Integrating a Philosophy

Although *Firebrand of Florence* had proven unsuccessful with critics, it did convince Weill that the values of European-style grand opera and American-style musical theater were not completely incompatible, or as he put it in 1947, that "the time was ripe for a real Broadway opera."[88] He nonetheless recognized that there were important conceptual differences between the two genres, and much of his work on *Street Scene* would involve trying to reconcile the high-art abstractions of opera and the accessible, informal qualities of the Broadway musical. "The great challenge for me [in *Street Scene*] was to find a form that translated the realism of the plot into music," he wrote to his former collaborator Caspar Neher. "The result is something entirely new and probably the most 'modern' form of musical theater, since it applies the technique of opera without ever falling into the artificiality [*Unnatürlichkeit*] of opera."[89] (Elsewhere he stated the problem more succinctly: "Nobody is going to want to hear 'I'll have a cup of coffee' sung."[90])

Weill had long explored the productive tension between such slippery concepts as "realism" and "artificiality," as well as other similarly structured binaries: "photographic representation" and "esotericism," "truth" and "poetry," "dramatic action" and "philosophy," and so on.[91] In his pioneering study of Weill, musicologist Stephen Hinton has argued that such pairings represent a recurring structural device in Weill's productions. He termed this feature "dramaturgical counterpoint," a technique that places the "real" (and related concepts) in productive tension with the "artificial" (and related concepts) and establishes musical analogues for each.[92] Shortly after arriving in New York, Weill described the general idea. He wrote, "the stage has a reason for existence today only if it aspires to a rarer level of truth, only if it restores poetry," and in language that preceded Hammerstein's theory of "heightened realism" (described in Chapter 3) by about six years, Weill wrote that music "projects the actions of the play to a different and higher level; over a stretch of scenes it provides a commentary on the action from a human, universal point of view; it lifts the characters out of the frame of the play and makes them express, directly or indirectly, the philosophy of the author."[93] In this case, Weill conceived of the music in his works as having two related functions: first, as cordoning off some portions of the drama from others, here creating a contrast between sections that are accompanied and those that are not; second, as suggesting to audiences that a change in music should entail a concomitant change of interpretive mode. He implied that whatever words or action accompanied the musical sections of the work were engaging in a different kind of meaning-making from the non-musicalized parts of the work: the one was "philosophical," the other was "realistic." And although in each subsequent production Weill would devise new conceptual, musical, and interpretive binaries, he would nevertheless retain the underlying goal of deploying contrasting musical idioms to toggle between different methods of hermeneutic engagement.

Such contrasting conceptual categories, along with their corresponding musical analogues, were fresh in mind when Weill composed *Street Scene*. Shortly after the show premiered, he wrote an essay describing it as the latest step in an ongoing progress toward Broadway opera. He implied that dramaturgical counterpoint linked each progressive step, including *Street Scene*, no matter how different it sounded from his previous works, no matter that it premiered in New York instead of Berlin:

> In the *Three-Penny Opera*, which was my first musical play, we deliberately stopped the action during the songs which were written to illustrate the "philosophy," the inner meaning of the play. *Mahogany* [i.e., *Aufstieg und Fall der Stadt Mahagonny*] was a sort of "dramatic review" [*sic*], using elements of the theatre from slapstick to opera. *The Silver Lake* was a serious musical which mixed realism and fantasy and used actors together with a singing chorus and a symphonic orchestra. But not until fifteen years later, not until *Street Scene*, did I achieve a real blending of drama and music, in which the singing continues naturally where the speaking stops and the spoken word as well as the dramatic action are embedded in overall musical structure.[94]

Weill emphasized the contrasting musical styles in each of his earlier works (song versus speech, music versus drama, slapstick versus opera, acting versus choral singing), each corresponding to different modes of "realism" ("action" versus "inner meaning," for example). Surviving correspondence reveals that Weill and his collaborators also conceived of *Street Scene* in two distinct levels of reality that corresponded to contrasting musical idioms: on the one hand, the torrid, violent "reality" of the Murrants' story, which ends in a double murder; on the other hand, what they called the play's "philosophy," a message of democratic "brotherhood" expressed in the slice-of-life scenes that surround the main story. In the final score, the former "realistic" level tends to feature music in a grand-opera style with extended arias and arioso passages; the latter "philosophical" level tends to feature folk and popular music in dialogue with standard thirty-two-bar forms.

According to Weill's essay, *Street Scene* differed from his other shows in that it "blended" the two levels of the story instead of juxtaposing them. Whether he was ultimately successful in this has long been a source of scholarly disagreement.[95] Yet, temporarily bracketing off that topic, a more fundamental issue emerges: The very attempt to blend the different levels of his dramaturgical counterpoint speaks to a broader reconsideration of how he was engaging his audiences. In his earlier works with Brecht, Weill had famously sought to dispel emotional identification, and he achieved this by deploying startlingly different kinds of music to jump abruptly from level to level (such as from the diegetic reality of stage action to the discursive reality of metatheatrical commentary delivered directly to the audience); likewise, in *Der Kuhhandel*, Weill had deployed popular tunes in a deeply ironic fashion to encourage audiences to critique the absurd characters onstage as analogues to real-life, present-day, warmongers. But *Street Scene* was designed to "follow the action and the emotional up-and-down" of the script, it "heightened and intensified" the "emotional power of the original play," along the lines of his lush, operetta sentimentality in *Firebrand of Florence*.[96] As will become clear, his goal in *Street Scene* was to deploy the emotional intensity of Viennese-style operetta toward "philosophical" ends: to engender a shared sense of community based on broad feelings of enthusiasm for abstract concepts of democratic "brotherhood."

Such accommodation between the "real" and "philosophical" may seem straightforward in theory, but it proved difficult in execution. Weill's and his collaborators' search for solutions to this challenge is borne out in surviving manuscript drafts from the show's development, a process that is unusually well documented. Not only does correspondence between the collaborators survive, and not only do Weill's diary and musical sketches survive, but lyricist Langston Hughes also kept hundreds of detailed, dated drafts for each lyric he wrote. On these he often jotted down feedback he received from his colleagues during meetings, over the phone, and at rehearsals. They amount to a day-by-day (and, at times, an hour-by-hour) account of their collaboration, revealing how difficult it was for the team to articulate what they called the play's "philosophy" in words and music that would also seem "realistic," and to avoid what they saw as a kind of grand-opera exaggerated mannerism that, they feared, would distract the audience and blunt the emotional impact of the show.

Weill launched his collaboration with Elmer Rice in the summer of 1945, and after securing the rights for their collaboration (from none other than Rodgers and Hammerstein, who had previously optioned it), Weill began work.[97] Befitting a show with civic intentions, he and Rice assembled a team that had experience in political musical theater. Rice himself had started his career in the politically engaged theater of the 1930s, and in 1935 was appointed the director of the New York office of the Federal Theatre Project (as described in Chapter 2); lyricist Langston Hughes had long been involved in left-wing causes and had helped establish the New York Suitcase Theater in 1936; director Charles Friedman had been part of a Shock Troupe during the Popular Front and later served as director of the political review *Pins and Needles*; and choreographer Anna Sokolow had formed her own troupe under the aegis of the radical Theater Union (where she collaborated with Mike Gold and Elie Siegmeister, introduced in Chapter 2) and the Federal Theatre Project.[98]

Also important to them was to gather a circle of people who would be able to blend high art and popular art. This was especially true for their lyricist, Hughes.[99] Hughes had written the yet unproduced *Troubled Island* with William Grant Still, which meant he had some limited experience in opera. But it is unclear whether Weill or Rice knew about this piece when they approached him. Rather, they probably considered Hughes for the role based on his poetry. Already in his breakout essay from 1926, "The Negro and the Racial Mountain" (written in the context of the Harlem Renaissance, described in Chapter 4), Hughes had argued that there could exist a form of high art that was not based on European standards, but instead on folk and popular music.[100] When Weill later described what drew him to Hughes, he said, "we decided that the lyrics should attempt to lift the everyday language of the people into a simple, unsophisticated poetry."[101] Rice agreed: "We asked Langston Hughes to come in because we didn't want any slick, wisecracking lyrics, and I felt this approach would be the right one.... It takes a more-or-less serious play out of the red plush and gilt of the opera house and puts it on The Street where people can see it."[102] Later, Hughes would recall that Weill asked for "a kind of synthesis of the language of New York City, the feeling of the sounds of our city, and of the—well, I guess you might say the folklorey feeling of New York."[103]

In very late August 1945, with the entire writing team in place, work began in earnest. The new version of the show was to follow the original script closely with only relatively minor changes, except for one, devised before Hughes had been hired: "musical sequences" amounting to a "song about the nation," performed during the first act.[104] Hughes was already calling this the "melting pot" number in the early September 1945.[105] In the final version of the show, this would become the graduation scene in which the neighborhood celebrates the high school children returning from their last day of school. Before it reached this final form, however, it went through many—and completely different—versions. Hughes later recalled that writing it took "almost as much time as it did to work out an entire act of the rest of the show."[106] (In fact, it took longer.) Given that the scene took so long (nearly fourteen months) to reach its final form, given how persistently they worked on it, and given that the disputes about it centered on form and philosophy, the scene's development can serve a log of the collaborators' evolving ideas about the show—and, by extension, their evolving ideas about Broadway opera.

In the first phase of work, the scene was to consist of two main parts, an entrance aria for the young scholar Sam, followed by a large, multi-section ensemble that would articulate the show's "philosophy," the paean to American democracy. Hughes would not produce a preliminary draft of the entire sequence until December 1945, but in the waning days of summer he began writing lyrics for the first part of it, the arietta (as he and Weill called it) for Sam's entrance, which he submitted as part of his first batch of lyrics to Rice and Weill in October 1945.[107] Hughes based the lyrics on a conversation from Rice's original play, a scene in which Sam tells his Italian neighbor that Neapolitan songs were shallow compared to the symphonies of Beethoven and Tchaikovsky.[108] By the middle of December, Hughes would submit three versions of the song: "Great Music," "If Life and Art Could Merge," and "Where Each Man Is a Friend," each on the same basic theme:

The way life is in books / Is more the way it ought to be. / The voices of men / Should borrow music's melody. / Instead of that around here—nothing but misery / If only art and life could merge / to lift humanity! / In art—and art alone—can man / Escape reality: / (Burst of beautiful and sensuous music) Music can open a gate / to a road of delight without end / Poetry can show the way / to a land where each man is a friend.[109]

There were three components of this version that would remain key points of discussion in the months ahead: first, that Sam should articulate the special loneliness one feels in the modern metropolis; second, that great art can alleviate these feelings by (somehow) disclosing a feeling of community spirit and universal brotherhood; and finally, that a "burst of beautiful and sensuous music" should coincide with these idealist concepts, suggesting that Weill's and Hughes's initial instinct was to couple "philosophical" meaning with classical-style music.

The team had doubts. At the top of a December 14 draft, presumably written in conference with Rice and Weill, Hughes scribbled "Discard" and "Too abstract," a critique that would become common during the rest of the show's development. On one undated page of notes for Sam's song from around this time, Hughes jotted, "make very personal" and described Sam's intense feeling of "esthetic starvation," suggesting that the song's delivery had struck the creative team as unnatural, unrealistic, unmotivated. Still unsatisfied on January 22, 1946, the creative team changed course altogether. They abandoned Sam's speech about art, focusing entirely on his loneliness.[110] Weill wrote to Hughes:

> Sam's Aria (unless you have a better idea) should be about the house (as Elmer lined it out the last we all met[)]—the house being a prison for the spirit, etc. It could almost become a theme song for the show. It should be passionate and very moving, but as personal as we can make it, that means: not abstract!!![111]

In response, Hughes wrote "Lonely House," which, with only a couple of minor changes, remained in the show on opening night (albeit in a different spot). The song opens with resolutely concrete lyrics that amount to a virtual catalogue of the tenement building's sounds: "neighbors snoring," "a baby cry[ing]," "a staircase creaking," "a distant telephone." It only reaches any kind of abstraction at the very end, when the music reaches its climax: "Unhook the stars and take them down." Gone from this song, however, are any descriptions of democratic universalism or the value of high art for a democracy.

Different, too, was the dramaturgical function of the music in the song. Instead of using a "burst of beautiful and sensuous music" to deliver idealist concepts, this music was now used as a vehicle for intense emotion, to make the scene more "passionate" and "moving." In fact, this was a topic they had been discussing for a while. In Hughes's notes for what appears to a very early conversation about the project (probably in early September 1945), Weill had explained that the central feature of the show was to be its "emotion," the "power of two love stories," and suggested *La Bohème* and *Louise* as models.[112] The rest of the show would follow this trend, such that the lush operatic style (as opposed to the popular style or the pastiche style) would serve mainly to intensify the emotional content of the show's central plot involving the murder of Mrs. Murrant.

As Sam's aria focused increasingly on his feelings of loneliness, the writers turned to the ensemble portions of the Melting Pot scene to express the "philosophy" of democratic optimism and universal brotherhood. The earliest drafts of these segments, dated December 1945, began with an argument about who first discovered America (dialogue from the original play, some of which remains in the final version of the show), and ended with a group affirmation of each nationality's contribution to American culture. One character (it is unclear who) was to sing, "Lippo's bound to have his way — / The Italians built New York, / But the Irish run it, / The Jews own it, / And the Negroes enjoy it — / So they say!" Then the chorus, sung by the ensemble, was to intone together: "There's uptown, downtown / The Bronx and Brooklyn, too. / Irish, German, Negro, / Chinese, Polish, Jew, / Italian, Swedish, Spanish — / And Hungarian, too! / ... That's New York! / That's New York! / It's you — / And me — / And we — / Who make New York!"[113] Taken together with the remainder of the scene, several inchoate structural principles appear to be at work: The scene was to feature an unclear number of short pieces, an ensemble number, Sam's solo, and a closing ensemble. Beyond this, any further, more specific details that Weill may have been considering at this point—recurring themes, referential harmonies, or standard song forms, for instance—have been lost to history.

In his letter from January 22, Weill wrote a new outline for this portion of the scene, which describes how he was developing the team's initial structural ideas. At the most basic level, Sam was now to enter during the argument, which presumably pushed "Lonely House" until after the scene. Ultimately, after each representative of the neighborhood's nationalities described their contribution to American culture, Sam was to enter and deliver the "melting pot" message, or as Hughes wrote it in one set of notes, "Let Sam build up to—'It's you and me and we who make New York.'"[114] This note was as literary as it was musical: It was the incremental intensity of the music that granted the characters license to deliver the philosophical lines.

In addition, Weill's letter offered some more information about large-scale musical form of the scene:

> The Melting Pot scene we have worked out somewhat on the following line: it should start out with a funny description of Columbus's trip by Lippo, always at the end of the stanza interrupted by Olsen's dry remark, "But Erickson was first." Then we'll have a number of rather short songs for the different nationalities, built on a refrain: "if it weren't for the Irish (Germans, Negroes, etc.), where would America be?" This would lead into a short fight. Then, we decided, Sam should come in and should give them the Melting Pot idea, and this leads into a big ensemble.—This has the great advantage that Sam has a very strong entrance.[115]

Although still inchoate, Weill was deploying two different "refrain" principles here: first, what was likely to be a short, repeated musical gag about Leif Erickson; second, a larger section of music (one phrase? one chorus?) that would follow each nationality's verse. These recurring, short, closed forms suggest that the context in which Weill was conceiving this song was not in the expanded "endless melody" of late nineteenth-century opera, but rather in the vein of operetta couplets, number opera, or even popular song. When Weill penned his first music for this scene (which he called "A Nation of Nations") in late April or May, he structured it as a series of interlocking verses, each written in a different, recognizable, national style (an Irish jig, a German waltz, jazz for Black characters), and each verse was to be followed by a recurring refrain to be sung by a member of the ensemble.[116] Despite all the changes to this scene that would follow in the next five months, this general refrain form would remain intact.

Once again, during the spring and summer of 1946, the creative team struggled to express a melting-pot philosophy in a naturalistic way. At this point, however, their strategy changed. Instead of expressing any "philosophy" outright, they started to devise more indirect ways of expressing the theme of democratic unity. The solution, as it took shape, was to rely upon emotion—upon the feeling of optimism for the diversity of New York City and the promise of future success—rather than any outright articulation of democratic principles. The argument between Lippo and Olsen about Christopher Columbus, for example, took on a much rosier tone, with Lippo singing: "When Captain Chris Colombo / Sailed up Fifth Avenue, / He sing, 'hello, America! I'm pleased to meet-a you!'"[117] Sam's entrance in this version of the sequence also changed. The specific scene that was to inspire Sam to deliver the show's philosophy was the sight of children in school. At this point, a group of passing kids would interrupt the argument about Columbus and Erikson. Sam, overcome, would join in their revelry and lead them in a dance around a maypole. The idea appears to have originated with Rice, who wrote down two of Robert Louis Stevenson's "Child's Garden of Verses" for Hughes on July 9.

> The rain is raining everywhere
> It falls on field and tree
> It falls on the umbrellas here
> And on the ship at sea
> The children sing in far Japan
> The children sing in Spain
> The organ with the organ man
> Is singing in the rain.

Hughes's lyrics followed suit: "When it's spring in New York / It's spring around the world. / When flowers bloom in central park / They bloom around the world. // The astors [*recte* asters] in New York / Are like astors everywhere — / They lift their happy heads to sing that spring is here. / The golden moon of June / Looks down on land and sea / And all the people in all lands / love that moon as much as me." In this version there was no overt reference to the "melting pot" philosophy, but nonetheless there remained an overall cheeriness about peaceful diversity.

Hughes seemed to be of two minds about this scene's material. As his biographer Arnold Rampersad has described, Hughes was struggling at this point in his career to balance an optimistic, conciliatory approach to American politics with the more radical political sympathies he had cultivated in the 1920s and 1930s.[118] This surfaced in especially stark terms as the writers tried to write the Black janitor's contribution to the scene. Starting in March 1946, his portion of the Melting Pot sequence was called "Happy to Be Alive," a song that eventually became "A Little Swing," which the authors would consider on and off as a potential part of the sequence throughout the summer of 1946. "When I came from Africa / Way back in times past, / I brought some things from Africa, / Looks like they bound to last: // I brought a little song for singing along: / I brought a little jive to jive, / I brought a little swing for swinging, / Happy just to be alive ... // I don't remember Africa, / Africa's forgot about me— / Three hundred years / And a lot o' tears— / Now, thank God-a-mighty— I'm free!"[119] Yet, perhaps because of Weill's and Hughes's own complex feelings about race relations in the United States, this song probably began to seem too optimistic to describe the character's situation adequately. Between July 9 and 13, the song became much more pessimistic. "Three hundred years / Picking in the cotton, / Three hundred years, / Chopping in the cane, / Three hundred years / Working on the road gang, / Digging in the sun / And shoveling in the rain. // The first two hundred years / I was not free. / You all came of your own free will— / but not me! ... // So *you* take your little talk / About how you made the U.S.A / I reckon I'll keep silent / You can have your say. // Some day all these years / Will be far away."[120] Yet for all the political potential that lay in the janitor's lyrics, this song seemed far removed from the overarching, "melting pot" philosophy of the show—in fact, these words effectively abnegated it.[121] Throughout July and August the authors considered both "A Little Swing" and a song called "Totin'" with lyrics similar to "Three Hundred Years," and eventually they cut this portion of the scene altogether.

Yet while they were still considering these options, they found that "A Little Swing" had not only an ideological appeal, but a musical one as well. As Hughes wrote to Weill, the song lent itself to "a nice catchy dance tune," again suggesting that refrain structures were central to Weill's thinking.[122] More than that, it suggests how thoroughly they had turned away from "the burst of sensual music" that had prepared the "philosophical" ideas in earlier drafts. At this point in the show's development, they were interested in expressing abstract, ideal content about democratic brotherhood, but they were trying to incorporate it into the show's popular-music components, into the "nice catchy dance tunes." This was an important development, a striking reversal of musical roles: By July 1946, the show's popular music components were expected to perform the idealist work typically thought more appropriate to classical music.

As the authors began to settle on the individual portions of the Melting Pot sequence, they turned their attention back to Sam, who, according to plan, should have made his entrance and delivered the philosophy of the Melting Pot sequence before singing "Lonely House." Once again, their concern was to find a way for Sam to deliver the melting pot philosophy realistically. As they had done with "Lonely House," they suggested that Hughes should start with concrete scenes from everyday life described in idealistic terms. During the first two weeks of August, he tried many different versions: one focused on baseball ("A home run for the human race / And a bright and brand new day / When we play the game of nations / In a sporting baseball way—"[123]), another focused on children in school ("Carmencita loves Patrick, / Waldemar loves Si Lan Chen / Xenophon loves Mary Jane / And Hildegarde loves Ben. . . . Ring around the Maypole! All around we go— / Waving our bright ribbons / Into a rainbow..."[124]), another was about the telephone book ("Nobody has priority— / it runs from A to Z. / A name like Rockefeller's / might even be behind me! . . . They're all in the telephone book! / They're all in the telephone book! / For information / As to who makes our nation / Just look in the telephone book!"[125]), and so on. All of these lyrics produced during the summer of 1946 held two things in common. First, they struggled (and, according to the authors, failed) to find natural ways to communicate the show's philosophy. Second, each individual section of the song was to be treated as a long verse with wildly varying melodies, harmonies, and accompaniments, yet they were all to be connected by a recurring refrain to be sung by the ensemble.

The writers rejected each new version. In August and September 1946, however, the collaborators began to work toward a different solution. Rather than state the melting pot philosophy outright, each character expressed some sense of optimism that they could achieve a better life in the United States than in their respective home countries. One refrain Hughes produced at this time was as follows: "Goodbye, Yesterday! / Hello, Tomorrow! / I am on my way! / I was all right yesterday— / But tomorrow's gonna be my day!"[126] After September 20, Hughes penned almost a dozen lyrics in this idealistic vein: "When I feel that Way," about smiling at one's neighbors;[127] "It's Fun to Go to a Party"[128] and "Just a Happy Bunch of Friends" for the children to sing;[129] "The Best of Everything to You"; "Just for Fun"; "What do you know, Joe?" and so on.[130] These lyrics mark an important milestone in the song's development. By this point, the emotional valence itself had come to take on vaguely political overtones, such that enthusiasm among the community was to stand in for what had earlier been an explicitly articulated philosophy about democratic brotherhood.

On October 5, in a meeting that Hughes had with Rice and director Charles Friedman, the plan changed subtly once again. In his notes, Hughes wrote in large letters across the center of the page, "Love Is The Thing," and at the bottom "When, if, if, if." In terms of words, the lyrics began to be not simply idealistic, but aspirational. In them the characters would describe their goals in life, and explain how inclusion, working together, and love would help them realize their dreams.[131] On October 6, Hughes wrote a letter to Weill to describe his new version of the song:

> The lyric, *That Happy Feeling* (or, if we wish to double up on the word "Happy" — *That Happy Happy Feeling*) has the advantage of lending itself to great lyrical variety within the framework of its form. Since it is a thirty-two bar, <u>two</u> part chorus, with a little release of two lines in each half, the release may be continually varied. If laughs are desired, it may be gagged up to suit each character. And only <u>one</u> half of the chorus need be repeated by the ensemble after each character sings.
>
> The first half of the chorus may be treated as a verse, and may be varied musically to suit the Irish, Italian, Negro, or Swedish characters, thus getting the qualities of their folk dancing into the song.
>
> Since the song has to be one suited to both children and adults, such a general theme of happiness would be suitable to both. Also it would offer a dramatic contrast with the quarrel that proceeds it, and the troubled feeling that is generated on Sankey's [Mrs. Murrant's lover] entrance. It also lends itself to dancing.[132]

Hughes's attention to form suggests how thoroughly musicalized his work with Weill had become: Even as they worked to articulate what the philosophy of the scene might have been, they also recognized how important it was to find a musical form that would express it adequately. Although the language is slightly unclear, it appears that Hughes envisioned a series of thirty-two-bar, parallel-period (AB||AC) choruses, indicated by his reference to "a little release of two lines in each half" (i.e., the B and the C sections). If this is true, it suggests that this sequence in the show was traveling farther away from the interlocking-verse form (operetta-style couplets?) Weill had originally suggested, and closer to familiar Broadway songs. In this plan, the first half of each chorus was to be individualized for each nationality, leading to the customary half cadence at the end of the B section; the second half, eventually leading to the perfect authentic cadence, was to be appropriate for everybody onstage—it was a musical analogue to the melting pot philosophy: The individual call invites a collective response. Again, it is notable that Weill and Hughes were entrusting the show's philosophy, not to the operatic portions of the show, but rather to a song conceived in a standard thirty-two-bar form.

The question that remained, however, was how to motivate this song within the plot. Their solution was to return to the idea of children in school. The scenario (which remains in the final version of the show) was that the argument onstage about who discovered America would be interrupted by a group of students returning home from their high school graduation, allowing everybody onstage to reflect about their hopes for the future. (By this point, Sam was no longer part of the scene, perhaps because his articulating the melting pot philosophy would have seemed out of place against his aria about loneliness that followed.) On October 12, Hughes wrote a lyric called "Stepping Stones," in which he attempted to tie together a number of previous ideas. Lippo, congratulating the graduates, began: "Honey, step on your stepping stone! / America's da land of da steppin' stone! / Me, myself, I'm stepping on a stepping stone!" The rest of the cast joined in, one by one:

> All god's chillun's got a stepping stone! / Leif Ericson, he laid the first stepping stone! / Naw! 'Twas Colombo laid that steppin' stone! Plymouth rock was a stepping stone! Thank God all mighty for that stepping stone! / George Washington, he laid a stepping stone! Old Tom Jefferson laid a stepping stone! / Abraham Lincoln laid a stepping stone! / (Henry) Ever since I been a-steppin on that / stepping stone! / Franklin D. he laid a stepping stone! / We're step, step, stepping on that / Stepping stone! / Stepping stones! America's a stepping stone! My heart is dancing on those / stepping stones / A diploma is a stepping stone! Education is a stepping stone! Brotherhood is a stepping stone! My heart is dancing on these stepping stones![133]

Two musical strategies remain in this version from previous versions. The first half of this song was to be individualized, and it appears that each participant was to receive one line of the song to sing. The second half, however, was to be collective, albeit if the song was to be in dialogue with the thirty-two-bar form one week earlier, given the sheer number of words, it would most likely have been an expanded version of that form. In addition, it was only after the song built to its climax (probably just before the cadence) that its most abstract, idealist words appear: "Brotherhood is a stepping stone!"

By the next day, however, they were back at the drawing board. At their meeting, Friedman felt the lyrics needed to be more "specific," and Rice felt that the song needed to be about "aspiration," but not about "grandiose things." Weill added that the lyric should be "folksy." The goal was to be idealistic without being unduly high-minded or naive, with Rice instructing Hughes to avoid the idea that "it's fun to be poor."[134] Contained in Hughes's notes are the seeds for the song that would eventually replace the Melting Pot sequence. Rice suggested that each character articulate as concretely as possible what he or she wanted out of life using similar, slangy words: "Jones: 100 - 1 hot / hot mazuma wrapped— Lippo: a bambino wrapped in a —," eventually becoming the number that remained in the show, "Wrapped in a Ribbon and Tied in a Bow."[135] Building on the form of "That Happy Happy Feeling," Weill instructed Hughes to write a single, repeating, thirty-two-bar refrain with the title in the fourth, eighth, and sixteenth line, this time with a single "release" "that goes off." Musically, then, Weill had changed his strategy, turning away from the parallel-period form chorus (AB||AC) and toward a AABA chorus, in which each A section was to repeat the title. Between October 13 and 21, Hughes produced dozens of potential stanzas that fit the mold, and at last, with viable set of lyrics in hand, Weill sketched the new song.

Why Weill ultimately landed upon this form is a matter of speculation. Scholars have noticed, however, that this song resembles Rodgers's music.[136] Like "The Surrey with the Fringe on Top" from *Oklahoma!*, this song also employs the modular technique described in Chapter 3, with each module of the phrases circling around a single pitch followed by a leap away. In fact, as Weill revised his initial sketches, this modular feature of the song became increasingly prominent (and therefore increasingly similar to Rodgers's song), so that eventually the phrase was almost entirely constructed of a small, repeating, long-short-short rhythmic cell (see Example 5.1).

Was this an emblem of Weill's sense of competition with Rodgers? Perhaps, although Weill was unlikely to sacrifice dramaturgy for what would amount to a private jab. Instead, he probably wrote in this style because of what it had come to represent: music that felt authentically Broadway, authentically American, authentically popular, especially when set against the more operatic components of *Street Scene*. Its very popularity would have

Example 5.1 Comparison of "Wrapped in a Ribbon and Tied in a Bow" and "Surry with the Fringe on Top."

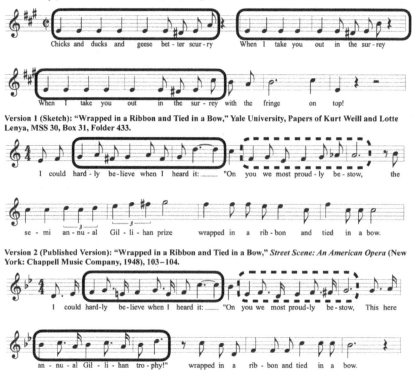

been a stylistic emblem of the melting pot philosophy, a kind of hit-parade music that had become familiar among all the different races and ethnicities of New York City during the mid-1940s.

By the end of October 1946, after nearly fourteen months of work, the Melting Pot sequence had reached its final form (although they would continue to make small edits throughout the rehearsal process). In the name of realism, they had drastically reduced the scope of the scene, and its "philosophy" had become far more understated than what they had originally planned to write. What was true of this scene was also true of the entire show, and shortly before it opened, the creative team harbored last-minute doubts about its integrated, high-low style. On December 21, Weill wrote a memo to the production staff saying that the show had not yet been integrated enough:

> But in some parts, specially [sic] in the first act, we have not succeeded yet in blending the elements of the show. In some places we try to be too legitimate, in other places too musical comedy. We are definitely using too much of the number technique of musical comedy instead of the flowing technique we had in mind.[137]

Here Weill referred to "blending" in two ways: first, he worried about the disparity between the musical elements (the "number technique" and the "flowing technique"); second, as a result, he worried that the show did not successfully blend the low and high elements (the "musical comedy" and the "legitimate" portions). The result would have been to jerk between different styles and different modes of presentation, which in turn would have vitiated any attempt at realism. Hughes had similar anxieties. On the same day, he wrote a memo complaining of the "ham-opera feeling," "melodrama," "gesturing," and "posturing."[138] He elaborated on this in another letter he wrote to his friend and collaborator Arna Bontemps one day later. He (unlike Weill) advocated eliminating the integrated technique altogether:

> If it was me I'd do it all stylized. Now, it is weakly half and half as to style and lighting— neither natural nor sufficiently unnatural to have a flavor. And as yet nobody is big and bad and bold enough to put a foot down flat and say it will be this or that OR ELSE. I wish I were running it. It would be one thing or another in a week. As it is now it sways back and forth between musical comedy, drama, and opera. (Which only a Meyerhold could make a unity—or ME![)] (Maybe!)[139]

Again, like Weill, Hughes worried that the elevated style and the naturalistic style did not blend, and tellingly, again like Weill, he associated the respective "stylized" and "natural" components with different musical modes of presentation: "musical comedy" and "opera" on the one hand, "drama" (no music; dialogue) on the other. As they prepared for the show's Broadway opening, it became clear that Weill and Hughes were concerned about more than the structural coherence of scene and score. They worried that if the show could not be identified as one genre or the other, then audiences would not understand how to interpret it: The "philosophy" would be lost in communication either because the lowbrow style of delivery would have precluded such a reading, or because the highbrow style would seem too overblown to be appropriate for the realistic characters and situations at hand. To encourage audiences to read the unusual production in a sympathetic or advantageous way, Weill turned to the press.

Politics and Emotion: Advertising *Street Scene*

As with so many other musicals in the mid-1940s—including *Oklahoma!* and *Beggar's Holiday*, as explained in the previous two chapters—the creative team of *Street Scene* struggled with how to label the show, given that it sat so conspicuously between opera and musical comedy. Choosing the right genre would help the audiences calibrate their expectations and would propose to them an appropriate set of interpretive parameters. Scattered glimpses into behind-the-scenes discussions suggest that the creative team disagreed about the best strategy. For example, the *New York Times* reported in May 1946 (nearly eight months before the production opened) "that if Co-Producer Dwight Deere Wiman prevails, the forthcoming musicalized 'Street Scene' will be called an opera."[140] Yet in communications with potential backers, the production team hedged: They described the show as both "off the beaten track of musical comedy," but also said it was "in no sense to be an 'art production' without respect to commercial possibilities."[141] As they entered rehearsals and prepared for their out-of-town tryout, they mostly avoided the term "opera" in public, even though in private Weill and Hughes continued to call to the piece a "popular Broadway opera."[142] They eventually settled on the designation "dramatic musical" by late November, and in December 1946, Weill gave an interview in which he said explicitly, "I am not calling my work an opera. I would rather term it a dramatic musical. There are certain things one usually expects from opera which cannot be done in a Broadway production."[143]

On December 22, however, this changed. The production team had recently returned to New York after a tumultuous tryout in Philadelphia, and Weill told producer Victor Samrock that the "critics were confused in reviewing *Street Scene*," and requested they "not say anything in any way to give critics or public here in New York the impression that this is a musical."[144] From that point on, *Street Scene* was to be referred to as Broadway opera. To clarify matters, Weill published an article for the *New York Times* just days before the show opened, which the producers also reprinted in the show's souvenir program. In a now familiar gambit, Weill announced his high-art bona fides as a "composer of grand opera" at the outset of the article.

He also cultivated his maverick pose, claiming he had "soon discovered the limitations of a form of entertainment in which almost all of the other demands of the theatre had to be sacrificed to the music or more often to the delicate condition of the vocal chords [sic] of the prima-donna." Splitting the difference between the two, he promised readers that he would import this high-art sophistication into the popular Broadway musical: "When I began to branch out into other fields of the musical theatre I discovered the simple truth that the varying categories of musical shows were actually nothing but different ways of mixing the same ingredients—music, drama and movement." Yet in addition to positioning himself somewhere between high art and popular culture, Weill was making a subtle interpretive claim. By focusing on the abstract qualities that were common to seemingly different kinds of musical shows (the "same ingredients"), and by turning his readers' attention to issues of form and construction (how the ingredients were mixed), he effectively displaced the show's compositional sophistication away from the musical surface—from the style, from the sound—toward the dramaturgical substrate: the strategies of blending music, word, and movement. This is to say that he decoupled sound and prestige, suggesting that even apparently popular culture could function as high culture without sacrificing seriousness—an argument he had been making about operetta since the 1920s, but this time applied to Broadway.

He achieved this by justifying the mixture of musical elements in civic terms. "As soon as I began to think about the music for *Street Scene*," he wrote, "I discovered that the play lent itself to a great variety of music, just as the streets of New York themselves embrace the music of many lands and people." By "variety," Weill meant two things. First, and most clearly, he alerted audiences to the fact that the production would feature the music of different ethnicities and nationalities. Second, he also drew their attention to the show's conspicuous mixture of popular and high-art music: "I had an opportunity to use different forms of musical expression, from popular songs to operatic and ensembles, music of mood and dramatic music, music of young love, music of passion and death—and, overall, the music of a hot summer evening in New York."[145] All of these kinds of music, Weill asserted, were worthy of equal attention and sympathy, and could stand equally as subjects of modern opera and as emblems of modern society.

If critics were to accept Weill's invitation to interpret *Street Scene* in this way, they would have had to accept that this piece was indeed both operatic and popular at once, capable of withstanding the formal and idealistic modes of interpretation Weill suggested, even while standing outside the European high-art tradition. Not all were willing to do this. Robert Garland of the *New York Journal-American*, for example, found *Street Scene* confusing because it "never manages to make up its mind about what it wants to be." He wrote, "I am sure it suffers by being neither drama, musical-comedy nor out-and-out grand opera." For him, the problem that arose from this had nothing to do with the show's entertainment value. "As home grown 'opera comique,' or whatever the American equivalent may come to be called, this be-lyric-ed and be-music-ed *Street Scene* is not unexciting theatergoing fare," he argued. The problem for him was that the operatic music seemed to demand from him a different kind of interpretation than the rest of the show, a purely musical interpretation, which he thought was incommensurable with dramatic qualities of theater: "[T]hese ... worthy tunes Kurt Weill composed are apt to demand attention on their own, not as an integral, if melodic, part of the musical drama 'Street Scene' aims to be."[146] Louis Kronenberger at *PM* used the same logic but reached a different conclusion. Like Garland, Kronenberger admitted that the score was "not without theater value," and especially praised Weill's "lighter music," the "strangely touching" underscoring, and the "choral effects" that "heighten things dramatically." Also like Garland, he believed that the operatic components demanded a specifically musical attention. However, applying that lens, he found the music unsophisticated. He wrote that the "strictly operatic side of *Street Scene* is *musically* not very rewarding," and complained that it was "pretentious," "facilely florid," full of "operatic posturing," adorned with recitative that was overwrought "to the point of bathos." Invoking this same split between theatrical values and purely musical values, he concluded, "*Street Scene* is not all it should be as folk opera. But it certainly stands up as a musical theater piece."[147] For each of these writers, the production's individual components were incommensurable, no matter how effective one or the other part may have been on its own.[148]

Most critics, however, did accept Weill's terms. Critic George Jean Nathan, for example, believed that *Street Scene* "represented an approach to American folk opera without the slightest pretentiousness, with an affecting book resolutely handled, with simple and appropriate lyrics."[149] His term "folk opera" probably conflates three slightly different ideas: first, that this show contained children's street songs, Italian tarantellas, and other snatches of folk-like material amid the popular-music and operatic components; second, that because of the mixture of different styles of music, *Street Scene* sat somewhere between opera, folk music, and popular culture, to the point where the word "opera" alone could not capture its effect; and third, that it stood as an authentic representation of a particular swath of American life. On these latter two points, John Lovell, Jr., in *The Crisis* largely agreed, writing that Weill's music "heightened" Rice's "drama of the crowded streets of New York," and he described the combination of operatic values and American culture as "important" (a word he used three times): "Think of the possibilities of that for important plays that have died and important dramatic ideas that are yet unborn."[150]

Moreover, most reviewers followed Weill's lead in arguing that the sophisticated, high-art touch in *Street Scene* lay, not necessarily in its sound or style (its melodies, harmonies, and orchestration), but rather in the structural values that linked seemingly disparate kinds of expression into a coherent whole—in other words, its formal integration. "Song and action become one and indivisible," wrote Elinor Hughes of the *Boston Herald*. She believed that the operatic music "really caught the feeling of Mr. Rice's story and characters," and stipulated that, despite the operatic music, it was not "lacking in popular value."[151] In *Musical America*, Quaintance Eaton acknowledged that there were individual songs throughout the evening, but claimed that "speech flows into music naturally and inevitably—Mr. Weill has mastered the Singspiel technique perfectly," resulting in a production so thoroughly integrated that "the play [i.e., Rice's drama] seems not to be a separate entity but one half of a whole—Mr. Weill's greatest achievement to date."[152]

Yet perhaps the most salient impression that emerged from the reviews was the intensity of the show's emotional force. "The unusual memory audiences carry away from *Street Scene* is that they have been through a real emotional experience. They can't remember many Broadway musicals that did that to them," wrote Shana Ager in *PM*.[153] Most critics also believed that the opera's point was not just to savor these feelings, but instead to bring vivid emotional life to characters—to people—in the United States who rarely rose to the level of artistic consideration. Its emotional valence was, in a word, civic. Elinor Hughes wrote, "It is not a pretty story, nor is it a pretty score. But it is life in New York—it might well be any metropolitan center—as that life has never been set forth before on stage."[154] Other reviewers agreed, calling it a "sidewalk opera" or a "metropolitan opera—a work that catches in both score and story the feel of the tenement house life," as one critic described it.[155] In a similar vein, *New York Times* music critic Olin Downes argued that

Weill's craftsmanship amplified the show's emotional effect. He noted that it "catered in places, deliberately and probably necessarily, to Broadway—prevailingly with fresh invention, a masterful and eclectic craftsmanship, and feeling, perhaps most tellingly revealed in the treatment of poignant details of the drama of the lives of the underdogs of modern society and their pitiful searchings for understanding and happiness." The result, for Downes, was civic, awakening intense sympathy for "the underdogs of modern society." He continued, referencing "Wrapped in a Ribbon and Tied in a Bow" specifically, "[Y]ou listened to the charming music and to Mr. Hughes' simple and moving lines, and looked on the squalor and humanity of it all with a lump in your throat."[156] Producer and columnist Billy Rose agreed. He had initially rejected an offer to invest in the show out of fear that it would be boring, but he saw *Street Scene* and wept. Once the curtain flew, he said that he witnessed "a world of trapped and hungering people who reached out for something pretty and got their fingers stepped on."[157]

The most explicit civic interpretation came from the Black press, especially in Lovell's review in the NAACP's magazine *The Crisis*. Like other reviewers, he noted that the songs were "natural expression of workers, haters, cheaters in fine clothes, beggers [sic], and slaves with swords in their hands." But he went further, noting, "In the original play, there were no Negroes in the tenement community; in the modern musical drama, there are three." For him, this play did not simply celebrate the American "melting pot" in an abstract or purportedly "objective" sense. Its goal, he argued, was progressive:

> The primary result of the play, however, it [sic] to show, very vividly, that the particular hammer under which all these people live daily, molds them into characters a great deal more alike than different. Thus democracy is shown in the fruitful sharing of ordinary, everyday experiences of pleasure, pain, and struggle, which foolish discriminations try to prevent.[158]

As described in Chapter 4, the Black press's theatrical coverage tended to advocate for equal employment for Black performers in roles that did not fall back into stereotypes. Therefore, Lovell's assertion that the characters onstage were "more alike than different" likely resonated beyond the diegetic world of the show, describing how *Street Scene* portrayed both the Black characters onstage and the Black actors who played them as part of a broad, shared, American community, regardless of their race.[159] "[I]t shows how the basic understandings of the American melting pot as a force for democracy are most effectively displayed," he wrote.

The strongest affirmation of middlebrow values came from Brooks Atkinson in the *New York Times*, whose review recognized the show's blend of seemingly incompatible genres of music, its civic intent, and its rejection of high-art opera. Regarding its middle path between high art and popular culture, Atkinson wrote, "Mr. Weill's *Street Scene* has been labeled folk opera out of respect for its musical integrity. But perhaps it would be more exact to regard his score as a sequence of related songs that convey in music the emotions of the characters and the moods of the streets."[160] The terms "folk opera" and "musical integrity" probably refer, once again, both to the variety of music (the popular music, the street cries, the ethnic songs, the operatic passages) and to the sophisticated way in which Weill combined them. Ultimately, however, Atkinson recognized that the point of including these kinds of music was to evoke sympathy for people of different classes, ethnicities, and races. He argued that this set the musicalized version of *Street Scene* apart from Rice's dramatic source material. "And perhaps this is something of what the opera contributes to the old drama [i.e., Rice's original play]. With its music and dances, its chorales and lyrics, it finds the song of humanity under the argot of the New York streets."[161] Yet he went further: It was not merely that this Broadway score accessed an idealist concept—the "song of humanity"—but rather that the emotional valence of the music also helped to purpose this idealist concept toward civic ends in the present day by providing an emotional point of contact between the theater audience and New York City's poor: "For [Weill] has listened to the main street cries of Mr. Rice's garish fable—the hopes, anxieties, and grief of people trying to beat a humane existence out of the squalor of a callous city."[162] This civic intent set the show apart from other musicals at the time, and, in Atkinson's estimation, even surpassed *Oklahoma!*. "Not since *Oklahoma!* has a stage play yielded so fine a musical. The aim and content of *Street Scene* give it complete superiority. Apart from its quality as theatre entertainment, it arouses pride, pity and interest in the vast human clutter of New York."[163]

Returning to the sense of competition that Weill felt with Rodgers, these reviews suggest that its stakes were higher than matters of form and genre. Instead, more fundamentally, their competition concerned the expressive scope of the Broadway musical: what kinds of topics it could potentially address, what kinds of music it could conceivably incorporate, what kinds of interpretation seemed appropriate to it. Both composers deployed different mixtures of popular culture, folk music, and highbrow music; both also sought (in different ways) to make the Broadway musical newly relevant to postwar New York. Weill was one of a group of creators who sought to grant the musical a civic importance that verged on political, even while eschewing any potentially divisive partisan ideology. Following the premiere of *Street Scene*, others would join this ongoing trend. The day after *Street Scene* opened, for example, E. Y. Harburg's, Fred Saidy's, and Burton Lane's *Finian's Rainbow* (1947) would premiere, and would once again mix present-day politics with folk music and popular culture. Afterward, Harburg and Saidy would reunite to produce *Flahooley* (1951, with a score by Sammy Fain), which was also politically minded and drew together seemingly incompatible kinds of music. And in the decade that followed, civic-minded (and even more overtly political) works would be especially well represented in the burgeoning Off-Broadway scene, including the revivals of Weill's *Threepenny Opera* (Theater de Lys, 1954) and *Johnny Johnson* (Carnegie Hall Playhouse, 1956), as well as Langston Hughes's and David Martin's *Simply Heavenly* (85th Street Playhouse, 1957).[164] Even Rodgers and Hammerstein would come to adopt parts of Weill's model: While *Oklahoma!* and *Carousel* were set in rural places and bygone times, many of their subsequent Broadway shows—including *Allegro* (1947), *South Pacific* (1949), *Pipe Dream* (1953), *Flower Drum Song* (1958), and *The Sound of Music* (1959)—were set in the recent historical past or the present day, bringing together wide-ranging genres of music (from opera to ethnic tunes to rock and roll) with a civic purpose of addressing pressing contemporary social issues such as the dehumanizing effects of modern business, racism, and immigration.

The broader historiographical point here has been to describe a self-conscious group of critics, writers, and composers, all in the widening circle surrounding cultural theorist Van Wyck Brooks (and, indirectly, Romain Rolland), who were bound together by shared cultural commitments. Such commitments were never monolithic, and the disagreements between Weill and Rodgers attest to just how deeply divisions could run. Nevertheless, the people featured in this chapter (and in this book) all rejected the obscurity of the most recent trends of the European high-art scene, adopting instead an attitude toward new music and theater that sought to situate it emphatically inside a received tradition. The purpose of this was to create musicals that on the one hand addressed serious topics that had been thought more proper to European high art, but on the other hand still engaged as broad a public as possible, namely the communities represented by folk and popular music.

The result was not only to open new topics, new styles, and new sounds to the mainstream Broadway musical, but also to envision a new function for the Broadway show. No longer was it primarily conceived of as an entertainment genre. In these composers' hands, the musical became a tool for gathering disparate cultural publics together to form a more cohesive social whole, even amid the contemporary divisions created by war and economic turmoil, by racism and poverty. What was novel in 1947 would become the norm: In subsequent years, even as Broadway turned toward new musical trends, toward new strategies of social engagement, and toward new cultural priorities, it nevertheless inherited from this generation the fundamental trait that the musical could, properly speaking, hold this civic function.

Conclusion

Further Steps Toward a Middlebrow Modernism

On its surface, this book has offered a new version of a familiar story, which describes the rise of the so-called integrated musical in the early 1940s, and which places Rodgers and Hammerstein's *Oklahoma!* at its center. Earlier studies had generally defined the integrated musical in formal terms as a kind of show in which all components were uniquely suited to the situations and characters at hand, as opposed to an older style of musical that supposedly comprised mostly interpolated numbers with only tenuous connections to the plot. As a result, compositional coherence and smooth transitions between scene, song, and dance have tended to stand as Broadway's primary achievement in the early 1940s, and claims of greater "maturity" or "sophistication" have usually followed. This study, however, has revealed that contemporary critics, writers, and composers used the term "integration" differently than previously thought. For them, it implied incorporating seemingly incompatible kinds of art—high art, folk art, and popular culture—into the same production, and doing so in ways that would avoid compromising the special qualities of each. For the people introduced in previous chapters, this mixing seemed to open strategies of interpretation that had once seemed foreclosed to the popular musical comedy because such modes of analysis had seemed more proper to high art or folk art. The result for many at the time was to reveal new "horizons" of potential meaning for the musical (to borrow a phrase from philosopher Hans Georg Gadamer).[1] And as the second half of this book demonstrated, contemporary critics believed that the horizon of potential meanings continued to expand throughout the decade.

Side by side with this story ran another one. It focused on early- to mid-twentieth-century debates about the proper distinctions between high art, folk art, and popular culture. Each writer, composer, and critic presented in this book sensed that these boundaries were shifting rapidly, and as they tried to describe the new Broadway musical, they were also forced to reconcile inherited aesthetic norms with a world they felt was utterly new. This was, in other words, a story about modernism. That such a discussion should emerge from a study of the Broadway musical may seem incongruous. After all, most studies of modernism have tended to focus on avowedly high art, avant-garde poetry, experimental music, and so on—genres that appear to lie far away from popular musical theater. Yet the Broadway musical was deeply invested in these debates. Its presumed distance from high art made it possible for the composers and critics introduced in previous chapters to reify the very concept of high art, to bracket it off conceptually from other kinds of culture as a monolithic (albeit complex) thing, at times to be the subject of adoration, at other times to bear the brunt of spoof. Regardless of the adopted attitude, this vantage point afforded Broadway writers and musicians a conceptual distance to observe the practices and boundaries of high art without becoming embroiled in internecine debates from within the art world. From a historiographical perspective, then, it has offered a fresh vantage point to think about the fundamental changes in the prevailing conceptions about high art during the early decades of the twentieth century.

Amid variegated research about modernist visual art, music, and literature over the past couple of decades, a methodological question about the relationship between modernism and artistic autonomy has emerged especially prominently as the subject of intense debate. One side has portrayed modernism as a radical cultural response to changes in bourgeois society, characterized above all by a commitment to aesthetic autonomy, which is to say, characterized by a series of practices that distanced art from the mundane world and cordoned it off into a space that resisted assimilation into the culture of modern capitalism.[2] Musicologist Richard Taruskin, for example, defined modernism as a "commitment" to modernity, which amounted to a rejection of Romanticism's nostalgia while still maintaining "the autonomous, socially divorced status" of high art familiar from the nineteenth century.[3] If autonomy is taken to be the central feature of modernism, the boundary between high art and popular art remains clearly demarcated: the "repudiation of *Trivialliteratur* has always been one of the constitutive features of a modernist aesthetic intent on distancing itself and its products from the trivialities and banalities of everyday life," according to literature scholar Andreas Huyssen.[4] If in the past, studies of modernism had tended to focus on emphatically experimental art, recent decades have opened up the field to art that did not fall to such stylistic extremes, even while maintaining autonomy as the central, constitutive feature. In his study of Jean Sibelius, for example, musicologist James Hepokoski argued that some music typically construed as a dying breath of Romanticism is actually better understood as an active reflection upon—and rejection of—the shocking developments of the younger generation's New Music.[5] He notes that Sibelius reaffirmed his alienated stance against what he sensed to be the modish one-upmanship of the contemporary musical marketplace: "Let's let the world go its own way," Sibelius wrote in his diary after hearing Stravinsky's music in 1911.[6] Even though Sibelius's symphonies generally do not sound like the extreme experiments of the New Music scene, they still belong to the modernist moment, bound to it (at least in part) by a commitment to autonomy.

Yet a different view of modernism (often described as the basic stance of the New Modernism Studies[7]) holds that despite the modernists' apparent distaste for popular or mass culture, their work is entirely suffused with it, incorporating everything from its content (modern slang, modern song, modern technology) to its modes of dissemination (modern periodicals, radio, film).[8] In cinema scholar Miriam Hansen's words, "just as modernist aesthetics are not reducible to a category of style, they tend to blur the boundaries of the institution of art in its traditional, eighteenth- and nineteenth-century incarnation that turns on the ideal of aesthetic autonomy and the distinction of 'high' vs. 'low,' of autonomous art vs. popular and mass culture." Instead of affirming the inherited boundaries between autonomous high art and popular culture, this version of modernism challenges them. With this definition in place, the study of modernism has broadened conceptually, geographically, and stylistically to include "a whole range of cultural and artistic practices that register, respond to, and reflect upon processes of modernism and the experience of modernity."[9] Scholars who conceive of modernism in this way tend to focus on how art of the time incorporated the quotidian, the ordinary, the utterly prosaic; the popular, the kitschy, the mass market; movies, popular jazz, cartoons all become part of modernism, properly speaking.[10]

Knotty historiographical questions accrue to both positions. For example, if modernism's defining feature is taken to be its autonomy, periodization becomes a central problem. Musicologist Peter Franklin was being deliberately provocative when he suggested that, if the concept of "autonomy" were the central defining feature of modernism, then modernism would become difficult to distinguish from Romanticism.[11] But the point was a serious one: Any critical lens that would wish to preserve modernism as its own distinct historical object of study (and not, as music theorist Leonard Meyer once famously called it, as a "late late Romanticism") would have to differentiate Romantic autonomy from modernist autonomy—in other words, would have to justify modernism's chronological boundaries.[12] If, however, modernism is construed more expansively as effacing institutional boundaries, one of the main problems lies in describing what is *not* modernism. In light of such bewildering breadth, literary theorist Rita Felski suggested imposing boundaries by fiat: "It is surely more useful to retain the term as a designation for those texts which display ... formally self-conscious, experimental, antimimetic features . . . while simultaneously questioning the assumption that such texts are necessarily the most important or representative works of the modern period."[13] This is to say that any approach to modernism would have to justify carefully the repertoire it chooses to include (and exclude) from its purview. Such historiographical issues as periodization and repertoire selection have proven so intractable that some recent writers have argued that the proper attitude of scholarship on this subject should be to accept that the contradictions cannot be resolved. Paul Saint-Amour, a scholar of British literature, argued that fuzzy concepts like "modernism" are best met as "weak theory" that does not try to explain away modernism's contradictions, but instead approaches the subject with "new modesty," at peace with irreducible complexity.[14]

Without trying to force clarity where none exists, musicologist Christopher Chowrimootoo has taken a different approach (and the title of this chapter pays homage to his book). He recommended displacing these problems from the realm of historiography (a problem of periodization and justification) to the realm of history (a problem that also rattled the art world of the early twentieth century).[15] For him, the study of middlebrow culture has proven particularly useful for this. In this scheme, fuzziness becomes, not a historiographical problem to overcome, but a historical fact to acknowledge: high and low, classical and popular, coterie and mass may have been constantly invoked as if they were clear in concept, but they were in fact always slippery in application. The concept of middlebrow can accommodate both. In Chowrimootoo's words, "the category of the middlebrow ... offers a chance to acknowledge the historical power of modernist critical oppositions on the one hand, while looking beyond them on the other—a chance, in other words, to deconstruct modernism from the 'inside,' balancing current desires to challenge modernist historiography with sensitivity to its history."[16]

As a heuristic—as a concept that enables scholars to study the tangled artistic strands of the early twentieth century without either succumbing to or suppressing the period's complexity—"middlebrow" offers a useful lens. As a term with any historical specificity—as something denoting a particular *kind* of complexity or ambivalence felt by a certain group of people at a specific time—it encounters many of the same foundational historiographical problems as the term "modernism." Musicologist Kate Guthrie summarized just how broadly the term "middlebrow" has been deployed: "In the hands of diverse writers, [the word "middlebrow"] was used to denote particular audiences; to explain modes of reception; to characterize institutions and cultural mediators; or to delineate artistic styles—literary, musical, and visual.... it was invoked with an array of contradictory connotations, from the disparaging to the defiant."[17] Returning to the historiographical aspect of the middlebrow, certain questions have remained unanswered: What, for example, separates the high-low ambivalence of the twentieth century from high-low ambivalence from earlier periods? What, for example, demarcates the middlebrow from the non-middlebrow? Perhaps as a symptom of the middlebrow's inherent in-between status, no stable body of generally agreed-upon middlebrow texts, artists, venues, or consumers has ever existed. In fact, even Russell Lynes, the journalist whose influential 1949 chart from *Life* purported to sort highbrow, lowbrow, and middlebrow taste, also admitted, "The problem with all this is that if you got any five people together and sat down to redo the chart, you'd probably come out with five different answers in every case."[18]

This book has tried to bring historical specificity to the historiographical theory. As a starting point, it acknowledged that, despite such variety, middlebrow has had one irreducible core feature: The term has implicated both "high art" and "low art," either by mixing them or by situating itself someplace in between them. As a basic first step, in this book I have sought to describe or delimit each component part ("high" and "low"), and to do so in a way that would be capacious enough to capture the many connotations each term has—denoting styles, audiences, venues, media, patterns of consumption—while nonetheless remaining conceptually coherent and historically grounded. To these ends, in Chapter 2 I defined each of these components as an "institution," which, in the words of literature scholar Peter Bürger, comprises "the notions about art (its functional determinants) which are generally valid in society" for a given historical period, and which take into account the "material conditions of the production and reception of art."[19] Put differently, an institution comprises the conceptual apparatus that separates capital-A "Art" from other kinds of culture at a specific historical moment, and therefore implicates the norms that legitimate certain forms of culture as art, that identify the apparatuses that promote art (the venues, the schools, the publishers, the societies), that describe the behaviors that accompany the consumption and creation of art, and that indicate the means by which people inculcate others with those values.[20] In this scheme, one of the central functional determinants of high art in the nineteenth and early twentieth centuries was its autonomy, and this informed many aspects of the high-art experience at that time: the style of a given work (often emphasizing its organic wholeness and completeness), the terms critics used to discuss it (emphasizing spiritual and intellectual distance from mundane life), the venues that supported it (a solemn space cordoned off from the profane), the way people learned to produce it (in conservatories and from authorized teachers, instead of, say, through oral tradition), and so on. Identifying the functional determinants of the institution of art does not allow a historian to label retroactively which individual cultural artifacts qualify as high art and which do not. This, after all, was often a source of disagreement among contemporary writers and artists. Nevertheless, it can describe the terms upon which such debates took place by identifying common vocabularies and shared concepts that, at the most fundamental level, made discussion (and disagreement) even possible.

Although in this book I have adopted institution theory as its main intellectual apparatus, I have also made two fundamental shifts away from established scholarship on this subject. First, while previous research has explored the functional determinants that have made high art possible, it has been less clear about non-art. Does this other form of culture also belong to an institution? Does it contain "functional determinants" that separate it from other forms of culture? Does it have apparatuses that reproduce its values? Or is it simply a gutter category, into which anything else collects by dint of not being art?[21] In this study I have proposed two additional institutions, each with their own functional determinants and their own apparatuses to preserve and cultivate these kinds of culture. Moreover, by the end of the nineteenth century each institution purported to do the kind of work that had generally seemed to be the purview of high art: the reconciliation of a fractured society into a unified, organic whole.

The first was folk art, a kind of culture that was equally as idealist as high art, but which was rooted in patterns of community feeling that supposedly spanned eons. To reiterate Chapter 2, if high art's main attribute was its purported "autonomy," which allocated art's meaning to some realm "beyond" the here-and-now, then folk art's main attribute was its purported "authenticity," which allocated art's meaning to some realm "before" the here-and-now. It stood emphatically apart from modern society. During the eighteenth and nineteenth centuries, folk art developed its own apparatuses—journals, academic departments, canonized repertoires, specialists, standards of performance, and highly developed vocabularies—all of which established a recurring set of principles that separated folk art from high art and popular culture, and which reproduced those values in successive generations. More than that, similar to highbrow artists, folk artists made claims that their work could heal the modern world. Philosopher Johann Gottfried Herder, whose writings supplied the central articles of faith for later folklorists, believed that folk song offered a glimpse of "a people in its *naked* simplicity," and he believed that with folk art, one could "[free] oneself from all the artificiality clinging to the heart and all the false politeness that has come to generate an inhumane sense of bourgeoise life, and one can finally breathe freely."[22]

The second institution was popular culture. During the late eighteenth century and early nineteenth century, popular culture had an ambiguous institutional status. Although it certainly had apparatuses, organizations, and venues for dissemination, it was not clear whether anybody recognized it as having functional determinants, or instead whether they conceived of it as culture whose central defining feature was simply that it was neither fine nor folk.[23] As demonstrated in Chapter 2, however, there gradually emerged a group of writers who endowed popular culture with its own positive values. By the early twentieth century, they were claiming that popular music was also capable of healing a fractured modern society, but that it could do so without adopting the alienated stance that typified other institutions. For these critics, popular culture was "vital" and "lively"; it could provide a rush of excitement or enthusiasm that would unite a community in feeling, and could do so without rejecting the modern world and its cultural marketplace.

"Middlebrow" is a concept that is distinct from the institutional categories of high art, folk art, and popular culture. It does not refer to a separate institution of art, but rather to an attitude toward the interaction among these institutions. Broadly speaking, critics and artists who called themselves middlebrow (and those who, while not calling themselves middlebrow outright, associated themselves with middlebrow writers) typically believed that the special properties of each institution could combine to create new interpretive strategies that otherwise would have been unavailable. For example, many believed that blending symphonic writing with popular music could make the idealist qualities of high-art music accessible, intelligible, and immediate, even to those with little experience in classical music. Meanwhile, opponents of middlebrow mixing believed that the special properties of each institution were incompatible. They were more likely to view popular music's present-day, marketplace appeal as conflicting with the idealist, autonomous meanings usually associated with symphonic music.

Why was such mixing (or fear of mixing) so important in the early twentieth century? After all, popular music, folk music, and art music have interacted as long as they have been known as such: Ländlers, minuets, and waltzes embedded within symphonies, bardic poetry, bucolic folk art of the late eighteenth century and early nineteenth century—each of these speak to this general idea of mixing institutions. Heated debates about mixing institutions were also common before the twentieth century; critics and artists have always viewed such mixtures enthusiastically or suspiciously. At first, the distinction might seem to be explained by new technology—the widespread reproducibility and distribution of cultural goods. Indeed, new means of production and dissemination held a firm grip on the imaginations of many artists and the experience of many consumers at the time. Yet technology alone cannot entirely distinguish the twentieth-century middlebrow from debates about high-low mixes in earlier periods. As Bürger has noted, mass-produced culture had been available since at least the seventeenth century, but "the idea of mass literature was not *a problem* for the culturally dominant class of high absolutist society." In his view, only when there developed a rival bourgeois institution of autonomous art did general accessibility become a problem for artists, who now had to differentiate themselves from those who produced widely available cultural goods, a moment that Bürger locates at the end of the eighteenth century.[24]

In this book I have suggested, rather, that one of the features that distinguished the middlebrow moment at the turn of the twentieth century from earlier periods was the new power that many artists and critics were granting to popular culture as an institution with its own positive values. In light of this change, middlebrow writers such as Van Wyck Brooks, Gilbert Seldes, Randolph Borne, Alain Locke, Brooks Atkinson, and others believed that high art and folk art could retain their idealism even as they benefited from the lively spark of popular culture. They believed that high art was more properly construed, not as autonomous, but rather as part of a community's traditions, akin to a ritual. They vehemently opposed any art that purported to stand apart from broader society. In context, the claim was audacious: Obscure high art and provincial folk art, far from curing the maladies of modern society, could actually make them worse by dividing the public between initiates and philistines, between highbrows and lowbrows.

In this light, writers who so shrilly denounced the middlebrow approach, writers such as Theodor Adorno, Dwight Macdonald, Virginia Woolf, and others, appear defensive, recoiling from new, startling claims that elevated popular art to a bona fide institution on par with high art. Such writers who parted ways with the middlebrow did not necessarily adopt a snobbish stance against popular culture as such. Instead, they tended to oppose mixing the values of the separate institutions, which would have had the effect of granting new cultural power and new interpretive possibilities to popular art. Art critic Clement Greenberg, for example, once wrote that middlebrow was worse than "old-time pulp" because "unlike [pulp], which has its social limits clearly marked out for it, middlebrow culture attacks distinctions as such and insinuates itself everywhere."[25] When Greenberg and his coterie praised artistic autonomy, it was a strategy to preserve the special qualities of each institution, to ward off the steady encroachment of commercial culture upon the few remaining parts of life that seemed to resist it—to forestall what they feared would amount to a cultural "grayout."

For the study of modernism, the middlebrow offers clarity without eradicating the period's inherent complexity and contradiction. It shifts scholarly attention away from categorizing cultural artifacts as high, low, or in between. Instead, it focuses on the diverging attitudes toward mixing established cultural institutions. For historians, this permits the traditional view of modernist studies (which takes autonomy to be modernism's central feature) to enter into conversation with the New Modernist Studies (which believes that modernism challenged the autonomous status of high art): Each side describes a different contemporary attitude toward institutional blending, one resisting it, the other embracing it. It also provides a relatively clear demarcation between the study of autonomy in the eighteenth and nineteenth centuries, and the study of autonomy in the beginning of the twentieth century: Around 1900, the new institutional claims about popular music reverberated outward to implicate the entire artistic field, rattling genres that had seemed squarely within the realm of high art and folk art, as well as those that stood just outside the conservatory, the art gallery, the literary journal—genres such as the Broadway musical.[26] With these new expanded claims about the power of popular culture, it became important for some artists to distinguish high art from low, to make claims that high art still remained capable of articulating something that popular culture could not.

This study has argued that Broadway cannot be held separate from the debates surrounding modernism in other fields because so many musicals thematized the distinctions that had traditionally separated high art, folk art, and popular culture at the time. The properties of each cultural institution became especially important as reviewers scrambled to figure out the appropriate terms with which to engage these musicals. In this context, the interpretive norms proper to high art did not necessarily enjoy any more cultural authority or deference than the norms afforded to folk art or popular culture. Critics, cited in previous chapters, frequently weighed the relative value of popular music against the prestige or sophistication of *soi-disant* classical music (and often found the latter wanting), while other critics weighed the relative value of classical music against the liveliness of *soi-disant* popular music (and often found the latter wanting).[27] For historians, this makes Broadway particularly useful for the study of broader trends in modernism. So many debates from other fields—from opera, from symphonic music, from the hit parade; from ballet, from the ballroom; from experimental theater, from lowbrow comedy—converged there with unusual intensity in the first half of the twentieth century when musical-theater composers and writers claimed for themselves a position that was emphatically, conspicuously, and provocatively in the middle.

Notes

Preface

1. Brooks can be seen as one of the foremost American writers taking part in what musicologist James Hepokoski called, in a different context, the "withdrawal phase" of European modernism. James Hepokoski, *Sibelius: Symphony No. 5* (Cambridge: Cambridge University Press, 1993), 8. See also Carl Dahlhaus, *Nineteenth-Century Music*, trans. J. Bradford Robinson (Berkeley: University of California Press, 1989), 366–67.
2. For example, see Raymond Knapp, *The American Musical and the Formation of National Identity* (Princeton, NJ: Princeton University Press, 2005), 123–24; Andrea Most, *Making Americans: Jews and the Broadway Musical* (Cambridge, MA: Harvard University Press, 2004), 104; Stacey Wolf, *Changed for Good: A Feminist History of the Broadway Musical* (New York and Oxford: Oxford University Press, 2011), 37ff.
3. This book expands on a trend in Broadway studies that emphasizes the musical's collaborative nature. See, for example, Dominic McHugh, "'I'll Never Know Exactly Who Did What': Broadway Composers as Musical Collaborators," *Journal of the American Musicological Society* 68 (2015): 605–52.
4. Geoffrey Block, *Enchanted Evenings: The Broadway Musical from* Show Boat *to Sondheim and Lloyd Webber* (New York and Oxford: Oxford University Press, 2009), 47–57. Block puts this succinctly: "Just as Beethovenian ideals of thematic unity and organicism became increasingly applied to dramatic works (culminating in Wagner's music dramas), Broadway musicals after Rodgers and Hammerstein's *Oklahoma!* (1943) would be evaluated on how convincingly they realized a new 'ideal type,' the integrated musical." See Block, "The Broadway Canon from *Show Boat* to *West Side Story* and the European Operatic Ideal," *Journal of Musicology* 11 (Autumn 1993): 525. The discussion of the "better book" revolution can be found in Scott McMillin, *The Musical as Drama* (Princeton, NJ: Princeton University Press, 2006), 15ff.

Chapter 1

1. Thomas Hischak, *The Oxford Companion to the American Musical: Theatre, Film, and Television* (New York and Oxford: Oxford University Press, 2008), 545.
2. Richard Rodgers, *Musical Stages: An Autobiography* (New York: Da Capo Press, 1995), 227.
3. Olin Downes, "Broadway's Gift to Opera," *New York Times*, June 6, 1943.
4. John Chapman, "Musicals Coming of Age: New Shows Have Creative Qualities Which Recent Dramas Lack," *Sunday News*, January 19, 1940.
5. Quoted in Gerald Bordman, *American Musical Comedy: From Adonis to Dreamgirls* (New York: Oxford University Press, 1982), 3.
6. Scott McMillin, *The Musical as Drama* (Princeton, NJ: Princeton University Press, 2006), 2, 8ff. See also David Van Leer, "Putting It Together: Sondheim and the Broadway Musical," *Raritan* 7, no. 2 (Fall 1987): 114–15; and Raymond Knapp's discussions of "camp" and "Musical Enhanced Reality Mode" in *The American Musical and the Formation of National Identity* (Princeton, NJ: Princeton University Press, 2005), 12–15; Raymond Knapp, *The American Musical and the Performance of Personal Identity* (Princeton, NJ: Princeton University Press, 2006), 67–68. This is also a recurring theme throughout Bradley Rogers, *The Song Is You: Musical Theater and the Politics of Bursting into Song and Dance* (Iowa City: University of Iowa Press, 2020).
7. Geoffrey Block, "Integration," in *The Oxford Handbook of The American Musical*, ed. Raymond Knapp, Mitchell Morris, and Stacy Wolf (New York and Oxford: Oxford University Press, 2011), 97–110; Bordman, *American Musical Comedy*, 159–60; Gerald Bordman and Richard Norton, *American Musical Theatre: A Chronicle* (New York and Oxford: Oxford University Press, 2010), 595; David Savran, *Highbrow/Lowdown: Theater, Jazz, and the Making of the New Middle Class* (Ann Arbor: University of Michigan Press, 2009), 81; Tim Carter, *Oklahoma!: The*

Making of an American Musical, rev. ed. (New Haven, CT: Yale University Press, 2020), 171–74; McMillin, *The Musical as Drama*, 2–3; Stephen Banfield, *Jerome Kern* (New Haven, CT: Yale University Press, 2006), 212; David Mark D'Andre, "The Theatre Guild, *Carousel*, and the Cultural Field of American Musical Theatre" (PhD diss., Yale University, 2000), 117–39; Kurt Gänzl, *The Encyclopedia of the Musical Theatre* (New York: Schirmer Books, 1994), 2:1085; Kim H. Kowalke, "Theorizing the Golden Age Musical: Genre, Structure, Syntax," *Gamut* 6, no. 2 (December 2013): 133–37. Dominic Symonds points out that the same claim has also been made about the vaudeville of Lew Fields from the turn of the twentieth century; see Dominic Symonds, *We'll Have Manhattan: The Early Works of Rodgers and Hart* (New York and Oxford: Oxford University Press, 2015), 22, and Dominic Symonds, "Coherency: Lew Fields, the Performer-Producer and Experimenter in Integration," in *The Palgrave Handbook of Musical Theatre Producers*, ed. Laura Macdonald and William Everett (New York: Palgrave MacMillan, 2017), 132–34.

8. "Institution" refers not to a venue or conservatory but more broadly to an "art world" as defined by Howard Becker, *Art Worlds* (Berkeley: University of California Press, 2008 [originally published 1982]), 1–39. See also Richard Taruskin, *The Oxford History of Western Music*, vol. 1 (Oxford and New York: Oxford University Press, 2010), xx–xxi. The topic of institutions will be covered in greater detail in Chapter 2.
9. Sam and Bella Spewack, "Introduction," in *Kiss Me Kate: A Musical Play*, by Sam and Bella Spewack, lyrics by Cole Porter (New York: Alfred A. Knopf, 1953), viii.
10. Dwight Macdonald, *Against the American Grain* (New York: Random House, 1962), 36–37.
11. Cited in Janice A. Radway, *A Feeling for Books: The Book-of-the-Month Club, Literary Taste, and Middle-Class Desire* (Chapel Hill: University of North Carolina Press, 1997), 161.
12. Macdonald, *Against the American Grain*, 37.
13. See, for example, Radway, *Feeling for Books*, 247–60; Birte Christ, "More Trouble with Diversity: Re-Dressing Poverty, Masking Class in Middlebrow Success Fiction," *Amerikastudien/American Studies* 55, no. 1 (2010): 22–23.
14. Radway, *Feeling for Books*, 163–75; Joan Shelley Rubin, *The Making of Middlebrow Culture* (Chapel Hill: University of North Carolina Press, 1992), 98–110.
15. Rubin, *Making of Middlebrow Culture*, 266–329. For a description of similar institutions in England, see Nicola Humble, *The Feminine Middlebrow Novel: Class, Domesticity, and Bohemianism, 1920s to 1950s* (Oxford and New York: Oxford University Press, 2001), 36–46.
16. Savran, *Highbrow/Lowdown*, 3–4.
17. Russell Lynes, "Highbrow, Lowbrow, Middlebrow," *Harper's Magazine* (February 1, 1949), 28.
18. Russell Lynes, *The Tastemakers* (New York: Harper and Brothers, 1954), 282.
19. The first recorded use of the word "middlebrow" comes from *Punch, or the London Charivari*, December 23, 1925, 673: "The B. B. C. claim to have discovered a new type, the 'middlebrow'. It consists of people who are hoping that some day they will get used to the stuff they ought to like."
20. Macdonald, *Against the American Grain*, 3.
21. Lawrence Levine, *Highbrow/Lowbrow: The Emergence of Cultural Hierarchy in America* (Cambridge, MA: Harvard University Press, 1988), chapters 1 and 2.
22. Ann Douglas, *The Feminization of American Culture* (New York: Alfred A. Knopf, 1977), 3–13; Lauren Berlant, *The Female Complaint: The Unfinished Business of Sentimentality in American Culture* (Durham, NC: Duke University Press, 2008); see also Humble, *Feminine Middlebrow Novel*; Jaime Harker, *America the Middlebrow: Women's Novels, Progressivism, and Middlebrow Authorship Between the Wars* (Amherst: University of Massachusetts Press, 2007), 4–15. For a recent collection of essays that reconsiders the gendered aspects of middlebrow culture, see Kate Macdonald, ed., *The Masculine Middlebrow, 1880–1950: What Mr. Miniver Read* (Basingstoke: Palgrave Macmillan, 2011).
23. Christopher Chowrimootoo, *Middlebrow Modernism: Britten's Operas and the Great Divide* (Oakland: University of California Press, 2018), 3. Tom Perrin makes a similar point regarding literature: middlebrow novels "at one and the same time allow readers an outlet for legitimate complaints about the hypocrisy of conventional values and also to maintain the irresistible appeal of belonging to mainstream society, an attraction that modernism is seen to repress." See Tom Perrin, "Rebuilding 'Bildung': The Middlebrow Novel of Aesthetic Education in the Mid-Twentieth-Century United States," *Novel: A Forum on Fiction* 44, no. 3 (Fall 2011): 384.
24. Andreas Huyssen, *After the Great Divide: Modernism, Mass Culture, Postmodernism* (Bloomington: Indiana University Press, 1986), viii.

25. Rubin, *Making of Middlebrow Culture*, 2–15. In cultural studies, this is usually framed as the distinction between "personality" and "character." The touchstone source is Warren Susman, *Culture as History: The Transformation of American Society in the Twentieth Century* (New York: Pantheon Books, 1984), 271–85.
26. Radway, *Feeling for Books*, 163.
27. The most famous studies of the process of "sacralization" of secular art in America are Paul DiMaggio, "Cultural Entrepreneurship in Nineteenth-Century Boston: The Creation of an Organizational Base for High Culture in America," *Media, Culture and Society* 4, no. 1 (1982): 33–50; Paul DiMaggio, "Cultural Entrepreneurship in Nineteenth-Century Boston, Part II: The Classification and Framing of American Art," *Media, Culture and Society* 4, no. 4 (1982): 303–22; and Lawrence Levine, "The Sacralization of Culture," in *Highbrow/Lowbrow*, 83–168.
28. John Guillory, "The Ordeal of Middlebrow Culture," *Transition* 67 (1995): 82–92. See also Humble, *Feminine Middlebrow Novel*, 57–107; Erica Brown, *Comedy and the Feminine Middlebrow Novel: Elizabeth von Arnim and Elizabeth Taylor* (London and New York: Routledge, 2016), 116–18. Studies that link middlebrow to undermining stable notions of identity include Christ, "More Trouble with Diversity"; Christoph Ehland and Cornelia Wächter, eds., *Middlebrow and Gender: 1890–1945* (Leiden: Brill Rodopi, 2016).
29. Rubin, *Making of Middlebrow Culture*, 26–33.
30. For example, see Casey Nelson Blake, *Beloved Community: The Cultural Criticism of Randolph Bourne, Van Wyck Brooks, Waldo Frank, and Lewis Mumford* (Chapel Hill: University of North Carolina Press, 1990); Rubin, *The Making of Middlebrow Culture*, especially xvii–xviii; Susan Hegeman, *Patterns for America: Modernism and the Concept of Culture* (Princeton, NJ: Princeton University Press, 1999); Victoria Grieve, *The Federal Art Project and the Creation of Middlebrow Culture* (Urbana: University of Illinois Press, 2009). I also join Elizabeth Crist in following what were generally thought to be ideas of the Progressive Movement into the post–World War I era. See *Music for the Common Man: Aaron Copland During the Depression and War* (Oxford and New York: Oxford University Press, 2005), 16.
31. Macdonald, *Against the American Grain*, 59.
32. I borrow the term "critical mood" from Rita Felski, *The Limits of Critique* (Chicago: University of Chicago Press, 2015), 20–22.
33. Macdonald, *Against the American Grain*, 12. It was common for writers to subdivide the "middlebrow" category. In addition to Macdonald, see Queenie Leavis, *Fiction and the Reading Public* (London: Chatto and Windus, 1932), 3–18, 23–24 (middlebrow read as literature, middlebrow not read as literature); Lynes, "Highbrow, Lowbrow, Middlebrow," 25–28 ("upper" and "lower" middlebrows). I do not adopt Macdonald's differentiation between "masscult" and "midcult" as two different kinds of middlebrow culture. After all, in much of his writing, Macdonald himself also tended to conflate these different categories under the umbrella term "middlebrow." For example, see Dwight Macdonald, "By Cozzens Possessed: A Review of Reviews," *Commentary* 25 (January 1958), 46. In this book I focus on common elements that united each of these subdivisions.
34. Thomas Wheatland, *The Frankfurt School in Exile* (Minneapolis: University of Minnesota Press, 2009), 165; Paul R. Gorman, *Left Intellectuals and Popular Culture in Twentieth-Century America* (Chapel Hill: University of North Carolina Press, 1996), 13–33. See also Richard A. Peterson, "The Rise and Fall of Highbrow Snobbery as a Status Marker," *Poetics* 25 (1997): 82–84, and Savran, *Highbrow/Lowdown*, 47–49.
35. On the perseverance of Victorian values in middlebrow culture, see Rubin, *Making of Middlebrow Culture*, xvii–xviii.
36. Margaret Widdemer, "Message and Middlebrow," *The Saturday Review of Literature* 9, no. 31 (February 18, 1933), 434. For the broader context of this kind of "dehumanizing" rhetoric in European art in the years surrounding World War I, see Richard Taruskin, *The Oxford History of Western Music*, vol. 4 (Oxford and New York: Oxford University Press, 2005), 467–78.
37. Daniel Tracy, "Investing in 'Modernism': Smart Magazines, Parody, and Middlebrow Professional Judgment," *Journal of Modern Periodical Studies* 1, no. 1 (2010): 40.
38. Radway, *Feeling for Books*, 163–68; Rubin, *Making of Middlebrow Culture*, 29–33; Tracy, "Investing in 'Modernism,'" 40–41; Marianne Conroy, "Acting Out: Method Acting, the National Culture, and the Middlebrow Disposition in Cold War America," *Criticism* 35, no. 2 (Spring 1993): 241.

39. Richard H. Pells, *Radical Visions and American Dreams: Culture and Social Thought in the Depression Years* (New York: Harper & Row, 1973), 335–40; Wheatland, *Frankfurt School in Exile*, 168–69.
40. Wheatland, *Frankfurt School in Exile*, 165–66, 172–77.
41. Alan Wald, *The New York Intellectuals: The Rise and Decline of the Anti-Stalinist Left from the 1930s to the 1980s* (Chapel Hill: University of North Carolina Press, 1987), 203–4.
42. Clement Greenberg, *Art and Culture: Critical Essays* (Boston: Beacon Press, 1961), 6 (emphasis original). Wald, *New York Intellectuals*, 207.
43. Macdonald, *Against the American Grain*, 6.
44. In part, these institutions will be the subject of Chapter 2. The locus classicus of studies that situate modernistic texts within a broad, commercial culture is Lawrence Rainey, *Institutions of Modernism* (New Haven, CT: Yale University Press, 1998). See also Catherine Turner, *Marketing Modernism Between the Two World Wars* (Amherst: University of Massachusetts Press, 2003); Mark Morrison, *The Public Face of Modernism: Little Magazine, Audiences, and Reception* (Madison: University of Wisconsin Press, 2001), 5–13, which provides an outline of the basic argument. See also the chapters written by Allison Pease and Lawrence Rainy in *The Cambridge Companion to Modernism*, ed. Michael Levenson (Cambridge: Cambridge University Press, 2011), 33–68 and 197–211, respectively.
45. Pells, *Radical Visions and American Dreams*, 334–46.
46. Wheatland, *Frankfurt School in Exile*, 171–87.
47. Ibid., 158–77.
48. Tracy, "Investing in 'Modernism,'" 52–53, 55. See also Michael Kammen, *The Lively Arts: Gilbert Seldes and the Transformation of Cultural Criticism in the United States* (New York and Oxford: Oxford University Press, 1996), 47–51, where he describes the backlash against one literary magazine in particular, *The Dial*. Linda J. Lumsden identifies this group as part of a "lyrical left," which comprised "community-builders among radical intellectuals largely outside the world of labor," and which she groups with "a number of prewar popular magazines [with] radical predilections." See Linda J. Lumsden, *Black, White, and Red All Over: A Cultural History of the Radical Press in Its Heyday* (Kent, OH: Kent State University Press, 2014), 187ff.
49. See, for example, Michael Kammen on the founding of *Time* magazine, which launched with the announcement that, according to rumor, "*The Waste Land* is a hoax." Kammen, *The Lively Arts*, 49 et passim.
50. Ehland and Wächter, eds., *Middlebrow and Gender*, 3. Similar descriptions (using different language) can be found in, among others, Radway, *Feeling for Books*, 9–10, 66–76; Humble, *Feminine Middlebrow Novel*, 5–6; Elizabeth Long, *Book Clubs: Women and the Uses of Reading in Everyday Life* (Chicago: University of Chicago Press, 2003), 145–48; Harker, *America the Middlebrow*, 19.
51. Lionel Trilling, "A Young Critic in a Younger America," *New York Times Book Review* (March 7, 1954), 1.
52. For more detail about this movement's general approach to art, see Richard Shusterman, *Pragmatist Aesthetics: Living Beauty, Rethinking Art*, 2nd ed. (Lanham, MD: Rowman and Littlefield, 2000), 6–33.
53. Van Wyck Brooks, *The Wine of the Puritans*, in *Van Wyck Brooks: The Early Years. A Selection from His Works, 1908–25*, ed. Claire Sprague (Boston: Northeastern University Press, 1993 [originally published 1908]), 37.
54. Van Wyck Brooks, *America's Coming of Age* (New York: Octagon Books, 1975 [1915]), 34.
55. Ibid., 9. Hegeman, *Patterns for America*, 7.
56. Brooks, *America's Coming of Age*, 33–34.
57. Blake, *Beloved Community*, 117–19.
58. Van Wyck Brooks, "On Creating a Usable Past," *The Dial* 64, no. 7 (April 11, 1918), 337.
59. Ibid., 339.
60. Quoted in Blake, *Beloved Community*, 61.
61. Brooks was part of a generation of critics who would reject this severe tendency in American criticism, which he had associated with the figure of Ralph Waldo Emerson. For more details, see Randall Fuller, *Emerson's Ghosts: Literature, Politics, and the Making of Americanists* (Oxford and New York: Oxford University Press, 2007), 54–59. Note that Fuller uses the term "oppositional criticism" (p. 54) differently than I do here.
62. Brooks, "On Creating a Usable Past," 337–38.
63. Ibid., 340.

64. James Gilbert, *Writers and Partisans: A History of Literary Radicalism in America* (New York: John Wiley and Sons, 1968), 161. This was to no avail; he resigned in protest in 1939. See Van Eyck Brooks, *An Autobiography* (New York: E. P. Dutton, 1965), 535.
65. He edited and then printed both talks in his book *The Opinions of Oliver Allston* that same year. According to Raymond Nelson, "On Literature Today" was more or less the same as a speech Brooks had given at Tufts College in 1937. See his *Van Wyck Brooks: A Writer's Life* (New York: E. P. Dutton, 1981), 236.
66. Van Wyck Brooks, *The Opinions of Oliver Allston* (New York: E. P. Dutton, 1941), 230.
67. Ibid., 243.
68. Lionel Trilling would later write that Brooks did not engage in a battle, but rather that his "abdication of his leadership of the modern movement was ... voluntary." Trilling, "Young Critic in a Younger America," 28. This seems incorrect given the combative language of *The Opinions of Oliver Allston* and Brooks's correspondence behind the scenes, which will be discussed in later chapters.
69. F. W. Dupee, "The Americanism of Van Wyck Brooks," *Partisan Review* (1939), reprinted in William Phillips and Philip Rahv, eds., *The Partisan Reader: Ten Years of Partisan Review 1934–1944: An Anthology* (New York: Dial Press, 1946), 377. Essays that attacked Brooks specifically include Dwight Macdonald, "Kulturbolschewismus Is Here," *Partisan Review* 8 no. 6 (November/December 1941): 224–51; Dupee, "The Americanism of Van Wyck Brooks" (1939); William Phillips, "The Intellectuals' Tradition," *Partisan Review* 8, no. 6 (November/December 1941): 481–90; and a symposium about Brooks's notion of a "usable past," published under the title "The Situation in American Writing" and spread out over two issues (1939), which included responses by Sherwood Anderson, R. P. Blackmur, Louise Bogan, John Dos Passos, James T. Farrell, Horace Gregory, Katherine Anne Porter, Gertrude Stein, Wallace Stevens, Allen Tate, and Lionel Trilling. These final three essays have been anthologized in Phillips and Rahv, eds., *The Partisan Reader*. In addition, others took up these debates. Herbert Marcuse wrote his famous 1937 description of "oppositional" and "affirmative" culture, in which he maintained that the affirmative stance represented a kind of "bourgeois culture" that asserted "a universally obligatory, eternally better and more valuable world that must be unconditionally affirmed," a type of culture that "celebrates" and "exalts" the status quo, thereby making it "regressive and apologetic." Herbert Marcuse, "The Affirmative Character of Culture," in *Negations: Essays in Critical Theory*, trans. Jeremy J. Shapiro (Boston: Beacon Press, 1968), 95, 103. Closer to Brooks stood (surprisingly) Eliot. He warned against the development of an upper class that was "deprived ... of its functional relationship to the rest of society," and the development of a kind of art that was "equally cut off from organic relation to the whole of society." He described such a group as "highbrow," and believed that their art and literature had become "frail." "The artist is, at best, making the best he can of a disintegrated society; at worst, he is merely the victim of it." T. S. Eliot, "Notes Towards a Definition of Culture," *Partisan Review* 11, no. 2 (Spring 1944): 146–47, 149.
70. Macdonald, "Kulturbolschewismus Is Here," 451.
71. For more detail on how Macdonald tried to enlist other writers in his cause against Brooks, both in public and in private correspondence, see Gilbert, *Writers and Partisans*, 221–31.
72. Michael Wreszin, ed., *A Moral Temper: The Letters of Dwight Macdonald* (Chicago: Ivan R. Dee, 2001), 106.
73. Macdonald, "Kulturbolschewismus Is Here," 448.
74. His picture was on the cover of *Time*, October 2, 1944.
75. Trilling, "Young Critic in Younger America," 1.
76. See Macdonald, "By Cozzens Possessed," 46.
77. Most writers argue that Brooks's influence waned in the 1920s, and often consider his mammoth and controversial *Opinions of Oliver Allston* peripheral (if they consider it at all). One representative opinion comes from intellectual historian Thomas Bender: "Van Wyck Brooks is one of those intellectuals whose work divides itself dramatically and clearly into two phases. For those who know him only by his later work, particularly his undiscriminating, fact-laden, and intellectually vacant multivolume celebration of American literary culture, the power and critical edge of this early criticism may come as a surprise." Thomas Bender, *New York Intellect: A History of Intellectual Life in New York City, from 1750 to the Beginnings of Our Own Time* (New York: Alfred A. Knopf, 1987), 239. In the present chapter I argue otherwise.
78. William Wasserstrom, *Van Wyck Brooks*, Pamphlets on American Writers, No. 71 (Minneapolis: University of Minnesota Press, 1968), 5.

79. William Wasserstrom, *The Legacy of Van Wyck Brooks: A Study of Maladies and Motives* (Carbondale: Southern Illinois University Press, 1971), 64.
80. Blake, *Beloved Community*, 6.
81. While Brooks remains a marginal figure, some scholars have performed essential groundwork on people who were in his circle, especially Paul Rosenfeld. See, for example, Michael Broyles, *Mavericks and Other Traditions in American Music* (New Haven, CT: Yale University Press, 2004), 102–106; Carol Oja, *Making Music Modern: New York in the 1920s* (New York and Oxford: Oxford University Press, 2000), 302–10.
82. Alfred Kazin, "Criticism and Isolation," *The Virginia Quarterly Review* 17, no. 3 (Summer 1941): 448 (for his position on Brooks specifically, see 450–51).
83. Alfred Kazin, *Starting Out in the Thirties* (Boston: Little Brown, 1962), 157. In this particular passage, he denounced his *Partisan Review* colleague Mary McCarthy as representing "the first," but hardly the last, "writer of my generation who made me realize that it would now be possible to be a radical without any idealism whatsoever." He described the far left-wing crowd in New York after the war: "Their boundless belief in criticism was actually their passport to the postwar world, for as society became more complex and intellectuals more consciously an elite, the old literary radicals were the few, in an age of academic criticism, who understood the relation of literature to institutions. Some of these writers even became the mass media, and presiding over the cultural rites of television and the slicks, delighted their most eager readers by insulting them to their faces as highbrows, the mass audience, the conformists, the herd. The intellectuals who failed at revolution were to succeed as intellectual arbiters. They had passion. They would never feel that they had compromised, for they believed in alienation, and would forever try to outdo conventional opinion even when they agreed with it" (pp. 155, 157).
84. John Brooks, "Highbrow, Lowbrows, Middlebrow, Now," *The American Heritage* 34, no. 4 (June/July 1983): 43. While this article says the revue was inspired by Lynes's article, it is more likely that only one sketch, called "Highbrow, Lowbrow," from the middle of Act I, was based on Lynes's article.
85. Lynes, "Highbrow, Lowbrow, Middlebrow," 20. "Lowbrow" for him meant something closer to "folk" art.
86. Russell Lynes, "The Taste-makers," *Harper's Magazine* 194, no. 1165 (June 1947), 491.
87. In correspondence, Lynes said that he did not know that Brooks had used the terms "highbrow" and "lowbrow" as far back as 1915, admitting that he only knew the "fine fury" of Virginia Woolf. Letter from Russell Lynes to Van Wyck Brooks, June 19, 1958, Van Wyck Brooks Papers, MSS Coll. 650, Box 25, Folder 1707.
88. Lynes, "Tastemakers," 491.

Chapter 2

1. In this chapter I define "institution" as "the set of basic assumptions and norms in a given historical context that validate particular [cultural] practices and denigrate others," following Russell Berman, "Introduction," in Peter Bürger and Crista Bürger, *The Institutions of Art*, tr. Loren Kruger (Lincoln: University of Nebraska Press, 1992), xiv. Sociologists tend to use the term "institution" more narrowly to refer to networks of organizations (or what Louis Althusser has called "apparatuses"), usually focusing on venues, organizations, societies, established parties, their relationships, their differences, and the way individuals interact with them. See Paul J. DiMaggio and Walter W. Powell, eds., *The New Institutionalism in Organizational Analysis* (Chicago: University of Chicago Press, 1991), 1–33. For a brief summary of these issues, see Peter Uwe Hohendahl, *Building a National Literature: The Case of Germany 1830–1870*, tr. Renate Baron Franciscono (Ithaca, NY: Cornell University Press, 1989), 16–43.
2. Bürger and Bürger, *The Institutions of Art*, 17.
3. This is borrowed, and slightly altered, from Arthur Danto. He described the patterns of thought that "[make] art possible" by drawing theoretical borders around the "art world": the kinds of thinking used to take up some cultural object "into the world of art, and [keep] it from collapsing into the real object which it is (in a sense of *is* other than that of artistic identification)." Arthur Danto, "The Artworld," *The Journal of Philosophy* 61, no. 19 (October 15, 1964): 572, 581.
4. Bürger and Bürger, *The Institutions of Art*, 17–18; see also Peter Bürger, *Theory of the Avant-Garde* (Minneapolis: University of Minnesota Press, 1984), 69–73.
5. For a brief summary of the web of meanings implied by "autonomy" in music, see Richard Taruskin, "Is There a Baby in the Bathwater? (Part I)," *Archiv für Musikwissenschaft* 63, no. 3 (2006): 163–70.

6. Philip Bohlman, *The Study of Folk Music in the Modern World* (Bloomington: Indiana University Press, 1988), 10–12. See also Matthew Gelbart, *The Invention of "Folk Music" and "Art Music": Emerging Categories from Ossian to Wagner* (Cambridge: Cambridge University Press, 2007), 9.
7. The word "lowbrow" could signify either folk art, as it did for Dwight Macdonald, Virginia Woolf, and Russell Lynes, among others; or popular culture, as it did for Van Wyck Brooks, Gilbert Seldes, and others.
8. Gelbart, *Invention of "Folk Music" and "Art Music,"* 204, 256–57. See also Brian Jones, "Finding the Avant-Garde in the Old-Time: John Cohen in the American Folk Revival," *American Music* 28, no. 4 (Winter 2010): 402–35. For the relationship between autonomy and folk music, see Allan Moore, "Authenticity as Authentication," *Popular Music* 21, no. 2 (May 2002): 217; Bohlman, *The Study of Folk Music*, xix.
9. Macdonald, *Against the American Grain*, 13. Although many of the authors cited below echo this position to varying degrees, the touchstone example remains Walter Benjamin, "The Work of Art in the Age of Mechanical Reproduction," in *Illuminations*, ed. Hannah Arendt, tr. Harry Zohn (New York: Harcourt, 1968), 214–18.
10. Brooks, *America's Coming of Age*, 10.
11. This was a common complaint about his work at the time. See Blake, *Beloved Community*, 131.
12. Brooks, *America's Coming of Age*, 26. Huyssen, *After the Great Divide*, viii.
13. Brooks, *America's Coming of Age*, 16–17.
14. Peter Bürger's word for this is the institution's "historicity." See *Institutions of Art*, 6.
15. Peter Bürger, *Theory of the Avant-Garde*, 35–46. In music, the *locus classicus* for discussing this *Stildualismus* is Carl Dahlhaus, *Nineteenth-Century Music*, tr. J. Bradford Robinson (Berkeley: University of California Press, 1989), 8–15.
16. Rubin dates this process at least as far back as the 1790s in the United States. See Rubin, *The Making of Middlebrow Culture*, 2. See also Levine, *Highbrow/Lowbrow*, 230–31.
17. J. Peter Burkholder, "Museum Pieces: The Historicist Mainstream in Music of the Last Hundred Years," *Nineteenth-Century Music* 2 (1983): 115–34; Levine, *Highbrow/Lowbrow*, 4; DiMaggio, "Cultural Entrepreneurship in Nineteenth-Century Boston: The Creation of an Organizational Base for High Culture in America," *Media, Culture, Society* 4, no. 1 (1982): 33–50.
18. Macdonald, *Against the American Grain*, 4.
19. Cf. Oja, *Making Music Modern*, 16.
20. Macdonald, *Against the American Grain*, 7.
21. Brooks, *America's Coming of Age*, 3, 7, 17.
22. Paul DiMaggio, "On Pierre Bourdieu," *American Journal of Sociology* 84, no. 6 (May 1979): 1461–62. Quoted in Karen Ahlquist, "Balance of Power: Music as Art and Social Class in the Late Nineteenth Century," in *Rethinking American Music*, ed. Tara Browner and Thomas Riis (Urbana: University of Illinois Press, 2019), 7–33.
23. Russell Berman has pointed out that typical institution theory suggests, at any time, a certain set of institutional norms and parameters tends to dominate. Berman calls this a subtle "Hegelian" element in the institutional model. Whether one set of parameters dominates others, and whether competing ideas "synthesize," is not of interest in this book. The point, rather, is that multiple institutions, with their own strategies of reproduction and validation, conflicted on Broadway at the time. See Berman, "Introduction," in *The Institutions of Art*, ed. Bürger and Bürger, xviii.
24. Benjamin Filene, *Romancing the Folk: Public Memory and American Roots Music* (Chapel Hill: University of North Carolina Press, 2000), 9. Contemporary accounts corroborate Filene's analysis. For example, influential critic Paul Rosenfeld wrote in 1929: "In view of the body of alleged American folk song, the contention that an American music is very young must appear fantastic. It is in fact anything but absurd. The belief that the Negro spirituals and the songs of the Appalachian mountains constitute an authentic folk music, like the English, the Russian, and the Magyar, flatters our vanities. But there is little realism in it." Paul Rosenfeld, "Beginnings of American Music," in *Musical Impressions: Selections from Paul Rosenfeld's Criticism*, ed. Herbert A. Leibowitz (New York: Hill and Wang, 1969), 228.
25. A study that served as a model for the following section (dealing largely with a later period of time) is Ron Eyerman and Scott Barretta, "From the 30s to the 60s: The Folk Music Revival in the United States," *Theory and Society* 25, no. 4 (August 1996): 501–43.
26. Filene, *Romancing the Folk*, 13.

27. Francis James Child, "Ballad Poetry," in *Johnson's Universal Cyclopædia* [originally published 1900], reprinted in *Journal of Folklore Research* 31 (1994): 214.
28. Robert Cantwell describes this as the primary motivation for the folk-song revival at the turn of the twentieth century and singles out Jane Addams as a leading figure. See Robert Cantwell, *When We Were Good: The Folk Revival* (Cambridge, MA: Harvard University Press, 1996), 26–29.
29. Child, "Ballad Poetry," 218. Emphasis original.
30. The subject of how folk songs change has long been one of the most controversial topics in folk studies, and a complete discussion lies beyond the scope of this book. For two brief overviews, see Bohlman, *Study of Folk Music*, 9, and Gelbart, *Invention of "Folk Music" and "Art Music,"* 186–90.
31. Quoted in Edward Lee, *Music of the People: A Study of Popular Music in Great Britain* (Bristol: Barrie and Jenkins, 1970), 118. Emphasis added. See also Becker, *Art Worlds*, 247; Bohlman, *Study of Folk Music*, 10. For more detail on Sharp and how folk music changes (through the processes of "continuity," "variation," and "selection"), see Richard Crawford, *America's Musical Life: A History* (New York: W. W. Norton, 2001), 599.
32. Gelbart, *The Invention of "Folk Music" and "Art Music,"* 256–59.
33. Child, "Ballad Poetry," 218; Filene, *Romancing the Folk*, 13.
34. Child, "Ballad Poetry," 214.
35. Filene, *Romancing the Folk*, 33–42. For another overview, which sums up earlier research on the subject, see Crawford, *America's Musical Life*, 597–618.
36. R. Serge Denisoff, *Great Day Coming: Folk Music and the American Left* (Urbana: University of Illinois Press, 1971), 19–38. Richard and Joanne Reuss, *American Music and Left-Wing Politics: 1927–1957* (Lanham, MD: Scarecrow Press, 2000), 81–114.
37. For a summary, see Crawford, *America's Musical Life*, 605–28.
38. Scholars have noticed that literature and visual art generally followed similar trends: Individual artists and writers drew inspiration from practices that seemed redolent of remote times and places, and sought to transfer them into an emphatically modern, urban setting without obliterating their folk qualities. This topic lies beyond the scope of this book. A touchstone study in the field of art remains Erika Doss, *Benton, Pollock, and the Politics of Modernism: From Regionalism to Abstract Expressionism* (Chicago: University of Chicago Press, 1991). In literature, especially illuminating is Rubin, *Constance Rourke and American Culture*.
39. Seldes does not use the word "authentic," but Michael Kammen uses the word in relation to Seldes. See Kammen, *The Lively Arts*, 97–98.
40. Gilbert Seldes, *The Seven Lively Arts* (Mineola, NY: Dover Publications, 2001), 77–78.
41. Ibid., 83, 95.
42. Ibid., 72, 38.
43. Ibid., 311, 313. Emphasis added.
44. Kammen, *The Lively Arts*, 10; Seldes, *Seven Lively Arts*, 191–92.
45. Seldes, *Seven Lively Arts*, 24, 78.
46. Ibid., 165–66.
47. Ibid., 98.
48. Ibid., 133. Emphasis original.
49. See Kammen, *The Lively Arts*, 5.
50. Brooks, *America's Coming of Age*, 33–34.
51. Seldes, *Seven Lively Arts*, 111.
52. Ibid., 311.
53. Gilbert Seldes, "This Can't Be Corn," *Esquire*, October 1, 1941, 160. The essay he refers to is Adorno's "On Popular Music," originally published in 1941 in the journal *Studies in Philosophy and Social Science*. Seldes did not read this essay, but rather excerpts from it that Virgil Thomson had quoted at length in his article "How Popular Music Works," *New York Herald-Tribune*, June 15, 1941. In fact, this would not be the last time Thomson used the *Herald-Tribune* to disseminate writing by members of the famous Institute for Social Research. See also his articles "The 'Hit' Parade," *New York Herald-Tribune*, June 26, 1941, and "Radio Examined," *New York Herald-Tribune*, February 8, 1942.
54. Quoted in Kammen, *The Lively Arts*, 9.
55. Maud Karpeles, "Some Reflections on Authenticity in Folk Music," *Journal of the International Folk Music Council* 3 (1951): 13–14.
56. Seldes, *Seven Lively Arts*, 310.

57. Ibid., 311. Emphasis added.
58. Studies describing the development of elite institutions for music in the United States is vast. For recent writing on this subject, see, for example, Ahlquist, "Balance of Power," 7-33. On its ramifications in popular music at the turn of the century, see Larry Hamberlin, *Tin Pan Opera: Operatic Novelty Songs in the Ragtime Era* (New York and Oxford: Oxford University Press, 2011), 5-8.
59. Levine, *Highbrow/Lowbrow*, 146.
60. Elie Siegmeister, *Music and Society* (New York: Critics Group Press, 1938), 59. The word "reintegration" was adapted from the introduction to *Music Vanguard: A Critical Review* 1, no. 1 (Mar.-Apr. 1935): 1. (It is spelled "redintegration" in the original source.) This was a short-lived journal (it produced only two issues) that contained writing by many associated with the Composers' Collective.
61. For recent research on this subject, see Victoria Von Arx, "The Third Street Music School Settlement: The Grand Tradition as Social Practice on New York's Lower East Side," *Journal of the Society for American Music* 5, no. 1 (Feb. 2011): 61-93.
62. For a brief summary of these developments, see Christopher Bigsby and Don B. Wilmeth, "Introduction," in *The Cambridge History of American Theatre*, ed. Don B. Wilmeth (Cambridge: Cambridge University Press, 2008), 10-14, and Mark Fearnow, "Theatre Groups and Their Playwrights," ibid., 348-61.
63. Harold Clurman, *The Fervent Years* (New York: Da Capo Press, 1983), 17.
64. Romain Rolland, "America and The Arts," trans. Waldo Frank, *Seven Arts* 1, no. 1 (1916): 47, 50.
65. The literature on this subject is once again large. For excellent, foundational overviews, see Michael Broyles, "The Community of the Ultramoderns," in Broyles, *Mavericks and Other Traditions in American Music*, 112-50, and Oja, *Making Music Modern*.
66. Claire Reis, "Contemporary Music and 'the Man on the Street,'" *Eolian Review* 2, no. 2 (March 1923): 27 (emphasis original). For more on American music as ultramodern, see David Metzer, "The League of Composers: The Initial Years," *American Music* 15, no. 1 (Spring 1997): 45-69, and John Gabriel, "There and Back Again: *Zeitoper* and the Transatlantic Search for a Uniquely American Opera in the 1920s," *Journal of the Society for American Music* 13, no. 2 (2019): 195-215.
67. I wish to thank Claire Leyden for suggesting this piece.
68. Jeffrey Magee, *Irving Berlin's Musical Theater* (New York and Oxford: Oxford University Press, 2012), 51-57.
69. A discussion of this song appears in Savran, *Highbrow/Lowdown*, 84-85.
70. See Magee, *Berlin's Musical Theater*, 52-57. See also Magee, "'Everybody Step': Irving Berlin, Jazz, and Broadway in the 1920s," *Journal of the American Musicological Society* 59 (2006): 697.
71. Quoted in Magee, *Berlin's Musical Theater*, 53.
72. David Savran, *Highbrow/Lowdown*, 101.
73. Quoted in Ray Allen, "An American Folk Opera? Triangulating Folkness, Blackness, and Americanness in Gershwin and Heyward's 'Porgy and Bess,'" *Journal of American Folklore* 117, no. 465 (Summer 2004): 248. (The first interpolation is by Allen; the second mine.)
74. George Gershwin, "Jazz is the Voice of the American Soul [originally published in 1925]," in *The George Gershwin Reader*, ed. Robert Wyatt and John Andrew Johnson (Oxford and New York: Oxford University Press, 2004), 91.
75. The Gershwins' very first song to be heard on Broadway in 1918 announces this institutional scramble in terms that would have appealed to Gilbert Seldes; it was called "The Real American Folk Song (Is a Rag)."
76. Philip Furia, "Lady, Be Good!," in *The George Gershwin Reader*, ed. Wyatt and Johnson, 66.
77. Quoted in Deena Rosenberg, *Fascinating Rhythm: The Collaboration of George and Ira Gershwin* ([Ann Arbor]: University of Michigan Press, 1997), 108.
78. Savran describes this as "a populist, vernacular, syncretic [form of modernism] (that regards jazz as the key to a distinctive national culture)," which was distinct from "a universalizing, high, pseudo-European modernism (that expects jazz to stay in its place)." Savran, *Highbrow/Lowdown*, 97.
79. Ibid., 89.
80. Richard Crawford, "Where Did Porgy and Bess Come from?," *The Journal of Interdisciplinary History* 36, no. 4 (Spring 2006): 697-734.

81. The foundational writing on the study of the reception of *Porgy and Bess* remains Richard Crawford, "It Ain't Necessarily Soul: Gershwin's 'Porgy and Bess' as a Symbol," *Anuario Interamericano de Investigación Musical* 8 (1972): 24–33.
82. Virgil Thomson, *A Virgil Thomson Reader* (Boston, MA: Houghton Mifflin, 1981), 25.
83. Ibid., 27.
84. Mark Tucker, ed., *The Duke Ellington Reader* (New York and Oxford: Oxford University Press, 1993), 115. Whether this quotation actually represents Ellington's point of view has been a matter of dispute among scholars. Tucker believes it represents Ellington's opinion, while Ray Allen and George P. Cunningham suggest otherwise. For this, and for more descriptions of the African American response to *Porgy and Bess*, see Ray Allen and George P. Cunningham, "Cultural Uplift and Double-Consciousness: African American Responses to the 1935 Opera *Porgy and Bess*," *The Musical Quarterly* 88 (2005): 359–62.
85. Quoted in Crawford, "It Ain't Necessarily Soul," 28; see also Allen, "An American Folk Opera?," 252.
86. Brooks Atkinson, "'Porgy and Bess,' Native Opera, Opens at the Alvin," *New York Times*, October 11, 1935.
87. Thomson, *A Virgil Thomson Reader*, 25.
88. For broad overviews of these various front organizations, see Michael Denning, *The Cultural Front: The Laboring of American Culture in the Twentieth Century* (London: Verso, 1998), 64–96; Morgan Y. Himmelstein, *Drama Was a Weapon: The Left-Wing Theatre in New York, 1929–1941* (New Brunswick, NJ: Rutgers University Press, 1963); Ellen Graff, *Stepping Left: Dance and Politics in New York City, 1928–1942* (Durham, NC: Duke University Press). Although this chapter is not specifically about the visual arts, Andrew Hemingway, *Artists on the Left: American Artists and the Communist Movement, 1926–1956* (New Haven, CT: Yale University Press, 2002), provided important background material that informed this chapter. For a contemporary account of the left-wing theatrical scene, see Bosley Crowther, "Theatre of the Left," *New York Times*, April 14, 1935.
89. These biographical details, including the disputed date of Gold's birth, can be found Michael Folsom, "Introduction: The Pariah of American Letters," in *Mike Gold: A Literary Anthology* (New York: International Publishers, 1972), 10–19.
90. In an article called "Proletarian Realism," originally published in 1930, Gold looked back and commented that his 1921 article still held true, and that the "little path" he suggested had "since become a highroad." See *Mike Gold: A Literary Anthology*, ed. Folsom, 203–4.
91. Ibid., 65.
92. Ibid., 70.
93. Ibid., 206, 208.
94. Ibid., 203.
95. For a summary of the complex position of avowed Communists toward folk music, see Cantwell, *When We Were Good*, 91–93.
96. Gold, in *Mike Gold: A Literary Anthology*, 206–7.
97. Quoted in Jeffrey Melnick, *A Right to Sing the Blues: African Americans, Jews, and American Popular Song* (Cambridge, MA: Harvard University Press, 1999), 146.
98. Quoted in Lewis A. Erenberg, *Swingin' the Dream: Big Band and the Rebirth of American Culture* (Chicago: University of Chicago Press, 1998), 132.
99. Mike Gold, "Change the World: Hats Off to the I. L. G. W. U. for Pins and Needles," *Daily Worker*, December 11, 1937. On the politics of *Pins and Needles*, see Trudi Wright, "*Pins and Needles* (1937): Everything in Moderation," *Studies in Musical Theatre* 7, no. 1 (January 2013): 61–73. I thank Professor Wright for supplying the Gold review.
100. Daniel Opler, "Music from the Vanguard: The Songs of the Composers Collective of New York, 1933–1936," *Journal for the Study of Radicalism* 10, no. 2 (Fall 2016): 126.
101. Quoted in Hemingway, *Artists on the Left*, 15.
102. Quoted in Graff, *Stepping Left*, 10. Originally published as Michael Gold, "Change the World," *Daily Worker*, June 14, 1934.
103. Michael Gold, "The Steam Hammer," *Daily Worker*, June 11, 1934. Quoted in Carol Oja, "Marc Blitzstein's 'The Cradle Will Rock' and Mass-Song Style of the 1930s," *The Musical Quarterly* 73 (1989): 460.
104. This two-part division can be found in Anne C. Shreffler, "'Music Left and Right': A Tale of Two Histories of Progressive Music," *Proceedings of the British Academy* 185 (2013): 70–72.

105. Charles Seeger, "Preface to All Linguist Treatment of Music," *Music Vanguard: A Critical Review*, 1, no. 1 (March–April 1935): 27.
106. Maria Cristina Fava, "The Composers' Collective of New York, 1932-1936: Bourgeois Modernism for the Proletariat," *American Music* 34, no. 3 (Fall 2016): 333.
107. Oja, "Marc Blitzstein's 'The Cradle Will Rock," 452–53.
108. David K. Dunaway, "Charles Seeger and Carl Sands: The Composers' Collective Years," *Ethnomusicology* 24, no. 2 (May 1980): 164.
109. Grant, *Rise and Fall*, 102.
110. Howard Pollack, *Marc Blitzstein: His Life, His Work, His World* (New York and Oxford: Oxford University Press, 2012), 152–53. This song is printed in Marc Blitzstein, *The Mark Blitzstein Songbook*, vol. 2, ed. Leonard Lehrman ([S. I.]: Boosey and Hawkes, 2001), 2–5.
111. Brooks Atkinson, "The Play: Jimmy Savo and 'Parade' Introduce the Theatre Guild to Revelry," *New York Times*, May 21, 1935.
112. Georgi Dimitrov, *The United Front: The Struggle Against Fascism and War* (London: Lawrence and Wishart, 1938), 91.
113. Morris Dickstein, *Dancing in the Dark: A Cultural History of the Great Depression* (New York: W. W. Norton, 2009), 125. The "Popular Front" is a confusing term in that it has two, somewhat related meanings. The first, used above, refers to the period in Communist history. However, Michael Denning uses the term in an expansive way, to refer to the cultural movement that was more or less sympathetic with the far left, but not affiliated or beholden to the dictates of the Comintern. As Denning writes, "the 'fellow travelers' *were* the popular front." See Denning, *The Cultural Front*, 5. While recognizing that the two senses of the term cannot be extricated, in this study I will generally limit its use to the first.
114. Elizabeth Osborne, *Staging the People: Community and Identity in the Federal Theatre Project* (New York: Palgrave Macmillan, 2011), 2–4.
115. John O'Connor and Lorraine Brown, eds., *The Federal Theatre Project: "Free, Adult, Uncensored"* (London: Eyre Methuen, 1980), 12.
116. Larry Stempel, *Showtime: A History of the Broadway Musical Theater* (New York: W. W. Norton, 2010), 470–80; Block, *Enchanted Evenings*, 129.
117. Willson Whitman, *Bread and Circuses: A Study of Federal Theatre* (Freeport, NY: Books for Libraries Press, 1972 [originally published 1937]), 19.
118. Ibid., 14. One notable exception was Lee Shubert, who thought he could profit by leasing dark theaters to the government for Federal Theatre Project shows. See Hallie Flanagan, *Arena* (New York: Duell, Sloan, and Pearce, 1985 [orig. published 1940]), 41.
119. Whitman, *Bread and Circuses*, 14.
120. Ibid., 4.
121. Flanagan, *Arena*, 45.
122. Hallie Flanagan, "What Are We Doing with Our Chance?," *Federal Theatre* 2, no. 3 ([January 15, 1937]): 5.
123. Hallie Flanagan, *Dynamo* (New York: Duell, Sloan and Pearce, 1943), 25.
124. Many of these are collected in Library of Congress, Washington, DC, Federal Theatre Collection, Container 24, "Publications."
125. Quoted in Hallie Flanagan, "Not in Despair," *Federal Theatre*, 2, no. 4 ([March 21, 1937]), 5.
126. Brooks Atkinson, "The Play," *New York Times*, May 21, 1937.
127. For a brief summary of these different origins stories, see Dan Isaac, "Introduction" to Arthur Arent, "'Ethiopia': The First 'Living Newspaper,'" *Educational Theatre Journal* 20, no. 1 (March 1968): 15–16.
128. John Vacha, "The Federal Theatre's Living Newspapers: New York's Docudramas of the Thirties," *New York History* 67, no. 1 (January 1986), 77–78.
129. For a list of surviving scripts, see Douglas McDermott, "The Living Newspaper as a Dramatic Form" (PhD diss., Graduate College of the State University of Iowa, 1963), 360–63. For more information about three unproduced scripts about the African American experience, see Paul Nadler, "Liberty Censored: Black Living Newspapers of the Federal Theatre Project," *African American Review* 29, no. 4 (Winter 1995): 615–22.
130. From "Writing the Living Newspaper," quoted in Laura Browder, "Finding a Collective Solution: The Living Newspaper Experiment," *Prologue: Quarterly Journal of the National Archives and Records Administration* 30, no. 2 (Summer 1998): 93. Emphasis added.
131. John W. Carson, "Living Newspaper: Theatre and Therapy," *TDR* (1988–) 44, no. 2 (Summer 2000): 109–12.

132. Quoted in Richard Drain, *Twentieth-Century Theatre: A Sourcebook* (London: Routledge, 1995), 181.
133. Ibid., 103.
134. NYPL, NCOF+ Arent, A., "Complete Working Script of 'Power,'" 2-6-8.
135. Brooks Atkinson, "'Power' Produced by the Living Newspaper under Federal Theatre Auspices," *New York Times*, February 24, 1937.
136. Brooks Atkinson, "Thoreau the Radical," *The Freeman* (July 28, 1920), 468; Brooks Atkinson, "Concerning Thoreau's Style," *The Freeman* (September 13, 1922), 8.
137. Francis Nielson, "The Story of 'The Freeman,'" *The American Journal of Economics and Sociology* 6, no. 1 supplement (October 1946): 27; on Atkinson and Brooks's meeting, see Atkinson, "Critic at Large: Death of Van Wyck Brooks Evokes Fond Memories of the Man and His Work," *New York Times*, May 10, 1963.
138. Letter from Van Wyck Brooks, December 12 (no year), New York Public Library, Billy Rose Theater Division, Brooks Atkinson Papers, Box 1, Folder 34. Also in the same folder is a letter dated September 8, 1961, in which Brooks wrote to Atkinson that his politics were the same as they have always been, that he was a "socialist" of the "Norman Thomas or British Socialist type."
139. Letter from Brooks Atkinson to Van Wyck Brooks, December 24 [1931], Van Wyck Brooks Papers.
140. Brooks, *The Opinions of Oliver Allston*, 228-46.
141. Brooks Atkinson, *Broadway Scrapbook* (New York: Theatre Arts, 1947 [article published in 1940]), 145.
142. Brooks Atkinson, "Early Summer Settles on the Broadway Theatre," *New York Times*, June 15, 1941.
143. Atkinson, *Broadway Scrapbook*, 122-23.
144. Brooks Atkinson, *The Lively Years* (New York: Association Press, 1973), 4. Note that his language comes very close to Hammerstein's "heightened realism," discussed in Chapter 3.
145. Brooks Atkinson, "The Coffee Bill Proposes to Set Up the Emergency Relief Projects into a Permanent Bureau of Fine Arts," *New York Times*, February 20, 1938. The Coffee Bill is discussed in the next section.
146. Brooks Atkinson, "Critic at Large: Modest and Positive Van Wyck Brooks, at 75, Returns to Literary Biographies," *New York Times*, September 22, 1961.
147. Atkinson, "Death of Van Wyck Brooks."
148. Ted Morgan, *Reds: McCarthyism in Twentieth-Century America* (New York: Random House, 2003), 520; Denning, *The Cultural Front*, 63; U.S. Congress, House of Representatives, Special Committee on Un-American Activities, "Investigation of Un-American Propaganda Activities," Seventy-Fifth Congress, Third Session, vol. 1, 1938, 540-41.
149. U.S. Congress, House of Representatives, Special Committee on Un-American Activities, "Investigation of Un-American Propaganda Activities," Seventy-Fifth Congress, Third Session, vol. 1, 1938, 409.
150. See Grieve, *The Federal Art Project*, 12-16, 166-72. The bill was named after its sponsors in the Senate and House of Representatives, respectively.
151. No author, "Damrosch Renews Attack on Art Bill," *New York Times*, April 10, 1938.
152. Macdonald, *Against the American Grain*, 76
153. Widdemer, "Message and Middlebrow," 433.
154. Louise Bogan, "The Defense of Belles-Lettres," *The Nation* (April 13, 1940): 480.
155. Greenberg, "Avant Garde and Kitsch," in *Art and Culture*, 6.
156. Richard Middleton, *Studying Popular Music* (Milton Keynes, UK: Open University Press, 1990), 14.
157. Macdonald, *Against the American Grain*, 14. In part this has probably been taken from his colleague Clement Greenberg's famous essay "Avant Garde and *Kitsch*," 10. Greenberg writes: "The peasants who settled in the cities as proletariat and petty bourgeois learned to read and write for the sake of efficiency, but they did not win the leisure and comfort necessary for the enjoyment of the city's traditional culture. Losing, nevertheless, their taste for the folk culture whose background was the countryside, and discovering a new capacity for boredom at the same time, the new urban masses set up a pressure on society to provide them with a kind of culture fit for their own consumption. To fill the demand of the new market, a new commodity was devised: ersatz culture, kitsch, destined for those who, insensible to the values of genuine culture, are hungry nevertheless for the diversion that only culture of

some sort can provide." See also Theodor Adorno and George Simpson, "On Popular Music," in *Essays on Music*, trans. Susan H. Gillespie (Berkeley: University of California Press, 2002 [orig. published 1941]), 437–69.
158. Louise Bogan, "Some Notes on Popular and Unpopular Art," *Partisan Review* 10, no. 5 (September 1943): 393; James Agee, "Pseudo-Folk," *Partisan Review* 11, no. 2 (Spring 1944): 220.
159. Agee, "Pseudo-Folk," 223.
160. Eric Bentley, *The Brecht Memoir* (New York: PAJ Publications, 1985), 11–17.
161. Quoted in Donald Lyons's introduction to Eric Bentley, *What Is Theatre? Incorporating the Dramatic Event and Other Reviews 1944–1967* (New York: Hill and Wang, 2000), xii.
162. Eric Bentley, *The Playwright as Thinker: A Study of Drama in Modern Times* (Cleveland, OH: World Publishing, 1955), xv.
163. Bentley, *Playwright as Thinker*, 242. Bentley never defines drama outright, but his description of it as a primarily literary art can be found on pp. 19, 61, 62, 240, and 244. On p. 241 he presents the succinct formula, "a drama not verbalized is a drama not dramatized." A definition of "theatricalism" can be found on p. 239.
164. Ibid., 239.
165. Ibid., 245. His most direct dig at Brooks (and Waldo Frank, Brooks's colleague) is on pp. 103, 307–308, but he also uses the term "coterie" and "secondary," which Brooks had coined to refer to literature written only for initiates. See pp. 103, 235, and 238. For Brooks, the terms were opprobrious; Bentley intended the opposite.
166. Bentley, *What Is Theatre?*, xxxvi–xxxvii.
167. Ibid., 323.
168. Ibid., 192.
169. Eric Bentley, "Broadway and Its Intelligentsia," *Harper's Magazine* (March 1947): 212.

Chapter 3

1. As Tim Carter writes, "This is perhaps the most frequent claim made for *Oklahoma!* and also the most significant: it was no mere musical comedy, nor even, as it was billed, a 'musical play,' but it tended toward the operatic" (*Oklahoma!: The Making of an American Musical*, 4). The link between *Oklahoma!* (and, more broadly, the integrated musical) and Wagnerism is common. The most in-depth analysis can be found in Gerald Mast, *Can't Help Singin': The American Musical on Stage and Screen* (Woodstock, NY: Overlook Press, 1987), 201–3, and in McMillin, *The Musical as Drama*, 1–6. See also John Bush Jones, *Our Musicals, Ourselves: A Social History of the American Musical Theatre* (Hanover, NH: Brandeis University Press, 2003), 46; Wolf, *Changed for Good*, 11.
2. For a catalogue of the typical uses of this term, see Block, "Integration," 98–99.
3. Quoted in Carter, *Oklahoma!*, 29.
4. Joseph Swain, *The Broadway Musical: A Critical and Musical Survey*, 2nd ed. (Lanham, MD: Scarecrow Press, 2002), 81.
5. Sheldon Patinkin, *"No Legs, No Jokes, No Chance": A History of the American Musical Theater* (Evanston, IL: Northwestern University Press, 2008), 9.
6. Ann Sears, "The Coming of the Musical Play: Rodgers and Hammerstein," in *The Cambridge Companion to the Musical*, ed. William A. Everett and Paul R. Laird (Cambridge: Cambridge University Press, 2008), 152. The term "musical play" did not originate with Rodgers and Hammerstein, nor, strictly speaking, did a "musical play" have to be formally integrated. For a concise history, see Stempel, *Showtime*, 291–93, which describes Moss Hart's and Kurt Weill's *Lady in the Dark* as a musical play that was not formally "integrated."
7. Stempel, *Showtime*, 309.
8. No author, "Stephen Sondheim: The Art of the Musical," *Paris Review*, no. 142 (Spring 1997): 267; Stephen Sondheim, "Introduction," in *Getting to Know Him: A Biography of Oscar Hammerstein II* (New York: Random House, 1977), xiii–xiv.
9. McMillin, *Musical as Drama*, 6–10, 31–33; D. A. Miller, *Place for Us: Essay on the Broadway Musical* (Cambridge, MA: Harvard University Press, 1998), 1–2. Knapp calls this the transition between "naturalism" and "Musically Enhanced Reality Mode" in the American film musical: see *The American Musical and the Performance of Personal Identity*, 67–70. Hannah Lewis describes integration as an "ideal" that most musicals only partially achieved. See "*Love Me Tonight* (1932) and the Development of the Integrated Film Musical," *Musical Quarterly* 100 (2017): 5.
10. See Chapter 1, n. 6.

11. See, for example, Stempel, *Showtime*, 291–93; Symonds, *We'll Have Manhattan*, 109. Symonds writes: "Despite the fact that we might assume the plot to be the quality that distinguishes vaudeville (plotless) from revue (thematic) and musical comedy (narrative), there was significant slippage between forms and practices, and in a Broadway melting pot whose creative artists worked variously in and with all three theatrical forms (and any other that periodically claimed the stage), boundaries were not blurred so much as whimsical. Critics got equally incensed lamenting the lack of plot in revue as they did in musical comedy."
12. Kowalke, "Theorizing the Golden Age Musical," 149.
13. Ibid., 149–50. See also Scott Miller, *Rebels with Applause* (Portsmouth, NH: Heinemann, 2001), 34. He writes, *Oklahoma!* "took all the innovations, experiments, and surprises that had shown up in numerous separate musicals over the previous twenty years and integrated them seamlessly and thoughtfully into the drama of the story." See also Swain, *The Broadway Musical*, 107; Gerald Bordman, *American Operetta: From H. M. S. Pinafore to Sweeney Todd* (New York and Oxford: Oxford University Press, 1981), 150; Patinkin, "No Legs, No Jokes, No Chance," 11; Ethan Mordden, *Better Foot Forward: The History of the American Musical Theatre* (New York: Grossman, 1976), 189; David Ewen, *Complete Book of the American Musical Theater* (New York: Holt, 1958), 248. There is another closely related way of phrasing this that tends to be a little more circumspect by claiming that previous (unsuccessful?) attempts at an integrated show had finally been achieved with *Oklahoma!*, sometimes implying that previous attempts had been ahead of their times. For example, David Ewen, *The Story of America's Musical Theater* (Philadelphia: Chilton, 1963), 183: "*Oklahoma!*, then, was in every way a revolutionary event in the musical theater. The musical play, first found with *Show Boat*, was here finally realized." See also David Walsh and Len Platt, *Musical Theater and American Culture* (Westport, CT: Praeger, 2003), 102; Ethan Mordden, *Broadway Babies: The People Who Made the American Musical* (New York and Oxford: Oxford University Press, 1983), 139; Meryle Secrest, *Somewhere for Me: A Biography of Richard Rodgers* (New York: Alfred A. Knopf, 2001), 255–56.
14. Carter, *Oklahoma!*, xv–xvii; quotation on p. xvi. In a similar vein, I explained the paradox by situating *Oklahoma!* in the heady atmosphere of World War II, in which claims of "organicism" and "integration" positioned the United States as the protector of so-called Western culture, which was under siege from fascism. James O'Leary, "*Oklahoma!*, 'Lousy Publicity,' and the Politics of Formal Integration in the American Musical Theater," *Journal of Musicology* 31, no. 1 (Winter 2014): 139–82. This chapter represents an update to those claims.
15. This chapter provides some of the historical and intellectual background for what Lydia Goehr describes as the "Folkloric Narrative" of American opera in "*Amerikamüde / Europamüde*: The Very Idea of American Opera," *The Opera Quarterly* 22 (2006): 412–13.
16. Richard Rodgers, "Mr. Rodgers Insists That It Ain't Luck," *New York Times*, August 1, 1943.
17. Quoted in Maya Cantu, "'Gilding the Guild': Art Theatre, the Broadway Revue and Cultural Parody in *The Garrick Gaieties* (1925–1930)," *Studies in Musical Theatre* 7, no. 1 (March 2013): 48.
18. Arnold Michaelis, "A Conversation with Richard Rodgers," *American Music* 27, no. 3 (Fall 2009): 279. For similar quotations, see Gary Marmorstein, *Ship Without a Sail: The Life of Lorenz Hart* (New York: Simon and Schuster, 2012), 55, 84–85; Richard Rodgers, "Introduction," in *Rodgers and Hart Song Book* (New York: Simon and Schuster, 1951), 2–3.
19. No author, "If You Must Write Lyrics Be Natural," *New York Herald Tribune*, March 21, 1926.
20. No author, "Innocents Abroad," *New York Times*, October 17, 1926. Quoted in Marmorstein, *Ship Without a Sail*, 55, 84–85, 115.
21. No author, "If You Must Write Lyrics." Emphasis added. See also Marmorstein, *Ship Without a Sail*, 110.
22. Quoted in Stempel, *Showtime*, 277. Some have criticized Hart for this. Lyricist Howard Dietz's famous quip: "Larry Hart can rhyme anything—and does!" Philip Furia, *The Poets of Tin Pan Alley* (Oxford and New York: Oxford University Press, 1990), 96. See also, for example, Stephen Sondheim, *Finishing the Hat: Collected Lyrics (1954–1981) with Attendant Comments, Principles, Heresies, Grudges, Whines and Anecdotes* (New York: Alfred A. Knopf, 2010), 153. Likewise, supposedly Buddy De Sylva wrote a parody of Hart's lyrics, set to Irving Berlin's "Always." "See how I dispense / Rhymes that are immense / But do they make sense? / Not always." No author, "The Lyric in Parody," *Dramatists Guild Quarterly* (Spring 1967): 8.
23. Alec Wilder describes a similar effect in *American Popular Song: The Great Innovators, 1900–1950* (New York and Oxford: Oxford University Press, 1990), 169.

24. As Geoffrey Block has shown, Rodgers's theory professor at the Musical Institute of America, Percy Goetschius, called this kind of repetition "confirmation of the melodic figures." See Block, *Richard Rodgers* (New Haven, CT: Yale University Press, 2003), 31–32.
25. Rodgers, *Musical Stages*, 80.
26. The locus classicus of this style of writing is "Tea for Two" from *No, No, Nanette* (1925), score by Vincent Youmans, lyrics by Irving Caesar and Otto Harbach, and book by Otto Harbach and Frank Mandel.
27. Dorothy Hart and Robert Kimball, eds. *The Complete Lyrics of Lorenz Hart* (New York: Alfred A. Knopf, 1986), 48–51. Emphasis added.
28. *Garrick Gaieties* souvenir program (1925), New York Public Library, Billy Rose Theatre Division, Scrapbooks NYPL MWEZ+ N. C., 5331, 3.
29. Ann Douglas, *Terrible Honesty: Mongrel Manhattan in the 1920s* (New York: Farrar, Straus and Giroux, 1995), 164–65.
30. Kimball and Hart, *Complete Lyrics of Lorenz Hart*, xv. Emphasis added. Fitzgerald's celebrated essay about the Jazz Age ends with a eulogy for liveliness: "it all seems rosy and romantic to us who were young then, because we will never quite *feel so intensely* about our surroundings anymore." F. Scott Fitzgerald, "Echoes of the Jazz Age," in *The Fitzgerald Reader*, ed. Arthur Mizener (New York: Charles Scribner's Sons, 1963), 331. Emphasis added. Likewise, H. L. Mencken contrasted slang with "proper" English in the United States during the early twentieth century. He claimed that "proper" English was "not their mother-tongue at all, but a dialect that [stood] quite outside their common experience, and into which they [had] to translate their thoughts, consciously and painfully." H. L. Mencken, *The American Language: An Inquiry into the Development of English in the United States*, 2nd ed. (New York: Alfred A. Knopf, 1921), 3–4.
31. For details on *The Nursery Ballet* and its relationship to *Jumbo*, see Geoffrey Block, "'Bigger than a Show—Better than a Circus': The Broadway Musical, Radio, and Billy Rose's *Jumbo*," *Musical Quarterly* 89 (2006): 187. In addition, Rodgers took on a solo project, the ballet *Ghost Town*, for the Ballets Russes de Monte Carlo, which premiered in 1939 at the Metropolitan Opera House in New York City. According to Rodgers, this project also offered something "creatively challenging" that his previous musical, *Too Many Girls*, had not. Rodgers, *Musical Stages*, 193. For a summary of the opening-night reviews (which generally describe the score as a "trifle light"), see William G. Hyland, *Richard Rodgers* (New Haven, CT, and London: Yale University Press, 1998), 123, and David Ewen, *Richard Rodgers* (New York: Henry Holt, 1951), 154.
32. Quoted in Rodgers, *Musical Stages*, 180.
33. Felix Cox, "'A Faltering Step in a Basically Right Direction': Richard Rodgers and *All Points West*,'" *American Music* 23, no. 3 (Fall 2005): 357.
34. Such sendups of high art were already common for them, and indeed, as described in Chapter 2, were common on Broadway at the time. Aside from the *Garrick Gaieties*, these included the song "Inspiration" for the Columbia University Varsity Show *Fly with Me* (1920); *Say It with Jazz* (1921) and *Jazz à la Carte* (1922), both written for the Institute of Musical Art, where Rodgers was a student; *The Melody Man* (1924); *One Dam Thing After Another* (1927), and even the three B's of *On Your Toes* (1936).
35. Rodgers and Hart had already worked with Whiteman in 1935 on the circus show *Jumbo*.
36. For a detailed description, see Symonds, *We'll Have Manhattan*, 220, and Marmorstein, *Ship Without a Sail*, 71.
37. Hugh Fordin, *Getting to Know Him: A Biography of Oscar Hammerstein II* (New York: Random House, 1977), 174. Thank you to Mark Horowitz for clarifying the exact dates of this correspondence.
38. No author, "'Always You' Is Amusing," *New York Times*, January 6, 1920; the reviewer wrote that the show "makes no bones about being a musical comedy." Likewise, his 1922 *Daffy Dill* was called "basically a musical comedy" and the reviewer noted that "the plot itself [was] something terrible, but by paying a minimum of attention to it [the producer] managed to get together a pretty good entertainment." Likewise, his 1922 *Queen of Hearts* was called "a thoroughly conventional musical comedy, equipped with a story whose complications manage to be even sillier than those things usually are, which is no faint praise." See no author, "Tinney Makes 'Daffy Dill,'" *New York Times*, August 23, 1922; no author, "'Queen of Hearts' Tuneful," *New York Times*, October 11, 1922.
39. Oscar Hammerstein II, *Lyrics*, ed. William Hammerstein (Milwaukee: Hal Leonard, 1985), 39, 41. This was also a recurring theme in his lyrics. For example, Hammerstein wrote a lyric called "A String of Girls" for his musical comedy *Always You* (1920): "Write in a well known joke, /

Use all the old time 'hoke' / For this is the surest plan / To entertain the tired business man." Hammerstein II, *The Complete Lyrics of Oscar Hammerstein II*, ed. Amy Asch (New York: Alfred A. Knopf, 2008), 15.
40. Hammerstein, *Lyrics*, 41.
41. Years later, Rodgers himself compared his two collaborators along these lines: "Well, I think the basic difference between the two men was that Oscar was interested in the 'what.' And I think Larry was more interested in the 'how.' [...] Larry had a peculiar, exciting way of saying things. Oscar said them with a great [deal] more purity." Michaelis, "A Conversation with Richard Rodgers," 287. In practice the contrast was not this stark. For example, Hammerstein commented that his song "When I Grow Too Old to Dream" did not make literal sense, but rather that his words "are like music superimposed on music," citing Gertrude Stein as another person writing this kind of poetry. See Hammerstein, *Lyrics*, 32.
42. Hammerstein himself would later cultivate his high-art bona fides by exaggerating certain parts of his career and downplaying others. For example, he once said, "After *Tickle Me* [1920], I don't believe I ever wrote another comedian vehicle. I found out early in my career that I preferred to write musical plays that did not depend on stars." Quoted in Stephen Citron, *The Wordsmiths: Oscar Hammerstein II and Alan Jay Lerner* (New York: Oxford University Press, 1995), 35. This was not true. Hammerstein had written and produced star vehicles for comedians such as Frank Tinney (*Tickle Me* and *Daffy Dill*, 1922), Frances White (*Jimmie*, 1920), Mary Hay (*Mary Jane McKane*, 1923), Nora Bayes (*Queen of Hearts*, 1922), Leo Carillo (the play *Gypsy Jim*, 1924), and Marilyn Miller (*Sunny*, 1925), among others, during the 1920s, just as Rodgers and Hart were doing at the same time, especially for Lew Fields (*Poor Little Ritz Girl*, 1920; *The Melody Man*, 1924).
43. Oscar Hammerstein II, "Voices Versus Feet: With the Triumph of Head over Heels, Operetta Regains Its Popularity," *Theatre Magazine* (May 1925), 70.
44. John Dizikes, *Opera in America: A Cultural History* (New Haven, CT: Yale University Press, 1993), 323.
45. Annegret Fauser, *Sounds of War: Music in the United States During World War II* (New York and Oxford: Oxford University Press, 2013), 162–77.
46. Fordin, *Getting to Know Him*, 81.
47. Sigmund Romberg wrote in a chromatically tinged minor mode to offset Moroccan and Vietnamese characters from their major-mode European counterparts in *The Desert Song* (1926) and *East Wind* (1928); he wrote a habañera for the Spanish character in *Desert Song* and a tango for the scene at Chez Creole in *The New Moon* (1928); and he wrote beer-hall and oom-pah waltzes for his film *Viennese Nights* (1930). William Everett, *Sigmund Romberg* (New Haven, CT: Yale University Press, 2007), 169–81, 193–209, 216–17, 248. Likewise, Jerome Kern's score for the musical *Three Sisters* (1934) used modal cadences as emblems of Englishness, his score for *Show Boat* (1927) included blues-inflected music for the African American characters, both *Show Boat* and *Sweet Adeline* (1929) interpolated actual songs from the 1890s, and his score for the film *High, Wide, and Handsome* (1937) included allusions to hillbilly guitar music. Banfield, *Jerome Kern*, 204ff. Hammerstein would later toy with including actual turn-of-the-century songs as background music in *Oklahoma!*, but abandoned the idea. See Carter, *Oklahoma!*, 91.
48. [Author illegible], "'Rainbow' Makes Bow at Chestnut," *Philadelphia Evening Public Ledger*, October 31, 1928. The critic continued, "'Show Boat' and 'Golden Dawn' have both stressed the importance of local color in a *musical-comedy* enterprise." Emphasis added.
49. Quoted in Fordin, *Getting to Know Him*, 53.
50. Banfield, *Jerome Kern*, 245. He cites "The Farmer and the Cowman" from *Oklahoma!* and "You've Got to be Carefully Taught" from *South Pacific*, among other examples. Fordin notes that this pattern of introducing a "universal theme" began in Hammerstein's shows with Sigmund Romberg. See Fordin, *Getting to Know Him*, 67.
51. No author, "'Wildflower' Is Melodious," *New York Times*, February 8, 1923; J. Brooks Atkinson, "The Play: Raising a New Curtain," *New York Times*, December 1, 1927; J. Brooks Atkinson, "The Play: Costumes, Music and Romance," *New York Times*, September 20, 1928. For information on *The Golden Dawn*, see Citron, *The Wordsmiths*, 59.
52. Mark N. Grant, *The Rise and Fall of the Broadway Musical* (Boston: Northeastern University Press, 2004), 60–61.
53. J. Brooks Atkinson, "The Play," *New York Times*, October 5, 1926.
54. Brooks Atkinson, "The Play: 'Show Boat' as Good as New," *New York Times*, May 20, 1932. Emphasis added.

NOTES 209

55. J. Brooks Atkinson, "Show-Folk Variously," *New York Times*, January 8, 1928. Emphasis added.
56. Brooks Atkinson, "The Play: 'Show Boat' as Good as New," *New York Times*, May 20, 1932.
57. J. Brooks Atkinson, "The Play: The Gay Nineties," *New York Times*, September 4, 1929. The language about sophistication also appeared in this review. The fuller citation: "But the mood is less sentimental than gay. Nor is the humor sophisticated, as you might expect; it is exuberantly good-natured."
58. Gilbert Gabriel, "Musical Comedy Is Stirring Treat, Gabriel's Verdict," [*Evening Sun*], no date; Robert Garland, "Philip Goodman Presents 'Rainbow' at Signor Gallow's," *New York Journal-American*, [no date]. The reviews of this show are collected in the New York Public Library clippings file, NCOF + "Rainbow."
59. Burns Mantle, "The Rainbow" [*New York Daily News*], [November 22, 1928]. Many other critics referred to this show as straddling the line between musical comedy and something more serious. For example, one critic wrote, "The plot assumes more importance than is expected in a musical comedy. The romance of the colonel's daughter and the disgraced army officer, whose error was the vehement defense of a woman's honor—when that honor was a quality that deserved no defense—moves through a series of incidents which, to a musical comedy, are highly effective." No author, "'Rainbow' Makes Bow at Chestnut," *Philadelphia Evening Public Ledger*, October 31, 1928.
60. St. John Ervine, "The New Play," [*The Observer*], [no date].
61. Herbert M. Miller, [no title], *The Dance*, January 1929, 58.
62. Howard Barnes, "'Rainbow' Curves in Brightly-Hued Joy over Broadway," *New York Herald-Tribune*, [no date].
63. J. Brooks Atkinson, "The Play," *New York Times*, November 22, 1928.
64. Ibid. Emphasis added. Mark Grant has argued that *Rainbow*, like *Show Boat*, represented Hammerstein's attempt to write the "Great American Musical." See *Rise and Fall of the Broadway Musical*, 61. The recurring metallurgic imagery was not limited to Atkinson. African American Studies scholar Paul Allen Anderson notes that many writers in the early decades of the twentieth century (including Alain Locke, discussed in Chapter 4) used mining imagery to describe folk music, and he traces this tendency back to imagery in Walter Pater's writing. See Anderson, *Deep River: Music and Memory in Harlem Renaissance Thought* (Durham, NC: Duke University Press, 2001), 147–48.
65. J. Brooks Atkinson, "The Play," *New York Times*, November 22, 1928; J. Brooks Atkinson, "Spilt Milk," *New York Times*, December 16, 1928. Earlier in the decade, as described above, Atkinson had often criticized Hammerstein's writing as stuffy, even when he praised the overall show.
66. Oscar Hammerstein II, *The Letters of Oscar Hammerstein II*, ed. Mark Horowitz (New York and Oxford: Oxford University Press, 2022), 42–43. Thank you to Mark Horowitz for an advance copy of this before his book was published.
67. Brooks Atkinson, "Music Being in the Air," *New York Times*, November 20, 1932.
68. Brooks Atkinson, "The Play: Emancipation of the Musical Drama in 'Music in the Air' by Kern and Hammerstein," *New York Times*, November 9, 1932.
69. For a summary of the differing accounts of the early stages of their work on *Oklahoma!*, see Carter, *Oklahoma!*, 84–86.
70. No author, "Broadway Report: Green Grow the Dancers," *PM*, February 4, 1943. This same newspaper continued to describe the show in similar terms in an article published on March 31, 1943, the day *Oklahoma!* opened on Broadway. It said that the show was "something a little different in the way of musical comedy," and "though the result[s] were aimed straight for Broadway and most of the people connected with the enterprise are old hands at show business, the production has such unusual features as a 28-piece orchestra (very large for a musical comedy), a generous sprinkling of graduates of the Juilliard School of Music and various ballet schools, and such people as the ballet's Agnes de Mille plotting the choreography and the movies' Rouben Mamoulian directing." See no author, "'Oklahoma! New Musical, Plays Up Homespun U.S.A.," *PM*, March 31, 1943. For an extended discussion of this article, see Carter, *Oklahoma!*, 1–5.
71. For this quotation and more information about the plot, production, and score of *Golden Dawn* (which was dubbed a "music drama"), see Citron, *The Wordsmiths*, 59.
72. Oscar Hammerstein II, "In Re 'Oklahoma!': The Adaptor-Lyricist Describes How the Musical Hit Came into Being," *New York Times*, May 23, 1943.
73. Likewise, Rodgers made a similar acknowledgment many years later. In his autobiography, he wrote that following the premiere of *Oklahoma!*, "everyone suddenly became

'integration'-conscious, as if the idea of welding together song, story, and dance had never been thought of before," the implication being that, of course, it had. Rodgers, *Musical Stages*, 229.
74. No author, "'Without Love' Gains; 'Lilacs' Ready to Go," *Daily News*, January 7, 1943.
75. Rouben Mamoulian Collection, Library of Congress, Washington, DC, Box 111, Folder 13, "Theatre Guild Production: Notes and Remarks," 4. Mamoulian signed his contract with the Theatre Guild to direct *Oklahoma!* on February 1, 1943, and details from these notes probably refer to a very early stage of production. A year later, after *Oklahoma!* had opened and the production team (comprised largely of the same group of people) was preparing to mount *Carousel*, director Joshua Logan wrote to Richard Rodgers to congratulate him on hiring Mamoulian again, but said that he hoped Mamoulian would avoid becoming "arty" in the way he had with *Porgy and Bess*, but rather hew closer to the style he developed in *Oklahoma!* Letter from Joshua Logan to Richard Rodgers, August 22, 1944, New York Public Library, Richard Rodgers Papers, T-MSS 1987-006, Box 3, Folder 22.
76. Ed Sullivan, "Little Old New York," *New York News*, April 18, 1943. Ellipses original. As early as December 20, 1935, Helburn expressed regret for having billed *Porgy and Bess* as an opera. In a letter to Mamoulian, she wrote, "*Porgy and Bess* just doesn't seem to get going no matter what we do. I'm afraid the word opera has hurt us more than we can estimate. George returned this week and is fine. I got him busy at once releasing the music for radio and dance floors." Letter from Theresa Helburn to Rouben Mamoulian, December 20, 1935, Library of Congress, Rouben Mamoulian Papers, Box 199, Folder 9, "Theatre Guild Correspondence."
77. These quotations, and more detail about this advertising campaign, can be found in O'Leary, "Lousy Publicity," 150.
78. Theatre Guild Archives, Yale Collection of American Literature, Beinecke Rare Book and Manuscript Library, Box 113, "Lynn Riggs" folder. See also Carter, *Oklahoma!*, 150.
79. Theresa Helburn, untitled, undated typescript, New York Public Library, MWEZ/+/ n.c./25, 609, folder titled "Undated," p. 27. She probably wrote this essay in late 1947 or early 1948; it mentions *Allegro*, which opened in October 1947, but was written before *Oklahoma!* closed on Broadway in May 1948. Essentially the same story appears in Agnes de Mille's account, *Dance to the Piper: Memoirs of the Ballet* (London: Columbus Books, 1952), 329–30.
80. Arthur Pollack, "The Theater: 'Oklahoma!' Opening at the St. James, Lives Up to Its Exclamation Point," *Brooklyn Eagle*, April 1, 1943. Gordon F. Allison, "The Stage: The Guild's 'Oklahoma!!' an Occasion for Dancing in the Streets," *Newark Sunday Call*, April 4, 1943.
81. Hammerstein, "In Re 'Oklahoma!'" This folk quality also attracted Teresa Helburn, who wrote, "Its American quality appealed to us. We felt a composer would find inspiration for new and different music from the kind of music and the period in American history with which [*Green Grow the Lilacs*] is concerned." Theresa Helburn, "TH on Greengrow" (undated typescript), NYPL, MWEZ/+/n.c./25, 609: Folder: "Undated."
82. Oscar Hammerstein II, "'Away We Go' Called Labor of Love," *Boston Globe*, March 14, 1943. Emphasis added.
83. Hammerstein, "In Re 'Oklahoma!'"
84. Hammerstein, "Labor of Love."
85. After the show opened, Mamoulian continued to describe the theory of heightened reality. In one interview, he said, "What I try to do is work with the essence of realism. It's like walking a tight-rope between life and fantasy." See Max Hill, "Mamoulian Still Glad He Came to U.S.," *Hartford Courant*, June 20, 1943. As Bradley Rogers has shown, "fantastic realism" was a concept developed by Evgeny Vakhtangov, one of Mamoulian's teachers at the Moscow Art Theater. Rodgers, *The Song Is You*, 95. The question of who was responsible for the theoretical foundation of *Oklahoma!* (Hammerstein and Rodgers on the one hand, or Mamoulian on the other) became the subject of an intense backstage dispute. See O'Leary, "Lousy Publicity," 167–72.
86. Many reviewers at the time describe the shadow effects in *Porgy and Bess*. One of the most vivid examples is Hall Johnson, "Porgy and Bess: A Folk Opera," *Opportunity* 14, no. 1 (January 1936): 27.
87. For details of the "Occupational Humoresque," see Charles Hamm, "The Theatre Guild Production of *Porgy and Bess*," *Journal of the American Musicological Society* 40 (1987): 509, 515, 530; see also 508–10 for more examples of Mamoulian's rhythmic staging in *Porgy and Bess*. A similar "occupational humoresque" appears in his film *Love Me Tonight*, with a score by Rodgers and Hart.

88. Although a complete discussion lies beyond the scope of this book, Mamoulian reiterated these ideas about "heightened realism" in the press after *Carousel* opened. See D'Andre, "The Theatre Guild,'" 234.
89. Rouben Mamoulian Papers, Library of Congress, Box 111, Folder 13, "Theatre Guild Production: Notes and Remarks," 1, 4.
90. This may refer to an earlier draft that does not survive, or it may be a mistake, an accidental substitution for the introduction of "It's a Scandal, It's an Outrage."
91. Carter, *Oklahoma!*, 149.
92. Graham Wood, "The Development of Song Forms in the Broadway and Hollywood Musicals of Richard Rodgers, 1919–1943" (PhD diss., University of Minnesota, 2000), 222–28.
93. Hammerstein, "In Re 'Oklahoma!'"
94. On May 23 he wrote substantially the same thing: "There are authentic figures and genuine hoe-down steps in the dancing, but it is better dancing, more exiting and varied than you would actually find in a barn or on a moonlit meadow."
95. *Musical Comedy Tonight*, Stan Harris, dir., featuring Sylvia Fine Kaye, Dena Pictures, Inc., originally aired October 1, 1979.
96. The phrase "slavish imitation" also appears in his article from March 14 in relation to the music. See Hammerstein, "Labor of Love." He wrote that he and Rodgers did not write "slavish imitations of folk ballads. They are songs which we hope may be liked for themselves, as songs of today. But the flavor of the time of our story and the viewpoints of the characters who sing are maintained in all the songs."
97. Richard Rodgers, *Musical Stages*, 220.
98. Carter, *Oklahoma!*, 86.
99. Wood, "Development of Song Forms," 238–39.
100. Charles Hamm, *Yesterdays: Popular Song in America* (New York: W. W. Norton, 1979), 292.
101. John A. Lomax, *Cowboy Songs and Other Frontier Ballads* (New York: Sturgis and Walton Company, 1917), 87–91.
102. Cf. Swain, *The Broadway Musical*, 90, where he describes this moment as a deceptive cadence.
103. According to Charles Hamm, it was typical for the refrain to repeat part of the verse in the mid-nineteenth century, although it was more common for the last four bars of the chorus to repeat the last four bars of the verse. See Hamm, *Yesterdays*, 224–25.
104. Lynn Riggs, *Green Grow the Lilacs* (New York: Samuel French, 1958), viii.
105. Ibid., viii.
106. Hammerstein, "In Re 'Oklahoma!'"
107. Hammerstein, "Labor of Love."
108. According to Hammerstein, "In his heart, [Rodgers] is far more a mystic than he knows he is." Hammerstein, "Foreword," in *The Rodgers and Hart Song Book* (New York: Simon and Schuster, 1951), xi.
109. Both quotations in Michaelis, "A Conversation with Richard Rodgers," 277.
110. Quoted in ibid., 293.
111. Quoted in Carter, *Oklahoma!*, 66. Hammerstein had tried to "train" his critics before. In 1924, for example, he had issued a broadside asking them not to cover the premiere of *Rose-Marie* because, he asserted, they were not qualified to judge it. "The critics' problem is that they do not recognize what a good libretto is, and do not realize that a good musical comedy must not necessarily be a good play." Quoted in Fordin, *Getting to Know Him*, 56–57.
112. E. R. S. "'Away We Go' Musical Is Hit at Shubert," *Waterbury, Connecticut American*, March 12, 1943. Emphasis added.
113. Henry Simon, "Musical Diary," *PM*, April 19, 1943. See also Stark Young, "Oklahoma with Details," *The New Republic*, April 19, 1943, 508–509. It would be difficult to understate just how common this assessment was. Howard Barnes's opening-night review in the *Herald-Tribune*, for example, described the middlebrow approach outright: "The point is that everybody concerned with this new offering has conspired to make it a striking piece of theatrical Americana as well as a series of musical-comedy numbers." Howard Barnes, "Lilacs to 'Oklahoma," *New York Herald-Tribune*, April 1, 1943. Burns Mantle of the *New York Daily News* wrote, "It is held to the native idiom and kept sufficiently clean to give it standing in the Western country from which it springs." Burns Mantle, "'Oklahoma' Links the Ballet with the Prairie Beautifully," *New York Daily News*, April 1, 1943. "Sufficiently clean" was high praise, meaning that Hammerstein mostly avoided musical comedy's familiar anything-goes

innuendo. Louis Kronenberger continued the trend in *PM*: "*Oklahoma!* is a little more than a musical comedy without being pretentiously so. [...] The whole show has just enough of an old-fashioned period quality to be pleasantly refreshing"; "It's Right Nice in Oklahoma," *PM*, April 1, 1943. Nichols also wrote in the final sentence (almost as an afterthought), "Possibly in addition to being a musical play, 'Oklahoma!' could be called a folk operetta; whatever it is, it is very good." This does not necessarily signify formal integration. The modifier "folk" suggests that he, too, was describing the tone of the musical. Lewis Nichols, "'Oklahoma!' a Musical Hailed as Delightful," *New York Times*, April 1, 1943.

114. Dizikes, *Opera in America*, 451–52.
115. Lewis Nichols, "Oklahoma!," *New York Times*, April 1, 1943.
116. No author, "American Grand Opera," *Boston Herald*, April 15, 1943.
117. Downes, "Introduction," *A Treasury of American Song*, 11–12.
118. Ibid., 17.
119. Ibid., 11.
120. Ibid., 13.
121. Glenda Dawn Goss, *Jean Sibelius and Olin Downes: Music, Friendship, Criticism* (Boston: Northeastern University Press, 1995), 25.
122. Olin Downes, "The Art of Romain Rolland," *New York Times*, January 7, 1945.
123. Downes, "Introduction," 17.
124. Ibid., 12.
125. Ibid.
126. Olin Downes, "Broadway's Gift to Opera," *New York Times*, June 6, 1943.
127. Ibid.
128. Ibid.
129. Ibid. Emphasis added.
130. George Beiswanger, "Broadway Letter," *The Kenyon Review* 6, no. 2 (Spring 1944): 320. In a similar manner, Deems Taylor wrote to Hammerstein, "If [people] are really looking for the 'significant,' 'American,' 'Folk' opera—'Oklahoma[!]' is it." He said that its novelty stemmed from the fact that, even though the show was "cast in [the] form of" a musical comedy, it was nonetheless "completely honest," and maintained this atmosphere without ever resorting to musical-comedy wit. "Everything belongs in the picture," he wrote. "The piece establishes a mood at the very start and that is never falsified or broken.... [Your lyrics] are so brilliant, without ever being smarty-pants, and, when the situation calls for poetry, so poetic." Hammerstein, *Letters of Oscar Hammerstein II*, ed. Horowitz, 304.
131. Cecil Smith, *Musical Comedy in America* (New York: Theatre Arts Books, 1950), 343. See also Timothy P. Donovan, "'Oh What a Beautiful Mornin'': The Musical *Oklahoma!* and the Popular Mind in 1943," *Journal of Popular Culture* 8, no. 3 (Winter 1974): 481–82.
132. Brooks Atkinson, "'Brigadoon' Arrives," *New York Times*, March 23, 1947.
133. Brooks, *Opinions of Oliver Allston*, 228–46.
134. Bentley, *The Playwright as Thinker*, 238.
135. Bentley, *What Is Theatre?*, 78.
136. Agee, "Pseudo-Folk," 221–22.
137. Ibid., 222.
138. Bentley, *The Playwright as Thinker*, 234.
139. Agee, "Pseudo-Folk," 220.
140. Bentley, *The Playwright as Thinker*, xv.
141. Ibid.
142. Romain Rolland, *The People's Theater*, trans. Barrett H. Clark (New York: Henry Holt, 1918), 115, 117.
143. Bentley, *The Playwright as Thinker*, 250.
144. Ibid., 243.
145. Ibid. For a definition of theatricalism, see p. 239. For a discussion of *Oklahoma!* as a theatricalist piece, see p. 238.

Chapter 4

1. The epigraph is from Wilella Waldorf, "'Bloomer Girl' a New Hit That Misses Now and Then," *New York Post*, October 6, 1944.
2. This show reunited Agnes de Mille (choreographer), Robert Russell Bennett (orchestrator), Lemuel Ayers (sets), Miles Whyte (costumes), and Celeste Holm and Joan McCracken (performers) from *Oklahoma!*.

3. According to musicologist Kate Edney, Kerr was inspired to write *Sing Out, Sweet Land* by the *Treasury of American Song* arranged by Elie Siegmeister and Olin Downes, quoted in the previous chapter. See Edney, "Making Sense of Integration: *Sing Out, Sweet Land* (1944), African Americans, and the Democratic Ideal," *New England Theater Journal* 28 (2017): 109. The original playbill also lists four newly composed songs alongside the folk material, three of which had music by Siegmeister.
4. More specifically, Teresa Helburn and Lawrence Langner of the Theatre Guild produced both, Rouben Mamoulian directed *Carousel*; Agnes de Mille choreographed *Carousel* and *Allegro*, the latter of which she also directed; Miles White designed the costumes for *Carousel*; Robert Russell Bennett orchestrated *Allegro* and worked with Don Walker on the orchestrations for *Carousel*. Rodgers and Hammerstein also ventured to Hollywood to produce the Midwestern musical film *State Fair* (1945). Slightly farther afield, but in a similar spirit, Rodgers and Hammerstein (via the League of Composers) offered a commission to Aaron Copland in 1952 for a television opera that would eventually become *The Tender Land*. Howard Pollack, *Aaron Copland: The Life and Work of an Uncommon Man* (New York: Henry Holt, 1999), 470.
5. Quoted in Max Wilk, *Ok!: The Story of* Oklahoma! (New York: Applause, 2002), 264.
6. Louis Kronenberger, "Bloomer Girl Here to Stay," *PM*, October 6, 1944.
7. Lewis Nichols, "Two Musicals," *New York Times*, January 7, 1945. An example of the humor in question, from a seventeenth-century Puritan locked in stocks: "Kissin' without huggin's like a verse without a chorus. You don't get to the pleasin' part." Walter Kerr, *Sing Out, Sweet Land: A Salute to American Folk and Popular Music*, New York Public Library, Billy Rose Theatre Collection, NCOF+ Kerr Sing Out Sweet Land, 1-1-3. Nichols also wrote, using language that would become very important in the reception of *Beggar's Holiday*, "The show had its choice of burlesque or, by playing it straight, nostalgia, and the choice was wrong." Lewis Nichols, "The Play," *New York Times*, December 28, 1945.
8. For details about the reception of *Carousel*, see Block, *Enchanted Evenings*, 198–99; Tim Carter, *Rodgers and Hammerstein's Carousel* (New York and Oxford: Oxford University Press, 2017), 97–106; D'Andre, "The Theatre Guild," 234–39.
9. Brooks Atkinson, "Evocation of a Man," *New York Times*, November 2, 1947
10. Brooks Atkinson, "Formula Is Broken," *New York Times*, January 26, 1947.
11. Brooks Atkinson, "'Brigadoon' Arrives," *New York Times*, March 23, 1947.
12. No author, "Three Musical Hits," *Life*, February 24, 1947, 75.
13. Robert Garland, "The Drama: Broadway Sings and Dances," *New York Journal American*, no date. Contained in the *Street Scene* scrapbooks of the Weill-Lenya Research Center, Series 50A/S6.
14. John Chapman, "Musicals Coming of Age: New Shows Have Creative Qualities Which Recent Dramas Lack," *Sunday News*, January 19, 1940.
15. Rosamond Gilder, "Rainbow Over Broadway," *Theatre Arts* 31, no. 3 (March 1947): 12.
16. Brooks Atkinson, "The New Play," *New York Times*, January 11, 1947.
17. George Freedley, "The Stage Today: Songs Outstanding in 'Rainbow'; Musical Is Colorful and Dashing," *Morning Telegraph*, January 13, 1947. He cited *Street Scene*, *Beggar's Holiday*, and *Finian's Rainbow* specifically, as well as *Call Me Mister*.
18. The bibliography on this subject is too vast to cite here. The most influential discussion of it (and with a compendious bibliography) is Jacquelyn Dowd Hall, "The Long Civil Rights Movement and the Political Uses of the Past," *Journal of American History* 91 (2005): 1233–63. The phrase "classic phase" comes from Bayard Rustin, "From Protest to Politics: The Future of the Civil Rights Movement," *Commentary Magazine* 39, no. 2 (February 1965): 25. The touchstone description of the major political issues addressed during the "long" civil rights movement in New York City is Martha Biondi, *To Stand and Fight: The Struggle for Civil Rights in Postwar New York City* (Cambridge, MA: Harvard University Press, 2003). For a summary of more recent work on the relationship between theater and the "long" civil rights movement's politics, see Paige A. McGinley, "Freedom Time: New Directions in Civil Rights Movement Scholarship," *American Quarterly* 75, no. 1 (March 2023): 153–62.
19. Duke Ellington, "Ellington in *Down Beat*: On Swing and Its Critics (1939)," in *The Duke Ellington Reader*, ed. Tucker, 132, 133, 138.
20. John Hammond, "The Tragedy of Duke Ellington," in ibid., 119, 120.
21. Ellington, "Ellington in *Down Beat*," 137, 138. For more on Hammond's "conflicts of interest," see Dustan Prial, *The Producer: John Hammond and the Soul of American Music* (New York: Farrar, Straus and Giroux, 2006), 68–70.

22. See David W. Stowe, *Swing Changes: Big-Band Jazz in New Deal America* (Cambridge, MA: Harvard University Press, 1994), 50–51.
23. Nathan Huggins, *Harlem Renaissance* (New York and Oxford: Oxford University Press, 2007 [originally published 1971]), 9–10; David Levering Lewis, *When Harlem Was in Vogue* (New York: Penguin Books, 1997 [originally published 1979]), 163, 173; Allen L. Woll, *Black Musical Theater: From* Coontown *to* Dreamgirls (Baton Rouge: Louisiana University Press, 1989), 111; Lawrence Levine, "Jazz and American Culture," *The Journal of American Folklore* 102, no. 403 (January–March 1989): 12–13; John Graziano, "Black Musical Theater and the Harlem Renaissance Movement," in *Black Music in the Harlem Renaissance*, ed. Samuel A. Floyd, Jr. (New York: Greenwood Press, 1990), 108; Guthrie P. Ramsey, Jr., *Race Music: Black Cultures from Bebop to Hip-Hop* (Berkeley: University of California Press, 2003), 117.
24. Samuel A. Floyd, Jr., "Music in the Harlem Renaissance: An Overview," *Black Music in the Harlem Renaissance*, 3–4; Jon Michael Spencer, *The New Negroes and Their Music: The Success of the Harlem Renaissance* (Knoxville: University of Tennessee Press, 1997); Guthrie Ramsey, Jr., *Who Hears Here? On Black Music, Pasts and Present* (Oakland: University of California Press, 2022), 29–33, 39–41.
25. See, for example, Erenberg, *Swingin' the Dream*, 137; John Gennari, *Blowin' Hot and Cool: Jazz and the Critics* (Chicago: University of Chicago Press, 2006), 32–34.
26. Quoted in Anderson, *Deep River*, 227. Hammond was not the only influential critic to divide jazz between "hot" and other forms. See, for example, Hughes Panassié, *Hot Jazz: The Guide to Swing Music* (New York: M. Whitmark and Sons, 1936) and Winthrop Sargeant, *Jazz, Hot and Hybrid* (New York: E. P. Dutton, 1946).
27. Quoted in Erenberg, *Swingin' the Dream*, 127.
28. James Dugan and John Hammond, "The Music Nobody Knows," reprinted as "An Early Black-Music Concert From Spirituals to Swing," *The Black Perspective in Music* 2, no. 2 (Autumn 1974): 194.
29. Anderson, *Deep River*, 233. According to Hammond, "George Gershwin, among other white audiences, made a sincere attempt to distill from its folk qualities a concert type of music that would be acceptable to prosaic audiences. It is doubtful, however, if this approach did anything more than suppress the genuine thing." Dugan and Hammond, "Music Nobody Knows," 191.
30. Dugan and Hammond, "Music Nobody Knows," 194.
31. Ibid., 191.
32. John Hammond, "The Tragedy of Duke Ellington," in *The Duke Ellington Reader*, ed. Tucker, 120.
33. John Hammond, "The Debate in Jazz (1943)" (originally titled "Is the Duke Deserting Jazz?"), ibid., 172.
34. Huggins, *Harlem Renaissance*, 57. For a summary of how Locke's theory of value fit intersected with his general cultural theories, see Charles Molesworth, "Introduction," in *The Works of Alain Locke* (Oxford and New York: Oxford University Press, 2012), xxix–xxxii.
35. Anderson, *Deep River*, 265. This was in direct competition with Hammond's famous concerts called "From Spirituals to Swing," which played in 1938 and 1939 in Carnegie Hall. Hammond did not invite Ellington.
36. Alain Locke, "Toward a Critique of Negro Music [1934]," anthologized in *The Works of Alain Locke*, ed. Molesworth, 142.
37. Locke entered Harvard as a member of the class of 1908 but graduated early in 1907. He even served as an informal editor of Brooks's 1905 collection of poetry, *Verses by Two Undergraduates*. For more information, see Leonard Harris and Charles Molesworth, *Alain L. Locke: Biography of a Philosopher* (Chicago: University of Chicago Press, 2008), 40.
38. Huggins, *Harlem Renaissance*, 60.
39. Alain Locke, *The Negro and His Music; Negro Art: Past and Present* (New York: Arno Press, 1969), 8–10. Occasionally Locke's attitude toward these institutions aligned with Hammond's. For example, Locke worried about the lure of popular culture, the "empty tricks of eccentric jazz," and the "musical shallows of diluted, sentimental 'sweet jazz.'" Locke also praised "Hot Clubs," founded by Hammond, for preserving folk music, which "rejuvenated old guard veterans . . . who are returning to their original traditions." Locke, *The Negro and His Music*, 102.
40. Locke, *The Negro and His Music*, 130.
41. The debates surrounding the topic of Black classical music in the early decades of the twentieth century are intricate, and a full explanation lies beyond the scope of this book. For a brief summary, see John Howland, *Ellington Uptown: Duke Ellington, James P. Johnson, and the Birth*

of Concert Jazz (Ann Arbor: University of Michigan Press, 2009), 108–10. Locke's arguments were situated within a broader debate about multiculturalism in the late nineteenth and early twentieth centuries—debates which also lie beyond the scope of this book. For a general overview, see Anderson, *Deep River*, 120–45; Ross Posnock, *Color and Culture: Black Writers and the Making of the Modern Intellectual* (Cambridge, MA: Harvard University Press, 1998), 191–201.
42. Quoted in Anderson, *Deep River*, 122.
43. Locke, *The Negro and His Music*, 2.
44. All quoted by Locke in "Toward a Critique of Negro Music," 142.
45. Locke, *The Negro and His Music*, 140.
46. Tucker, *The Duke Ellington Reader*, 114.
47. Duke Ellington, "The Duke Steps Out," in *The Duke Ellington Reader*, 49.
48. Ellington, "We, too, Sing America [1941]," ibid., 146.
49. Quotation (and a brief description of other extended works) from Howland, *Ellington Uptown*, 251–52.
50. Edward Kennedy Ellington, *Music Is My Mistress* (New York: Da Capo Press, 1973), 17.
51. No author, "Duke Ellington Defends His Music [1933]," in *Duke Ellington Reader*, 80.
52. Duke Ellington, "Where Is Jazz Going? [1962]," in *Duke Ellington Reader*, 326.
53. The phrase "beyond category" comes originally from Billy Strayhorn. Mark Tucker, *Ellington: The Early Years* (Urbana: University of Illinois Press, 1991), 6. Another example: "We take our American music seriously. If *serious* means European music, I'm not interested in that. Some people mix up the words *serious* and *classical*. They're a lot different. Classical music is supposed to be 200 years old. There is no such thing as modern classical music. There is great, serious music. That is all." Quoted in Graham Lock, *Blutopia: Visions of the Future and Revisions of the Past in the Work of Sun Ra, Duke Ellington, and Anthony Braxton* (Durham, NC: Duke University Press, 1999), 128. So familiar is the idea of being "beyond category" that an entire biography about Ellington bears this phrase as a title: John Edward Hasse, *Beyond Category: The Life and Genius of Duke Ellington* (New York: Simon and Schuster, 1993).
54. Locke, *The Negro and His Music*, 93.
55. Howland, *Ellington Uptown*, 156–76.
56. Howard Taubman, "The 'Duke' Invades Carnegie Hall [1943]," in *Duke Ellington Reader*, 159. Punctuation altered.
57. Quoted in Lock, *Blutopia*, 127.
58. Brent Hayes Edwards, "The Literary Ellington," in *Uptown Conversation: The New Jazz Studies*, ed. Robert G. O'Meally, Brent Hayes Edwards, and Farah Jasmine Griffin (New York: Columbia University Press, 2004), 337.
59. Ibid., 336–38.
60. Lock, *Blutopia*, 2.
61. Ellington, *Music Is My Mistress*, 193.
62. Helen M. Oakley, "Ellington to Offer 'Tone Parallel,'" in *Duke Ellington Reader*, 157.
63. Ibid., 156. Punctuation altered.
64. Duke Ellington, "Swing Is My Beat! [1944]," in *Duke Ellington Reader*, 249. See also Richard O. Boyer, "The Hot Bach," in *Duke Ellington Reader*, 226–27.
65. Hammond, "Is the Duke Deserting Jazz," in *Duke Ellington Reader*, 173.
66. Gary Giddins and Scott Deveaux, *Jazz* (New York: W. W. Norton, 2009), 187–88; Anderson, *Deep River*, 224.
67. Leonard Feather, "Goffin, *Esquire*, and the Moldy Figs," in *Reading Jazz: A Gathering of Autobiography, Reportage, and Criticism from 1919 to Now*, ed. Robert Gottlieb (New York: Vintage Books, 1996), 733. See also Bernard Gendron, "'Moldy Figs' and Modernists: Jazz at War (1942–1946)," in *Jazz Among the Discourses*, ed. Ken Grabbard (Durham, NC: Duke University Press, 1995), 31–56.
68. Ernest Borneman, "The Jazz Cult II: War Among the Critics," *Harper's Magazine*, March 1947, 261.
69. Barry Ulanov, *Duke Ellington* (New York: Creative Edge Press, 1946), 274; Gunther Schuller, *The Swing Era: The Development of Jazz, 1930–1945* (New York and Oxford: Oxford University Press, 1989), 142; Lock, *Blutopia*, 127; Anna Harwell Celenza, "The 1940s: The Blanton-Webster Band, Carnegie Hall, and the Challenge of the Postwar Era," in *The Cambridge Companion to Duke Ellington*, ed. Edward Green (Cambridge: Cambridge University Press, 2014), 130; Howland, *Ellington Uptown*, 197–99. Harvey Cohen, *Duke Ellington's America* (Chicago: University of Chicago Press, 2010), 236.

70. Ellington, "Certainly It's Music!," in *Duke Ellington Reader*, 247.
71. A fleeting detail in Howard Pollack's biography of librettist John Latouche suggests that the phrase "in tempo" may also have been familiar to Latouche, but in a different sense. Blevins Davis, producer of the operetta *Rhapsody*, suggested that its source material be brought "up to date in tempo and situation." Pollack, *The Ballad of John Latouche: An American Lyricist's Life and Work* (New York and Oxford: Oxford University Press, 2017), 193.
72. Dale Wasserman Papers, Wisconsin Center for Film and Theater Research (hereafter DWP), Box 1, Folder "Scripts; Contracts; Correspondence, 1945; Notes; Programs."
73. No author, "Up-to-Date Beggar's Opera," unknown publication, September 29, 1945. This clipping is housed in the New York Public Library, Billy Rose Theatre Division, NYPL MWEZ + n.c. 10,371.
74. Unknown author and title, [*New York Daily*] *News*, November 11, 1945, NYPL MWEZ + n.c. 10,371. The earliest synopsis states that the production would combine both *Beggar's Opera* and *Polly*. John Latouche, "The Beggar's Opera (Outline by John Latouche)," Duke Ellington Collection, Smithsonian Museum, Washington, DC, Series 16, Box 5, Folder 5, cover sheet, 1 (hereafter DEC). Even after Ellington signed his contract, one synopsis still claimed that "portions of 'Polly' are being incorporated into the present production." Dale Wasserman, "The Beggar's Opera (Prospectus by Dale Wasserman)," DWP, Box 1, Folder "Beggar's Holiday Outlines and Prospectus," [p. 1].
75. No author, "Up-to-Date Beggar's Opera."
76. Draft version of the synopsis; the document has no title page, but the front page is labeled "Generally." DWP, Folder "Scripts: *Beggar's Holiday*: Outlines and Prospectus."
77. Ibid. The document has no title page, and the page number has been covered by the letter x. DWP, "*Beggar's Holiday* Outlines and Prospectus."
78. David Hajdu, *Lush Life: A Biography of Billy Strayhorn* (New York: North Point Press, 1996), 101.
79. The authors and sources are unknown; dated September 12, 1945, and possibly January 1946. They can be found in NYPL MWEZ + n.c. 10,371. This language remained consistent both before and after Ellington signed his contract.
80. Latouche, DWP, Folder "*Beggar's Holiday* Outlines and Prospectus," "The Beggar's Opera (Outline by John Latouche)," [1].
81. A narrator who argues with his central character was also a feature of *Knickerbocker Holiday* (1938) by Maxwell Anderson and Kurt Weill.
82. No author, "Synopsis," DWP, Box 1, Folder "*Beggar's Holiday* Outlines and Prospectus," typewritten document labeled "Synopsis," [1].
83. Joyce Aschenbrenner, *Katherine Dunham: Dancing a Life* (Urbana: University of Illinois Press, 2002), 140. For more on Latouche's earlier work in the left-wing theater, see Pollack, *Ballad of John Latouche*, 46–52, 69–71, 74–86.
84. Bernard Eisenschitz, *Nicholas Ray: An American Journey*, trans. Tom Milne (Minneapolis: University of Minnesota Press, 1993), 88.
85. John Latouche, "Radio," *Mademoiselle* (September 1942), 147.
86. John Latouche, "The *Beggar's Opera* (Outline by John Latouche)," document section called "The Place," DWP, Folder "Beggar's Holiday Outlines and Prospectus," no page number.
87. Latouche, "The *Beggar's Opera* (Outline by John Latouche)," document section called "Intention," DWP, Folder "Beggar's Holiday Outlines and Prospectus," 1.
88. John Latouche, "Letter to John Gay," *New York Times*, February 9, 1947. In the general (as opposed to specific) nature of its critique, it resembles the 1928 version of Weill's and Brecht's *Die Dreigroschenoper*. See Stephen Hinton, "Misunderstanding 'The Threepenny Opera,'" in *Kurt Weill: The Threepenny Opera* (Cambridge: Cambridge University Press, 1990), 189–90.
89. Ellington, *Music Is My Mistress*, 175.
90. Ibid., 180.
91. Ibid., 185.
92. Lock, *Blutopia*, 95; the full discussion can be found on pp. 95–102.
93. No author, "Locale * Period [early draft of synopsis]," DWP, Folder: "*Beggar's Holiday* Outlines and Prospectus," [1].
94. Latouche, "Outline," "The Place."
95. NYPL MWEZ + n.c. 10,371: press release dated January 22 [1946] [presumably from Lorella Val-Mery, based on the fact that the address at the top of the page is the same as her signed press releases]. NYPL MWEZ + n.c. 10,371: Unknown, 9/29/1945, "Up-to-Date Beggar's

Opera." In September 1946, Douglas Watt wrote an article claiming that *Beggar's Holiday* was originally planned as an all-Black production until "various Negro spokesmen" protested at "having a gallery of corrupt characters portrayed by Negroes." NYPL MWEZ + n.c. 10,371: "Beggars Opera' Had to Drop Plans for All-Negro Version" from *Sunday News* by Douglas Watt, September 15, 1946. Another article appeared shortly thereafter called "Duke's 'Beggar's Opera' Drops Plans for All-Colored Cast," *Afro-American*, September 28, 1946. These were obviously false; the show had already been planned as interracial for at least a year. See also Wisconsin Center for Film and Theater Research, DWP, Box 1, "Scripts: Beggar's Holiday: Outlines and Prospectus," "Casting."
96. No author, "Locale * Period [early draft of synopsis]," [1].
97. Final quotation in John Franceschina, *Duke Ellington's Music for the Theatre* (Jefferson, NC: McFarland, 2001), 59.
98. John Latouche, "The Muse and the Mike," *Vogue*, March 1, 1941, 64.
99. Pollack, *The Ballad of John Latouche*, 199.
100. Dale Wasserman, "The Beggar's Opera (Prospectus by Dale Wasserman)," DWP, Box 1, Folder "Beggar's Holiday Outlines and Prospectus," [p. 3]. One early synopsis even called it "expressionistic" outright: "Free in scope, realism and fussiness to be abjured. Style, expressionism, selection of dominat [sic] features with exaggeration and comic distortion of these. Arbitrary in design, frankly theatrical, broad." Draft version of the synopsis, same folder, labeled "Generally."
101. Latouche, "Outline," "The Characters," p. 5. Emphasis added. In an earlier version, probably written before Ellington signed his contract, the synopsis claims about the ballad singer: "Great imagination (otherwise how could he dream this opera?) and great phraseology." No author, "Character Sketches," DWP, Folder "*Beggar's Holiday* Outlines and Prospectus," 5. This synopsis is missing the first three pages.
102. No author, "Character Sketches," 17. Emphasis added.
103. Ibid., 5.
104. John Latouche, "Letter to John Gay," *New York Times*, February 9, 1947. "Big Rock Candy Mountain" was probably a nod to the show's song "Tomorrow Mountain."
105. Latouche, "Outline," "Intention," 2.
106. See Mark Tucker, "The Genesis of *Black, Brown, and Beige*," *Black Music Research Journal* 13, no. 2 (Autumn 1993): 133.
107. Wasserman, "The Beggar's Opera," 2.
108. Presumably written by Lorella Val-Mery, press release dated January 22 [1946], NYPL MWEZ + n.c. 10,371.
109. Archibald MacLeish, "The Irresponsibles," in *A Time to Speak: The Selected Prose of Archibald MacLeish* (Boston: Houghton Mifflin, 1941), 109.
110. Ibid., 113 (second quotation), 118 (first quotation).
111. Scott Donaldson, *Archibald MacLeish: An American Life* (Boston: Houghton Mifflin, 1992), 335, 394. Nelson, *Van Wyck Brooks*, 236. Dwight Macdonald, for his part, so thoroughly detested the speech that he started calling it the "Brooks-MacLeish Thesis" in *Partisan Review* and churning out articles in opposition. For example, seven authors (including John Crowe Ransom, Louise Bogan, and Lionel Trilling) contributed to a collection of responses called "On the Brooks-MacLeish Thesis," *Partisan Review* 9, no. 1 (January–February 1942): 38–47.
112. Latouche, "The Muse and the Mike," 64.
113. Ibid.
114. Both can be found in NYPL MWEZ + n.c. 10,371: the first is a clipping from the *New York News* dated November 11, 1945, which begins, "John LaTouche came bouncing by and said that he and Duke Ellington have started work on a musical show which may be called 'The Beggars Opera' but which will actually be based on the suppressed sequel of the ancient piece." The second is a press release dated January [1946].
115. NYPL MWEZ + n.c. 10,371, press release dated January 22 [1946].
116. This announcement appeared in the *New York Tribune* on March 12, 1946, and is contained in NYPL MWEZ + n.c. 10,371.
117. Pollack notes that Latouche wrote a piece for drummer Gene Krupa that premiered on May 16, 1946. See Pollack, *Ballad of John Latouche*, 218. Composer Kurt Weill, who was considering collaborating with Latouche, corroborates this general impression in letters that he

wrote to choreographer Ruth Page between May and August 1945. On June 28, Weill wrote, "Every time I meet him he has a terrible hangover, but he says that is purely accidental." By August 18, the situation had deteriorated entirely. "I couldn't work with anybody so dishonest and unreliable as a worker and as a person," he wrote, complaining that Latouche had all but disappeared, and had lied about working concurrently with composer Vernon Duke. "So let's forget about that little louse." Letters from Kurt Weill to Ruth Page dated June 28, 1946, and August 18, 1946, Weill-Lenya Research Center, ser. 40.
118. These survive in the Dule Ellington Collection at the Smithsonian Museum, Series 1: Music Manuscripts, Boxes 33–35.
119. [John Latouche], "The Beggar's Opera (First Draft)," DEC, Series 4, Box 3, Folder 4, 1–2. These lyrics differ slightly from the lyrics in Ellington's sheet music.
120. Latouche, "First Draft," 7.
121. Ibid., 2-3-11–2-3-12.
122. Ellington, *Music Is My Mistress*, 185–86.
123. Cf. Pollack, *Ballad of John Latouche*, 224.
124. Latouche, "First Draft," 2-1-26.
125. Ibid., 2-3-4.
126. McMillin, *The Musical as Drama*, 6–10.
127. The manuscript for "Inbetween" can be found in the DEC, Box 33 (Series 1), Folder 14–15. (The text underlay is occasionally unclear in the surviving scores.) The printed sheet music for "Tomorrow Mountain" is held in the Music Division of the New York Public Library.
128. Duke Ellington, *Beggar's Holiday*. Perf: Alfred Drake, Bernice Parks, Libby Holman. Blue Pear-1013, [1946], LP. This album can be found in Yale University's Historical Sound Recordings Archive.
129. John Houseman, *Front and Center* (New York: Simon and Schuster, 1979), 191. In the same section (on p. 193), he continued, "The quality and color of Ellington's music and the energy of our mixed cast almost made us forget the inadequacies of our book and the absence of a structured score."
130. Hajdu, *Lush Life*, 102.
131. Pollack, *Ballad of John Latouche*, 219.
132. These can be found in a miscellaneous set of handwritten notes and drafts on microfilm *ZC-50 at the New York Public Library, Billy Rose Theater Collection.
133. Houseman, *Front and Center*, 191.
134. One exception, reminiscent of the original draft, occurs in the second act. When Peachum and Lockit argue, instead of yelling at one another, they are ventriloquized by two instruments, an E-flat clarinet for the former, and double bass for the latter. See John Latouche, "Beggar's Holiday [marked "Gift of Gore Vidal]," in the New York Public Library, Billy Rose Theatre Collection, *NCOF + 03-65, 114.
135. Ibid., 1.
136. Ibid., 35–36.
137. Ibid., 140.
138. Ibid., 142.
139. John Gay, *The Beggar's Opera*, in *Norton Anthology of English Literature*, 7th ed., vol.1C (New York: W. W. Norton, 2000), 2652.
140. Undated press release, found in NYPL *Beggar's Holiday* Clippings File. This script contains rewrites dating from November 2, while the show was still in rehearsals.
141. Louis Calta, "Frank's 'Mr. Adam' to Be Staged Here," *New York Times*, November 9, 1946.
142. No author, no title, *Tribune*, November 23, 1946, contained in the New York Public Library, MWEZ+ n.c. 10,371.
143. No author, no title, no journal, September 12, 1945, contained in NYPL MWEZ+ n.c. 10,371.
144. No author, no title, *Daily News*, December 9, 1946, contained in NYPL MWEZ+ n.c. 10,371
145. Louis Calta, "2 Shows Opening Runs Here Tonight," *New York Times*, December 26, 1946.
146. Louis Calta, "To Offer Two Plays," *New York Times*, December 19, 1946.
147. No author, no title, *Daily News*, November 4, 1946, contained in NYPL MWEZ+ n.c. 10,371.
148. The ledgers for this musical can be found in DWP, Box 1, Folder "Scripts: *Beggar's Holiday*: Budget, Business Records, Cast List, Clippings."
149. Some of these title changes may have happened at the request of Kurt Weill and his producers, who were in the middle of assembling their new musical *Street Scene*, and who did not want

audiences to be confused. Letter from unknown author to Benjamin M. Shankman of Cohen, Cole, Weiss and Wharton, dated June 5, 1946, ser. 40, Weill-Lenya Research Center.
150. Marilyn Berger, "George Abbott, Broadway Giant with Hit After Hit, Is Dead at 107," *New York Times*, February 5, 1995. According to Mary Rodgers, Abbott's line was "Your paycheck," and he said it to Joe Bova during rehearsals for *Once Upon a Mattress*. See Mary Rodgers and Jesse Green, *Shy: The Alarmingly Outspoken Memoirs of Mary Rodgers* (New York: Farrar, Straus and Giroux, 2022), 233.
151. No author, "Overhauls 'Beggar's Holiday,'" *New York Tribune*, December 23, 1946.
152. The first press release to mention that Libby Holman may be replaced was in the *Daily News*, December 17, 1946 (no author or title listed). On December 22, 1946, a Western Union telegram, signed by Marvin Kohn, was sent to Sam Zolotow of the *New York Times* confirming that Bernice Parks was replacing Holman, and that she "has been given only three days to learn this difficult role." This news was printed the next morning in many newspapers. All of these are preserved in NYPL MWEZ + n.c. 10,371.
153. Latouche, "Beggar' Holiday," DEC, Number 301, Series 4, Box 3, Folder 4. Originally this had appeared in the middle of Act II as "Utopiaville." See Latouche, "Beggar's Holiday" ["Gift of Gore Vidal"], 101–4.
154. Francescina, *Duke Ellington's Music for Theater*, 67. See also George Abbott, *"Mister Abbott"* (New York: Random House, 1963), 217.
155. John Latouche, "Beggar's Holiday," DEC, Number 301, Series 4, Box 3, Folder 4, 2-8-38.
156. Ibid., 2-9-1–2-9-2. Once again, this lies very close to Gay's original dialogue in the final scene *Beggar's Opera*.
157. Atkinson, "Formula Is Broken." In a copy of the script held in the Luther Henderson Collection, there is a note that states, "IN BETWEEN was the curtain raiser in [the] earlier version but was cut from the Broadway show. It's a damn good song so I typed up the lyrics." This could refer to a proposed 1969 revival that never took place. John Latouche, "Beggar's Holiday," Luther Henderson Papers, Schomburg Center for Research in Black Culture, New York Public Library, Box 10, Folder 7.
158. This was an Associated Press article, "New Musical Satisfies," *Los Angeles Times*, December 28, 1946.
159. Louis Kronenberger, "A Classic Is Done Over and Partially Done In," *PM*, December 29, 1946.
160. George Freedley, "'Beggar's Holiday' Unique Musical by Duke Ellington, John Latouche," *Morning Telegraph*, December 28, 1946.
161. John Chapman, "'Beggar's Holiday' Tops New Shows on Broadway," *Chicago Daily Tribune*, January 5, 1947.
162. Howard Barnes, "Cold Night for Beggars," *New York Herald Tribune*, December 27, 1946.
163. Chapman, "Ellington's 'Beggar's Holiday.'"
164. THP, "New Musical Is Presented at Bushnell," *Hartford Courant*, November 28, 1946. Along these lines, another critic maintained that it was "'Holiday' and not 'Opera' in Duke's book." See no author, "It's 'Holiday' and Not 'Opera' in Duke's Book," *Chicago Defender*, November 2, 1946.
165. Kronenberger, "Classic Is Done Over," *PM*, December 29, 1946.
166. Earlier in this chapter, the word "burlesque" appeared in Brooks Atkinson's review of *Allegro* by Rodgers and Hammerstein. In that context, it referred to a show that may have had pretentions toward high art or folk art, but collapsed into mere entertainment. The connotations are similar here. See n. 7.
167. Elliott Norton, no title, *Boston Post*, December 4, 1946, contained in NYPL MWEZ + n.c. 10,371. Elinor Hughes wrote a similar critique. She noted that the original Gay opera was "a savage lampoon of corrupt judges and politicians, and but little secret was made of the author's targets," while *Beggar's Holiday* "seem[ed] curiously soft-pedaled." See Elinor Hughes, "'Beggar's Opera' Remodeled," *Boston Herald*, December 8, 1946.
168. Richard Watts Jr., "A Colorful but Confused Show Based on 'Beggar's Opera,'" *New York Post*, December 27, 1946. This was a very common theme in the reviews. "If satire, it misses. If bawdy entertainment, it may attract a public when it has been smoothed out and stepped up." Hughes, "'Beggar's Opera' Remodeled." A reviewer from Connecticut maintained that "the satire which [Gay] intended has been but palely carried over into the present opus." THP, "New Musical Is Presented." The critic for *Variety* wrote that the show "almost becomes burlesque in its wide distortions of the original Gay opera." Kahn, "Beggar's Holiday," *Variety*, January 1, 1947.

169. Izzy, "Izzy Dubs 'Beggar's Holiday' Colorful, Entertaining Show," *Pittsburgh Courier*, January 4, 1947.
170. Robert Garland, "'Beggar's Holiday' at the Broadway," *New York Journal-American*, December 27, 1946.
171. Bentley, "Broadway and Its Intelligentsia," 213.
172. William Eben Shultz, *Gay's Beggar's Opera: Its Content, History, and Influence* (New Haven, CT: Yale University Press, 1923), 204. This is housed in the Columbia University Library, John Latouche Papers, MS#0746, Box 2, "Beggar's Holiday."
173. As described in Chapter 2, the word "sophisticated" had held negative connotations in his correspondence with Van Wyck Brooks.
174. Brooks Atkinson, "The Play," *New York Times*, December 27, 1946.
175. Ibid.
176. Brooks Atkinson, "Formula Is Broken," *New York Times*, January 26, 1947. As described in Chapter 2, this was the same word he used to praise the Federal Theatre Project's production of *Power*.
177. Woll, *Black Musical Theater*, 210–11, 215–18. For a contemporary account, see Charles Grutzner, "The Arts vs. Bias," *New York Times*, March 16, 1947; no author, "Forecast: Mixed Shows Rule Broadway This Fall," *Chicago Defender*, August 23, 1947.
178. Woll, *Black Musical Theater*, 193.
179. Ibid., 200. For information about the broader movement to end discrimination, see Biondi, *Stand and Fight*, 18–20. Such debates over representation took place in other media, and indeed, had been taking place for more than a century. For an overview, see Barbara Dianne Savage, *Broadcasting Freedom: Radio, War, and the Politics of Race, 1938–1948* (Chapel Hill: University of North Carolina Press, 1999), 7–12.
180. Luther Townsley, "Drama 'Beggar's Holiday' Slated for 20 Weeks," *New Journal and Guide*, April 19, 1947. See also, no author, "'Beggar's Holiday' Producer Pioneer," *New Journal and Guide*, April 5, 1947; Lillian Scott, "Negro Renaissance Seen on Broadway," *Los Angeles Sentinel*, February 20, 1947.
181. No author, "'Beggar's Holiday' Show All Should Attempt to View," *New York Amsterdam News*, January 4, 1947. Likewise, as one of the major industry magazines, *Variety*, put it, *Beggar's Holiday* "has failed to 'stereotype' its colored characters." Kahn, "Beggar's Holiday," *Variety*, January 1, 1947.
182. Richard Dier, "Color Line Fades as Duke's New Opus Thrills Gotham," *Afro-American*, January 4, 1947.
183. Brooks Atkinson, "Negro Drama," *New York Times*, March 1, 1947.
184. In a follow-up column about *Beggar's Holiday* and *Finian's Rainbow*, Atkinson addressed the latter show's explicit political dialogue, which he felt was so obvious as to avoid the problem of alienating: "This column is also in favor of the Bible," he wrote. Atkinson, "Formula Is Broken."
185. Eileen Southern, *The Music of Black Americans: A History*, 3rd ed. (New York: W. W. Norton, 1997), 471–73; Burton W. Peretti, *Lift Every Voice: The History of African American Music* (Lanham, MD: Rowman and Littlefield, 2009), 143–45.
186. Julius Fleming, *Black Patience: Performance, Civil Rights, and the Unfinished Project of Emancipation* (New York: New York University Press, 2022), 71–72; Cohen, *Duke Ellington's America*, 298–308, 379–407.
187. Mercer Ellington and Stanley Dance, *Duke Ellington in Person: An Intimate Memoir* (Boston: Houghton Mifflin, 1978), 97.

Chapter 5

1. Hinton, *Stages of Reform*, 46–48.
2. The original German: "Ich meine besonders die Kapitel [in *Jean-Christophe*], wo sich der junge geniale Musiker gegen die Lüge, gegen die Überempfindsamkeit in der deutschen Musik, selbst bei Bach, Wagner u.a. auflehnt." Kurt Weill, *Briefe an die Familie (1914–1950)*, ed. Lys Symonette and Elmar Juchem (Stuttgart: J. B. Metzler, 2000), 167.
3. Translated and quoted in Max Paddison, "The Critique Criticised: Adorno and Popular Music," *Popular Music* 2 (1982): 214. For other accounts of Weill's divided stance on the German idealist tradition, see David Drew, "Kurt Weill and His Critics," *Times Literary Supplement*, October 3, 1975; Kim H. Kowalke, *Kurt Weill in Europe* (Ann Arbor, MI: University Microfilms International, 1979), 98–106; Kim H. Kowalke, "Kurt Weill, Modernism, and Popular Culture: *Öffentlichkeit als Stil*," *Modernism/Modernity* 2, no. 1 (January 1995): 29–30; Hinton,

Stages of Reform, 45–47; Larry Stempel, "*Street Scene* and the Enigma of Broadway Opera," in *A New Orpheus: Essays on Kurt Weill*, ed. Kim H. Kowalke (New Haven, CT: Yale University Press, 1986), 331.

4. Kurt Weill, "What Is Musical Theater?," lecture for the Group Theatre, July 27, 1936, manuscript contained in Weill-Lenya Research Center, New York, New York, Ser. 31, Box 2, original held in the Papers of Kurt Weill and Lotte Lenya, Yale University, Irving S. Gilmore Music Library, New Haven, Connecticut, Series VIII, Box 68, Folder 17 (hereafter, the Weill-Lenya Research Center will be abbreviated as WLRC).

5. Kurt Weill, "The Future of Opera in America," trans. Joel Lifflander, *Modern Music* 14, no. 4 (May–June 1937): 183.

6. Weill's insistence that he was an "insider" culminated in an often-cited letter he published in *Life* magazine about two months after *Street Scene* opened. Kurt Weill, Letter to the editor, *Life* 22, no. 11 (March 17, 1947): 17. Weill's enthusiastic but complex relationship to his American identity has been the subject of two books: Hermann Danuser and Hermann Gottschewski, eds., *Amerikanismus, Americanism, Weill: Die Suche nach kultureller Identität in der Moderne* (Schliengen: Edition Argus, 2003), and Naomi Graber, *Kurt Weill's America* (New York and Oxford: Oxford University Press, 2021). See also Jürgen Thym, "The Enigma of Kurt Weill's Whitman Songs," in *A Stranger Here Myself: Kurt Weill-Studien*, ed. Kim H. Kowalke and Horst Edler (Hildesheim: Georg Olms Verlag, 1993), 289–91; Fauser, *Sounds of War*, 59–60.

7. Weill, "The Future of Opera in America." See also Tim Carter, "Celebrating the Nation: Kurt Weill, Paul Green, and the Federal Theatre Project," *Journal for the Society for American Music* 5, no. 3 (2011): 298 n. 3.

8. The most complete account of Weill's competition with Rodgers, where it is a running theme throughout the book, is Graber, *Kurt Weill's America*. See also Joel Galand, "Introduction" to *Firebrand of Florence*, vol. 1, by Kurt Weill, Ira Gershwin, and Edwin Justus Meyer (New York: Kurt Weill Foundation for Music, 2002), 17–18.

9. Kurt Weill and Lotte Lenya, *Speak Low (When You Speak Love): The Letters of Kurt Weill and Lotte Lenya*, ed. and trans. Lys Symonette and Kim H. Kowalke (Berkeley: University of California Press, 1996), 460.

10. Kowalke, "Kurt Weill, Modernism, and Popular Culture," 37.

11. Letter from Weill to Rouben Mamoulian, January 22, 1946, WLRC, Series 30 IV.A, Box 47, Folder 11, original held in Yale University, Irving Gilmore library (same call number). Emphasis added. For other examples, see Kurt Weill, "Score for a Play," *New York Times*, January 5, 1947; Kurt Weill, liner notes for *Street Scene*, original cast recording, 1947, Columbia Masterworks M-MM-683. All of Weill's published American writings and interviews have been collected on the Kurt Weill Foundation's website, https://www.kwf.org/research-center/weill-bibliography/.

12. Weill, "Score for a Play." In another article (published about five months after *Street Scene* opened), Weill combined both senses of the word explicitly: "[W]e find on Broadway a definite trend away from the traditional musical comedy towards a more integrated form of musical theatre, and the big successes of the season have been shows which are unorthodox in form and content." Kurt Weill, "Broadway and the Musical Theatre," *The Composer's News-Record* no. 2 (May 1947): 1.

13. Weill, "Score for a Play."

14. Stempel, "*Street Scene*," 325.

15. Weill, "Score for a Play."

16. Kurt Weill, "Über den gestischen Charakter der Musik [1929]," in *Musik und musikalisches Theater: Gesammelte Schriften*, ed. Stephen Hinton, Jürgen Schebera, and Elmar Juchem (Mainz: Schott Musik International, 2000), 84. This collection is hereafter abbreviated MTT. A translation can be found in Kowalke, *Kurt Weill in Europe*, 491. This is hereafter abbreviated KWE. I have translated *gesellschaftlichen* as "coterie" to conform to terminology in previous chapters.

17. He probably adopted this term from critic Paul Bekker, whom he had once described as "the most significant writer on music next to Rolland." Weill, *Briefe and die Familie*, 209. For Weill's distinction between "gesellschaftlichen" and "gemeinschaftsbildenden" art, see "Verschiebungen in der musikalischen Produktion [1927]," MTT 62, KWE, 479–80. For more on these terms, see Hinton, *Stages of Reform*, 56–58.

18. Kurt Weill, "Die neue Oper [1926]," MTT 44, KWE, 465, where it is translated as "intermediary genre."

19. This distinction comes from a suggestion made by Larry Stempel after a talk I gave on this subject in 2017 at the Society for American Music; I thank him for it. See also Stempel, *Showtime*, 259, where he distinguishes between "farce with a political setting" and "satire with a real political agenda."
20. Quoted in bruce d. mcclung, "Psicosi per musica: Re-examining *Lady in the Dark*," in *A Stranger Here Myself: Kurt Weill-Studien*, ed. Kim H. Kowalke and Horst Edler (Hildesheim: Georg Olms Verlag, 1993), 235.
21. Weill and Lenya, *Speak Low*, 388.
22. Galand, "Introduction," 19.
23. Kurt Weill, "Lortzings *Zar und Zimmermann* und Offenbachs *Orpheus in der Unterwelt* als Sendespiele [1925]," MTT, 242. In a similar vein, he had written a letter to his brother dated July 12, 1918, which said: "Ganz wie der 'Orpheus' eine Veräppelung der griechischen Mythe mit äußerst geistreicher, schwungvoller Musik, aber für meinen heutigen Standpunkt albernen Witzen." Weill, *Briefe an die Familie*, 165.
24. Guy Stern, "Der literarisch-kulturelle Horizont des jungen Weill: Eine Analyse seiner ungedruckten frühen Briefe," in *A Stranger Here Myself*, 95; Andreas Eichhorn, "Auf der Suche nach der Moderne: Kurt Weills Rolland-Lektüre," in *Kurt Weill und Frankreich*, ed. Andreas Eichhorn (Münster: Waxman, 2014), 27–29. For more information on Weill's role in any cultural rapprochement between France and Germany during the mid-1920s, see Pascal Huynh, *Kurt Weill ou la conquête des masses* (Arles: Actes Sud, 2000), 179–83.
25. Kurt Weill, "Die fehlende Operette [1925]," MMT, 286–87.
26. Kurt Weill, "Offenbachs *Großherzogin von Gerolstein* [1926]," MTT, 335.
27. "Offenbachs Persiflage ist auf mancherlei Weise auszudeuten, sie muß sich nicht auf seine Zeit beschränken, sie hätte mit Leichtigkeit auf gewisse lächerliche Dinge unserer Tage angewandt werden können." Weill, "[Lortzings *Zar und Zimmermann*]," MMT, 242.
28. Kurt Weill, "Johann Strauß' II *Waldmeister* als Sendespiel [1925]," MMT, 290–91. A partial translation can be found in Joel Galand, "Operetta as Revenant: *The Firebrand of Florence*," *Kurt Weill Newsletter* 17, nos. 1–2 (Fall 1999): 25.
29. Quoted in Hinton, *Weill's Musical Theater*, 45. For more on the term "classicality," see pp. 53–54.
30. Quoted in Gunther Diehl, *Der junge Kurt Weill und seine Opera "Der Protagonist*," vol. 1 (Kassel: Bärenreiter, 1994), 95. The entire sentence (pp. 95–96): "Zur 'jungen Klassizität' rechne ich noch den definitiven Abschied vom Thematischen und das Wiedergreifen der Melodie—(nicht im Sinne eines gefälligen Motives)—als Beherrscherin aller Stimmen, aller Regungen, als Trägerin der Idee und Erzeugerin der Harmonie, kurz: der höchst entwickelten (nicht kompliziertesten) Polyphonie." Weill attributed this idea to Busoni in "Busonis *Faust* und die Erneuerung der Opernform [1926]," MMT, 54–58, KWE, 468–74.
31. Tamara Levitz, *Teaching New Classicality: Ferruccio Busoni's Master Class in Composition* (Frankfurt am Main: Peter Lang GmbH, 1996), 74–82, 247–50.
32. Hinton, *Weill's Musical Theater*, 59–63.
33. Levitz, *Teaching New Classicality*, 203. Busoni also believed that folk melody could provide access to this urform; for him, folk melodies were a "basic melodic essence." See pp. 203–4.
34. "Der Walzer wird ihm zur musikalischen Form, zum wertvollen Gefäß, in das er die edlen Empfindungen seiner bedeutenden Persönlichkeit ausströmen läßt. Ihn stattet er mit Melodien aus von einer Intensität, von einer Linienführung, wie wir sie nur in den genialsten Eingebungen der größten Musiker finden. Wien aber ist der Boden, der einzig eine solche Begabung hervorbringen konnte, der seinen Willen zum Tanz, seine leichte, unbeschwerte Lebensauffassung bis zu einer tänzerischen Schöpferkraft von solchem Ausmaß steigern konnte." Kurt Weill, "Johann Strauß: Zum Gedenken seines 100. Geburtstages im Rundfunk [1925]," MTT, 289.
35. Kurt Weill, *Briefwechsel mit der Universal Edition*, ed. Nils Grosch (Stuttgart: Verlag J. B. Metzler, 2002), 147. Cf. David Drew, "*Der Kuhhandel* as a Key Work," in *A New Orpheus: Essays on Kurt Weill*, ed. Kim H. Kowalke (New Haven, CT: Yale University Press, 1986), 244–45.
36. Weill and Lenya, *Speak Low*, 113.
37. Quoted in David Drew, *Kurt Weill: A Handbook* (London: Faber and Faber, 1987), 255.
38. Weill, "Die fehlende Operetta," MTT, 286.
39. This remains the standard classification in scholarship today. See Stempel, *Showtime*, 71–74, 98–105.
40. Weill and Lenya, *Speak Low*, 185.
41. Weill, "The Future of Opera in America,", 187–88.

42. Weill, "Über den gestischen Charakter der Musik," MMT 84, KWE 491.
43. N.S., "Kurt Weill's New Score Music for 'Road of Promise' Written in Modern Contemporary Style," *New York Times*, October 27, 1935.
44. Letter dated July 2, 1946, quoted in Kim Kowalke, "'The Threepenny Opera' in America," in *Kurt Weill: The Threepenny Opera*, ed. Stephen Hinton (Cambridge: Cambridge University Press, 1990), 95.
45. "I'm an American! Interview with Kurt Weill," program broadcast March 9, 1941, on NBC Blue Network. Transcription available on the Kurt Weill Foundation Website.
46. On the gradual divergence of opera and operetta, see Dizikes, *Opera in America*, 200. See also Christopher Lynch, "Opera and Broadway: The Debate over the Essence of Opera in New York City, 1900–1960" (PhD diss., State University of New York at Buffalo, 2013), 19–20.
47. Quoted in Stanley Green, *The World of Musical Comedy*, 4th ed. (San Diego, CA: Da Capo Press, 1980), 38. See also Dizikes, *Opera in America*, 448.
48. Lewis Nichols, "The Play," *New York Times*, September 6, 1943; Louis Kronenberger, "Music Hath Charms, but Its Charms Have Limits," *PM*, September 7, 1943. The most complete description of the gradual disappearance of American romantic operetta is Bordman, *American Operetta*, 143–48. See also Lehman Engel, *The American Musical Theater: A Consideration* (New York: CBS Records, 1967), 38–44. Historians have noted that Jerome Kern and George Gershwin mixed the lush operetta style with Broadway jazz in a style that Alec Wilder has called "swinging operetta." Wilder, *American Popular Song*, 152.
49. No author, "Light Opera Boom," *Time*, November 9, 1942, 44.
50. Fauser, *Sounds of War*, 161–62. In the field of operetta, this began with the Federal Theatre's famous production of *Swing Mikado* (1938), followed by Mike Todd's commercial production of the *Hot Mikado* (1939).
51. S. J. Wolf, "Opera for Everybody," *New York Times*, November 15, 1942; no author, "The Mérö-Irion," *Time*, November 16, 1942, 73.
52. No author, "New Opera Company," *New York Times*, June 1, 1941. The company originally planned a ballet season alongside its opera season, but those productions seem never to have materialized. See also Bernhard Dopheide, *Fritz Busch: Sein Leben und Wirken in Deutschland mit einem Ausblick auf die Zeit seiner Emigration* (Tutzing: Hans Schneider, 1970), 174.
53. Antal Doráti, *Notes of Seven Decades*, rev. ed. (Detroit, MI: Wayne State University Press, 1981), 186.
54. No author, "New Opera Company Drops Spring Season," *New York Times*, February 26, 1942.
55. Sam Zolotow, "'Rosalinda' Shows Profit of $138,000," *New York Times*, October 27, 1943.
56. Howard Barnes, "A Very Merry Widow," *New York Herald Tribune*, August 5, 1943. This was similar to Olin Downes's review of "La vie parisienne" in the first season, which described the show as "an American musical comedy, done in a rather inferior American way, though with much muscularity and a tremendous display of energy." Olin Downes, "'La vie parisienne' Is Given in English," *New York Times*, November 6, 1941.
57. No author, "Light-Opera Boom," *Time*, November 9, 1942, 44.
58. Cf. Galand, "Introduction," 15–16, and Graber, *Kurt Weill's America*, 169. Both argue that the Italian setting probably contributed to the show's critical failure because, in Graber's phrasing, "U.S. audiences of 1945 were in no mood to be international."
59. Robert Bagar, "Max Reinhardt Version of The Bat Presented by New Opera Company," *New York World-Telegram*, October 29, 1942.
60. Quoted Ronald Sanders, *The Days Grow Short: The Life and Music of Kurt Weill* (New York: Holt, Reinhart and Winston: 1980), 323. Galand, "Introduction," 16.
61. This would eventually open on Broadway under the title *Helen Goes to Troy* in 1944, produced by the New Opera Company.
62. Letter from Kurt Weill to Russell Lewis dated November 14, 1942. WLRC Series 30 IV.A, Box 47, Folder 9; original held at Yale University, Irving S. Gilmore Library, Papers of Kurt Weill and Lotte Lenya (same call number). I thank Dave Stein for helping to differentiate this cluster of operetta projects.
63. No author, "What News on the Rialto?" *New York Times*, August 16, 1942. No author, "Eleanor Lynn Gets Role in New Show," *New York Times*, August 22, 1942; no author, "Rialto Gossip: Grace Moore Will be La Belle Helene in a Production Set for May," *New York Times*, December 27, 1942.
64. Galand, "Introduction," 16–17.
65. Quoted in ibid., 17.
66. Letter from Weill to Ira Gershwin, April 3, 1944, quoted in Graber, *Kurt Weill's America*, 167.

67. John Chapman, "New York Has Another Theater Hit: 'Carmen Jones,'" *Chicago Daily Tribune*, December 12, 1943; no author, "'Carmen Jones': An All-Negro Cast Makes Oscar Hammerstein II's Modernization of Bizet's Opera Memorable Theater," *Time*, December 13, 1943, 111.
68. This was one of the most common arguments surrounding *Carmen Jones* at its premiere. Some examples: "Opera is fundamentally a rather ponderous business and even its best humor has a glum and oppressive quality not unlike the jokes made by Shakespeare's clowns. The music may be very gay, but the behavior of the singers, while sometimes heavily skittish, doesn't exactly suggest that they have a very high opinion of comedy. Billy Rose [the producer], I think, has fixed all that." Wolcott Gibbs, "Funny and Wonderful," *New Yorker*, December 11, 1943, 69. "One of the extraordinary things about 'Carmen Jones' . . . is that the actors in it do not act like opera singers. They do not sing like opera singers either, for the opera people have bigger and better voices. But as the girls and boys in 'Carmen Jones' act out their roles you believe them. They seem to be people." Arthur Pollock, "The Theater," *Brooklyn Eagle*, February 2, 1944. "I felt deeply sorry for poor, distraught Joe, who had to do his no-good Carmen in with a snapper. Never at the Opera Comique, the Met or the Manhattan Opera House, had I felt disturbed because some Jon Jose was constrained to stab some soprano." John Chapman, "'Carmen,' Now 'Carmen Jones,' Is Thrilling as Presented at Broadway Theatre," *Sunday News*, December 12, 1943. Peggy Doyle described it a "shot in the arm to the grand opera tradition" that combined opera with the "refreshing aliveness" of popular culture. Peggy Doyle, "Smash-Hit Future for 'Carmen Jones,'" *Boston Evening American*, November 10, 1943. For more on the trend toward popular opera in the early 1940s, see Annegret Fauser, "'Dixie Carmen': War, Race, and Identity in Oscar Hammerstein's *Carmen Jones* (1943)," *Journal for the Society for American Music* 4, no. 2 (May 2010): 129; Fauser, *Sounds of War*, 161–77.
69. Elsa Maxwell, "Leave Them Classics Lay," *Toledo Blade*, January 18, 1946. Again, it would be difficult to overstate how common such reviews were. Some examples: "In fact, Mr. Rose may yet save the Metropolitan. The strictly theater-going public well may take a trip south of the Forty-Second Street deadline to see how long anything that could suggest such a show as 'Carmen Jones' has been going on." Lewis Nichols, "About 'Carmen Jones,'" *New York Times*, December 12, 1943. "The first of these lessons is that the music of many operas imposes no great strain upon even the untutored listener. . . . The other, and far more important lesson, is that the two things that chiefly militate against a more widespread liking for opera in this country are (1) the prevailing use of foreign texts and (2) the fact that these performances are, as a rule, wretched theatre." Warren Storey Smith, "Of 'Carmen Jones' and 'Carmen' a Comparison," *Boston Post*, November 14, 1943.
70. Weill and Lenya, *Speak Low*, 382. Spelling and punctuation original.
71. Graber, *Kurt Weill's America*, 83–127; Hinton, *Stages of Reform*, 392; Carter, "Celebrating the Nation," 301. Thank you to Professor Graber for discussing this issue with me.
72. Weill and Lenya, *Speak Low*, 404.
73. Ibid., 378. In a similar vein, Weill wrote to his parents on April 30, 1945: "Musikalisch war es das beste was ich in Jahren geschrieben habe, ein richtige Opera mit grossen Chören und Ensemble-Nummern, voll von melodischer Erfindung, unter Ausnutzung des ganzen handwerklichen Könnens, das ich durch die Jahre mir angeeignet habe." Weill, *Briefe an die Familie*, 397.
74. Weill and Lenya, *Speak Low*, 397, 432.
75. Ibid., 398.
76. Ibid., 376.
77. Ibid., 411.
78. Ibid., 401.
79. Ibid., 416.
80. Ibid., 391.
81. Ibid., 388.
82. Ibid., 374. As Fauser notes, most critics were wary of shows that did too much updating or were too slangy. See Fauser, *Sounds of War*, 163–65.
83. Lewis Nichols, "The Firebrand of Florence," *New York Times*, March 23, 1945. Again, critics were nearly unanimous in this. Another example: the *PM* reviewer described it as "much more operetta than musical comedy," with "a big romantic score, much of it full-bodied and tuneful." Yet, he argued, "the music lacks . . . character and variety; the songs do not rise above a tradition, and they are not effectively set off against one another," the lyrics "lack [Gershwin's] usual gaiety and sparkle," and the book, in keeping with operetta tradition "where librettos as

a rule are even sadder than they are in musical comedy," boasts "some witty lines, but there is a frail wit, lost among puerile antics." Louis Kronenberger, "Cellini Proves Dull Company," *PM*, March 23, 1945. Even critics who enjoyed the production agreed. "'The Firebrand of Florence' is a high, wide and handsome show in Max Gordon's [the producer's] most expansive manner. The first audience adored the greater part of it, even if, as I suspect, many a modern may find it unduly dated." Robert Garland, "Cellini Set to Music at Alvin Theatre," *New York Journal-American*, March 23, 1945.

84. Weill, "Score for a Play."
85. WLRC Ser. 33, 1945–46.
86. For more about Robeson's involvement in *Ulysses Africanus* in 1945, see Drew, *Kurt Weill: A Handbook*, 310. Regarding the potential collaborations with Brecht: Negotiations were complex, and wrapped up in a proposed all-Black revival of *Dreigroschenoper* and a proposed collaboration on what would eventually become *Schweyk im Zweiten Weltkrieg*. For details, see Drew, *Kurt Weill: A Handbook*, 406–16.
87. Joseph Horowitz, "Lenya Recalls 'Scene' with Weill," *International Herald Tribune*, October 31, 1979.
88. Kurt Weill, "Liner Notes" for *Street Scene*, original cast recording, 1947. Columbia Masterworks M-MM-683. Although *Firebrand of Florence* was unsuccessful, he did note, "*Porgy and Bess* [probably the 1942 revival] became a big popular success, *Carousel* and *Carmen Jones* introduced operatic elements, and the American public became more and more opera-conscious."
89. Quoted in Hinton, *Stages of Reform*, 369. Brackets added.
90. Harriett Johnson, "Personal Appearance: Street Scene Idea Comes from Verdi, Says Composer Weill," *New York Post*, January 24, 1947. He repeated this in Ager, "Broadway's First Real Opera."
91. Weill most likely began developing this approach when he was a student of Busoni. According to musicologist Gunther Diehl, the language Busoni used was to reflect the world either as a magic mirror ("Zauberspiegel") or as a fun-house mirror ("Lachspiegel"). Diehl, *Der junge Kurt Weill*, 95. Shortly after Busoni died, Weill embarked on his early collaborations with Bertolt Brecht and repurposed this metaphor: "we can represent the world view that we see . . . no longer as a photograph, but as a mirror reflection. In most cases it will be a concave or convex mirror, which reproduces life in a magnification or reduction proportionate to how it appears in reality." The original German can be found in Kurt Weill, "Zeitoper [1928]," MTT, 65; KWE, 482.
92. Hinton, *Stages of Reform*, 407.
93. Kurt Weill, "Alchemy of Music," *Stage* 14, no. 2 (November 1936): 63–64.
94. Weill, liner notes for *Street Scene*.
95. Stempel, "*Street Scene*"; Kowalke, "Kurt Weill, Modernism, and Popular Culture," 37–42; Hinton, *Stages of Reform*, 372–73.
96. Weill, liner notes for *Street Scene*.
97. David Kilroy, "Kurt Weill on Broadway: The Postwar Years (1945–1950)" (PhD diss., Harvard University, 1992), 76.
98. For more on Sokolow, see Graff, *Stepping Left*, 65–74.
99. Originally, Weill's frequent collaborator Maxwell Anderson had been hired to write lyrics. Although Anderson helped produce a detailed outline of *Street Scene* in early August 1945, he left the project a few days later for reasons that remain unclear. For speculation about why he left, see Kilroy, "Kurt Weill on Broadway," 79–84, and Arnold Rampersad, *The Life of Langston Hughes*, vol. 2: *1941–1967, I Dream a World* (New York and Oxford: Oxford University Press, 2002), 110–11. The terms, at first, were contingent: Hughes was asked to submit four sample lyrics on a trial basis (which he did on September 4, 1945), and then to submit nine lyrics for use in the show by November 1 (he actually submitted fourteen by October 23, 1945). Both Rice and Weill were pleased, and on November 15 they hired Hughes as a permanent member of the team. For details about the arrangement, see Hughes's letter describing the agreement and listing his lyrics, dated November 1, 1945, in Langston Hughes Papers, James Weldon Johnson Collection in the Yale Collection of American Literature, Beinecke Rare Book and Manuscript Library, Yale University, Folder 2535 (hereafter designated LHP).
100. Langston Hughes, "The Negro Artist and the Racial Mountain [1926]," in *The Collected Works of Langston Hughes*, vol. 9: *Essays on Art, Race, Politics, and World Affairs* (Columbia: University of Missouri Press, 2002), 33.
101. Kurt Weill, "Score for a Play."

102. From an unidentified article and photo spread in the *Street Scene* scrapbooks in the WLRC Ser.50A/S6/1947/New York.
103. Langston Hughes, "A Living Liner," issued with "Two Worlds of Kurt Weill," RCA LSC-2863, 1966.
104. The outline is held in WLRC Ser. 31, Box 1; the original is held in the Harry Ransom Humanities Research Center, University of Texas at Austin, Maxwell Anderson Collection. Weill's annotated script is located at the WLRC Ser. 20/S6/194-.
105. In LHP Folder 5743 there is a sheet of paper that contains no title, but has a sequence of songs, probably written before any lyrics were put to paper. Item 13 reads "Melting Pot Ensemble (p. 53–55)," most likely referring to pages in the original script. Since Hughes began writing after Labor Day 1945, when he received the first script, this list probably came from early September 1945. For another such list made around the same time, see Kilroy, "Kurt Weill on Broadway," 79.
106. Langston Hughes, "Kurt Weill, My Collaborator," reprinted in *Kurt Weill Newsletter* 13, no. 1 (Spring 1995): 8. This essay was originally printed in the program booklet for the 1955 Düsseldorf production of *Street Scene*.
107. In LHP Folder 5743, there is a sheet titled "List of lyrics submitted to Kurt Weill and Elmer Rice," dated October 1945. On it the "Melting Pot Song" appears among the songs that remained to be drafted.
108. Elmer Rice, *Street Scene in Three Plays* (New York: Hill and Wang, 1965), 88.
109. LHP Folder 5741, draft dated December 14. Many of these ideas appear in Hughes's lyrics from the October 15 batch, LHP Folder 5735: "Little light airs, / Polite little airs, / Sweet sentimental ditties / Like tamed and caged canaries! / No! / Music should be / A great veil of mystery! / Sometimes the veil is torn / And the soul of music is born! / The secret is revealed, / And the heart is healed. // [... Music] Must be the known here / And the unknown there, / The earth / And the vast nowhere, / The dross dissolved, / The real gold coined, / Man and God / And the Universe / Joined!"
110. In LHP Folder 5730 there was an undated intermediate version that still tried to include hints of Sam's erudition, yet that nonetheless focused more on his loneliness and restlessness. Called "Can't Sleep," it was written during the month of February 1946. Soon after, Hughes started work on the version that would eventually become "Lonely House" (the final version of which dates from July 13; see LHP, Folder 5730). Hughes refers to a version of this song, probably this one, in a letter to Rice dated March 1, 1946, contained in LHP Folder 2535.
111. Letter from Kurt Weill to Langston Hughes, January 22, 1936, LHP Folder 3801.
112. LHP Folder 5744. Although undated, these appear to be handwritten notes from one of the earliest conversations Weill had with Hughes, which means that it probably dated from August 1945. It could, in fact, represent a conversation they had when they hired Hughes on a "trial" basis. The notes Hughes took are basic, describing broad characterization and fundamental strategy. All other surviving notes from other phone calls, which are often dated, are more specific, dealing with particular changes to songs or lines, or dealing with contracts, royalties, advertising, and other logistical matters.
113. LHP Folder 5737.
114. LHP Folder 5738.
115. Letter from Weill to Hughes, dated January 22, 1946, LHP Folder 3801.
116. MSS 30, Papers of Kurt Weill and Lotte Lenya in the Irving S. Gilmore library, Yale University, Box 31, Folder 434. The cut-time refrains are found on pp. 3, 8, and 12.
117. Draft dated July 11 [1946], LHP Folder 5738.
118. Rampersad, *Life of Langston Hughes*, 117–23.
119. Draft dated March 14, LHP Folder 5738.
120. LHP, Folder 5738. Emphasis original.
121. Perhaps knowing that this would be controversial, Hughes also produced another, more idealistic lyric at the same time, in keeping with the food theme, called "Southern Fried." "This old earth's enormous, / Yes, it's big and wide— / But there's nothing in it nowhere like / Southern fried." LHP Folder 5738.
122. Letter from Hughes to Weill, dated March 14, 1946, LHP Folder 3081.
123. Draft dated August 9, 1946, LHP Folder 5737.
124. LHP, Folder 5739.
125. Draft dated August 13 [1946], LHP Folder 5739. Other versions focused on public schools. "When I studied my A-B-C's / And learned arithmetic, / I also learned in public school / What

makes America tick. / There were rich kids there and poor kids, / From varied homes they came— / But in our class in public school / Every one was just the same..." LHP Folder 5736. The original ideas for this came from a song Hughes had written on March 23 called "P.S. 93," also in LHP Folder 5736. There were two intermediate versions, in which Hughes turned back to the idea of brotherhood and music from earlier in the year: "Everybody Loves Music" and "Music of America." LHP Folder 5737.

126. LHP Folder 5737, draft dated September 5; they began this on August 15.
127. LHP Folder 5739, dated October 1.
128. LHP Folder 5736, written on a draft called "Block Party," dated October 4.
129. LHP Folder 5739, drafts dated October 3, 4, 5.
130. All of these are in LHP Folder 5739.
131. LHP Folder 5736.
132. LHP Folder 5739.
133. LHP Folder 5733.
134. LHP Folder 5733, page of notes dated October 16.
135. LHP Folder 5733, dated October 13.
136. Stempel, "*Street Scene*," 331–32; Kilroy, "Kurt Weill on Broadway," 98; Kowalke, "Kurt Weill, Modernism, and Popular Culture," 44; Huynh, *Kurt Weill*, 386. Cf. William R. Thornhill, "Kurt Weill's *Street Scene*" (PhD diss., University of North Carolina at Chapel Hill, 1990), 86.
137. Thornhill, "Kurt Weill's *Street Scene*," 27–28.
138. Letter dated December 21, LHP Folder 5745.
139. The entire letter appears in Kilroy, "Kurt Weill on Broadway," 105. Vsevolod Meyerhold (1874–1940) was a director whose works Hughes encountered on his nearly yearlong trip to the Soviet Union starting in 1932. Meyerhold was known in part for blending seemingly incompatible styles of theater. For more information about his lasting impression on Hughes, see Leslie Sanders, "'Interesting Ways of Staging Plays': Hughes and the Russian Theatre," *The Langston Hughes Review* 15, no. 1 (1997): 7–9.
140. Lewis Funke, no title, *New York Times*, May 26, 1946.
141. LHP Folder 2424.
142. Rampersad, *Life of Langston Hughes*, 123–24.
143. Letter from Weill to Rouben Mamoulian, January 22, 1946, WLRC, Series 30 IV.A, Box 47, Folder 11; original held in Yale University, Irving Gilmore library (same call number).
144. Quoted in Kilroy, "Kurt Weill on Broadway," 108.
145. Weill, "Score for a Play," *New York Times*, January 5, 1947.
146. Robert Garland, "'Street Scene' Bows at Adelphi Theatre," *New York Journal-American*, no date. Louis Kronenberger made a similar point. "It is captioned a 'dramatic musical' (it could just as easily have been captioned a folk opera) ..." Kronenberger, "'Street Scene,' Set to Music Is Still Lively Theater," *PM*, no date. Unless otherwise noted, all reviews can be found in the *Street Scene* production folder, WLRC Ser.50A/S6/1947/New York.
147. Kronenberger, "Street Scene," Emphasis original. Other writers also commented on the show's recitative to similar effect. *Newsweek* maintained that, despite being called a "dramatic musical," one "must first face the fact that it is actually an opera," and, "unqualified enjoyment of it will therefore be limited to those who like their dramatic dialogue sung to them." No author, "Street Opera," *Newsweek*, January 20, 1947.
148. Other critics followed suit. For example, one wrote, "Not, to be sure, that the melodramatics are any harder to take than those accepted nightly over at the Metropolitan. But it is unfortunate that the Messrs. Rice, Weill and Langston Hughes (who wrote lyrics that soar frequently into the realm of pure poetry) have chosen to borrow some of the irritations of 'grand' opera along with its virtues." B. F., "New Plays: Music Ascendant," *Cue*, January 18, 1947.
149. George Jean Nathan, "Read On—There's Some Good News Coming," no journal, no date. This clipping can be found in the *Street Scene* scrapbook at the Weill-Lenya Research Center, Ser.50A/S6/1947/New York.
150. John Lovell, Jr., "Singing in the Streets," *The Crisis*, June 1947.
151. Elinor Hughes, "'Street Scene' Becomes an Opera with Striking Results," *Boston Herald*, May 4, 1947.
152. Other critics made the same point. In *Variety*, for example, the reviewer seemed to want to distance Weill's score from popular music, and yet maintain the prestige of opera. "There are no hit tunes as such, in the juke box sense, but there are notable solos, as well as some fine duets, quartets and groups, and ensemble numbers. But each song is an integral part of

the production and advances it accordingly." Bron., "Plays on Broadway," *Variety*, January 15, 1947.
153. Shana Ager, "Kurt Weill's Music Has Made Something New out of 'Street Scene,'" *PM*, February 9, 1947.
154. Edward J. Smith, *Musical Digest* 29, no. 6 (February 1947): 39.
155. John Chapman, "Musical 'Street Scene' a Splendid and Courageous Sidewalk Opera," *New York Daily News*, January 10, 1947.
156. Olin Downes, "Opera on Broadway," *New York Times*, January 26, 1947.
157. Billy Rose, "Pitching Horseshoes," *Variety*, January 22, 1947.
158. Lovell, "Singing in the Streets."
159. In fact, Lovell explicitly addressed the employment issue elsewhere in his article: ""[T]he emergence of young people like Helen Ferguson is a challenge to talented Negro adolescents to become presentation-worthy, for the opportunities are surely available."
160. Brooks Atkinson, "Words and Music: Menotti's Two Operas, 'The Telephone' and 'The Medium,' Come to Broadway," *New York Times*, May 11, 1947.
161. Brooks Atkinson, "The New Play," *New York Times*, January 10, 1947.
162. Ibid.
163. Brooks Atkinson, "New York to Music," *New York Times*, January 19, 1947.
164. Other productions on Broadway and Off-Broadway also deploy similar strategies toward civic or political ends. These include Elie Siegmeister's *Sandhog* (Phoenix Theater, 1954), Aaron Copland's *The Tender Land* (New York City Opera, 1954), a revival of Virgil Thomson's *The Mother of Us All* (Phoenix Theater, 1956), *West Side Story* (Broadway, 1957), and Robert Kurka's and Lewis Allen's *The Good Soldier Schweik* (New York City Center, 1958).

Conclusion

1. Hans Georg Gadamer, *Truth and Method*, trans. Joel Weinsheimer and Donald G. Marshall (London: Bloomsbury, 2013), 313–15.
2. A touchstone example of a study that explains the phenomenon of "modernism" by looking to contemporary political changes is Matei Calinescu, *Five Faces of Modernity: Modernism, Avant-Garde, Decadence, Kitsch, Postmodernism* (Durham, NC: Duke University Press, 1987). For a more recent assessment of this book's influence on the field of modernism studies, see Mark Wollaeger, "Modernism Under Review: Matei Calinescu's *Five Faces of Modernity: Modernism, Avant-Garde, Decadence, Kitsch, Postmodernism* (1987)," *Modernist Cultures* 8, no. 2 (2013): 163–78.
3. Taruskin, *Oxford History of Western Music*, vol. 4: 1–5. See also Walter Frisch, *German Modernism: Music and the Arts* (Berkeley: University of California Press, 2005), 3–4. In a similar vein, Daniel Albright has described modernism as "testing the limits of aesthetic construction," arguing that "the nineteenth century had established a remarkably safe, intimate center" but that modernism "reache[d] out to art's freakish circumferences." Yet even at these edges, Albright contends, the field of modernism was, however tenuously, "monistic": squarely within the field of high art. Daniel Albright, *Music's Monisms: Disarticulating Modernism* (Chicago: University of Chicago Press, 2021), 2.
4. Huyssen, *After the Great Divide*, 47. In a similar vein, Peter Franklin writes that modernism is "a mode of art whose innovative aspect is associated with an explicitly or implicitly critical attitude to past and present norms and manners of artistic production and consumption, and the restricted imaginative world of its frequently (to the artist) insensitive consumers." Peter Franklin, "Modernismus and the Philistines," *Journal of the Royal Musical Association* 139 (2014): 185.
5. Hepokoski, *Sibelius Symphony No. 5*, 7–9. See also Richard Taruskin, "Not Modern and Loving It," in *Russian Music at Home and Abroad: New Essays* (New York and Oxford: Oxford University Press, 2016), 120–33. Hepokoski's approach has proven especially influential in the study of British modernism. See, for example, Daniel Grimley, "Modernism and Closure: Nielsen's Fifth Symphony," *The Musical Quarterly* 86 (2002): 151–52; Eric Saylor, *English Pastoral Music: From Arcadia to Utopia, 1900–1955* (Urbana: University of Illinois Press, 2017), 10–12.
6. Hepokoski, *Sibelius Symphony No. 5*, 16.
7. Douglas Mao, "Introduction: The New Modernist Studies," in *History of New Modernism Studies*, ed. Douglas Mao (Cambridge: Cambridge University Press, 2021), 1–21.
8. See, for example, Michael North, "Against the Standard: Linguistic Imitation, Racial Masquerade, and the Modernist Rebellion," in *The New Modernist Studies Reader: An Anthology of Essential Criticism*, ed. Sean Latham and Gayle Rogers (London: Bloomsbury Academic,

2021), 41–74 (hereafter, this collection is abbreviated *NMSR*); Miriam Bratu Hansen, "The Mass Production of the Senses," *NMSR*, 121–136; Mark S. Morrison, "Youth in Public: The *Little Review* and Commercial Culture in Chicago," *NMSR*, 137–61; Brent Hayes Edwards, "Variations on a Preface," *NMSR*, 162–98.

9. Both quotations come from Hansen, "Mass Production of the Senses," 122.
10. Hannah Freed-Thall, *Spoiled Distinctions: Aesthetics and the Ordinary in French Modernism* (New York and Oxford: Oxford University Press, 2015). For a larger bibliography on this subject, see p. 150 n. 11.
11. Franklin, "Modernismus and the Philistines," 184.
12. Leonard B. Meyer, "A Pride of Prejudices; or, Delight in Diversity," *Music Theory Spectrum*, 13 no. 2 (Autumn 1991): 241.
13. Rita Felski, "Modernity and Feminism," *NSMR*, 84–85.
14. Paul K. Saint-Amour, "Weak Theory, Weak Modernism," *NMSR*, 355.
15. Chowrimootoo, *Middlebrow Modernism*, 190.
16. Ibid. Likewise, from Tom Perrin, "if for middlebrow authors modernists texts were characterized by the rejection of literary conventions, seeming to call on readers to reject their society, middlebrow texts challenged such conventions but did not reject them—as that would be as impossible as abandoning one's society." Perrin, "Rebuilding *Bildung*," 384.
17. Kate Guthrie, *The Art of Appreciation: Music and Middlebrow Culture in Modern Britain* (Oakland: University of California Press, 2021), 12.
18. Brooks, "Highbrow, Lowbrows, Middlebrow, Now," 47.
19. Bürger and Bürger, *Institutions of Art*, 5. For a succinct definition, see Hohendahl, *Building a National Literature*, 34.
20. Jacques Dubois, *L'Institution de la littérature: Introduction à une sociologie* (Brussels: Editions Labor, 1986), 32–33.
21. By Bürger's criteria, it seemed unlikely that other culture had functional determinants that would make it a coherent institution: "What is decisive in this context is the fact that, in the period in which the essential founding principles of the emergent bourgeois society (instrumental reason and the division of labor) become apparent, art is in turn understood as the single possible field in which the lost totality of humanity can be regained." Bürger and Bürger, *Institutions of Art*, 7.
22. Johann Gottfried Herder, "From *Alte Volkslieder / Ancient Folk Songs*," trans. Philip V. Bohlman, in Johann Gottfried Herder and Philip V. Bolhman, *Song Loves the Masses: Herder on Music and Nationalism* (Berkeley: University of California Press, 2017), 43.
23. Emblematic of this was, once again, Herder. His description of popular music, for which he did not have a word; whatever he meant by "folk," he did not mean "folk songs of our own time." Herder, ibid., 27. The original passage is in italics, removed here.
24. See Bürger and Bürger, *The Institutions of Art*, 10. Michael Kammen, however, differentiates between proto-mass culture, mass culture, and popular culture, and claims that true mass culture did not appear until the 1960s. See Michael Kammen, *American Culture, American Tastes: Social Change and the Twentieth Century* (New York: Alfred A. Knopf, 1999), 162–89. The present book makes no distinction between these categories.
25. Quoted in Christopher Chowrimootoo, "Reviving the Middlebrow, or: Deconstructing Modernism from the Inside," *Journal of the Royal Musical Association* 139 (2014): 187.
26. A thorough discussion of the end of the middlebrow era lies beyond the scope of this book. Preliminary research in this field has been done by sociologist Richard Peterson, who suggested that institutional attitudes changed drastically in the middle of the twentieth century—the same era that witnessed the rise of the New Left, the early articulations of postmodernism, and so on. In his telling, there remains a group of people who are willing to mingle folk and highbrow culture, but that increasingly cultural sophistication became marked by omnivorousness. See Richard Peterson and Roger M. Kern, "Changing Highbrow Taste: From Snob to Omnivore," *American Sociological Review* 6, no. 5 (October 1996): 900–907, and Peterson, "The Rise and Fall of Highbrow Snobbery as a Status Marker."
27. Cf. Susan McClary, "Terminal Prestige: The Case of Avant-Garde Music Composition," *Cultural Critique* 12 (Spring 1989): 57–81.

Bibliography

Archival Sources

Brooks Atkinson Papers, New York Public Library, Billy Rose Theater Division, New York, NY.
Dale Wasserman Papers, Wisconsin Center for Film and Theater Research, Madison, WI.
Duke Ellington Collection, Smithsonian Museum, Washington, DC.
Federal Theatre Collection, Library of Congress, Washington, DC.
John Latouche Papers, MS 0746, Columbia University Library, New York, NY.
Kurt Weill and Lotte Lenya Papers, MSS 30, Irving S. Gilmore Music Library, Yale University, New Haven, CT.
Kurt Weill Collection, Weill-Lenya Research Center, New York, NY.
Langston Hughes Papers, James Weldon Johnson Collection in the Yale Collection of American Literature, Beinecke Rare Book and Manuscript Library, Yale University, New Haven, CT.
Luther Henderson Papers, Schomburg Center for Research in Black Culture, New York Public Library, New York, NY.
Oscar Hammerstein II Collection, Library of Congress, Washington, DC.
Richard Rodgers Papers, T-MSS 1987-006, New York Public Library, Billy Rose Theater Division, New York, NY.
Rouben Mamoulian Collection, Library of Congress, Washington, DC.
Theatre Guild Archives, Yale Collection of American Literature, Beinecke Rare Book and Manuscript Library, Yale University, New Haven, CT.
Van Wyck Brooks Papers, MSS Coll. 650, Kislak Center for Special Collections, Rare Books and Manuscripts, University of Pennsylvania, Philadelphia, PA.

Works Cited

Unless they are drawn from anthologies, individual newspaper and magazine articles do not appear in the list below. Their citations can be found in the notes for each chapter.

Abbott, George. *"Mister Abbott."* New York: Random House, 1963.
Adorno, Theodor, and George Simpson. "On Popular Music." In *Essays on Music*, trans. Susan H. Gillespie, 437–69. Berkeley: University of California Press, 2002.
Agee, James. "Pseudo-Folk." *Partisan Review* 11, no. 2 (Spring 1944): 219–23.
Ahlquist, Karen. "Balance of Power: Music as Art and Social Class in the Late Nineteenth Century." In *Rethinking American Music*, ed. Tara Browner and Thomas Riis, 7–33. Urbana: University of Illinois Press, 2019.
Albright, Daniel. *Music's Monisms: Disarticulating Modernism*. Chicago: University of Chicago Press, 2021.
Allen, Ray. "An American Folk Opera? Triangulating Folkness, Blackness, and Americanness in Gershwin and Heyward's 'Porgy and Bess.'" *Journal of American Folklore* 117, no. 465 (Summer 2004): 243–61.
Allen, Ray, and George P. Cunningham. "Cultural Uplift and Double-Consciousness: African American Responses to the 1935 Opera *Porgy and Bess*." *The Musical Quarterly* 88 (2005): 342–69.

Anderson, Paul Allen. *Deep River: Music and Memory in Harlem Renaissance Thought.* Durham, NC: Duke University Press, 2001.
Aschenbrenner, Joyce. *Katherine Dunham: Dancing a Life.* Urbana: University of Illinois Press, 2002.
Atkinson, Brooks. *Broadway Scrapbook.* New York: Theatre Arts, 1947.
Atkinson, Brooks. *The Lively Years.* New York: Association Press, 1973.
Banfield, Stephen. *Jerome Kern.* New Haven, CT: Yale University Press, 2006.
Becker, Howard. *Art Worlds.* Berkeley: University of California Press, 2008.
Beiswanger, George. "Broadway Letter." *The Kenyon Review* 6, no. 2 (Spring 1944): 318–20.
Bender, Thomas. *New York Intellect: A History of Intellectual Life in New York City, from 1750 to the Beginnings of Our Own Time.* New York: Alfred A. Knopf, 1987.
Benjamin, Walter. *Illuminations,* ed. Hannah Arendt, trans. Harry Zohn. New York: Harcourt, 1968.
Bentley, Eric. "Broadway and Its Intelligentsia." *Harper's Magazine* (March 1947): 211–21.
Bentley, Eric. *The Brecht Memoir.* New York: PAJ Publications, 1985.
Bentley, Eric. *The Playwright as Thinker: A Study of Drama in Modern Times.* Cleveland, OH: World Publishing, 1955.
Bentley, Eric. *What Is Theatre? Incorporating the Dramatic Event and Other Reviews 1944–1967.* New York: Hill and Wang, 2000.
Berlant, Lauren. *The Female Complaint: The Unfinished Business of Sentimentality in American Culture.* Durham, NC: Duke University Press, 2008.
Berman, Russell. "Introduction." In *The Institutions of Art,* ed. Peter Bürger and Christa Bürger, trans. Loren Kruger, xi–xx. Lincoln: University of Nebraska Press, 1992.
Bernstein, Leonard. *The Joy of Music.* New York: Simon and Schuster, 1959.
Bigsby, Christopher, and Don B. Wilmeth. "Introduction." In *The Cambridge History of American Theatre,* ed. Don B. Wilmeth, 1–23. Cambridge: Cambridge University Press, 2008.
Biondi, Martha. *To Stand and Fight: The Struggle for Civil Rights in Postwar New York City.* Cambridge, MA: Harvard University Press, 2003.
Blake, Casey Nelson. *Beloved Community: The Cultural Criticism of Randolph Bourne, Van Wyck Brooks, Waldo Frank, and Lewis Mumford.* Chapel Hill: University of North Carolina Press, 1990.
Blitzstein, Marc. *The Mark Blitzstein Songbook,* vol. 2, ed. Leonard Lehrman. [S. I.]: Boosey and Hawkes, 2001.
Block, Geoffrey. "'Bigger than a Show—Better than a Circus': The Broadway Musical, Radio, and Billy Rose's *Jumbo*." *Musical Quarterly* 89 (2006): 164–98.
Block, Geoffrey. "The Broadway Canon from *Show Boat* to *West Side Story* and the European Operatic Ideal." *The Journal of Musicology* 11 (1993): 525–44.
Block, Geoffrey. *Enchanted Evenings: The Broadway Musical from* Show Boat *to Sondheim and Lloyd Webber.* New York and Oxford: Oxford University Press, 2009.
Block, Geoffrey. "Integration." In *The Oxford Handbook of The American Musical,* ed. Raymond Knapp, Mitchell Morris, and Stacy Wolf, 97–110. New York and Oxford: Oxford University Press, 2011.
Block, Geoffrey. *Richard Rodgers.* New Haven, CT: Yale University Press, 2003.
Bogan, Louise. "Some Notes on Popular and Unpopular Art." *Partisan Review* 10, no. 5 (September 1943): 391–401.
Bogan, Louise. "The Defense of Belles-Lettres." *The Nation* 150 (April 13, 1940): 480–81.
Bohlman, Philip. *The Study of Folk Music in the Modern World.* Bloomington: Indiana University Press, 1988.
Bordman, Gerald. *American Musical Comedy: From Adonis to Dreamgirls.* New York: Oxford University Press, 1982.
Bordman, Gerald. *American Operetta: From H. M. S. Pinafore to Sweeney Todd.* New York and Oxford: Oxford University Press, 1981.

Bordman, Gerald, and Richard Norton. *American Musical Theatre: A Chronicle*, 4th edition. Oxford: Oxford University Press, 2010.
Brooks, John. "Highbrow, Lowbrows, Middlebrow, Now." *The American Heritage* 34, no. 4 (June/July 1983): 42–47.
Brooks, Van Wyck. *America's Coming of Age*. New York: Octagon Books, 1975.
Brooks, Van Wyck. *An Autobiography*. New York: E. P. Dutton, 1965.
Brooks, Van Wyck. "On Creating a Usable Past." *The Dial* 64, no. 7 (April 11, 1918): 337–41.
Brooks, Van Wyck. *The Opinions of Oliver Allston*. New York: E. P. Dutton, 1941.
Brooks, Van Wyck. *Van Wyck Brooks: The Early Years*, ed. Claire Sprague. Boston: Northeastern University Press, 1968.
Browder, Laura. "Finding a Collective Solution: The Living Newspaper Experiment." *Prologue: Quarterly Journal of the National Archives and Records Administration* 30, no. 2 (Summer 1998): 87–97.
Brown, Erica. *Comedy and the Feminine Middlebrow Novel: Elizabeth von Arnim and Elizabeth Taylor*. London and New York: Routledge, 2016.
Broyles, Michael. *Mavericks and Other Traditions in American Music*. New Haven, CT: Yale University Press, 2004.
Bürger, Peter. *Theory of the Avant-Garde*. Minneapolis: University of Minnesota Press, 1984.
Bürger, Peter, and Christa Bürger. *The Institutions of Art*, trans. Loren Kruger. Lincoln: University of Nebraska Press, 1992.
Burkholder, J. Peter. "Museum Pieces: The Historicist Mainstream in Music of the Last Hundred Years." *Nineteenth-Century Music* 2. no. 2 (Spring 1983): 115–34.
Calinescu, Matei. *Five Faces of Modernity: Modernism, Avant-Garde, Decadence, Kitsch, Postmodernism*. Durham, NC: Duke University Press, 1987.
Cantu, Maya. "'Gilding the Guild': Art Theatre, the Broadway Revue and Cultural Parody in the *Garrick Gaieties* (1925–1930)." *Studies in Musical Theatre* 7, no. 1 (March 2013): 45–60.
Cantwell, Robert. *When We Were Good: The Folk Revival*. Cambridge, MA: Harvard University Press, 1996.
Carson, John W. "Living Newspaper: Theatre and Therapy." *TDR* (1988–) 44, no. 2 (Summer 2000): 107–22.
Carter, Tim. "Celebrating the Nation: Kurt Weill, Paul Green, and the Federal Theatre Project." *Journal for the Society for American Music* 5, no. 3 (August 2011): 297–334.
Carter, Tim. *Oklahoma!: The Making of an American Musical*. Revised edition. New Haven, CT: Yale University Press, 2020.
Carter, Tim. *Rodgers and Hammerstein's Carousel*. New York and Oxford: Oxford University Press, 2017.
Celenza, Anna Harwell. "The 1940s: The Blanton-Webster Band, Carnegie Hall, and the Challenge of the Postwar Era." In *The Cambridge Companion to Duke Ellington*, ed. Edward Green, 121–33. Cambridge: Cambridge University Press, 2014.
Child, Francis James. "Ballad Poetry." *Johnson's Universal Cyclopœdia* [originally published 1900], reprinted in *Journal of Folklore Research* 31, nos. 1–3 (January–December 1994): 214–22.
Chowrimootoo, Christopher. *Middlebrow Modernism: Britten's Operas and the Great Divide*. Oakland: University of California Press, 2018.
Chowrimootoo, Christopher. "Reviving the Middlebrow, or: Deconstructing Modernism from the Inside," *Journal of the Royal Musical Association* 139 (2014): 187–93.
Christ, Birte. "More Trouble with Diversity: Re-Dressing Poverty, Masking Class in Middlebrow Success Fiction." *Amerikastudien / American Studies* 55, no. 1 (2010): 19–44.
Citron, Stephen. *The Wordsmiths: Oscar Hammerstein II and Alan Jay Lerner*. New York: Oxford University Press, 1995.
Clurman, Harold. *The Fervent Years*. New York: Da Capo Press, 1983.
Cohen, Harvey. *Duke Ellington's America*. Chicago: University of Chicago Press, 2010.
Conroy, Marianne. "Acting Out: Method Acting, the National Culture, and the Middlebrow Disposition in Cold War America." *Criticism* 35, no. 2 (Spring 1993): 239–63.

Cox, Felix. "'A Faltering Step in a Basically Right Direction': Richard Rodgers and *All Points West.*" *American Music* 23, no. 3 (2005): 355–76.
Crawford, Richard. *America's Musical Life: A History.* New York: W. W. Norton, 2001.
Crawford, Richard. "It Ain't Necessarily Soul: Gershwin's 'Porgy and Bess' as a Symbol." *Anuario Interamericano de Investigación Musical* 8 (1972): 17–38.
Crawford, Richard. "Where Did Porgy and Bess Come from?" *The Journal of Interdisciplinary History* 36, no. 4 (Spring 2006): 697–734.
Crist, Elizabeth Bergman. *Music for the Common Man: Aaron Copland During the Depression and War.* Oxford and New York: Oxford University Press, 2005.
Dahlhaus, Carl. *Nineteenth-Century Music,* trans. J. Bradford Robinson. Berkeley: University of California Press, 1989.
D'Andre, David Mark. "The Theatre Guild, *Carousel,* and the Cultural Field of American Musical Theatre." PhD dissertation, Yale University, 2000.
Danto, Arthur. "The Artworld." *The Journal of Philosophy* 61, no. 19 (October 15, 1964): 571–84.
Danuser, Hermann, and Hermann Gottschewski, eds. *Amerikanismus, Americanism, Weill: Die Suche nach kultureller Identität in der Moderne.* Schliengen: Edition Argus, 2003.
de Mille, Agnes. *Dance to the Piper: Memoirs of the Ballet.* London: Columbus Books, 1952.
Denisoff, R. Serge. *Great Day Coming: Folk Music and the American Left.* Urbana: University of Illinois Press, 1971.
Denning, Michael. *The Cultural Front: The Laboring of American Culture in the Twentieth Century.* London: Verso, 1998.
Dickstein, Morris. *Dancing in the Dark: A Cultural History of the Great Depression.* New York: W. W. Norton, 2009.
Diehl, Gunther. *Der junge Kurt Weill und seine Opera "Der Protagonist",* vol. 1. Kassel: Bärenreiter, 1994.
DiMaggio, Paul. "Cultural Entrepreneurship in Nineteenth-Century Boston: The Creation of an Organizational Base for High Culture in America." *Media, Culture and Society* 4, no. 1 (1982): 33–50.
DiMaggio, Paul. "Cultural Entrepreneurship in Nineteenth-Century Boston, Part II: The Classification and Framing of American Art." *Media, Culture and Society* 4, no. 4 (1982): 303–22.
DiMaggio, Paul. "On Pierre Bourdieu." *American Journal of Sociology* 84, no. 6 (May 1979): 1460–74.
DiMaggio, Paul J., and Walter W. Powell, eds. *The New Institutionalism in Organizational Analysis.* Chicago: University of Chicago Press, 1991.
Dimitrov, Georgi. *The United Front: The Struggle Against Fascism and War.* London: Lawrence and Wishart, 1938.
Dizikes, John. *Opera in America: A Cultural History.* New Haven, CT: Yale University Press, 1993.
Donaldson, Scott. *Archibald MacLeish: An American Life.* Boston: Houghton Mifflin, 1992.
Donovan, Timothy P. "'Oh What a Beautiful Mornin'': The Musical *Oklahoma!* and the Popular Mind in 1943." *Journal of Popular Culture* 8, no. 3 (Winter 1974): 477–88.
Dopheide, Bernhard. *Fritz Busch: Sein Leben und Wirken in Deutschland mit einem Ausblick auf die Zeit seiner Emigration.* Tutzing: Hans Schneider, 1970.
Doráti, Antal. *Notes of Seven Decades,* revised edition. Detroit, MI: Wayne State University Press, 1981.
Doss, Erika. *Benton, Pollock, and the Politics of Modernism: From Regionalism to Abstract Expressionism.* Chicago: University of Chicago Press, 1991.
Douglas, Ann. *The Feminization of American Culture.* New York: Alfred A. Knopf, 1977.
Douglas, Ann. *Terrible Honesty: Mongrel Manhattan in the 1920s.* New York: Farrar, Straus and Giroux, 1995.
Downes, Olin. "Introduction." In *Treasury of American Song,* ed. Olin Downs and Elie Siegmeister, 11–18. New York: Alfred A. Knopf, 1943.

Drain, Richard. *Twentieth-Century Theatre: A Sourcebook*. London: Routledge, 1995.
Drew, David. "*Der Kuhhandel* as a Key Work." In *A New Orpheus: Essays on Kurt Weill*, ed. Kim H. Kowalke, 217–67. New Haven, CT: Yale University Press, 1986.
Drew, David. *Kurt Weill: A Handbook*. London: Faber and Faber, 1987.
Drew, David. "Kurt Weill and His Critics." *Times Literary Supplement*, October 3, 1975.
Dubois, Jacques. *L'Institution de la littérature: Introduction à une sociologie*. Brussels: Editions Labor, 1986.
Dugan, James, and John Hammond. "The Music Nobody Knows." Reprinted as "An Early Black-Music Concert From Spirituals to Swing," *The Black Perspective in Music* 2, no. 2 (Autumn 1974): 191–207.
Dunaway, David K. "Charles Seeger and Carl Sands: The Composers' Collective Years." *Ethnomusicology*, 24, no. 2 (May 1980): 159–68.
Edney, Kate. "Making Sense of Integration: *Sing Out, Sweet Land* (1944), African Americans, and the Democratic Ideal." *New England Theater Journal* 28 (2017): 105–22.
Edwards, Brent Hayes. "The Literary Ellington." In *Uptown Conversation: The New Jazz Studies*, ed. Robert G. O'Meally, Brent Hayes Edwards, and Farah Jasmine Griffin, 326–56. New York: Columbia University Press, 2004.
Edwards, Brent Hayes. "Variations on a Preface." In *The New Modernist Studies Reader: An Anthology of Essential Criticism*, ed. Sean Latham and Gayle Rogers, 162–98. London: Bloomsbury Academic, 2021.
Ehland, Christoph, and Cornelia Wächter, eds. *Middlebrow and Gender: 1890–1945*. Leiden: Brill Rodopi, 2016.
Eichhorn, Andreas. "Auf der Suche nach der Moderne: Kurt Weills Rolland-Lektüre." In *Kurt Weill und Frankreich*, ed. Andreas Eichhorn, 25–38. Münster: Waxman, 2014.
Eisenschitz, Bernard. *Nicholas Ray: An American Journey*, trans. Tom Milne. Minneapolis: University of Minnesota Press, 1993.
Eliot, T. S. "Notes Towards a Definition of Culture." *Partisan Review* 11, no. 2 (Spring 1944): 145–57.
Ellington, [Edward Kennedy]. *Beggar's Holiday*. Performers: Alfred Drake, Bernice Parks, Libby Holman. Blue Pear-1013, [1946], LP.
Ellington, Edward Kennedy. *Music Is My Mistress*. New York: Da Capo Press, 1973.
Ellington, Mercer, and Stanley Dance. *Duke Ellington in Person: An Intimate Memoir*. Boston: Houghton Mifflin, 1978.
Engel, Lehman. *The American Musical Theater: A Consideration*. New York: CBS Records, 1967.
Erenberg, Lewis A. *Swingin' the Dream: Big Band Jazz and the Rebirth of American Culture*. Chicago: University of Chicago Press, 1998.
Everett, William. *Sigmund Romberg*. New Haven, CT: Yale University Press, 2007.
Ewen, David. *Complete Book of the American Musical Theater*. New York: Henry Holt, 1958.
Ewen, David. *Richard Rodgers*. New York: Henry Holt, 1951.
Ewen, David. *The Story of America's Musical Theater*. Philadelphia: Chilton, 1963.
Eyerman, Ron, and Scott Barretta. "From the 30s to the 60s: The Folk Music Revival in the United States." *Theory and Society* 25, no. 4 (August 1996): 501–43.
Fauser, Annegret. "'Dixie Carmen': War, Race, and Identity in Oscar Hammerstein's *Carmen Jones* (1943)." *Journal for the Society for American Music* 4, no. 2 (May 2010): 127–74.
Fauser, Annegret. *Sounds of War: Music in the United States During World War II*. New York and Oxford: Oxford University Press, 2013.
Fava, Maria Cristina. "The Composers' Collective of New York, 1932–1936: Bourgeois Modernism for the Proletariat." *American Music* 34, no. 3 (Fall 2016): 301–43.
Fearnow, Mark. "Theatre Groups and Their Playwrights." In *The Cambridge History of American Theatre*, ed. Don B. Wilmeth, 348–61. Cambridge: Cambridge University Press, 2008.
Feather, Leonard. "Goffin, *Esquire*, and the Moldy Figs." In *Reading Jazz: A Gathering of Autobiography, Reportage, and Criticism from 1919 to Now*, ed. Robert Gottlieb, 722–40. New York: Vintage Books, 1996.

Felski, Rita. *The Limits of Critique*. Chicago: University of Chicago Press, 2015.
Felski, Rita. "Modernity and Feminism." In *The New Modernist Studies Reader: An Anthology of Essential Criticism*, ed. Sean Latham and Gayle Rogers, 75–93. London: Bloomsbury Academic, 2021.
Filene, Benjamin. *Romancing the Folk: Public Memory and American Roots Music*. Chapel Hill: University of North Carolina Press, 2000.
Fitzgerald, F. Scott. "Echoes of the Jazz Age." In *The Fitzgerald Reader*, ed. Arthur Mizener, 323–31. New York: Charles Scribner's Sons, 1963.
Flanagan, Hallie. *Arena*. New York: Duell, Sloan, and Pearce, 1985.
Flanagan, Hallie. *Dynamo*. New York: Duell, Sloan, and Pearce, 1943.
Flanagan, Hallie. "Not in Despair." *Federal Theatre* 2, no. 4 ([21 March 1937]): 5, 28.
Flanagan, Hallie. "What Are We Doing with Our Chance?" *Federal Theatre* 2, no. 3 ([January 15, 1937]): 5–6.
Fleming, Julius. *Black Patience: Performance, Civil Rights, and the Unfinished Project of Emancipation*. New York: New York University Press, 2022.
Floyd, Samuel A., Jr. "Music in the Harlem Renaissance: An Overview." In *Black Music in the Harlem Renaissance*, ed. Samuel A. Floyd, Jr., 1–29. New York: Greenwood Press, 1990.
Folsom, Michael. "Introduction: The Pariah of American Letters." In *Mike Gold: A Literary Anthology*, ed. Folsom, 7–20. New York: International Publishers, 1972.
Fordin, Hugh. *Getting to Know Him: A Biography of Oscar Hammerstein II*. New York: Random House, 1977.
Franceschina, John. *Duke Ellington's Music for the Theatre*. Jefferson, NC: McFarland, 2001.
Franklin, Peter. "Modernismus and the Philistines." *Journal of the Royal Musical Association* 139 (2014): 183–87.
Freed-Thall, Hannah. *Spoiled Distinctions: Aesthetics and the Ordinary in French Modernism*. New York and Oxford: Oxford University Press, 2015.
Frisch, Walter. *German Modernism: Music and the Arts*. Berkeley: University of California Press, 2005.
Fuller, Randall. *Emerson's Ghosts: Literature, Politics, and the Making of Americanists*. Oxford and New York: Oxford University Press, 2007.
Furia, Philip. "Lady, Be Good!" In *The George Gershwin Reader*, ed. Robert Wyatt and John Andrew Johnson, 65–72. Oxford and New York: Oxford University Press, 2004.
Furia, Philip. *The Poets of Tin Pan Alley: A History of America's Great Lyricists*. Oxford and New York: Oxford University Press, 1992.
Gabriel, John. "There and Back Again: *Zeitoper* and the Transatlantic Search for a Uniquely American Opera in the 1920s." *Journal of the Society for American Music* 13, no. 2 (2019): 195–215.
Gadamer, Hans Georg. *Truth and Method*, trans. Joel Weinsheimer and Donald G. Marshall. London: Bloomsbury, 2013.
Galand, Joel. "Introduction." In *Firebrand of Florence*, vol. 1, by Kurt Weill, Ira Gershwin, and Edwin Justus Meyer, 13–54. New York: Kurt Weill Foundation for Music, 2002.
Galand, Joel. "Operetta as Revenant: *The Firebrand of Florence*." *Kurt Weill Newsletter* 17, nos. 1–2 (Fall 1999): 25–28.
Gänzl, Kurt. *The Encyclopedia of the Musical Theatre*, vol. 2. New York: Schirmer Books, 1994.
Gay, John. *The Beggar's Opera*. In *Norton Anthology of English Literature*, 7th edition, vol. 1C. New York: W. W. Norton, 2000.
Gelbart, Matthew. *The Invention of "Folk Music" and "Art Music": Emerging Categories from Ossian to Wagner*. Cambridge: Cambridge University Press, 2007.
Gendron, Bernard. "'Moldy Figs' and Modernists: Jazz at War (1942–1946)." In *Jazz Among the Discourses*, ed. Ken Grabbard, 31–56. Durham, NC: Duke University Press, 1995.
Gennari, John. *Blowin' Hot and Cool: Jazz and the Critics*. Chicago: University of Chicago Press, 2006.
Giddins, Gary, and Scott Deveaux. *Jazz*. New York: W. W. Norton, 2009.

Gilbert, James. *Writers and Partisans: A History of Literary Radicalism in America.* New York: John Wiley and Sons, 1968.

Goehr, Lydia. "*Amerikamüde / Europamüde*: The Very Idea of American Opera." *The Opera Quarterly* 22 (2006): 398–432.

Gorman, Paul R. *Left Intellectuals and Popular Culture in Twentieth-Century America.* Chapel Hill: University of North Carolina Press, 1996.

Goss, Glenda Dawn. *Jean Sibelius and Olin Downes: Music, Friendship, Criticism.* Boston: Northeastern University Press, 1995.

Graber, Naomi. *Kurt Weill's America.* New York and Oxford: Oxford University Press, 2021.

Graff, Ellen. *Stepping Left: Dance and Politics in New York City, 1928–1842.* Durham, NC: Duke University Press.

Grant, Mark. *The Rise and Fall of the Broadway Musical.* Boston: Northeastern University Press, 2004.

Graziano, John. "Black Musical Theater and the Harlem Renaissance Movement." In *Black Music in the Harlem Renaissance*, ed. Samuel A. Floyd, Jr., 87–110. New York: Greenwood Press, 1990.

Green, Stanley. *The World of Musical Comedy*, 4th edition. San Diego, CA: Da Capo Press, 1980.

Greenberg, Clement. *Art and Culture: Critical Essays.* Boston: Beacon Press, 1961.

Grieve, Victoria. *The Federal Art Project and the Creation of Middlebrow Culture.* Urbana: University of Illinois Press, 2009.

Grimley, Daniel. "Modernism and Closure: Nielsen's Fifth Symphony." *The Musical Quarterly* 86 (2002): 149–73.

Guillory, John. "The Ordeal of Middlebrow Culture." *Transition* 67 (1995): 82–92.

Guthrie, Kate. *The Art of Appreciation: Music and Middlebrow Culture in Modern Britain.* Oakland: University of California Press, 2021.

Hajdu, David. *Lush Life: A Biography of Billy Strayhorn.* New York: North Point Press, 1996.

Hall, Jacquelyn Dowd. "The Long Civil Rights Movement and the Political Uses of the Past." *Journal of American History* 91 (2005): 1233–63.

Hamm, Charles. "The Theatre Guild Production of *Porgy and Bess*." *Journal of the American Musicological Society* 40 (1987): 495–532.

Hamm, Charles. *Yesterdays: Popular Song in America.* New York: W. W. Norton, 1979.

Hamberlin, Larry. *Tin Pan Opera: Operatic Novelty Songs in the Ragtime Era.* New York and Oxford: Oxford University Press, 2011.

Hammerstein, Oscar, II. *The Complete Lyrics of Oscar Hammerstein II*, ed. Amy Asch. New York: Alfred A. Knopf, 2008.

Hammerstein, Oscar, II. "Foreword." In *The Rodgers and Hart Song Book*, ix–xii. New York: Simon and Schuster, 1951.

Hammerstein, Oscar, II. *The Letters of Oscar Hammerstein II*, ed. Mark Horowitz. New York and Oxford: Oxford University Press, 2022.

Hammerstein, Oscar, II. *Lyrics*, ed. William Hammerstein. Milwaukee: Hal Leonard, 1985.

Hammerstein, Oscar, II. "Voices Versus Feet: With the Triumph of Head over Heels, Operetta Regains Its Popularity." *Theatre Magazine* (May 1925): 14, 70.

Hammond, John. "The Debate in Jazz (1943)." In *The Duke Ellington Reader*, ed. Mark Tucker, 170–78. New York and Oxford: Oxford University Press, 1993.

Hammond, John. "The Tragedy of Duke Ellington." In *The Duke Ellington Reader*, ed. Mark Tucker, 118–20. New York and Oxford: Oxford University Press, 1993.

Hansen, Miriam Bratu. "The Mass Production of the Senses." In *The New Modernist Studies Reader: An Anthology of Essential Criticism*, ed. Sean Latham and Gayle Rogers, 121–46. London: Bloomsbury Academic, 2021.

Harker, Jaime. *America the Middlebrow: Women's Novels, Progressivism, and Middlebrow Authorship Between the Wars.* Amherst: University of Massachusetts Press, 2007.

Harris, Leonard, and Charles Molesworth. *Alain L. Locke: Biography of a Philosopher.* Chicago: University of Chicago Press, 2008.
Harris, Stan, dir. *Musical Comedy Tonight*, featuring Sylvia Fine Kaye. Dena Pictures, originally aired October 1, 1979.
Hart, Dorothy, and Robert Kimball, eds. *The Complete Lyrics of Lorenz Hart.* New York: Alfred A. Knopf, 1986.
Hasse, John Edward. *Beyond Category: The Life and Genius of Duke Ellington.* New York: Simon and Schuster, 1993.
Hegeman, Susan. *Patterns for America: Modernism and the Concept of Culture.* Princeton, NJ: Princeton University Press, 1999.
Hemingway, Andrew. *Artists on the Left: American Artists and the Communist Movement, 1926–1956.* New Haven, CT: Yale University Press, 2002.
Hepokoski, James. *Sibelius: Symphony No. 5.* Cambridge: Cambridge University Press, 1993.
Herder, Johann Gottfried. "From *Alte Volkslieder / Ancient Folk Songs*." In Johann Gottfried Herder and Philip V. Bohlman, *Song Loves the Masses: Herder on Music and Nationalism*, 36–43. Berkeley: University of California Press, 2017.
Himmelstein, Morgan Y. *Drama Was a Weapon: The Left-Wing Theatre in New York, 1929–1941.* New Brunswick, NJ: Rutgers University Press, 1963.
Hinton, Stephen. *Stages of Reform: Weill's Musical Theater.* Berkeley: University of California Press, 2012.
Hischak, Thomas. *The Oxford Companion to the American Musical: Theatre, Film, and Television.* New York and Oxford: Oxford University Press, 2008.
Hohendahl, Peter Uwe. *Building a National Literature: The Case of Germany 1830–1870*, trans. Renate Baron Franciscono. Ithaca, NY: Cornell University Press, 1989.
Houseman, John. *Front and Center.* New York: Simon and Schuster, 1979.
Howland, John. *Ellington Uptown: Duke Ellington, James P. Johnson, and the Birth of Concert Jazz.* Ann Arbor: University of Michigan Press, 2009.
Huggins, Nathan Irving. *Harlem Renaissance.* New York and Oxford: Oxford University Press, 2007.
Hughes, Langston. "Kurt Weill, My Collaborator." Reprinted in *Kurt Weill Newsletter* 13, no. 1 (Spring 1995): 7–8.
Hughes, Langston. "A Living Liner" issued with "Two Worlds of Kurt Weill." RCA LSC-2863, 1966.
Hughes, Langston. "The Negro Artist and the Racial Mountain [1926]." In *The Collected Works of Langston Hughes*, vol. 9: *Essays on Art, Race, Politics, and World Affairs*, 31–36. Columbia: University of Missouri Press, 2002.
Humble, Nicola. *The Feminine Middlebrow Novel, 1920s to 1950s: Class, Domesticity, and Bohemianism.* Oxford and New York: Oxford University Press, 2001.
Huynh, Pascal. *Kurt Weill ou la conquête des masses.* Arles: Actes Sud, 2000.
Huyssen, Andreas. *After the Great Divide: Modernism, Mass Culture, Postmodernism.* Bloomington: Indiana University Press, 1986.
Hyland, William G. *Richard Rodgers.* New Haven, CT, and London: Yale University Press, 1998.
"Introduction." *Music Vanguard: A Critical Review* 1, no. 1 (March–April 1935): 1–2.
Isaac, Dan. "Introduction" to Arthur Arent, "'Ethiopia': The First 'Living Newspaper.'" *Educational Theatre Journal* 20, no. 1 (March 1968): 15–31.
Johnson, Hall. "Porgy and Bess: A Folk Opera." *Opportunity* 14, no. 1 (Jan. 1936): 24–28.
Jones, Brian. "Finding the Avant-Garde in the Old-Time: John Cohen in the American Folk Revival." *American Music* 28, no. 4 (Winter 2010): 402–35.
Jones, John Bush. *Our Musicals, Ourselves: A Social History of the American Musical Theatre.* Hanover, NH: Brandeis University Press, 2003.
Kammen, Michael. *American Culture, American Tastes: Social Change and the Twentieth Century.* New York: Alfred A. Knopf, 1999.

Kammen, Michael. *The Lively Arts: Gilbert Seldes and the Transformation of Cultural Criticism in the United States*. New York and Oxford: Oxford University Press, 1996.
Karpeles, Maud. "Some Reflections on Authenticity in Folk Music." *Journal of the International Folk Music Council* 3 (1951): 10-16.
Kazin, Alfred. "Criticism and Isolation." *The Virginia Quarterly Review* 17, no. 3 (Summer 1941): 448-53.
Kazin, Alfred. *Starting Out in the Thirties*. Boston: Little Brown, 1962.
Kilroy, David. "Kurt Weill on Broadway: The Postwar Years (1945-1950)." PhD dissertation, Harvard University, 1992.
Knapp, Raymond. *The American Musical and the Formation of National Identity*. Princeton, NJ: Princeton University Press, 2005.
Knapp, Raymond. *The American Musical and the Performance of Personal Identity*. Princeton, NJ: Princeton University Press, 2006.
Kowalke, Kim H. *Kurt Weill in Europe*. Ann Arbor, MI: University Microfilms International, 1979.
Kowalke, Kim H. "Kurt Weill, Modernism, and Popular Culture: *Offentlichkeit als Stil*." *Modernism / Modernity* 2, no. 1 (January 1995): 27-69.
Kowalke, Kim H. "Theorizing the Golden Age Musical: Genre, Structure, Syntax." *Gamut* 6, no. 2 (2013): 133-84.
Kowalke, Kim H. "'The Threepenny Opera' in America." In *Kurt Weill: The Threepenny Opera*, ed. Stephen Hinton, 78-119. Cambridge: Cambridge University Press, 1990.
Leavis, Queenie. *Fiction and the Reading Public*. London: Chatto and Windus, 1932.
Lee, Edward. *Music of the People: A Study of Popular Music in Great Britain*. Bristol: Barrie and Jenkins, 1970.
Levenson, Michael, ed. *The Cambridge Companion to Modernism*. Cambridge: Cambridge University Press, 2011.
Levine, Lawrence. *Highbrow/Lowbrow: The Emergence of Cultural Hierarchy in America*. Cambridge, MA: Harvard University Press, 1988.
Levine, Lawrence. "Jazz and American Culture." *The Journal of American Folklore* 102, no. 403 (January-March 1989), 6-22.
Levitz, Tamara. *Teaching New Classicality: Ferruccio Busoni's Master Class in Composition*. Frankfurt am Main: Peter Lang GmbH, 1996.
Lewis, David Levering. *When Harlem Was in Vogue*. New York: Penguin Books, 1997 (originally published 1979).
Lewis, Hannah. "*Love Me Tonight* (1932) and the Development of the Integrated Film Musical." *Musical Quarterly* 100 (2017): 3-32.
Lock, Graham. *Blutopia: Visions of the Future and Revisions of the Past in the Work of Sun Ra, Duke Ellington, and Anthony Braxton*. Durham, NC: Duke University Press, 1999.
Locke, Alain. *The Negro and His Music; Negro Art: Past and Present*. New York: Arno Press, 1969.
Locke, Alain. *The Works of Alain Locke*, ed. Charles Molesworth. New York and Oxford: Oxford University Press, 2012.
Lomax, John A. *Cowboy Songs and Other Frontier Ballads*. New York: Sturgis and Walton, 1917.
Long, Elizabeth. *Book Clubs: Women and the Uses of Reading in Everyday Life*. Chicago: University of Chicago Press, 2003.
Lumsden, Linda J. *Black, White, and Red All Over: A Cultural History of the Radical Press in Its Heyday*. Kent, OH: Kent State University Press, 2014.
Lynch, Christopher. "Opera and Broadway: The Debate over the Essence of Opera in New York City, 1900-1960." PhD dissertation, State University of New York at Buffalo, 2013.
Lynes, Russell. "Highbrow, Middlebrow, Lowbrow." *Harper's Magazine* (February 1, 1949): 19-28.
Lynes, Russell. "The Taste-makers." *Harper's Magazine* 194, no. 1165 (June 1947): 481-91.
Lynes, Russell. *The Tastemakers*. New York: Harper and Brothers, 1954.

Lyons, Donald. "Introduction." In Eric Bentley, *What Is Theatre? Incorporating the Dramatic Event and Other Reviews 1944-1967*, ix-xxxii. New York: Hill and Wang, 2000.
Macdonald, Dwight. *Against the American Grain*. New York: Random House, 1962.
Macdonald, Dwight. "By Cozzens Possessed: A Review of Reviews." *Commentary* 25 (January 1958): 36-47.
Macdonald, Dwight. "Kulturbolschewismus Is Here." *Partisan Review* 8, no. 6 (November-December 1941): 442-51.
Macdonald, Kate, ed. *The Masculine Middlebrow, 1880-1950: What Mr. Miniver Read*. Basingstoke, UK: Palgrave Macmillan, 2011.
MacLeish, Archibald. *A Time to Speak: The Selected Prose of Archibald MacLeish*. Boston: Houghton Mifflin Co., 1941.
Magee, Jeffrey. "'Everybody Step': Irving Berlin, Jazz, and Broadway in the 1920s." *Journal of the American Musicological Society* 59 (2006): 697-732.
Magee, Jeffrey. *Irving Berlin's Musical Theater*. New York and Oxford: Oxford University Press, 2012.
Mao, Douglas. "Introduction: The New Modernist Studies." In *History of New Modernism Studies*, ed. Douglas Mao, 1-12. Cambridge: Cambridge University Press, 2021.
Marcuse, Herbert. "The Affirmative Character of Culture." In *Negations: Essays in Critical Theory*, trans. Jeremy J. Shapiro, 88-133. Boston: Beacon Press, 1968.
Marmorstein, Gary. *A Ship Without a Sail: The Life of Lorenz Hart*. New York: Simon and Schuster, 2012.
Mast, Gerald. *Can't Help Singin': The American Musical on Stage and Screen*. Woodstock, NY: Overlook Press, 1987.
McClary, Susan. "Terminal Prestige: The Case of Avant-Garde Music Composition." *Cultural Critique* 12 (Spring 1989): 57-81.
mcclung, bruce d. "Psicosi per musica: Re-examining *Lady in the Dark*." In *Stranger Here Myself: Kurt Weill-Studien*, ed. Kim H. Kowalke and Horst Edler, 235-65. Hildesheim: Georg Olms Verlag, 1993.
McDermott, Douglas. "The Living Newspaper as a Dramatic Form." PhD dissertation, Graduate College of the State University of Iowa, 1963.
McHugh, Dominic. "'I'll Never Know Exactly Who Did What': Broadway Composers as Musical Collaborators." *Journal of the American Musicological Society* 68 (2015): 605-52.
McMillin, Scott. *The Musical as Drama*. Princeton, NJ: Princeton University Press, 2006.
Melnick, Jeffrey. *A Right to Sing the Blues: African Americans, Jews, and American Popular Song*. Cambridge, MA: Harvard University Press, 1999.
Mencken, H. L. *The American Language: An Inquiry into the Development of English in the United States*. 2nd edition. New York: Alfred A. Knopf, 1921.
Metzer, David. "The League of Composers: The Initial Years." *American Music* 15, no. 1 (Spring 1997): 45-69.
Meyer, Leonard B. "A Pride of Prejudices; or, Delight in Diversity." *Music Theory Spectrum* 13, no. 2 (Autumn 1991): 241-51.
Michaelis, Arnold. "A Conversation with Richard Rodgers." *American Music* 27, no. 3 (Fall 2009): 267-301.
Middleton, Richard. *Studying Popular Music*. Milton Keynes, UK: Open University Press, 1990.
Miller, D. A. *Place for Us: Essay on the Broadway Musical*. Cambridge: Cambridge University Press.
Miller, Scott. *Rebels with Applause*. Portsmouth, NH: Heinemann, 2001.
Molesworth, Charles. "Introduction." In *The Works of Alain Locke*, xi-xxxvi. Oxford and New York: Oxford University Press, 2012.
Moore, Allan. "Authenticity as Authentication." *Popular Music* 21, no. 2 (May 2002): 209-23.
Mordden, Ethan. *Better Foot Forward: The History of the American Musical Theater*. New York: Grossman Publishers, 1958.

Mordden, Ethan. *Broadway Babies: The People Who Made the American Musical*. New York and Oxford: Oxford University Press, 1983.

Morgan, Ted. *Reds: McCarthyism in Twentieth-Century America*. New York: Random House, 2003.

Morrison, Mark. *The Public Face of Modernism: Little Magazine, Audiences, and Reception*. Madison: University of Wisconsin Press, 2001.

Morrison, Mark S. "Youth in Public: The *Little Review* and Commercial Culture in Chicago." In *The New Modernist Studies Reader: An Anthology of Essential Criticism*, ed. Sean Latham and Gayle Rogers, 137–61. London: Bloomsbury Academic, 2021.

Most, Andrea. *Making Americans: Jews and the Broadway Musical*. Cambridge, MA: Harvard University Press, 2004.

Nadler, Paul. "Liberty Censored: Black Living Newspapers of the Federal Theatre Project." *African American Review* 29, no. 4 (Winter 1995): 615–22.

Nelson, Raymond. *Van Wyck Brooks: A Writer's Life*. New York: E. P. Dutton, 1981.

Nielson, Francis. "The Story of 'The Freeman.'" *The American Journal of Economics and Sociology* 6, no. 1 supplement (October 1946): 3–53.

No author. "The Lyric in Parody." *Dramatists Guild Quarterly* (Spring 1967): 8.

No author. "Stephen Sondheim: The Art of the Musical." *Paris Review*, no. 142 (Spring 1997): 258–78.North, Michael. "Against the Standard: Linguistic Imitation, Racial Masquerade, and the Modernist Rebellion," *The New Modernist Studies Reader: An Anthology of Essential Criticism*, ed. Sean Latham and Gayle Rogers, 41–74. London: Bloomsbury Academic, 2021.

O'Connor, John, and Lorraine Brown, eds. *The Federal Theatre Project: "Free, Adult, Uncensored."* London: Eyre Methuen, 1980.

Oja, Carol. *Making Music Modern: New York in the 1920s*. New York and Oxford: Oxford University Press, 2000.

Oja, Carol. "Marc Blitzstein's 'The Cradle Will Rock' and Mass-Song Style of the 1930s." *The Musical Quarterly* 73 (1989), 445–75.

O'Leary, James. "*Oklahoma!*, 'Lousy Publicity,' and the Politics of Formal Integration in the American Musical Theater." *Journal of Musicology* 31, no. 1 (Winter 2014): 139–82.

Opler, Daniel. "Music from the Vanguard: The Songs of the Composers Collective of New York, 1933–1936." *Journal for the Study of Radicalism* 10, no. 2 (Fall 2016): 123–52.

Osborne, Elizabeth. *Staging the People: Community and Identity in the Federal Theatre Project*. New York: Palgrave Macmillan, 2011.

Paddison, Max. "The Critique Criticised: Adorno and Popular Music." *Popular Music* 2 (1982): 201–18.

Panassié, Hughes. *Hot Jazz: The Guide to Swing Music*. New York: M. Whitmark and Sons, 1936.

Patinkin, Sheldon. *"No Legs, No Jokes, No Chance": A History of the American Musical Theater*. Evanston, IL: Northwestern University Press, 2008.

Pease, Allison. "Modernism and Mass Culture." In *The Cambridge Companion to Modernism*, 197–211. Cambridge: Cambridge University Press, 2011.

Pells, Richard H. *Radical Visions and American Dreams: Culture and Social Thought in the Depression Years*. New York: Harper & Row, 1973.

Peretti, Burton W. *Lift Every Voice: The History of African American Music*. Lanham, MD: Rowman and Littlefield, 2009.

Perrin, Tom. "Rebuilding *Bildung*: The Middlebrow Novel of Aesthetic Education in the Mid-Twentieth-Century United States." *Novel: A Forum on Fiction* 44, no. 3 (Fall 2011): 382–401.

Peterson, Richard A. "The Rise and Fall of Highbrow Snobbery as a Status Marker." *Poetics* 25 (1997): 75–92.

Peterson, Richard A., and Roger M. Kern. "Changing Highbrow Taste: From Snob to Omnivore." *American Sociological Review* 61, no. 5 (Oct. 1996): 900–7.

Phillips, William, and Philip Rahv, eds. *The Partisan Reader: Ten Years of Partisan Review 1934–1944: An Anthology*. New York: Dial Press, 1946.

Pollack, Howard. *Aaron Copland: The Life and Work of an Uncommon Man.* New York: Henry Holt, 1999.
Pollack, Howard. *The Ballad of John Latouche: An American Lyricist's Life and Work.* New York and Oxford: Oxford University Press, 2017.
Pollack, Howard. *Marc Blitzstein: His Life, His Work, His World.* New York and Oxford: Oxford University Press, 2012.
Posnock, Ross. *Color and Culture: Black Writers and the Making of the Modern Intellectual.* Cambridge, MA: Harvard University Press, 1998.
Prial, Dustan. *The Producer: John Hammond and the Soul of American Music.* New York: Farrar, Straus and Giroux, 2006.
Radway, Janice. *A Feeling for Books: The Book-of-the-Month Club, Literary Taste, and Middle-Class Desire.* Chapel Hill: University of North Carolina Press, 1997.
Rainey, Lawrence. *Institutions of Modernism.* New Haven, CT: Yale University Press, 1998.
Rampersad, Arnold. *The Life of Langston Hughes*, vol. 2: *1941–1967, I Dream a World.* New York and Oxford: Oxford University Press, 2002.
Ramsey, Guthrie, Jr., *Who Hears Here? On Black Music, Pasts and Present.* Oakland: University of California Press, 2022.
Reis, Claire. "Contemporary Music and 'the Man on the Street.'" *Eolian Review* 2, no. 2 (March 1923): 24–27.
Reuss, Richard, and Joanne. *American Music and Left-Wing Politics: 1927–1957.* Lanham, MD: Scarecrow Press, 2000.
Rice, Elmer. *Street Scene in Three Plays.* New York: Hill and Wang, 1965.
Riggs, Lynn. *Green Grow the Lilacs.* New York: Samuel French, 1958.
Rodgers, Mary, and Jesse Green. *Shy: The Alarmingly Outspoken Memoirs of Mary Rodgers.* New York: Farrar, Straus and Giroux, 2022.
Rodgers, Richard. "Introduction." In *Rodgers and Hart Song Book*, 1–4. New York: Simon and Schuster, 1951.
Rodgers, Richard. *Musical Stages: An Autobiography.* New York: Da Capo Press, 1995.
Rogers, Bradley. *The Song Is You: Musical Theatre and the Politics of Bursting into Song and Dance.* Iowa City: University of Iowa Press, 2020.
Rolland, Romain. "America and The Arts," trans. Waldo Frank. *Seven Arts* 1, no. 1 (1916): 47–51.
Rolland, Romain. *The People's Theater*, trans. Barrett H. Clark. New York: Henry Holt, 1918.
Rosenberg, Deena. *Fascinating Rhythm: The Collaboration of George and Ira Gershwin.* [Ann Arbor]: University of Michigan Press, 1997.
Rosenfeld, Paul. *Musical Impressions: Selections from Paul Rosenfeld's Criticism*, ed. Herbert A. Leibowitz. New York: Hill and Wang, 1969.
Rubin, Joan Shelley. *Constance Rourke and American Culture.* Chapel Hill: University of North Carolina Press, 1980.
Rubin, Joan Shelley. *The Making of Middlebrow Culture.* Chapel Hill: University of North Carolina Press, 1992.
Saint-Amour, Paul K. "Weak Theory, Weak Modernism." *The New Modernist Studies Reader: An Anthology of Essential Criticism*, ed. Sean Latham and Gayle Rogers, 353–70. London: Bloomsbury Academic, 2021.
Sanders, Ronald. *The Days Grow Short: The Life and Music of Kurt Weill.* New York: Holt, Reinhart and Winston, 1980.
Sargeant, Winthrop. *Jazz, Hot and Hybrid.* New York: E. P. Dutton, 1946.
Savage, Barbara Dianne. *Broadcasting Freedom: Radio, War, and the Politics of Race, 1938–1948.* Chapel Hill: University of North Carolina Press, 1999.
Savran, David. *Highbrow/Lowdown: Theater, Jazz, and the Making of the New Middle Class.* Ann Arbor: University of Michigan Press, 2009.
Saylor, Eric. *English Pastoral Music: From Arcadia to Utopia, 1900–1955.* Urbana: University of Illinois Press, 2017.

Schreffler, Anne C. "'Music Left and Right': A Tale of Two Histories of Progressive Music." *Proceedings of the British Academy* 185 (2013): 70–72.
Schuller, Gunther. *The Swing Era: The Development of Jazz, 1930–1945*. New York and Oxford: Oxford University Press, 1989.
Sears, Ann. "The Coming of the Musical Play." In *The Cambridge Companion to the Musical*, ed. William A. Everett and Paul Laird, 147–63. Cambridge: Cambridge University Press, 2008.
Secrest, Meryle. *Somewhere for Me: A Biography of Richard Rodgers*. New York: Alfred A. Knopf, 2001.
Seeger, Charles. "Preface to All Linguist Treatment of Music." *Music Vanguard: A Critical Review*, 1, no. 1 (March–April 1935): 17–31.
Seldes, Gilbert. *The Seven Lively Arts*. Mineola, NY: Dover Publications, 2001 (originally published 1924).
Seldes, Gilbert. "This Can't Be Corn." *Esquire*, October 1, 1941, 51, 160.
Shultz, William Eben. *Gay's Beggar's Opera: Its Content, History, and Influence*. New Haven, CT: Yale University Press, 1923.
Shusterman, Richard. *Pragmatist Aesthetics: Living Beauty, Rethinking Art*. 2nd edition. Lanham, MD: Rowman and Littlefield, 2000.
Siegmeister, Elie. *Music and Society*. New York: Critics Group Press, 1938.
Smith, Cecil. *Musical Comedy in America*. New York: Theatre Arts Books, 1950.
Sondheim, Stephen. *Finishing the Hat: Collected Lyrics (1954–1981) with Attendant Comments, Principles, Heresies, Grudges, Whines and Anecdotes*. New York: Alfred A. Knopf, 2010.
Sondheim, Stephen. "Introduction." In *Getting to Know Him: A Biography of Oscar Hammerstein II*, xi–xiv. New York: Random House, 1977.
Southern, Eileen. *The Music of Black Americans: A History*. 3rd edition. New York: W. W. Norton, 1997.
Spencer, Jon Michael. *The New Negroes and Their Music: The Success of the Harlem Renaissance*. Knoxville: University of Tennessee Press, 1997.
Spewack, Sam, and Bella Spewack. "Introduction." In *Kiss Me Kate: A Musical Play*, by Sam and Bella Spewack, lyrics by Cole Porter, vii–xix. New York: Alfred A. Knopf, 1953.
Sprague, Claire, ed. *Van Wyck Brooks: The Early Years*. Boston: Northeastern University Press, 1993.
Stempel, Larry. *Showtime: A History of the Broadway Musical Theater*. New York: W. W. Norton, 2010.
Stempel, Larry. "*Street Scene* and the Enigma of Broadway Opera." In *A New Orpheus: Essays on Kurt Weill*, ed. Kim H. Kowalke, 321–41. New Haven, CT: Yale University Press, 1986.
Stern, Guy. "Der literarisch-kulturelle Horizont des jungen Weill: Eine Analyse seiner ungedruckten frühen Briefe." In *A Stranger Here Myself: Kurt Weill-Studien*, ed. Kim H. Kowalke and Horst Edler, 73–105. Hildesheim: Georg Olms Verlag, 1993.
Stowe, David W. *Swing Changes: Big-Band Jazz in New Deal America*. Cambridge, MA: Harvard University Press, 1994.
Susman, Warren. *Culture as History: The Transformation of American Society in the Twentieth Century*. New York: Pantheon Books, 1984.
Swain, Joseph. *The Broadway Musical: A Critical and Musical Survey*. 2nd edition. Lanham, MD: Scarecrow Press, 2002.
Symonds, Dominic. "Coherency: Lew Fields, the Performer-Producer and Experimenter in Integration." In *The Palgrave Handbook of Musical Theatre Producers*, ed. Laura Macdonald and William Everett, 127–35. New York: Palgrave MacMillan, 2017.
Symonds, Dominic. *We'll Have Manhattan: The Early Works of Rodgers and Hart*. New York and Oxford: Oxford University Press, 2015.
Taruskin, Richard. "Is There a Baby in the Bathwater? (Part I)." *Archiv für Musikwissenschaft* 63, no. 3 (2006): 163–85.

Taruskin, Richard. "Not Modern and Loving It." In *Russian Music at Home and Abroad: New Essays*, 120–33. New York and Oxford: Oxford University Press, 2016.

Taruskin, Richard. *The Oxford History of Western Music*, vol. 1. Oxford and New York: Oxford University Press, 2010.

Taruskin, Richard. *The Oxford History of Western Music*, vol. 4. Oxford and New York: Oxford University Press, 2010.

Thomson, Virgil. "How Popular Music Works." *New York Herald-Tribune*, June 15, 1941.

Thomson, Virgil. *A Virgil Thomson Reader*. Boston: Houghton Mifflin, 1981.

Thornhill, William R. "Kurt Weill's *Street Scene*." PhD dissertation, University of North Carolina at Chapel Hill, 1990.

Thym, Jürgen. "The Enigma of Kurt Weill's Whitman Songs." In *A Stranger Here Myself: Kurt Weill-Studien*, ed. Kim H. Kowalke and Horst Edler, 289–91. Hildesheim: Georg Olms Verlag, 1993.

Tracy, Daniel. "Investing in 'Modernism': Smart Magazines, Parody, and Middlebrow Professional Judgment." *Journal of Modern Periodical Studies* 1, no. 1 (2010): 38–63.

Trilling, Lionel. "A Young Critic in a Younger America." *New York Times Book Review* (March 7, 1954): 1, 28.

Tucker, Mark, ed. *The Duke Ellington Reader*. New York and Oxford: Oxford University Press, 1993.

Tucker, Mark. *Ellington: The Early Years*. Urbana: University of Illinois Press, 1991.

Tucker, Mark. "The Genesis of *Black, Brown, and Beige*." *Black Music Research Journal* 13, no. 2 (Autumn 1993): 131–50.

Turner, Catherine. *Marketing Modernism between the Two World Wars*. Amherst: University of Massachusetts Press, 2003.

Ulanov, Barry. *Duke Ellington*. New York: Creative Edge Press, 1946.

United States Congress, House of Representatives, Special Committee on Un-American Activities. "Investigation of Un-American Propaganda Activities." Seventy-Fifth Congress, Third Session, volume 1, 1938.

Vacha, John. "The Federal Theatre's Living Newspapers: New York's Docudramas of the Thirties," *New York History* 67, no. 1 (January 1986): 66–88.

Van Leer, David. "Putting It Together: Sondheim and the Broadway Musical." *Raritan* 7, no. 2 (Fall 1987): 113–28.

Von Arx, Victoria. "The Third Street Music School Settlement: The Grand Tradition as Social Practice on New York's Lower East Side." *Journal of the Society for American Music* 5, no. 1 (February 2011): 61–93.

Wald, Alan M. *The New York Intellectuals: The Rise and Fall of the Anti-Stalinist Left from the 1930s to the 1980s*. Chapel Hill: University of North Carolina Press, 1987.

Walsh, David, and Len Platt. *Musical Theater and American Culture*. Westport, CT: Praeger, 2003.

Wasserstrom, William. *The Legacy of Van Wyck Brooks: A Study of Maladies and Motives*. Carbondale: Southern Illinois University Press, 1971.

Wasserstrom, William. *Van Wyck Brooks*. Pamphlets on American Writers, No. 71. Minneapolis: University of Minnesota Press, 1968.

Weill, Kurt. "Alchemy of Music." *Stage* 14, no. 2 (November 1936): 63–64.

Weill, Kurt. *Briefe an die Familie (1914–1950)*, ed. Lys Symonette and Elmar Juchem. Stuttgart: J. B. Metzler, 2000.

Weill, Kurt. *Briefwechsel mit der Universal Edition*, ed. Nils Grosch. Stuttgart: Verlag J. B. Metzler, 2002.

Weill, Kurt. "Broadway and the Musical Theatre." *The Composer's News-Record* no. 2 (May 1947): 1.

Weill, Kurt. "The Future of Opera in America," trans. Joel Lifflander, *Modern Music* 14, no. 4 (May–June 1937): 183–88.

Weill, Kurt. "I'm an American! Interview with Kurt Weill." Program broadcast, March 9, 1941, NBC Blue Network (transcription available on the Kurt Weill Foundation Website, August 13, 2017, https://www.kwf.org/kurt-weill/recommended/im-an-american/).
Weill, Kurt. Liner notes for *Street Scene*, original cast recording, 1947. Columbia Masterworks M-MM-683.
Weill, Kurt. *Musik und musikalisches Theater: Gesammelte Schriften*, ed. Stephen Hinton, Jürgen Schebera, and Elmar Juchem. Mainz: Schott Musik International, 2000.
Weill, Kurt., and Lotte Lenya, *Speak Low (When You Speak Love): The Letters of Kurt Weill and Lotte Lenya*, ed. and trans. Lys Symonette and Kim H. Kowalke. Berkeley: University of California Press, 1996.
Weill, Kurt, and Edward J. Smith. "Broadway Opera: Our Composers' Hope for the Future." *Musical Digest* 29, no. 4 (December 1946): 16, 42.
Wheatland, Thomas. *The Frankfurt School in Exile*. Minneapolis: University of Minnesota Press, 2009.
Whitman, Willson. *Bread and Circuses: A Study of Federal Theatre*. Freeport, NY: Books for Libraries Press, 1972.
Widdemer, Margaret. "Message and Middlebrow." *The Saturday Review of Literature* 9, no. 31 (February 18, 1933): 433–34.
Wilder, Alec. *American Popular Song: The Great Innovators, 1900–1950*. New York and Oxford: Oxford University Press, 1990.
Wilk, Max. *Ok!: The Story of* Oklahoma!. New York: Applause, 2002.
Wolf, Stacy. *Changed for Good: A Feminist History of the Broadway Musical*. New York and Oxford: Oxford University Press, 2011.
Woll, Allen L. *Black Musical Theatre: From Coontown to Dreamgirls*. Baton Rouge: Louisiana State University Press, 1989.
Wollaeger, Mark. "Modernism under Review: Matei Calinescu's *Five Faces of Modernity: Modernism, Avant-Garde, Decadence, Kitsch, Postmodernism* (1987)." *Modernist Cultures* 8, no. 2 (2013): 163–78.
Wood, Graham. "The Development of Song Forms in the Broadway and Hollywood Musicals of Richard Rodgers, 1919–1943." PhD dissertation, University of Minnesota, 2000.
Wreszin, Michael, ed. *A Moral Temper: The Letters of Dwight Macdonald*. Chicago: Ivan R. Dee, 2001.
Wright, Trudi. "*Pins and Needles* (1937): Everything in Moderation." *Studies in Musical Theatre* 7, no. 1 (January 2013): 61–73.

Credits

The following publishers and individuals have generously given permission to reprint articles, excerpts, lyrics, and music from longer works.

Excerpt from Renata Adler, *Speedboat* (New York: New York Review Books, 2013), 48. Copyright © 2024 by Renata Adler.
"Oh, What a Beautiful Mornin'" from *Oklahoma!*, lyrics by Oscar Hammerstein II, music by Richard Rodgers. Copyright © 1943 by Williamson Music Company c/o Concord Music Publishing. Copyright renewed. All Rights Reserved. Used by Permission.
"The Surrey With the Fringe on Top" from *Oklahoma!*, lyrics by Oscar Hammerstein II, music by Richard Rodgers. Copyright © 1943 by Williamson Music Company c/o Concord Music Publishing. Copyright Renewed. All Rights Reserved. Used by Permission.
Published excerpts from John Latouche's writing appearing in the *New York Times* (February 9, 1947) and *Vogue* (March 1, 1941), and for those previously unpublished excerpts belonging solely to John Latouche from the archives of the New York Public Library for the Performing Arts, Billy Rose Theatre Division and Music Division; Smithsonian Institution, Duke

246 BIBLIOGRAPHY

Ellington Collection; Wisconsin Center for Film and Theater Research, Dale Wasserman Papers, are reprinted by consent of The Barbara Hogenson Agency, Inc. All rights reserved.

Permission to use archival excerpts by Dale Wasserman has been granted by Martha Wasserman on behalf of the Estate of Dale Wasserman.

Permission to use archival excerpts by Duke Ellington has been granted by the Estate of Duke Ellington.

"Tomorrow Mountain," words by John Latouche, music by Duke Ellington. Copyright © 1947, 1955 Sony Music Publishing (US) LLC. Copyright renewed. All rights on behalf of Sony Music Publishing (US) LLC administered by Sony Music Publishing (US) LLC 424 Church Street, Suite 1200, Nashville, TN 37219. International Copyright Secured. All Rights Reserved.

"In Between" from *Beggar's Holiday*, words and Music by John Latouche and Duke Ellington. Copyright © 1947, Sony Music Publishing (US) LLC. Copyright renewed. All rights on behalf of Sony Music Publishing (US) LLC administered by Sony Music Publishing (US) LLC 424 Church Street, Suite 1200, Nashville, TN 37219. International Copyright Secured. All Rights Reserved.

"Wrapped in a Ribbon and Tied in a Bow" from *Street Scene*, lyrics by Langston Hughes, music by Kurt Weill. © 1945 (renewed) Chappell & Co., Inc., and Tro-Hampshire House Publishing Corp, New York, NY. All rights for the world outside of the U.S. administered by Chappell & Co., Inc. All rights reserved. Used by permission of Alfred Music.

"Wrapped in a Ribbon and Tied in a Bow" from the Musical Production *Street Scene*, words by Langston Hughes, music by Kurt Weill. TRO – © copyright 1947 (renewed) Hampshire House Publishing Corp., New York and Warner Chappell Music, Inc., Los Angeles, CA. International copyright secured. Made in U.S.A. All rights reserved including public performance for profit. Used by permission.

Archival excerpts from and related to *Street Scene* by Langston Hughes, copyright © 2023, used by permission of Harold Ober Associates and International Literary Properties LLC.

Published and archival texts by Kurt Weill © The Kurt Weill Foundation for Music, Inc.

Index

For the benefit of digital users, indexed terms that span two pages (e.g., 52–53) may, on occasion, appear on only one of those pages.

Figures are indicated by an italic *f* following the page number.

Abbott, George, 132, 136
  revision of *Beggar's Holiday*, 132–34
Adams, Samuel Hopkins, 7
Addams, Jane, 7
Adorno, Theodor, 10–11, 30–31, 56–57, 142, 190
affirmative culture, xi–xii, 11–14, 16–17, 23–24, 30, 36
  Brooks Atkinson and, 51–52
  Communist attitude toward, 38, 44–45
  Olin Downes and, 91–92
  See also middlebrow culture
Agee, James, 10–11, 55–56, 58
  review of *Oklahoma!*, 96–97
Ager, Shana, 177–78
All Points West (Rodgers and Hart), 67–69
Allegro (Rodgers and Hammerstein), 100–1, 179–80
Almanac Singers, 27–28
American Lullaby (Ellington), 111
American Negro Theater, 139
America's Coming of Age (Brooks), 12–13
Anderson, Maxwell, 73–74, 157–58
anti-Semitism, 36–37
art. *See* high art
Atkinson, Brooks, 11–12, 15–16, 24–25, 48–53, 63–64, 72–73, 75, 101–2, 146, 189–90
  on the Federal Theater Project, 52–53
  and integration, 72–73, 75, 96, 137–38
  and Oscar Hammerstein II, 74–75
  on politics in the theater, 52–53, 139, 146–47
  review of *Allegro*, 100–1
  review of *Beggar's Holiday*, 134, 137–38, 139
  review of *Deep River*, 72
  review of *Music in the Air*, 74–75
  review of *Oklahoma!*, 96
  review of *Parade*, 43–44
  review of *Porgy and Bess*, 37, 72
  review of *Power*, 48–51
  review of *Rainbow*, 73, 74
  review of *Show Boat*, 72–73, 80–81
  review of *Street Scene*, 179
  review of *Sweet Adeline*, 80–81
  on "sophistication," 51–52, 72–73, 80–81, 137
  and Van Wyck Brooks, 51–52, 53, 80–81
Aufstieg und Fall der Stadt Mahagonny (Brecht and Weill), 159
authenticity, definition of, 20–22, 23, 25–32, 36–37, 47, 55–56, 187–88
  See also folk, institutional definition of
autonomy, 10–11, 20–22, 32–38, 54–55, 186–87, 190
  as a feature of modernism, 183–85, 190–91
avant-garde, 9–10, 11, 14–17

Balanchine, George, 152–53
ballet, 39, 82, 93–94, 96
Banfield, Stephen, 71–72
Barnes, Howard, 73–74, 152–53
Bay, Howard, 152–53
beauty, 22–23, 33–34, 58
Beggar's Holiday (Ellington and Latouche), 2
  cost, 131–32
  early sketches, 114–23
  final version, 132–34
  first complete draft script, 123–27
  genre of (satire or burlesque), 135–37, 174
  legacy of, 101–2, 103, 140–41
  as middlebrow, 109, 114, 121, 122, 137–39, 140–41
  press reception of, 134–41
  rehearsal version of script, 127–31
  score, 121–22, 123–24, 125–27, 134
  and social commentary, 121, 130–31, 133, 136–37, 138–39
  song form in, 126, 133
Beggar's Opera (Gay), 103, 114–15, 131, 137
Beiswanger, George, 95
belle Hélène, La (Offenbach), 153–54

Bentley, Eric, 24–25, 56–57, 58, 136–37
  review of *Oklahoma!*, 96–97, 98–99
Berkeley, Busby, 93–94
Berlant, Lauren, 5
Berlin, Irving, 34–35
  See also Watch Your Step
Bernstein, Leonard, 1
"Big Rock Candy Mountain," 121
Bird of Paradise (Ellington), 111
Black actors on Broadway, 138–39
Black, Brown, and Beige: A Tone Parallel to the History of the American Negro (Ellington), 109–10, 111–14
Bledsoe, Jules, 72
Blitzstein, Marc, 43–44, 46
  See also Cradle Will Rock, The
Bloomer Girl (Arlen, Harburg, Herzig, and Saidy), 100–1
Blue Bells of Harlem (Ellington), 111
Blue Blouse troupes, 48
"Blue Room" (Rodgers and Hart), 65–66, 66f
Blutopia (Ellington), 109–10
Bogan, Louise, 55–56, 58
bogus art (Seldes), 30–31, 32
Bohlman, Philip, 20
Bontemps, Arna, 173
Bordman, Gerald, 151–52
Borneman, Ernest, 113–14
Bourne, Randolph, 13–14
Brecht, Bertold, 56–57, 115–16, 148–49, 150–51, 160
  See also Aufstieg und Fall der Stadt Mahagonny; Dreigroschenoper, Die; gute Mensch von Sezuan, Der
Britten, Benjamin, 5
Broadway musicals
  and classical music, 34–35, 36
  and Communism, 38, 40–41, 42–44
  and folk authenticity, 25–32, 72, 89–90, 100–1
  Golden Age, 2–3, 59
  historiography, 1–4, 18, 60–62
  interpretive norms, 1, 2–4, 59, 180–81, 182, 191
  jazz musicals, 151–52
  Leonard Bernstein on, 1
  and politics, 102–3, 180–81
  relationship to the Federal Theatre Project, 45
  See also integration
Brooks, Van Wyck, 4–5, 11–18, 19–22, 23–24, 33–34, 54–55, 91–92, 97–98, 180–81, 189–90
  and affirmative culture, 11–14, 23–25, 30
  and Alain Locke, 107–8
  and Archibald MacLeish, 122
  biographical background, 11–12
  and Brooks Atkinson, 24–25, 51–53, 72–73
  on civic art, 13
  criticism of avant-garde, 14
  dispute with Dwight Macdonald, 14–16, 23–24
  and Gilbert Seldes, 30
  on high art, 12–13, 21f, 70–71
  on literary tradition, 11–13, 22
  "middle path," 12–13, 17, 23–24, 30–31, 41–42, 49–51, 53, 54–55, 63–64
  and Mike Gold, 39–40
  reputation, 16–18
  and "sophistication," 51–52, 72–73, 80–81
  See also America's Coming of Age; coterie literature; "On Creating a Usable Past"; *Wine of the Puritans*
Broyles, Michael, 33–34
Bruskin, Perry, 116–17
Bryant, Marie, 132–33
Bürger, Crista, 19–20
Bürger, Peter, 19–20, 186–87, 189
Burlesque, 57–58
Busoni, Ferruccio, 149

Cabin in the Sky (Duke and Latouche), 121
Carmen (Bizet), 154
Carmen Jones (Hammerstein), 154, 155f
Carousel (Rodgers and Hammerstein), 81, 100, 143–44, 179–80
Carrol, Walter, 139
  See also Tin Top Valley
Carter, Tim, 61–62
Chapman, John, 2, 101–2
Chee-Chee (Rodgers and Hart), 2–3, 68–69, 76
Child, Cecil, 28–30
Child, Francis James, 26–27
Chowrimootoo, Christopher, 5, 185
civil rights movement, 103
classical music, institutional definition of, 59, 102
  Alain Locke's definition of, 107–8
  Communist Party's relationship to, 38–39, 42, 44–45
  See also high art
Cohan, George M., 2–3, 61
comedy, musical. *See* Broadway musical
Communism
  and the arts, 38–45
  Popular Front, 44–45
  Third Period, 41–42
Communists' Workers Music League, 42
Composers' Collective, 39, 42–45, 46, 48–49
Contes d'Hoffmann, Les (Offenbach), 156
coterie literature, 14, 15, 51–52, 96, 146, 185

INDEX

couleur locale, 69–75
Cowley, Malcolm, 14
Cradle Will Rock, The (Blitzstein), 46
Creole Rhapsody (Ellington), 111
Cullen, Countee, 109–10

Damrosch, Walter, 54–55, 152–53
dance, 39, 41, 76, 82, 90, 93–94, 95, 102
 See also ballet
Darrell, R. D., 108–9
Debutante, The (Herbert Victor), 34
de Mille, Agnes, 76, 82, 90, 100
Deep River (Harling), 72
Deep South Suite (Ellington), 109–10
Depression. *See* Great Depression
Desert Song, The (Hammerstein), 71, 76
Dickstein, Morris, 44
Dier, Richard, 138–39
Dies Committee, 53–54
DiMaggio, Paul, 25
Dimitrov, Georgi, 44
Diminuendo and Crescendo in Blue (Ellington), 111
Doráti, Antal, 152
Douglas, Ann, 5, 67
Down in the Valley (Weill and Downes), 146, 156
Downes, Olin, 1–2, 91–95, 146
 compared to Van Wyck Brooks, 91–93
 on integration, 95
 review of *Oklahoma!*, 94–95
 review of *Porgy and Bess*, 95
 review of *Sing Out, Sweet Land*, 100–1
 review of *Street Scene*, 177–78
 and Romain Rolland, 93–94
dramaturgical counterpoint, 158–60
Dreigroschenoper, Die (Brecht and Weill), 115–16, 179–80
Dunham, Katherine, 116–17

Eaton, Quaintance, 177
Eisler, Hanns, 42–43
Ellington, Duke, 2, 36–37, 103–4, 109
 as middlebrow, 104–5, 109–12, 121–22
 and politics, 109–10, 118–19, 140–41
 and symphonic music, 111
 See also American Lullaby; *Bird of Paradise*; *Black, Brown, and Beige*; *Blue Bells of Harlem*; *Blutopia*; *Creole Rhapsody*; *Diminuendo and Crescendo in Blue*; *Harlem*; *Jump for Joy*; parallel; *Reminiscing in Tempo*; *Rhapsody Jr.*; *Symphony in Black: A Rhapsody of Negro Life*
Ellington, Mercer, 140–41

Ervine, St. John, 73–74
Ethiopia, 46–47

Fain, Sammy, 179–80
Fauser, Annegret, 70
Federal Music Project, 152
Federal Theater Project, 44–46, 52–53, 54–55, 102–3, 116–17, 152, 161
Felski, Rita, 184–85
Ferber, Edna, 69
Filene, Benjamin, 25–26
Finian's Rainbow (Harburg, Saidy, and Lane), 2, 101–2, 179–80
Firebrand, The (Meyer), 153–54
Firebrand of Florence (Weill), 143–44, 147–48, 156–58, 160
Fitzgerald, F. Scott, 67
Flahooley (Harburg, Saidy, and Fain), 179–80
Flanagan, Hallie, 45–47, 48
Fledermaus, Die (Strauss), 152–53
Fleming, Julius, 140–41
Florrell, Walter, 152–53
Flower Drum Song (Rodgers and Hammerstein), 179–80
folk, 3–4, 9–10, 182–83, 189–90
 Alain Locke on, 107–8
 and American opera, 93–94
 Black folk music, 105–6, 121
 and Broadway, 25, 28–29, 59, 70–71, 72–74, 86–87, 100–1, 102–3, 140, 179–81, 191
 Communism and, 38–39, 40–41, 44–45
 Duke Ellington on, 110, 111–12, 121–22
 George Gershwin and, 35, 36–37
 and the Harlem Renaissance, 105
 historical definition, 25–28, 47
 institutional definition of, 20–22, 21f, 23–24, 55–56, 102, 187–88
 and jazz, 104, 114
 John Latouche and, 120
 Kurt Weill and, 156, 159–60
 Langston Hughes and, 161–62, 169
 Living Newspapers and, 47, 48–51
 modern ("urban") folk, 28–30, 66–67
 and *Oklahoma!*, 63–64, 76, 77, 78–87, 88–91, 94, 102
 Olin Downes on, 92–93, 94–95
 Oscar Hammerstein II and, 70–71, 72–73, 75, 78–79, 80–81
 relationship to high art, 22–25, 31–33, 35, 92–93
 relationship to popular culture, 23–24, 28–29, 32–33, 45
 See also authenticity; Child, Francis James; Seldes, Gilbert

folk opera, 36, 77, 95, 146, 175–77, 179
　See also Porgy and Bess
folk operetta, 91
Fontanne, Lynne, 153–54
Foreman, Larry, 46
Frank, Waldo, 15–16
Frankfurt School, 10–11
Franklin, Peter, 184–85
Freedly, George, 102–3
Freeman, The, 51–52
Friedman, Charles, 161, 169, 171
Friml, Rudolph, 151–52
Fulda, Ludwig, 153–54. See also Seeräuber, Der

Garland, Robert, 101–2, 136–37
　review of Street Scene, 175–76
Garrick Gaieties, The (Rodgers and Hart), 66–68
Gay, John, 103, 116
　See also Beggar's Opera; Polly
Gershwin, George, 61, 77, 106, 111, 144–45
　concert music, 35
　as "crossover" artist, 35–36
　and folk music, 35, 36–37
　Of Thee I Sing, 95
　Porgy and Bess, 36–38, 77, 95
　"When Do We Dance?", 34
Gershwin, Ira, 153–54, 156–57
Gilder, Rosamond, 101–2
Girl Friend, The (Rodgers and Hart), 65–66
Goebbels, Josef, 97
Goffin, Robert, 108–9
Gold, Mike, 24, 39–42, 44
　See also "Proletarian Realism"; "Toward a Proletarian Revolution"
Golden Age Broadway. See Broadway musicals
Golden Dawn (Hammerstein), 71–72
Gordon, Robert Winslow, 27
Graham, Martha, 41
Grant, Mark, 72
Great Depression, 38, 45–46
Green Grow the Lilacs (Riggs), 76, 79–80, 83, 87–88
Greenberg, Clement, 9–11, 55, 190
Grieve, Victoria, 54–55
Gropper, Milton, 71–72
Guillory, John, 5–6
gute Mensch von Sezuan, Der (Brecht), 157–58
Guthrie, Kate, 185–86
Guthrie, Woody, 27–28
Guys and Dolls, 57
Gwynn, Nell, Weill's proposed operetta on, 153–54

Gypsy Jim (Hammerstein), 71–72

Hammerstein II, Oscar, 1–2, 60, 69–70, 89–90, 179–80
　and Brooks Atkinson, 63–64, 74–75
　couleur locale, 69–75
　and Donaldson Awards, 154
　and folk, 70–71, 72–73, 75, 78–79, 80–81
　and folk musicals of the 1920s, 72–74
　on Green Grow the Lilacs, 79–80
　and heightened realism, 62, 63–64, 79–83, 86–87, 88, 158–59
　and integration, 60, 62, 72–73, 74, 75, 76–77, 79, 102
　as middlebrow, 63–64, 70–71
　and operetta, 71
　relationship to high art (opera), 70
　reputation, 60–61, 96–97
　See also Carousel; Carmen Jones; Desert Song; Golden Dawn; Gypsy Jim; Oklahoma!; New Moon, The; Rainbow; Rose-Marie; Wildflower
Hammond, Jr., John, 104
　critique of Ellington, 105–8, 113–14
Handcox, John, 27–28
Hansen, Miriam, 184
Harburg, E. Y., 2, 101–2, 179–80
　See also Finian's Rainbow; Flahooley
Harlem (Ellington), 111
Harling, W. Franke, 72
Hart, Dorothy, 67
Hart, Lorenz, 64, 69, 70
　on music lyrics, 65–66
　on musical comedy, 69–70
Hartt, Rollin Lynde, 7
Hayes, Lee, 27–28
Hearst, Willian Randolph, 97
Heidt, Jo, 77
heightened realism, 62, 63–64, 79–83, 86–87, 88, 158–59
Helburn, Theresa, 78
Hepokoski, James, 183–84
Herbert, Victor. See Debutante, The
Herder, Johann Gottfried, 187–88
high art
　and autonomy, 20–23, 32
　and Broadway, 34–35, 182–83
　institutional definition of, 20–24, 186–88
　relationship to folk, 22–25, 32–33, 189–90
　relationship to popular culture, 23–24, 32–33
　See also classical music; highbrow; opera; reintegration

highbrow (definitions), 6–7, 11, 12–13, 19–22, 21f
   See also autonomy; high art
Hill, Joe, 27–28
Hinton, Stephen, 158–59
Holman, Libby, 132
Horkheimer, Max, 10–11
Hot Mikado (Cooke), 70
House Committee on Un-American Activities, 53–54
Houseman, John, 116–17, 127, 132
Huggins, Nathan, 107–8
Hughes, Elinor, review of *Street Scene*, 177–78
Hughes, Langston, 2, 101–2, 109–10, 179–80
   and *Street Scene*, 160–71
   See also "Negro and the Racial Mountain, The"; *Simply Heavenly*; *Troubled Island*
Huyssen, Andreas, 22, 183–84

"Inbetween" (Ellington and Latouche), 116, 124, 126, 128f, 133, 134
Injunction Granted (Federal Theatre Project), 46–47
institution, definition of, 12–13, 19–22, 21f, 25, 186–87
   See also authenticity; autonomy; high art; folk; popular culture
institution theory, 187–88
integration
   formal integration, 74–75, 144, 177
   and *Oklahoma!*, 1–3, 60–63, 76–77, 81, 93–94, 96, 182
   institutional integration, 70–71, 72–73, 74–75, 95, 137–38, 144–45, 172–73
   and *Oklahoma!*, 62–63, 79, 81, 88–90, 98–99, 182
International Ladies Garment Workers' Union, 40–41
International Union of Revolutionary Music, 41

Jackson, Aunt Molly, 27–28
jazz, 28–29, 67–69, 72–73, 104–5
   Alain Locke and, 107, 108–9
   and classical or symphonic music, 106, 107–8, 111–12, 121–22
   Duke Ellington and, 104–7, 108–9, 110–14, 121–22
   folk ("hot"), 24, 25–26, 28–29, 105–6
   George Gershwin and, 35–36
   jazz musicals, 30, 70, 151–52
   John Hammond and, 105–6, 111, 113–14
   Kurt Weill and, 148–49, 165
   sweet, 106

Johnny Johnson (Weill and Green), 179–80
Johnson, Hall, 36–37
Joplin, Scott, 35
"Joy Spreader, The" (Rodgers and Hart), 66–68
Jumbo (Rodgers and Hart), 67–68
Jump for Joy (Ellington), 109–10, 118

Kant, Immanuel, 58
Karpeles, Maude, 31–32
Kazin, Alfred, 15–17
Kern, Jerome, 30–31, 61, 72–73
Kerr, Walter, 17, 56–57
Kerr, Jean, 17
King and I, The (Rodgers and Hammerstein), 57
Kingdom for a Cow (Weill). See *Kuhhandel, Der*
Kittredge, George Lyman, 27
Knapp, Raymond, 2–3
Korngold, Erich, 152–53
Kowalke, Kim, 61
Kronenberger, Louis, 100–1, 151–52
   review of *Street Scene*, 175–76
Kuhhandel, Der (*Kingdom for a Cow*) (Weill), 149–51, 163–64

Lahr, Bert, 57–58
Lambert, Constant, 108–9
Lane, Burton, 2, 101–2, 179–80
Lantz, Lou, 46. See also *Revolt of the Beavers*
Lardner, Ring, 30, 67
Larkin, Margaret, 27–28
Latouche, John, 2, 46, 122–23, 140
   as librettist for *Beggar's Holiday*, 103, 114–31, 135, 136–37
Leadbelly, 121
League of American Writers, 14
League of Composers, 34
Lebedinsky, Lev, 41
Lenya, Lotte, 143–44, 154–58
Lerner, Alan Jay, 100
Levine, Lawrence, 5, 32–33
Levitz, Tamara, 149
Lewis, Russell, 153–54
Liberty Deferred (Federal Theatre Project), 46–47
Living Newspapers, 46–49
Lock, Graham, 111–12, 119
Locke, Alain, 11–12, 15–16, 189–90
   on Duke Ellington, 104, 107–11
   See also parallel evolution
Lomax, John, 27, 28, 84f
Long, Avon, 132–33
Lovell, Jr., John, review of *Street Scene*, 176–77, 178–79

Lowenthal, Leo, 10–11
Lunt, Alfred, 153–54
Lynes, Russell, 17, 185–86

Macdonald, Dwight, 4–5, 19, 20–23, 54–55, 58, 97, 190
  compared to Van Wyck Brooks, 11–13, 19–22, 23–24, 54–55
  criticism of middlebrow, 6–7, 9–10
  criticism of Van Wyck Brooks, 15–17
  and New York Intellectuals, 8–11, 55–57
MacLeish, Archibald, 15–16, 122–23
Magee, Jeffrey, 35
Mamoulian, Rouben, 77, 81
Manhattan Opera House, 70
Mantle, Burns, 73–74
Martin, David, 179–80
Martin, Linton, 36
Maxwell, Elsa, 154
McCarthy, Mary, 10–11
McMillin, Scott, 2–3, 61
McPherson, Aimee Semple, 97
Meier, Edith, 67
Mencken, H. L., 67
Meyer, Edwin Justus, 153–54
  See also Firebrand, The; Firebrand of Florence, The
Meyer, Leonard, 184–85
middlebrow
  Alain Locke as, 107–8, 110–11, 189–90
  Archibald MacLeish and, 122
  Black, 104–14, 138–39
  and Broadway, 3–4, 19, 42–53, 59, 115, 144, 145
  Brooks Atkinson and, 24–25, 51–53, 179, 189–90
  communism and, 38–39, 41–42, 44–45
  controversy about, 14–18, 54–58
  definition of, 4–7, 23–24, 188–89
  Duke Ellington as, 104–5, 109–12, 121–22
  Dwight Macdonald on, 6–11, 15, 19, 23–24, 54–56, 190
  Eric Bentley and, 24–25, 56–58
  Federal Theatre Project as, 45–46, 48–49
  George Gershwin and, 35–36
  "middle path" (*see under* Brooks, Van Wyck)
  modernism and, 11, 15, 185–87, 189–91
  Oklahoma!, 62–64, 100
  Olin Downes and, 91–92
  Van Wyck Brooks on, 11–14, 15, 19, 23–24, 189–90
  See under Beggar's Holiday
Middleton, Richard, 55

Miller, Herbert, 73–74
minstrel shows, 105–6
modernism, 11, 14–18, 36, 91–92, 182–83, 191
  definitions of, 183–85
  middlebrow modernism, 185, 190–91
Moore, Grace, 153–54
Moreno, Jacob, 47
Mostel, Zero, 130, 137
Mumford, Lewis, 14
Music in the Air (Hammerstein and Kern), 62, 74–75
Music Man, The (Willson), 100
musical comedy. *See* Broadway musicals
musicals. *See* Broadway musicals

Nathan, George Jean, 176–77
"Negro and the Racial Mountain, The" (Hughes), 161–62
Negro Theater, 116–17
Neher, Caspar, 158
New Dance Group, 39
New Modernist Studies, 184, 190–91
New Moon, The (Hammerstein), 71–72
New Opera Company, 152–54, 156–57
New York Intellectuals, 8–11
New York Suitcase Theater, 161
Newell, William Wells, 27
Nichols, Lewis, 91, 100–1, 151–52
Norton, Elliott, 135
Nursery Ballet (Rodgers and Hart), 67–69

"Oh, What a Beautiful Morning," (Rodgers and Hammerstein), 83–86, 84f, 85f, 86f
Of Thee I Sing (Gershwin), 95
Offenbach, Jacques, operettas, 148–49
  See also La belle Hélène; La vie parisienne; Les Contes d'Hoffmann
Oja, Carol, 42–43
Oklahoma! (Rodgers and Hammerstein), 100, 154–56, 179–80
  advertising, 76–79
  Brooks Atkinson on, 96
  critical reception, 89–99
  dance in, 82, 90, 93–94, 96
  design of, 81
  Eric Bentley on, 96–97, 98–99
  heightened realism in, 79–89
  legacy, 99, 100–1, 102–3, 115, 137, 143–44, 145–47
  as middlebrow, 62–64, 75, 100
  Olin Downes on, 94–95
  as opera, 90–96, 144–45
  score, 82–86
  as watershed, 1–4, 60–62, 182

See also integration
"Ol' Man River" (Kern and Hammerstein), 93
"On Creating a Usable Past" (Brooks), 13–14
On Your Toes (Rodgers and Hart), 2–3
One-Third of a Nation (Federal Theatre Project), 46–47
One Touch of Venus (Weill), 153–54
opera, 70
   American folk opera, 72, 77, 89–99
   Brooks Atkinson on, 72, 74–75
   Duke Ellington and, 114–15, 121–22
   jazz, 121–22
   Kurt Weill and, 142–47, 156–58, 159–60, 165
   Langston Hughes and, 161–62, 173–74
   light opera. See operetta
   Oklahoma! as, 59, 60, 61–62, 63–64, 90–96, 144–45
   Oscar Hammerstein II on, 70–71
   Porgy and Bess as, 36–38, 49–51, 77
   relationship to Broadway, 1–2, 3, 34, 56–57, 144
   Richard Rodgers and Lorenz Hart and, 67–68
   Street Scene as, 158, 159, 174–78, 179
operetta, 147–54, 156–57
   classic and Viennese, 149–50
   Oscar Hammerstein II on, 71
   revival of, 152–54
oppositional culture, 7–11, 15–16, 24–25, 53–59, 97–98
   communism and, 38–39
   Dwight Macdonald and, 7, 16–17, 19, 23–24
   John Hammond and, 106–7
   middlebrow rejection of, 11, 15, 51–52

Paint Your Wagon (Lerner and Loewe), 100
Parade (revue), 43–44
parallel (Ellington), 104–14, 115–16, 117
parallel evolution (Locke), 108, 111–12
Parker, Dorothy, 67
Partisan Review, 10–11, 15–16
   against middlebrow culture, 15
Patinkin, Sheldon, 60–61
Peer, Ralph, 27
"People's Theater" (Rolland), 97–98
Pergolesi, Giovanni Battista, La serva padrona, 94–95
Pierre Degeyter Club, 39
Pins and Needles (revue), 40–41, 116–17, 161
Pipe Dream (Rodgers and Hammerstein), 179–80
Pirate, The (Weill), 153–54
Piscator, Erwin, 48
poets, modernist, 122–23
Pollack, Howard, 120

Polly (John Gay), 114–15
Poor Little Ritz Girl (Rodgers and Hart), 68–69
popular culture
   institutional definition of, 21f, 22–23, 34, 102, 182–83, 188, 189–90
   relationship to folk culture, 27, 28–29
Popular Front, 38–39, 44
Porgy and Bess (Gershwin), 43–44, 76–77, 121–22
   criticism of, 36–38, 72, 95
   as highbrow opera, 37
Porter, Cole, 30–31
Power (Federal Theatre Project), 44–45, 46–47, 48–51, 49f
pragmatism, philosophical, 11–12
Princess Musicals, 2–3
Prolet Bühne, 39, 48
"Proletarian Realism" (Gold), 41–42
Proust, Marcel, 40

Radway, Janice, 5–6
ragtime, 25–26, 28–29, 34–35
ragtime folk music, 28
Rainbow (Hammerstein), 62, 71, 72, 73–74
Rampersad, Arnold, 166–67
Ray, Nicholas, 116–17
realism. See heightened realism
reintegration, 32–34, 42–43, 45–46, 54–55
Reiss, Claire, 33–34
Reminiscing in Tempo (Ellington), 104, 111
Revolt of the Beavers (Lantz and Walzer), 46
Rhapsody Jr. (Ellington), 111
rhyme, 65–66
Rice, Elmer, 2, 46–47, 101–2, 161–62, 171, 179
Riggs, Lynn, 76, 78, 79–80, 87–88
   See also Green Grow the Lilacs
Robinson, Earl, 46
Rodgers, Richard, 30–31, 63–64, 96–97, 100–1
   collaboration with Hammerstein, 69, 75–76, 80–81, 82–86, 89, 100, 143–44 (see also Allegro; Carousel; Flower Drum Song; Oklahoma!; Pipe Dream; Sound of Music, The; South Pacific)
   collaboration with Hart, 64–69 (see also All Points West; Chee-Chee; Jumbo; Nursery Ballet; Poor Little Rich Girl)
   compositional practice, 65–66, 83–86
   and folk music, 82–83, 90, 94, 96
   and the integrated musical, 1–2, 61, 182
   and Kurt Weill, 143–45, 156, 171–72, 179–81
Rolland, Romain, 33–34, 92–93, 97–98, 142, 146

Rome, Harold, 40–41
Rosalinda (Strauss), 152–53
Rose, Billy, 177–78
Rose-Marie (Hammerstein), 70, 76
Rosenfeld, Paul, 15–16
Rosenkavalier, Der (Strauss), 156
Rubin, Joan Shelley, 5–6, 22–23

Saidy, Fred, 2, 101–2, 179–80
Saint-Amour, Paul, 184–85
Samrock, Victor, 174–75
Saul, Oscar, 46
Savo, Jimmy, 43–44
Savran, David, 35, 36
Schultz, William Eben, 137
Sears, Ann, 60–61
Seeger, Charles, 42–43
Seeger, Pete, 27–28
Seeräuber, Der (Fulda), 153–54
Seldes, Gilbert, 11–12, 15–16, 24, 28–32, 35, 51, 63–64, 66–67
Seven Arts, 33–34
"Sezhuan". *See gute Mensch von Sezuan, Der*
Shakespeare, William, 111–12
Shapiro, Meyer, 10–11
Sharp, Cecil, 26–27
Sheppard, John R., 131–32
Show Boat (Hammerstein and Kern), 2–3, 62, 69, 72–73
Sibelius, Jean, 183–84
Siegmeister, Elie, 32–33
Silbersee, Der (Weill), 159
Simon, Henry, 90
Simply Heavenly (Hughes and Martin), 179–80
Sing for Your Supper (Federal Theatre Project), 46
Sing Out, Sweet Land (Kerr and Siegmeister), 100–1
Silver Lake, The (Weill), 159
Smith, Cecil, review of *Oklahoma!*, 96
Sokolow, Anna, 161
Sondheim, Stephen, 60–61
songs, popular, and opera, 93–94
Sound of Music, The (Rodgers and Hammerstein), 179–80
South Pacific (Rodgers and Hammerstein), 179–80
Spewack, Sam and Bella, 2–4
spirituals, concert, 111–12
Spirochete (Federal Theatre Project), 46–47
Stallings, Laurence, 72, 73
   See also What Price Glory?

Stempel, Larry, 60–61
Still, William Grant, 161–62
Stowe, Harriet Beecher, 5
Strauss II, Johann, operettas, 148–49
   See also Rosalinda; Fledermaus, Die
Strayhorn, Billy, 111–12, 127, 133
Street Scene (Hughes, Rice, and Weill), 2, 101–2, 144–47, 159–81
   advertising, 174–75
   as Broadway opera, 144–45, 158
   critical reception of, 175–81
   as opera, 158, 159, 174–78, 179
Such Sweet Thunder (Strayhorn and Ellington), 111–12
"Surrey with the Fringe on Top, The" (Rodgers and Hammerstein), 171, 172*f*
Swain, Joseph, 60–61
Swing Mikado (Federal Theatre Project), 70
swing music, 104
Swingin' the Dream (Seldes, et al.), 30
Symonds, Dominic, 68–69
Symphony in Black: A Rhapsody of Negro Life (Ellington), 111

Taruskin, Richard, 183–84
Taylor, Deems, 67–68
theater, popular, and opera, 74–75
"Theater of Spontaneity," 47
Theater Union, 161
Theatre Arts Committee, 116–17
Theatre Guild, 43–44, 69, 77
   and *Oklahoma!*, 77–78
Theatre Union, 39
theatricalism, 98–99
Thomson, Virgil, 36–38
Thoreau, Henry David, 51
"Thou Swell," 65–66, 66*f*
Threepenny Opera (Brecht and Weill). *See Dreigroschenoper, Die*
Tin Pan Alley, 28–29, 40–41
Tin Top Valley (Carrol), 139
Tinted Venus, The (Weill), 153–54
Tippett, Tom, 27–28
Tip-Toes, 34
"Tomorrow Mountain" (Ellington and Latouche), 128*f*, 132–33, 134
tone parallel. *See* parallel (Ellington)
Toscanini, Arturo, 111
Touch and Go (revue), 17
"Toward Proletarian Art" (Gold), 39–40
Treemonisha (Joplin), 35
Trilling, Lionel, 15–16

INDEX   255

Triple-A Plowed Under (Federal Theatre Project), 46–47
Troubled Island (Hughes and Still), 161–62
Tucker, Mark, 109
"T.V.A. Song" (Wainer), 49f

Ulysses Africanus (Weill and Anderson), 157–58
Unsinkable Molly Brown, The (Willson), 100
"Utopiaville" (Ellington and Latouche), 132–33

Verdi, Giuseppe, 34
vie parisienne, La (Offenbach), 152, 153–54

Waldorf, Wilella, 100
Walpole, Horace, 118
Walzer, Oscar, 46
Wasserman, Dale, 114–15, 116–17, 121, 131–32
Watch Your Step (Berlin), 34
Watkins, Perry, 114–15, 116–17, 119–20, 121
Watson, Morris, 46–47
Watts, Richard, 135
Weill, Kurt, 2, 101–2, 115–16
    and Bertolt Brecht, 150–51, 160
    emigration, 142–43
    and integration, 144
    and Olin Downes, 156
    and opera, 142–47, 156–58, 159–60, 165
    and operetta, 147–51, 153–54, 156–57
    and Richard Rodgers, 143–45, 156, 171–72, 179–81
    and Romain Rolland, 142, 146
    See also dramaturgical counterpoint; *Dreigroschenoper, Die*; *Firebrand of Florence*; *Johnny Johnson*; *Kuhhandel, Der*; *One Touch of Venus*; *Silbersee, Der*; *Pirate, The*; *Street Scene*; *Tinted Venus, The*; *Ulysses Africanus*
Wellek, René, 15–16
What Price Glory? (Stallings), 73–74
Whiteman, Paul, 68–69, 106, 111
Whitman, Willson, 45
"Whoopee Ti-Yi-Yo, Git Along Little Dogies," 83–84, 84f, 86, 87f
Widdemer, Margaret, 7–9, 55
Wiggins, Ella May, 27–28
Wildflower (Hammerstein), 71–72
Williams, Claude, 27–28
Wilson, Edmund, 15
Wiman, Dwight Deere, 174
Winchell, Walter, 71–72
Wine of the Puritans, The (Brooks), 11–12
Winsor, Frederick, 7
Woll, Allen, 138–39
Wood, Graham, 83
Woolf, Virginia, 190
Woollcott, Alexander, 71–72
Workers' Dance League, 39
Workers' Laboratory Theater (Theater of Action), 39
Workers' Music League, 39
"Wrapped in a Ribbon and Tied in a Bow" (Weill), 171, 172f, 177–78